W9-DGS-361

Political Science: Looking to the Future
Edited by William Crotty

Volume Two
Comparative Politics, Policy, and International Relations

Northwestern University Press
Evanston, Illinois

Northwestern University Press
Evanston, Illinois 60201

Copyright © 1991 by Northwestern University Press
All rights reserved. Published 1991
Printed in the United States of America

First printing, 1991

ISBN: 0-8101-0924-7 (cloth)
    0-8101-0950-6 (paper)

Library of Congress Cataloging-in-Publication Data

Political science : looking to the future / edited by William Crotty.
    p.   cm.
    Includes bibliographical references.
    Contents: v. 1. The theory and practice of political science — v.
2. Comparative politics, policy, and international relations — v.
3. Political behavior — v. 4. American institutions.
    ISBN 0-8101-0922-0 (v. 1 : alk. paper). — ISBN 0-8101-0923-9 (v.
1 : pbk. : alk. paper)
    1. Political science.   2. International relations.   3. United
States—Politics and government.   I. Crotty, William J.
JA37.P75   1991
320—dc20   91-7988
                                                              CIP

Political Science: Looking to the Future

Volume Two

Political Science: Looking to the Future
William Crotty, General Editor

Contents

Acknowledgments

A project of this magnitude involves the efforts of a large number of people. Among those contributing in significant ways to the publication of these volumes have been Alan D. Monroe, Richard P. Farkas, Ruth S. Jones, Catherine E. Rudder, Molly Crotty, Dale D. Vasiliauskas, M. L. Hauch, Lucille Mayer, Laura Olson, and Ada W. Finifter, whose advice in the preliminary stages of the undertaking was of great assistance. The evaluations of the entire manuscript by Jonathan D. Caspar, Leon D. Epstein, and Joseph M. Schwartz were deeply appreciated.

Those at Northwestern University Press who were particularly helpful include: Jonathan Brent, the press's director; Susan Harris, Managing Editor, who oversaw the editorial process; Nan Crotty, Jill Shimabukuro, Amy Schroeder, Rina Ranalli, and Rachel Inger.

To all, we are grateful.

Introduction: Setting the Stage

William Crotty

Political science, like much of academia, is at a crossroads.[1] The causes are many.

First is the problem of generational change. Estimates vary, but one-half or more of the practicing political scientists in the United States are expected to retire roughly by the year 2000 (give or take five years or so). A new generation of academicians will take over, with consequences uncertain. The loss of the postwar giants that shaped the modern era of political science will be keenly felt. It is always tricky to select a few names to illustrate a trend, but the legacy of those such as William H. Riker, Robert A. Dahl, Warren E. Miller, Gabriel A. Almond, Harold Guetzkow, Richard F. Fenno, Jr., Donald R. Matthews, Samuel J. Eldersveld, Dwaine Marvick, Philip E. Converse, Donald E. Stokes, Heinz Eulau, David Easton, Joseph LaPalombara, Harry H. Eckstein, and their colleagues is compelling, as the papers published in these volumes make clear. The list of names is obviously incomplete; yet it does illustrate the magnitude—in terms of intellectual force and disciplinary impact—of those for whom replacements must be found.

Where the discipline is to go, who are to be its intellectual patrons, and what concepts, theories, problem areas, or approaches are likely to dominate its collective consciousness—these are some of the questions that led to the explorations contained in these volumes. The aim is not to answer these questions with a degree of certainty: intellectual dogmatism serves no good purpose, and no one point of view (as will become readily apparent) guided these efforts. The idea was to explore options, ask questions, sort through subfields, and attempt to separate that which may be useful and productive from that which may be old, worn-out, or misleading. Each author had license to do this in the manner he

1

or she found most appropriate. There were no preconditions concerning the points to be raised or the intellectual forces to be addressed. The intent was to raise issues and advance ideas, to force people to think. What does the future hold? How should we in political science prepare for it? What is the best we have to offer, and what can most conveniently be left behind?

Generational concerns are also reflected in the balance of authors chosen to write the subfield essays. Most significantly, each was a scholar of stature in his or her subfield. In addition, however, the likelihood is that most of the contributors should be around for the next several decades to help set in broad relief the future directions the discipline will pursue. Thus, there is a heavier reliance than otherwise might be the case on respectable scholars from middle-level age groups who have already made substantial contributions to their particular specialties. Clearly, many who could have qualified have not been included. This is not the point. Those who were chosen must wrestle in the near future with precisely the types of concerns they address in their papers. The selection strategy was intentional.

These essays will be controversial—some more than others. Each, however, represents an author's (or authors') perspective on the broader questions raised as exemplified by his or her subfield. Each author, in turn, is considered an expert in his or her field with something of importance to say concerning its present condition and its likely future course of development. Their ideas are worth considering; they are meant to stimulate, to serve as a basis for discussion and contention, and to force a reexamination, however modest, of a discipline entering a critical phase in its development. If they accomplish these ends, they will have served their purpose.

Social science, like all of academia, has gone through a difficult period. Support for education, funding of original research, and an emphasis on the qualitative development of knowledge have not been priorities in American culture and politics since at least the late 1960s. The predictable result has been a drop-off in the initiation of research and a stabilization, and even decline, in the number of students seeking Ph.D.s. Teaching and research have not been prized career objectives over the last several decades. It is also probable that, with scholarship support decreased and many universities severely restricted in their hiring, graduate schools have not only had fewer applicants, but the quality of those seeking entrance has not been of the caliber it might be. Law, medical, and business and professional schools may be proving more attractive to the abler undergraduates. Little of this can be directly and quantifiably proven. Still, the difficult times faced by the academic community have been real, and the fears expressed about the long-term consequences reflect those heard on campuses throughout the nation.

In more specific relation to political science, there has also been a mood of disenchantment. The unity, cohesiveness, and commonalities of the field seem to be in eclipse; perhaps they have already been abandoned.[2] This is a common theme in many of the essays that follow. Frequently, the approaches or substantive concerns that have held a subfield together and contributed to its distinctiveness are now in doubt. There is change in the redefinition of boundary areas, in what is significant and should continue to be so in contrast to what has been considered important in the past. The subfields are in flux: some are assuming greater importance; the interest in others is declining. Political science is a discipline in transition.

The question of seeking a broader identity for the field is raised in varying contexts by a number of authors. What distinguishes political science as an integrative whole, a bounded and coherent intellectual pursuit? What makes the discipline distinctive? What constitutes its particular problems? What should be the central focus and common bonds among its practitioners? These concerns are addressed in differing contexts and, in particular, served as the basis for those contributing to Volume 1, *The Theory and Practice of Political Science,* arguably the most contentious of the four. These questions are the mega-issues, the ones that concern all of us as practicing academicians. Whether it is preferable to achieve the coherence, stability, and self-assurance that some found in the past, or whether a more eclectic, exploratory, and innovative practice is preferable is debatable. Whether conceptual approaches ("power," "politics," "markets," "representation," "democracy"), subject matter (the study of government, institutions, political behavior), or definitional guides ("the authoritative allocation of values," "who gets what, when, and how") are the best indicators of relevance is also arguable.

Both approaches have their costs: in one, smugness, perhaps, and a hint as to what can or "should" be done, contrasted in the other with a disparate, shotgunlike scattering of interests that raises questions about the interests or bonds that political scientists share. What distinguishes political scientists from sociologists, economists, historians, or anthropologists (or, for that matter, from those who work in professional schools of law, journalism, management, or policy)? Should distinctions among them be made? Can they communicate intellectually with each other? What do they have to share, borrow, or contribute that is distinctive to their respective disciplines? Or, conversely, are those valid concerns? Some believe that each subfield should follow its own road. Eventually, they argue, all—or at least knowledge writ large—should prosper. The role of graduate education—what skills and perspectives are transmitted to future generations of practitioners—in such a scheme is unclear—a further sign of a discipline's indecision. Many believe that this indecision typifies the mood that has been progressively enveloping the discipline over the last generation.

The questions raised in the essays that follow are basic. No effort has been made to supply answers—should they even exist at this point in time—on which the balance of contributors might agree. The purpose is to encourage critical thought at a convenient summing-up point in a discipline's development.

Finally, a note on what the essays that follow are not. They are not intended to be comprehensive reviews of the literature in any given area.[3] In fact, the authors were specifically asked not to do this. These instructions, however, did not exclude the compiling of bibliographies to many of the essays that might provide a reasonable starting point for serious inquiry into the subfield being discussed. Many of these are extensive.

The authors were also asked not to restrict themselves to the need to present a balanced or thorough examination of their respective fields. This type of directive is a little unusual in academia. One result may be the intentional omission of works of stature, the contributions of major scholars. The editor, not the authors, takes full responsibility for such deficiencies. Rather than comprehensiveness, fairness, or balance, we wanted ideas—a freshness of perspective, a personal signature on the observations made. The goal has been to raise issues of significance for discussion and debate. Where are we? Where are we going? What could prove useful to us as we move toward an uncertain future? These are the comments that unite the chapters.

The papers were commissioned for a special series of theme panels held at the 1989 annual meeting of the Midwest Political Science Association. At that time, William Crotty was serving as president of the association and assumed the principal responsibility for organizing these panels. Alan D. Monroe served as program chair for the meeting. In addition, significant support was provided by Richard P. Farkas, then executive director of the Midwest Political Science Association, and Catherine E. Rudder, executive director of the American Political Science Association.

The idea behind the theme panels was to have a distinguished practitioner in a field prepare a paper on his or her specialty written in the context described above. A panel was then built around each paper and included three to four discussants, also individuals of prominence in the subfield, who commented on the paper, challenging its assumptions and often advancing alternative explanations, relevant criteria, or scenarios for future exploration. Most of the individuals who contributed in these ways are acknowledged by the authors in their essays.

The papers were then read before a group presumed to be expert in most cases, or at least interested enough as teachers or researchers in the area under discussion to participate in such a specialized critique. In general, the sessions were well attended. Surprisingly, perhaps, many of the panels had standing-room-only audiences, and in a few cases the meeting rooms were unable to accommodate all those wishing to attend. In most cases, too, the exchanges were lively, perhaps indicating that the issues being addressed and the questions raised reflected generally felt concerns in the discipline.

The authors were asked to incorporate into their essays the points they considered most relevant from the resulting exchanges and, specifically, to address in some fashion any issues that might appear to have been deficiencies in their original presentations. In some cases, the editor also advanced suggestions, but always with the understanding that the author's judgment as to relevance and importance, and the issues and themes that he or she preferred to emphasize, took precedence. No two essayists address the same questions within the same format. Some of the papers are lengthy; others are relatively brief. Some are opinionated; others preferred to mute their approach while allowing their personal preferences to remain clear. Some are cautiously optimistic; others are not. Some attempted to document their arguments extensively; others opted for a simpler thematic presentation. All in all, though, we trust that the essays taken together serve to highlight many of the most significant issues facing the discipline today, and that they provide a starting point for a serious discussion about where we as political scientists now are, what we have to contribute, and where we, as a discipline, may be headed.

IN THIS VOLUME . . .

Russell J. Dalton ("Comparative Politics of the Industrial Democracies: From the Golden Age to Island Hopping") begins by arguing the centrality of comparative politics to political science, even though it can be argued that comparative politics did not emerge as a well-defined subfield until the 1960s, late in the discipline's evolution. A few short decades after what may be considered the flowering of its most influential work, the field is in disarray, lacking a clear focus, integrative theories and methodologies, and a clear agenda of research questions to address. Such criticisms are shared by many in the area, though they are advanced with varying degrees of fervor.

Comparing conditions over the last several decades, Dalton finds (1) a major increase in the depth and comprehensiveness of knowledge available about societies, including those specifically beyond the traditional concentration on Britain and Western Europe; (2) a greater willingness to use a variety of methodological tools, from survey research to qualitative case studies; (3) a tightening of academic standards and a marked improvement in the quality of information available; (4) the creation of an institutional infrastructure for scholars to build on; and (5) a greater sensitivity to engaging in truly comparative research.

The present disquiet concerns the weakness of theorizing in the subfield. As research in the area has grown in sophistication and quality, the demands placed upon practitioners have also increased. These include (1) the need to find unifying theoretical perspectives, questions to be explored, and research agendas; (2) the development of explanatory theories of greater precision, clarity, and empirical utility; (3) a move away from all-inclusive megatheorizing; (4) a distrust with employing the American experience as the starting point for comparative evaluations; and (5) a new appreciation for the complexity and unpredictability of evolving political processes. One consequence has been a shift in research emphasis to more modest objectives, to efforts to explain the contributions of institutions or behavior patterns within a polity rather than to explicate the operations of the system as a whole. Data collection and the generation of knowledge then have sought more limited, but more realistic and achievable, ends.

Dalton illustrates the benefit of the newer empirically based, middle-range theorizing for studying advanced industrial societies with references to the contributions made by postmaterial and neocorporate perspectives employed in comparative research.

Nonetheless, discontent with the way in which the field has evolved continues. Critics find a fragmentation, a lack of a commonly accepted focus, and a disintegration of the bonds and the cumulative pool of knowledge and concepts that once defined the area's distinctiveness. Such criticisms may be a natural by-product of any subfield's intellectual growth. A middle-range strategy and a diversity of interests and research undertakings should not be the bases for pessimism. Breakthrough research undertakings, ostensibly the next step in the development of the subfield, and of political science more generally, await fundamental structural and institutional changes in how we approach the accumulation of knowledge. The prospects for such a reorientation in approach are limited at present.

Barbara Geddes ("Paradigms and Sand Castles in the Comparative Politics of Developing Areas") attempts to answer such questions as why the creation of sophisticated explanatory theories relevant to understanding the politics of developing nations has proven so unproductive, why it has significantly lagged behind the collection of data, and why the theories put forth to guide inquiries have such limited staying power. Geddes looks in particular depth at modernization theory—including variations such as diffusion theory and others with economic and Marxist orientations—and dependency theory, meant to be a revision of and a challenge to the thinking on modernization. Each has failed to account for or predict the developments experienced in Latin America, Asia, and Africa. The manner in which each theory misjudged the economic consequences of change and the inability of political structures and democratic practices to match economic growth is explained. The economic orientation of theorizing on Third World relationships during the 1970s and the early 1980s is particularly pronounced.

The reasons for the failure of theorizing to supply consistent insight, explanatory power, and research focus for any sustained period of time are many. Theoretical development often did not call on the data available to help shape propositions or discouraged the empirical testing of assumptions. To an extent, the use of case studies or national experiences on which to base observations was selective; that which did not fit with the perspective being proposed was ignored. Ideology played a role; critics attacked theories they found personally offensive and chose not to contest ones whose objectives they admired. Aesthetics, too, played a role. Some theoretical perspectives have an elegance that is attractive, although their empirical utility is limited and the rationale underlying their construction faulty.

Most recently a pluralism of approaches has vied for attention in the study of the comparative polities of nonindustrialized nations. These approaches include a new emphasis on comparative historical sociology; an emphasis on explaining economic strategies, and particularly industrialization, in relation to state influences and class interests; an emphasis on studying the context of political decision-making and the actors and institutions that immediately influence it; and an application of rational actor models to developing area concerns. Each has its strengths as well as its limitations. Several of these are not necessarily theoretical orientations, but more basically are perspectives that signal sensitivities to certain types of problems, the institutions influencing them, and the nature of the explanation likely to emerge.

The current diversity of approaches is in large part dictated by fundamental problems—specifically, democratization and Third World debt—that remain impervious to the more elegant and simplified interpretations put forth by conventional theorizing. Much of the work on these problems has remained descriptive. The old has proved inadequate; more resilient theoretical approaches are barely beyond the design stage.

Ellen Comisso ("Where Have We Been and Where Are We Going? Analyzing the Politics of Socialism in the 1990s") reviews the study of communist and related socialist systems, primarily the Soviet Union and Eastern European countries, in terms of what we know, how such research has been approached, and what its limits are. Second, Comisso looks at the subfield in relation to the likely effect political liberalization and the introduction of market mechanisms will have on communist studies and the directions in which the field is likely to move.

Despite a variety of intellectual approaches to the subject matter and the problems inherent in data collection, a broad consensus exists as to what is known about communist systems, how they operate, and the reasoning underlying variations in Communist party rule and a nation's behavior.

The boundaries between state and economy are not well articulated in a communist order, and the society or state, not the individual, dominates in the ownership of property. The bureaucratic control of the economy and the dominant role of a Leninist party in state decision-making define the socialist system.

The different methodological and conceptual approaches to communist studies have usually evolved in efforts to overcome gaps in substantive knowledge. As a consequence, they have played a supplemental role in adding to the common knowledge, rather than provoking controversies or dividing scholars, as has occurred in other subfields. There area centrality of subject matter and a commonality of interest not often found in the discipline.

Among the approaches that have gained currency are historically oriented studies, which explain a nation's behavior in terms of its evolution and long-term political needs and practices; the totalitarian school, with its emphasis on state terror; Marxist analyses, in which access to power replaces economics as a class divider; and an emphasis on group politics and interests as they influence political choices. Additional perspectives include an organizational-bureaucratic concentration, which looks at the bargaining process among institutional elites and the forces that influence policy outcomes; a "limits of state" model (our term), reflecting the pluralism in societies and the power that nonstate and nonofficial forces have in effectuating decisions; and an emphasis on explaining behavior in relation to the conflicts and cleavages apparent within the political leadership.

Each of these approaches is broad-gauged, several supplying little more than a focus for research attention and a presumption that this is the critical point of attack for understanding a socialist nation's actions. They are not necessarily theoretical orientations; more basically, they represent perspectives and sensibilities intended to guide research efforts. Each has its assets and its liabilities. Comisso critiques the various schools and their utility for expanding our base of knowledge. Some are more common in past studies; others, in modified form, are enjoying a resurgence of attention; still others are relatively new efforts to approach an understanding of communist political systems.

The future should prove challenging to a field where the subject matter is undergoing substantial and fast-moving change. There is the problem of explaining discrepancies in performance among socialist nations (East Germany, Yugoslavia, Czechoslovakia) that have not been successfully addressed. A fundamental concern will be to redefine what socialist studies includes: Is it a field witnessing its own death? Given the traditional definition of communist studies in relation to Leninist party control and a state/economy nexus, what happens if these undergo a transformation, as they so clearly appear to be doing? A redefinition of interests would appear to be one likelihood. An alternative approach, favored by Comisso, would draw on the more avowedly comparative work in other fields to provide the perspectives required to understand change in socialist systems. Taking this position, the many comparative research approaches and research questions that suggest themselves offer a variety of ways for attacking transitional political and economic questions in socialist nations.

Communist studies has been a subfield known for its flexibility. It is now facing a challenge to its identity. How it reacts will dictate its future viability.

Deborah J. Gerner ("Foreign Policy Analysis: Renaissance, Routine, or Rubbish?") begins her critique of the intellectual currents in the research on foreign policy by asking if a consensus exists as to the area's central questions, methodologies, and theories—the essence of what the field involves. The answer is an emphatic No! It is a wide-ranging subfield difficult to distinguish from other areas of public policy and noted for its inclusiveness and diversity rather than for the clarity of its focus or the interrelatedness of its concerns.

Research in the field ranges from the abstract modeling of crisis situations to expository essays in prestigious journals influential with governmental decision-makers, from concerns with affairs in other nations and international bodies to domestic policy-making. It is a full menu. The connecting link is that foreign policy deals with the objectives and motivations of national policy focusing on the nation-state as the unit of analysis.

Gerner traces the history of the field, including its separatism from the more behavioralist and scientifically oriented international relations specialists. Foreign policy students place greater value on less quantifiable, policy-relevant, and qualitative strains in their analyses. Gerner critiques the intellectual development of research relevant to foreign policy concerns, including such approaches as legal, historical, and institutional; rational actor; decision-making; organizational processes and collective group behavior; societal pressures and public opinion influences; the psychological makeup, cognitive screening, and belief systems of relevant foreign policy influentials; crisis decision-making; artificial intelligence modeling of decision processes; and the compara-

tive foreign policy analyses of events data, a distinct subfield within
the field.

Gerner recommends a joining of classical and behavioral perspectives: a reexamination of the basic issues and fundamental questions
that define the field and the adoption of a flexibility and tolerance toward the approaches most likely to yield the best results. Steps in this
direction have been taken. For scholars of foreign policy, it could mean
an expansion of boundaries, the inclusion of dimensions of analysis
once neglected, and a reorientation of thinking along newly negotiated
paths. The cumulative advancement of knowledge would be the objective. Could a "renaissance" of sorts be in the offing?

Jacek Kugler ("The Study of War and Peace: Quo Vadis?") examines conflict studies within international relations, the strain that has
defined world politics for decades and one of two (the other is political
economy; see below) that dominates the field. The research on war and
peace has produced a verifiable and acceptable data base. More generally, however, there is little consensus on many issues of concern to the
field and there is a large body of unrelated findings that needs incorporation into some kind of organic whole. No acceptable paradigm has
been advanced to place conflict studies within an understandable context in international relations. There is little agreement on what has
proven successful in the past or what should prove productive in the
future. Competing theoretical explanations are put forward, but there is
little agreement on how these should be judged. It is a "developing"
rather than mature subfield, one with significant problems to overcome.

Kugler traces the origins of the field, looking at schools of thought
that emphasize the impact of power distributions (balance of power
versus hegemony) on conflict among nations, theories of nuclear deterrence and nuclear proliferation, explanations for arms races, the relationship of domestic to international conflict, and cycle patterns in the
relations among nations.

Kugler concludes that progress has been made in war and peace research, in particular relating to the employment of more empirical studies to sift through the mass of propositions and alternative explanations
that characterize the knowledge in the field. Broader theoretical exposi-
tion seems attainable, as does access to more inclusive data banks to test
propositions. A greater attention to specifying the conditions that lead
to cooperation and the peaceful resolution of conflict, as against the
factors that produce war, would be welcome.

This generation of political scientists may have been the one to first
demonstrate the value of scientific investigation in approaching such
mega-problems as war and peace. The likelihood is that the advances
made should be even more pronounced in future years.

One of the most influential of the newer thrusts in political science is in many respects one of the oldest. Political economy was proposed in the nineteenth century as a unity of the concerns that eventually fed into two distinctive disciplines, political science and economics. More recently, political scientists have begun to use the tools and perspectives of economics in attempting to increase their understanding of the economic factors that influence political behavior. This emphasis is now visible in different degrees in virtually every aspect of the discipline. William R. Keech, Robert Bates, and Peter Lange ("Political Economy within Nations") look at the benefits to the discipline from employing economic perspectives, or what they call "choice-theoretic reasoning"; and the substantive implications of the relationship between economics and political phenomena, governments, and markets. The end result of such studies may well be a more comprehensive and unified social science enterprise.

The authors discuss the utility of the approach and the substantive and theoretical interrelationship between politics and the state and between economics and markets. The contributions to knowledge made along these lines are treated in three sections devoted to American politics, European studies, and Third World research, each written by the specialist in that particular area. The chapter has a scope and systematic thematic development that is rare in such ventures. In large part, this is a consequence of a collaboration between three authors sharing related theoretical orientations but expert in different substantive fields. As they indicate, they would like to contribute to breaking down the barriers between economics and political science as well as among subfields of political science. The way to do so is by emphasizing the commonalities in research and the strength of a shared intellectual orientation in approaching research questions.

The authors review the three basic components of choice-theoretic reasoning: individuals as the basic unit of analysis and individual choice as the principal variable; the aggregation and optimization of choice through elections, markets, and voluntary associations; and the costs and constraints implicit in such actions.

The authors analyze choice-theoretic perspectives used in understanding American electoral behavior and legislative policy-making; its role in establishing societal goals, especially apparent in the theorizing on the limitations of markets in failing to fulfill such a function; institutional factors as they affect decision-making and the distribution of resources; and the political resources and structures that shape macroeconomic policy.

In a related overview, the authors examine how similar choice-theoretic approaches have been applied to the problems of advanced industrial democracies. They make a particular effort to show how this research relates to that on American politics. The areas reviewed in this

context include questions of macro and microlinkage in political economy, especially as related to issues of democracy, capitalism, and the
role of the state; historical institutional analyses of state and societal
structures, political processes, and economic markets; the representations of class interests and the evaluation of democratic capitalism; societal corporatism (to be distinguished from the older strain of a state
corporation with its overtones of authoritarianism) as a mediating influence between class and the modern democratic state; and the conflict
between democratic rights of associations, organization and the advancement of interests, and the use of the vote and political parties as
mitigating factors influencing the efficient operation of the market or
economic management and distributional mechanism.

In an associated vein, the authors explore how choice-theoretic perspectives aid in understanding political development and Third World
politics. The approach has been applied to questions raised by rural radicalism and political violence. Decision-based theories of peasant revolution (decidedly anti-market in tone) or neoclassical political economy
explanations of resource allocation and societal decision-making (pro-
market in orientation) have proven unable to explain such activity.
Both approaches fail to offer an adequate explanation of how individual
choice aggregates into public policy. Both perspectives also suffer from
an inability to account for the interdependence of choice—that is, the
anticipation in decision-making of what others might do.

Choice-theoretic reasoning in political economy helps bridge the
distance between the disciplines of economics and political science and
between the study of markets and politics. It has something of importance to add to our understanding of democratic and nondemocratic
systems of governing. It would appear that its unique contributions to
political science, already significant, should continue to grow.

Similar to political economy, the study of public policy can be an
integrative force within political science. It provides a comprehensive
emphasis and has demonstrated an ability to draw from all of the social
science disciplines and each of the political science subfields. Paul A.
Sabatier ("Public Policy: Toward Better Theories of the Policy Process") points out that policy studies has only enjoyed the status of being
considered a major field within political science for the last two decades.
Its subject matter is complex and the approaches to studying it eclectic.

Policy analyses can be divided into four areas: research focusing on
individual policy areas (crime, health, transportation, as examples);
evaluation and impact studies; examination of policy-making processes,
the most productive of the emphases; and a concern with policy design
and its consequences, the most recent approach.

Sabatier notes that policy research has been described as atheoretical, a criticism more relevant to earlier periods than at present. In rang-

ing across traditional subfield boundaries, policy studies has drawn attention to otherwise neglected areas of concern. These include: the integrative institution of networks involved in the development and application of policy; the importance of substantive information for decision-making; the dominant role of elites in shaping policy outcomes; the importance of longitudinal analyses for policy evaluation; and the differences in behavior, costs, and benefits that affect types of policy areas (Theodore Lowi's distributive, redistributive, and regulatory classifications can serve as examples).

Sabatier argues that the discipline and the subfield share a common interest in encouraging better theorizing and, in particular, in developing theoretical perspectives that combine policy interests with conventional areas of political science concern. Specific efforts in those regards examined in greater depth are "open systems" theory, a rational actor within institutions focus, a "policy streams" perspective, and "advocacy coalitions" developments. Each is associated with the work of particular policy analysts.

The challenge for the next wave of policy specialists may well be to test empirically the broader theories now current and to adapt or replace these with others of greater precision, predictive ability, and explanatory power.

The volume concludes with brief biographical sketches of the authors.

NOTES

1. William G. Boyer and Julie Ann Sosa, *Prospects for Faculty in the Arts and Sciences: A Study of Factors Affecting Demand and Supply, 1987 to 2012* (Princeton, N.J.: Princeton University Press, 1989).

2. Gabriel A. Almond, *A Divided Discipline* (San Mateo, Calif.: Sage Publications, 1989), and idem, "Separate Tables: Schools and Sects in Political Science?" *PS* 21:828–42. See also Kristen Monroe, Gabriel A. Almond, John Gunnell, Ian Shapiro, George Graham, Benjamin Barber, Kenneth Shepsle, and Joseph Cropsey, "The Nature of Contemporary Political Science: A Roundtable Discussion," *PS: Political Science and Politics* 23 (1):34–43.

3. These are needed and welcome. See, as examples, Ada W. Finifter, ed., *Political Science: The State of the Discipline* (Washington, D.C.: American Political Science Association, 1983), and Fred I. Greenstein and Nelson W. Polsby, eds., *Handbook of Political Science*, 4 vols. (Reading, Pa.: Addison-Wesley Publishing Company, 1975). See also Herbert S. Weisberg, *Political Science: The Science of Politics* (New York: Agathon Press, 1986). A guide to the relevant literature critiquing the discipline can be found in Donald M. Freeman's "The Making of a Discipline" in volume 1.

REFERENCES

Almond, Gabriel A. 1989a. *A Divided Discipline*. San Mateo, Calif.: Sage Publications.

————. 1989b. "Separate Tables: Schools and Sects in Political Science?" *PS* 21:828-42.

Boyer, William G., and Julie Ann Sosa. 1989. *Prospects for Faculty in the Arts and Sciences: A Study of Factors Affecting Demand and Supply, 1987 to 2012*. Princeton, N.J.: Princeton University Press.

Finifter, Ada W., ed. 1983. *Political Science: The State of the Discipline*. Washington, D.C.: American Political Science Association.

Greenstein, Fred I., and Nelson W. Polsby, eds. 1975. *Handbook of Political Science*. 8 vols. Reading, Pa.: Addison-Wesley.

Monroe, Kristen, Gabriel A. Almond, John Gunnell, Benjamin Barber, Kenneth Shepsle, Joseph Cropsey, George Graham, and Ian Shapiro. "The Nature of Contemporary Political Science: A Roundtable Discussion." *PS: Political Science and Politics* 23 (1):34-43.

Weisberg, Herbert F., ed. 1986. *Political Science: The Science of Politics*. New York: Agathon Press.

1

Comparative Politics of the Industrial Democracies: From the Golden Age to Island Hopping

Russell J. Dalton

Perhaps no area is so central to the discipline of political science as the field of comparative politics. We trace our origins back to Aristotle, whose study of politics involved the comparison of Greek city-states to examine variations in political structures and the political process. Throughout the evolution of political science as a descriptive and then an analytic method, comparison frequently has been a central part of these endeavors. A reliance on the comparative approach can be traced to the nature of our inquiry as social scientists. A social scientist who wishes to study causal relationship must explore variation. Depending on one's research question, cross-national comparisons often provide the only source of this variation. Even when we are interested in only a single nation, cross-national research allows us to determine what is unique and distinctive about political processes in the nation.[1] Social scientists are also drawn to the comparative approach because of our interest in developing general theories of politics. If human behavior and organizational behavior are governed by general laws, then the comparative approach provides a vehicle for assessing whether such gen-

I would like to thank Samuel Barnes, Harry Eckstein, Scott Flanagan, Joseph LaPalombara, Larry LeDuc, Mark Lichbach, and W. P. Shively for their advice in preparing this chapter.

15

eral patterns of behavior exist. Even if our general theories do not function in the same manner across nations, we learn a great deal. Science frequently progresses by finding exceptions to general theory, which ne-
(cessitate further theoretical work. The same applies to social science.

Despite these early beginnings and the ability to trace the comparative method throughout the evolution of political science as a discipline, comparative politics has a fairly short history as a systematic field of study. Public administration, legal and institutional studies, and the other subfields discussed in this series were developing a scientific and empirical base early in this century, but comparative politics had not yet crystallized as a distinct subfield in political science.[2]

A variety of factors converged in the 1960s, however, to produce the subfield of comparative politics as an integral part of modern political science.(Probably the most prominent factor was the emergence of research questions that focused the attention of the profession on matters that were intrinsically cross-national or international in scope. Understanding what led to the collapse of democracy in interwar Europe and the inhumanity of the Third Reich were major research themes for postwar social science in Western Europe and America. Similarly, the experiences of decolonialization and national independence raised the theme of political development to the top of the research agenda.)

These questions stimulated a burst of intellectual energy that envitalized the comparative politics subfield. Many of the best scholars in political science were drawn to the comparative field, and their efforts produced what are still considered landmark works. Gabriel Almond and James Coleman edited the tremendously influential *The Politics of Developing Areas* (1960), which introduced the structural-functional framework and influenced the course of research on political development for the next generation. S. M. Lipset's *Political Man* (1959) was the first modern treatise on political economy, statistically relating socioeconomic development to political democracy. Almond and Sidney Verba's *The Civic Culture* (1963) had a profound impact on the study of individual political behavior. Research by Lipset and Stein Rokkan (1967) created the conceptual framework that still structures contemporary research on party systems and voter alignments. David Easton's (1965) application of systems theory to the political realm offered an extremely valuable framework for conceptualizing the political process. Karl Deutsch (1963; Deutsch and Edinger 1959) directed a series of projects that explored the conditions of nation-building and international cooperation in postwar Europe. Henry Ehrmann (1957), Harry Eckstein (1960), and Joseph LaPalombara (1964) produced important studies of interest group politics·in Western democracies. This list can be extended to nearly overwhelming length.

Support from research foundations and other institutions facilitated the surge of creativity and grew as a result of this activity. There was relatively generous government support for area studies and international research projects, and fellowship opportunities drew students into the comparative field. In 1968, the two major journals in the comparative politics field were established. Truly, these must have been heady times to be a comparativist.

It is apparently becoming conventional lore to look back upon the late 1950s and early 1960s as the Golden Age of comparative politics, while lamenting the stagnation and lack of progress of subsequent years. Some critics see the field of comparative politics in fundamental disarray, as Howard Wiarda exclaims in his recent review:

> The field of comparative politics . . . is in a state of crisis. Few scholars are now able to define the field's parameters precisely, its methodology has been subjected to searching criticism, there is no longer a single integrating set of theories on which scholars in the field can agree, students are put off by the lack of a clear focus, and the field itself has become fragmented and disjointed. (1985, xi)

Although Wiarda's sentiments are extreme, they are by no means unique. Similar views are expressed in the other chapters of Wiarda's edited volume (also see Mayer 1989 and the inaugural issue of *Comparative Politics*, vol. 1, no. 1, 1968). Gabriel Almond (1988a, 1988b) has voiced similar views in recent essays on the state of the discipline. There is a common refrain that the field has lost its theoretical focus and is in disarray. From other sectors (especially Washington), we hear that even basic knowledge is eroding, as the decline in area studies and the retirement of the postwar generation of social scientists diminish the available expertise on comparative politics.

How have we moved from the Golden Age of the 1960s to a crisis of fundamental proportions in such a short time, or have we? Is the life span of our theories and findings in the social sciences so short, or did we overestimate the vitality of these initial steps? These are the questions addressed in this chapter. It is difficult, if not impossible, to provide definitive answers within a limited space, but the chapter examines some of the claims and counterclaims upon which this debate rests. It also reviews the accomplishments of the field, and the developments that lead some to question its vitality.

LAYING FOUNDATIONS

Slightly more than two decades ago, Joseph LaPalombara concluded that "one of the great problems we confront in comparative politics today is that of the enormous imbalance in the amount of . . . informa-

tion available for the United States, on the one hand, and the rest of the
world, on the other" (1968, 62). I think most scholars would agree that
the field has made substantial and relatively steady progress in narrow-
ing this information gap and building an infrastructure for comparative
politics research. Therefore, let us begin on a positive note and a point
of relative consensus, by discussing the physical growth of the field.

When one looks back over the past quarter-century, there is undeniable evidence of tremendous *advances in the breadth and depth of our
knowledge* about society and the political process in Western industrial
democracies (Verba 1985). Until fairly recently, the limited resources of
comparative scholarship narrowed the focus of research activities primarily to the major European states. Knowledge about Britain was relatively abundant, followed by research on France, Germany, and Italy.
But for the rest of Europe, even basic factual information was often difficult to retrieve. Large areas of our research map of Europe (and Japan)
were like medieval maps containing dark, uncharted areas (lacking only
the warning: "Beware, there be dragons here"). But as comparative politics has grown, research teams have explored these unknown areas, so
that nation size is no longer a good predictor of our information level.
Moreover, analyses of the smaller European democracies have highlighted aspects of the democratic process that were less apparent in
the set of larger European states. This research ranges from Arend
Lijphart's analysis of consociational democracy (1975, 1977) to Peter
Katzenstein's recent political economy studies (1984, 1985).

The depth of our knowledge about Western societies has also
expanded dramatically. The legalistic approach of early comparative
research, focusing on constitutional arrangements and institutional relationships, left numerous politically relevant aspects of society and the
political system understudied. I am not just referring to the absence of
empirical data; anthropological studies of culture, systematic descrip-
tions of the legislative process, detailed knowledge of the workings of
interest groups, and information on other fundamental features of the
political process were in short supply. The modern surge in comparative
politics expanded our knowledge of these various elements of the policy
process by almost geometric rates of increase. Let me draw but a single
example from my own area of study: Almond and Verba's (1963) *Civic
Culture* represented a major stride forward in our knowledge about
mass politics. Still, this volume's sweeping conclusions about contemporary democracy were based on a single multination survey (admittedly the only such data that were then widely available to academic
researchers). When this topic was revisited two decades later (Almond
and Verba 1980), the number of national and cross-national surveys
available to scholars had reached an impressive scale, leading to a more
refined, complex (and accurate) view of the significance of political cul-

ture. The same could be said, I believe, for most areas of research on Western industrial democracies. If judged by the standards of the contemporary field, many of the early classic works are almost fragile antiques—valuable for their ideas but limited in their information base and methods.

⌐Besides growth in the quantity of information on Western political systems, I would argue that there have been equal methodological advances in the quality of our research. This progress has been most noticeable in the area of empirical research, because there was a synergistic relationship between the behavioral revolution and the growth of the comparative politics field. Not only did empirical researchers collect data on various features of society and national politics, but the empirical approach also provided a common methodology, and often a theoretical paradigm, that facilitated systematic cross-national comparison.⌐ The empirical advances are clearly evident for research on mass electoral behavior. Through the Institute for Social Research (ISR) at the University of Michigan and the Inter-university Consortium for Political and Social Research (ICPSR), the methodology of scientific sampling à la Leslie Kish and the research approach of Angus Campbell and his colleagues (1960) diffused across the industrialized democracies. Later advances in sampling, questionnaire construction, and statistical analysis pushed the quality of electoral research far beyond the level of the first election studies (cf. the data sources and methodology in Lipset and Rokkan 1967 versus those in Dalton et al. 1984).⌐Public opinion research represents one of the clearest examples of the diffusion of methodological innovation in the social sciences, though similar progress can be noted in other areas of comparative politics. Early elite studies, for example, often relied solely upon published biographical sources and limited their interests to those questions which could be answered by such data; extensive personal interviewing of elites was quite rare, and seldom based on systematic sampling principles. Contemporary elite research is both cross-national in scope and based on scientifically sound data collection methods (e.g. Putnam 1973; Aberbach, Putnam, and Rockman 1981; Verba et al. 1987; Hoffman-Lange et al. 1980; Miller and Jennings 1987). Research on the legislative process and policy outcomes similarly draws upon a much improved base of information (e.g. Loewenberg et al. 1985; DiPalma 1977; Norton 1981; Livingston and Thaysen 1990).⌐I think the same story could be told for most aspects of comparative politics: We not only know more about the politics of Western industrial democracies, but the quality of our information—its reliability and validity—has also improved.⌐

⌐Another major advance in the field of comparative politics has been the *institutionalization of a research infrastructure*. With the passage of time, many basic data collections have become institutionalized, providing an infrastructure for continuing and expanding research. Again, election studies and public opinion research are at the forefront of this development. Ad hoc research studies of voting behavior in a specific election have gradually developed into institutionalized election study teams in most European states. There are now long ongoing election study series in West Germany, Britain, the Netherlands, Sweden, Norway, and Denmark, often with sources of continual funding. Since 1974 the European Community has supported semiannual public opinion surveys in all EC member states. Over three hundred separate national surveys have been conducted as part of the Eurobarometer series, yielding an incomparably rich resource for comparative scholarship. Public policy analysts have benefited from ongoing data collection efforts such as the Historical Indicators of West European Development (HIWED) project (Flora et al. 1983; Flora 1986; Flora and Heidenheimer 1981), the *World Handbook* (Taylor and Jodice 1983), and the standardized national statistics provided by the OECD, the EC, and other international organizations.

This institutionalization of a research infrastructure also involves the development of historical archives and data repositories. Following the model of the ICPSR, national data archives now exist in most West European states.[3] These archives ensure the routine and widespread dissemination of research materials, and their activities involve a significant level of international exchange and cooperation. The development of centralized data repositories maximizes the productivity of comparative research through the sharing of resources, but more important it instills norms of professionalism and encourages cumulative research because of the use of common data bases. In the few nations where this infrastructure has been slow to evolve (mostly in Mediterranean Europe), research has lagged as a consequence. The institutional infrastructure has developed in other ways, too. The European Consortium for Political Research, for example, was founded in the early 1970s; its annual conferences provide a uniquely valuable forum for discussing cross-national research on Western industrial societies.[4] Research institutes such as the Zentrum fuer Umfragen, Methoden und Analysen (ZUMA) in Mannheim, and Social and Community Planning Research (SCPR) in London further contribute to this institutional support base. In addition, a number of journals now provide an identity to the field and respected outlets for research findings, e.g. *Comparative Politics* (established in 1968), *Comparative Political Studies* (1968), the *European Journal of Political Research* (1973), and *West European Politics* (1978). All of these developments represent relatively recent advances in the field—they did not exist a quarter-century ago.

In my mind, more significant than the progress in data collection and infrastructural development has been the *growth of a comparative*

approach within the field of comparative politics. Historically, comparative politics consisted largely of non-American country studies, rather
than truly comparative analyses. To study the comparative politics of
Western democracies meant to study Britain, or France, but not necessarily to compare. Only infrequently did scholars attempt to generalize
beyond a single nation, and when they did, the base of knowledge was
woefully inadequate for systematic comparative study.

Although country studies are still an essential part of comparative
politics, increasing efforts are devoted to developing and testing generalized theories of politics in multi-national settings. Not only are we
searching for what is unique about each nation, but also what is common across nations. Moreover, when nations do differ, there is an attempt to understand the processes that produce these differences, what
Adam Przeworski and Jacob Teune (1970) label "the elimination of
proper names" from comparative politics. There are abundant examples
of this comparative approach in research on mass political behavior
(e.g. Inglehart 1977, 1990; Dalton et al. 1984; Franklin et al. 1991),
political economy (see the review by Keech et al. in this volume), party
research (Harmel and Janda 1982; Merkl and Lawson 1988; Taageperra
and Shugart 1989; Budge et al. 1987), collective violence (Hibbs 1973;
Barnes and Kaase 1979; Muller 1979; Powell 1982; Jennings and van
Deth 1989), coalition formation (Dodd 1976; DeSwaan 1973; Daalder
and Mueller-Rommel 1989), and indeed most aspects of the comparative field. This approach does not imply a rejection of the traditional
case study, but an awareness of the greater scientific value of generalized
theory and the by-product of advances in the field that provide the research base for such generalizations. With the development of this comparative approach, moreover, there is more conscious attention to the
theory and methodology of comparative, cross-national research (e.g.
Przeworski and Teune 1970; Holt and Turner 1970). In short, comparative politics is developing a logic of comparative inquiry.

These advances in the research infrastructure should improve the
scholarship in the study of Western industrial democracies, since the
base of our knowledge has expanded tremendously in the past several
decades. But although a celebration of our progress in these areas is
deserved, it should not obscure what remains to be done. A retrospective view inevitably highlights the advances that have been made over
the past few decades. When one thinks about where the research resources of the field stood in the early 1960s, or what was considered
path-breaking research at that time, the evidence of progress is impressive. But when one considers the contemporary questions that concern
us (as is our normal mode of thinking) and what is needed to address
these questions, our present resources still appear meager. As the resource base of the field has prospered and grown, the complexity of our

research interests has displayed concomitant growth. Past gains can not
be an end point and a source of contentment, but provide a base for
further advances.

THE BODY IS WILLING, BUT IS THE SPIRIT WEAK?

Despite the progress chronicled in the last section, concerns about a
malaise of comparative politics are a recurring, and apparently spread-
ing, feeling within the discipline. The source of the presumed infirmity
is not the research infrastructure, but the theoretical state of the field. In
colloquial terms, the critics of the field may acknowledge that the *body*
of the discipline is in good health, but they fear its theoretical *spirit* is
suffering. Critics such as Wiarda (1985) and Almond (1988a, 1988b)
feel that something the field once possessed has been lost—and our efforts suffer as a result.

It is undoubtedly true that the spirit of the comparative politics
field has changed in the past generation, though each practitioner might
differ on the nature and dimensions of this change. This section out-
lines what I believe are the major trends that give rise to these criticisms
of theoretical devolution and then evaluates these criticisms.

In Search of a Unified Theory of Politics

Perhaps the most distinctive feature of the spirit of comparative politics
research in the 1950s and early 1960s was the importance of a single
research question—what are the prerequisites of democracy?—to a
broad range of American and European social scientists. On the one
hand, this research focus represented a liberal enthusiasm for democracy
in reaction to recent wartime experiences and continuing international
instability in nondemocratic states. On the other hand, previous and
current threats to the democratic political order focused research on the
necessary and sufficient conditions for democracy to take root and endure. For instance, the collapse of Weimar democracy and the subsequent horrors of the Third Reich stimulated study of the general social
and political conditions facilitating fascism and right-wing extremism.
Adorno's studies of the authoritarian personality (1950), Milgram's experimental analyses of obedience to authority (1974), Lipset and Earl
Raab's research on right-wing extremism (1970), and the *Civic Culture*
study (Almond and Verba 1963; Verba, 1965) illustrate the efforts directed to this topic by sociologists, psychologists, and political scientists. At the same time, the political tensions of the Cold War raised the
specter of the communist threat to democracy, which stimulated serious academic research on this threat (e.g. Almond. 1954; Pye 1956).

⌜Another spiritual trait of the comparative politics field arose in reaction to the national independence movements that were transforming the postwar international system. The creation of new nation-states in Africa and Asia stimulated concern about the status and political future of developing countries. The topic of comparative politics in the developing world might seem tangential to the politics of Western industrial democracies (just as the two fields are covered by separate chapters in this volume), but in fact, the intellectual overlap between these research areas was considerable. The very term "political development" implied that nations followed an evolutionary and perhaps predictable pattern of social and political growth. Implicitly, and often explicitly, the historical experience of Western societies served as the model that Third World nations should and could follow—and the ideal end point in this evolutionary process was the Western democratic political system (e.g. Grew 1978; Lipset 1959). A considerable amount of academic research dealt with the question of what social forces, institutional structures, and political processes could move the developing world most rapidly through this evolutionary process (e.g. Almond and Coleman 1960; Apter 1965; Rostow 1960).

These orientations reinforced a tendency to develop large macro-level (or metalevel) theories about politics that could explain the political process on the grand scale of these research interests. David Easton's systems theory of political life (1965), Almond and Coleman's structural-functional model (1960), Talcott Parsons's (Parsons and Shils 1951) pattern variables, or Karl Deutsch's cybernetic model (1953, 1963) can be viewed in this light (also see Eckstein 1966). These attempts to generalize at a high level of abstraction probably received further encouragement from the behavioral revolution in political science, in which the identification of behavioral regularities and general laws became the objective of scientific inquiry. Some scholars saw their goal as developing a *unified theory of politics* similar to the unified theory of natural forces that the physicists pursue.[5] In the unified theory of politics the various elements of the political process—public opinion, interest groups, political parties, political institutions, and the like—would be linked together; the goal was to develop a metatheory that would explain these linkages and the evolutionary course that political systems were supposedly following. ⌟

At the core of these activities was a small group of behavioralists—Almond, Coleman, Deutsch, Eckstein, LaPalombara, Macridis, Pye, Ward, Verba, and others—who exerted an intellectual influence on the discipline that was many times greater than their numbers. An informal linking of these scholars began at Northwestern University's Inter-university Research Seminar on Comparative Politics in 1952. Soon thereafter, the Social Science Research Council's Committee on Com-

parative Politics (SSRC/CCP) provided an institutional base *and fi-*
nancial support for this network of scholars.[6] Over the next decade,
the SSRC/CCP served as a focal point for scholars and scholarship in
the comparative field. The SSRC/CCP publication list not only was the
cutting edge of research on comparative politics but also illustrated
the grand theorizing that characterized the field. These were universal,
synthesizing volumes that merged issues of democratic politics, political development, and general theory: *Political Culture and Political De-*
velopment, Political Parties and Political Development, Bureaucracy and
Political Development, Education and Political Development, and so
forth.[7]

These scholars did not succeed in creating a unified theory of politics, a fact that is now generally acknowledged. But at the same time, the
SSRC/CCP network of scholars came close to creating a Kuhnian paradigm of a behavioral approach to comparative politics derived from a
theoretical framework embedded in their studies and research reports
(though see discussion below). Undoubtedly a legion of graduate students have written doctoral theses that apply concepts such as political
culture, structural/functionalism, or systems theory in a comparative
setting. Even those behavioralists working outside the SSRC network
often adopted these global orientations to theory-building, built upon
their own metatheory of politics (e.g. Dahl 1966; Lijphart 1977).

The burst of theory and knowledge of the Golden Age was not limited to the behavioral approach to comparative politics espoused by the
SSRC/CCP network. At roughly the same time, a public choice model of
politics and the democratic process was emerging among political economists (Buchannan and Tullock 1965; Riker 1962; Olson 1965; Downs
1957). This approach has subsequently guided comparative research on
voting choice (e.g. Fiorina 1981), coalition formation (DeSwaan 1973;
Dodd 1976), and interest group activity (Moe 1980; Frohlich and Oppenheimer 1981; Olson 1982). Indeed, the rational choice approach is
one of the most vibrant areas of growth in contemporary comparative
politics. The antibehavioralist Straussian school also was coalescing in
the early 1960s (Storing 1962). Unfortunately, these other theoretical
traditions sometimes go unmentioned and unrecognized in accounts of
the intellectual history of comparative politics.

The behavioralists may have exterted disproportionate influence on
the discipline through their control of the commanding heights of the
discipline and research resources, but the theoretical richness of the
Golden Age was multifaceted. Moreover, these new approaches joined
the existing methods of comparative political analysis, such as historical, legalistic, and Marxist studies. We should, in fact, be clear that the
majority of scholars continued to work within these traditional research
approaches. For instance, Barrington Moore's study (1962) of the so-

cial origins of dictatorship and democracy and Hannah Arendt's (1951) investigation of the origins of totalitarianism represented traditional analytic methods of political science at their best. Thus the unifying element of this seminal research on comparative politics was a common spiritual quest for grand theorizing.

The Devolution of Theory

Just as the surge of intellectual activity within comparative politics was reaching a peak in the late 1960s, the theoretical spirit of the field began to shift. The broad, conceptual models of comparative politics came under increasing challenge on several fronts—both for their analytic value and for their internal integrity.

In large part, the very progress of comparative politics as a field provided the seeds of this discontent. There were growing feelings that broad, all-encompassing theories of political systems often proved too vague or too abstract to guide productively the specific research activities that were proliferating within the field. LaPalombara quotes a reaction from Heinz Eulau, a founding behavioralist who still sympathizes with broad theoretical approaches, that captures the sentiments at the time: "I have yet to read—and that includes David Easton's new book—a systems analysis from which one can derive testable propositions about politics" (LaPalombara 1968, 70). The same might be said of Parsons's pattern variables, structural-functionalism, or most other unified theories of politics.[8]

When relevant empirical data could be collected, the accumulating evidence, and political events, often undercut the apparent validity of prior macrotheories. For example, efforts to empirically separate the concepts of diffuse and specific support have yielded uncertain results (e.g. Miller 1974; Citrin 1974; Muller and Jukam 1977). The "progressive" model of political development came under heavy attack by those who questioned the inevitability of socioeconomic change producing political development (Huntington 1968) and by dependency theorists who raised even more fundamental questions about the basic premises of the model (e.g. Cardosa and Faletto 1979; Chilcote 1981). Evidence of substantial change in the American and West German political cultures eroded at least a part of the theoretical underpinnings of the concept of national cultures (Almond and Verba 1980).

There was also a growing awareness (especially among Third World specialists) that early attempts to develop general theory were often too heavily influenced by the specific conditions of American politics and the perspectives of American political scientists. This ethnocentrism may have been inadvertent, but it was still present—even in research on Western industrial democracies. Critics of Almond and Verba's research ʃon political culture argued that the concept of a "civic culture" was itself culture-bound, rooted in American conceptions of how democracy should function (Pateman 1970; Barry 1970). In the critics' views, different variants of culture could be conducive to a stable democratic order, not just the pattern identified with Anglo-American traditions.[9] At a lower level of theorizing, a similar situation existed for early voting studies. Attempts to export the American concept of party identification to the European context showed that basic elements of the party identification concept were uniquely American (Budge et al. 1976). Similarly, the Miller and Stokes representation study (1963) is one of the seminal works in political behavior research, and the basic design of the study was replicated in nearly a dozen other industrial democracies (e.g. Barnes 1977; Farah 1980; Converse and Pierce 1986). Yet one of the major findings of this research was the distinctiveness of the American pattern of political representation as captured in the theory and design of the Miller-Stokes study (Dalton 1988). This tale can be repeated in several different forms: research on European interest groups, political parties, legislative behavior, public administration, and policy outputs illustrated the distinctiveness of the American experience (e.g. Lehmbruch and Schmitter 1978; Berger 1981; Harmel and Janda 1982; Loewenberg et al. 1985; Flora and Heidenheimer 1981). At a one level, such findings are a significant product of the comparative approach—comparison enabled us to learn about American exceptionalism. But it was ironic that the exceptional American case initially provided the reference system for many early attempts to develop general theory of political phenomena.

Finally, Western democracies were themselves undergoing fundamental changes throughout the postwar period—developing characteristics of advanced industrial or postindustrial societies—which transformed basic elements of the political process and presented new analytic questions (Bell 1973; Inglehart 1977, 1990). Prior grand theories of the political system tended to portray politics in stable, evolutionary terms (e.g. Easton and Dennis 1969): They had provided little advance warning of the student protests that swept through most Western democracies in the 1960s, or the plethora of new issue interests and new political movements that followed in their wake (Dalton and Kuechler 1990; Klandermans 1989). The expanding sophistication of contemporary electorates and the participatory revolution of the 1970s projected a new model of citizen politics (Barnes and Kaase 1979; Dalton 1988) that was at odds with the models derived from *The Civic Culture* or *The American Voter*. Within a single decade, the major question in political party research changed from explaining the persistence of party systems (Lipset and Rokkan 1967; Rose and Urwin 1970) to explaining their instability (Dalton et al. 1984; Merkl and Lawson 1988).

Government action in creating the welfare state and addressing new quality-of-life issues transformed the scope and scale of the political process (Offe 1984; Flora, 1986). In short, earlier metatheories seemed drawn from a more halcyon period of Western political development and appeared less adequate in explaining the newly emerging forces and process of advanced industrial societies.

The combined impact of these factors shifted the course of the comparative politics field in a direction in which it is still proceeding today. Instead of defining the research problem in terms of describing the entire political system, with a resulting emphasis on macrotheories, there was a turning away from such efforts. Given existing knowledge about reality and the complexities of politics, such theorizing was an valuable intellectual exercise but less valuable as an investment in the science of politics. A general theory of politics still represented the ultimate goal of scientific method, but many felt that productive efforts in this direction must be based upon firmer scientific knowledge. Karl Deutsch (1966) and others were beginning to argue that we were theory-rich, but data-poor.

These sentiments narrowed the focus of research attention to more specific subunits of the political process—explaining the actions of voters, political parties, or political elites—rather than attempting to explain the entire process. This shift in research questions also led to a greater emphasis on "middle-range" theory that was tailored to these middle-range research topics (LaPalombara 1968; Macridis 1968). Instead of grand theories of politics, the discipline generally focused its attention on developing a better understanding of the separate elements of the political process; for example, constructing *and testing* theories at the level of voting behavior, political participation, interest groups, elite action, and similar mid-level concepts.

This shift in the spirit of research was a major factor in the rapid expansion of scientific knowledge in the comparative politics field that was discussed earlier in the chapter. This approach led scholars to collect new information and build modest models to explain how subunits of the political system functioned. The research interests of the field proliferated, sometimes building on insights drawn from earlier macrotheories and sometimes moving in new directions. The discipline became more eclectic, but it also became richer and more varied in its knowledge.

It is impossible to review all the progress the middle-level approach has yielded, but we can illustrate how this has produced substantial gains in our knowledge with two examples: postmaterialism and neocorporatism. The choice of these two cases was predicated on several factors. In preparing this essay, I found that these two theories were nearly uniformly cited (at least among my network of colleagues) as major conceptual advances in the recent study of Western industrial democracies. While one theory—postmaterialism—reflects a new approach to new political phenomena, the other—neocorporatism—represents a revival of previous theorizing. Most important, both examples illustrate the success of middle-level theory in developing a conceptual framework that generates testable research hypotheses, and which, once validated, reaches beyond its initial starting point to other aspects of the political system.

Ronald Inglehart's thesis of postmaterial value change (e.g. 1971, 1977, 1981, 1990) is one of the major theoretical and empirical innovations in the recent study of Western industrial democracies. Inglehart began his research on value change as an attempt to explain the generational and educational patterns in popular support for European integration; this effort soon expanded to a broader theory of the changing value priorities of Western publics. His explanation of value change is based on two premises. First, he suggests that the public's basic value priorities are determined by a scarcity hypothesis: individuals place the greatest value on those things that are in relatively short supply.[10] The second component of Inglehart's theory is a socialization hypothesis: individual value priorities reflect the conditions that prevailed during one's preadult years. The combination of both hypotheses produces a general model of value formation: an individual's basic value priorities are formed early in life in reaction to the socioeconomic conditions (personal and societal) of this period, and, once formed, these values tend to endure in the face of subsequent changes in life conditions. Thus the socioeconomic forces transforming Western industrial societies are changing the relative scarcity of valued goals, and consequently the value priorities of Western publics. Older generations are still more likely to emphasize traditional "material" social goals, such as economic well-being, social security, law and order, religious values, and national security. Having grown up in an environment where these traditional goals seem relatively assured, younger generations of Westerners are shifting their attention toward "postmaterial" goals of self-expression, personal freedom, social equality, self-fulfillment, and maintaining the quality of life.

Although Inglehart presents his concept of postmaterial values in the context of the broad social forces transforming advanced industrial societies, I think this is still an example of middle-level theorizing. The value change theory focuses on one aspect of public opinion: how value priorities are formed, and how they change in reaction to external stimuli. This theoretical focus leads to testable predictions about public opinion: expectations about value differences across generations, other sociodemographic groups, national boundaries, and over time. Moreover, in contrast to grand macrotheories of politics, Inglehart developed an impressive store of public opinion data supporting the basic assumptions of his postmaterial thesis.

What is most significant about Inglehart's postmaterial thesis, how-ever, is its broad relevance to the study of contemporary Western industrial societies. His concept of value change was immediately useful in explaining generational differences in public attitudes toward the Common Market. But in addition, the underlying dimension of material/ postmaterial values is related to the public's growing interest in environmental and quality-of-life issues, leading to the instability of voting patterns and the eventual formation of New Left and Green parties (Inglehart 1984; Buerklin 1984; Mueller-Rommel 1989). Postmaterialism appears to be an explanatory factor in the changing action repertoires of Western publics (Barnes and Kaase 1979) and the proliferation of new social movements (Dalton and Kuechler 1990). In short, the "reach" of the concept has been much broader than its original application.

Another current focal point for research on advanced industrial societies is the neocorporatist thesis. During the past decade, a growing awareness of the limitations of pluralist interest group theory led to the revival of alternative corporatist theories (Chalmers 1985). Since corporatist theories have a long history in the study of European politics, often identified with fascist or authoritarian systems, this more recent variant was labeled as "liberal corporatism" or "neocorporatism" (Schmitter 1982; Lehmbruch and Schmitter 1979; Berger 1981). There are two basic elements of neocorporatist theory. First, neocorporatism is characterized by the consolidation and institutionalization of social interests into a highly structured, monopolistic system of interest representation; this is in contrast to the relatively fluid nature of interest groups under the pluralist model. Second, under a neocorporatist system, interest groups develop more formal ties with government, including direct involvement in the policy process ("concertation"); in contrast to the open, competitive nature of interest group politics in the pluralist model and the government's neutral position in this process.

The concept of neocorporatism was of immediate value in orienting research on interest group activities, such, as studies of unions, business associations, and industrial policy (e.g. Katzenstein 1984, 1985; Gourevitch 1986; Gourevitch et al. 1984; Grant 1985, 1987; Markovits 1984). Neocorporatism also provided a framework for explaining the patterns of interest intermediation within several European democracies, patterns that often carried over to noncorporatist interest groups.

At a more general level, patterns of interest intermediation were linked to basic policy outputs and systemic characteristics of nations. The nature of industrial relations and levels of strike activity are related to the existence of neocorporatist structures (Schmidt 1979). Schmitter (1981) presented further evidence that corporatism moderates general

levels of political conflict in a nation. Harold Wilensky (1975) corre-
lated national levels of corporatism with support for welfare state policies; others have examined the relationship between corporatism and
policy outputs such as unemployment levels, inflation, and overall government expenditures (Castles 1987). Indeed, corporatist structures
not only facilitated the expansion of the European welfare state in the
1960s, but apparently also furthered the retrenchment of the welfare
state in the 1980s (Rochon 1988). In sum, like postmaterialism, the
neocorporatist concept has been applied to political phenomena and
areas of research beyond its initial origins.[11]

Certainly, other mid-level theories have advanced the study of Western industrial societies, so this is not an inclusive list.[12] But other areas
of considerable research activity—for example, political economy and
research on the state—lack the unifying theoretical model that postmaterialism and neocorporatism have provided for research on mass
politics and interest intermediation. Postmaterialism and neocorporatism thus stand out as examples because they have influenced a broad
range of research on contemporary democracies. And although neither
postmaterialism nor neocorporatism are comprehensive systemic
(macrolevel) theories of the structure and organization of contemporary societies, both theories provide valuable tools in predicting (or explaining) a variety of political phenomena identified with advanced
industrial societies. Isn't this the measure by which we judge the value
of our theorizing?

A Debate on Spiritual Grounds

Despite the advances represented by postmaterialism, neocorporatism,
and other middle-range research in comparative politics, a substantial
number of critics now openly worry about the course we are following.
The frequently used imagery is that we have created *islands of theory*, unconnected to one another in their interests and findings. In a recent essay,
Gabriel Almond (1988a) observes that comparativists now sit at separate
tables, isolated by our methodology and ideological orientations. Even
stronger views are found in Wiarda (1985). Wiarda, and several other
contributors to his edited volume, maintain that the decline of macrotheorizing has placed the field of comparative politics in a crisis. It is argued
that by losing our grand theoretical perspectives, the field now lacks focus; graduate students can no longer identify the field's "central core,"
knowledge is not cumulative, and scholars are multiplying but scholarship is suffering. Thus they ask us to change course in the future, and try
to recapture the grand theorizing of earlier times.

This is a debate over our spirit. It concerns our judgments of how
research should be done, and how the field should develop in the future.

Will we continue along the course of middle-level research and theorizing that has characterized the past two decades? Or, are we losing our theoretical soul by following this path? After several decades of middle-level theory building and data collection, should we reemphasize the development of systemic theory?

I agree that there is at least an element of truth to these criticisms: the comparative politics field has fragmented as a consequence of the shift toward middle-range research, and therefore it is more difficult to identify the central core of comparative politics. But at the same time, I think that the sharpest criticisms of our present spiritual orientations are somewhat flawed in their depiction of past events and the scientific process.

Those who lament the devolution in research interests and theorizing often premise their arguments on a romanticized image of the intellectual history of comparative politics. These critiques are built upon the implicit assumption that there once was a unifying theory (or even set of theories) that gave a higher order meaning to the field of comparative politics during its Golden Age—this is not so. As we noted above, during the 1950s and 1960s a large portion of the field shared a common interest in research questions involving democratic development, which encouraged the search for grand theory. But a single, accepted theory was a goal, not an accomplished fact. On the one hand, many comparative politics scholars at the time, probably most, did not share an interest in the development question or the behavioralist persuasion of the SSRC/CCP network. Even my brief, cursory check of comparative politics books reviewed in the *American Political Science Review* in the early 1960s found that most studies utilized historical, institutional, or classical-theory approaches, rather than behavioralism. The emerging schools of public choice theorists and Straussians directly challenged the behavioralist method. In many historical accounts of the comparative politics field written by behavioralists, the origins of the field become synonymous with behavioralism. This tendency to define the entire discipline in terms of one's own approach appears common among academics, as Alker and Biersteker (1984) have illustrated for the field of international relations, but this tendency oversimplifies the richness and diversity of scholarship—especially when it is projected back two or three decades. On the other hand, even behavioralists during the Golden Age did not agree upon a single, grand theory; systems theory, structural-functionalism, pattern variables, and other macro-theories competed against one another. Gabriel Almond's own conceptual framework evolved from a group-based approach, to structural-functionalism, to a political culture framework, as Almond himself acknowledges. Was there really greater unity and clarity in the field when the leading behavioralist scholars championed contrasting macro-

theories of the political process that differed in fundamental elements
and basic structure, and that could not be verified?

Those who see middle-level research and theorizing as producing a
crisis of comparative politics also err, in my opinion, in their understanding of the relationship between theory and the scientific process.
Robert Merton (1949) held that the construction of macrotheories is
necessary at the beginning of a scientific discipline. This theorizing provides a general frame of reference, a rough celestial map to guide our
explorations. Such grand theories are inevitably crude and imperfect,
given our initial knowledge of the world, but they provide a general
framework for research as the discipline moves to mid-level theorizing
and the collection of knowledge that in the long run may lead to the
construction of a new paradigm. The Golden Age represented an
attempt to provide these initial orientations for scholars in the comparative politics field. At some point, which we have passed, global theorizing reached the limits of our knowledge and the discipline naturally
turned to a more productive line of scientific inquiry.[13] We can continue
to admire prior macrotheories for their intellectual complexity and
creativity: Parsons (or Marx) will always be an intellectual challenge
for graduate students. But theories are not deities; they should be
judged on their functional value in providing us a model for understanding the world, whose validity can be determined by testing it
against reality.

TOWARD THE FUTURE

In reflecting on the field of comparative politics, Sidney Verba (1985)
speculates that the supposed crisis of comparative politics may be a
function of the age of the critics *or* the age of the discipline. I think he is
correct on both counts. The Golden Age of the 1950s and early 1960s
was marked by a exhilarating feeling that fundamental scientific advances were being made in comparative politics and a revolutionary
new political science was on the horizon. This revolution never materi-
alized, at least as envisioned, and some participants of the period now
project a sense of failure or unfulfilled potential onto the field. It is true,
the behavioral revolution did not supplant the ancien régime—though
it has transformed the nature of comparative political science. Moreover, this unfulfilled revolution does not mean that the field of comparative politics has failed. Indeed, the past quarter-century is marked by
impressive (though perhaps not revolutionary) advances in our knowledge and theorizing about comparative politics.

I would thus describe the devolution of the field not in pejorative
terms, but as creating diversity and pluralism in the study of compara-

tive politics. The behavioral approach has joined more traditional modes of comparative analysis; more recently, formal modeling and rational choice perspectives may be broadening our analytic scope still further.[14] While I might be critical of some of these other schools, and wish that they would accept "my" view of comparative politics, I am also glad that the diversity of the field means that I am not forced to accept "their" view. This variation strengthens the field of comparative politics through the competition of ideas and alternative paradigms. Theories and research approaches are judged by their value, thus attracting more support for some approaches or leading to declining support for others. In short, at the present state of the discipline it is not always harmful for scholars to be able to choose between separate tables (Mayer 1989).

This essay has also stressed the diversity in the level of defining research questions, and therefore theorizing, in comparative politics. Some scholars will continue to work on grand, systemic theories, while others toil on their separate islands of theory. The choice between macrolevel and middle-level theorizing reflects our personal and collective judgment on the reasonable possible returns from both strategies, as well as the institutional structure in which research is conducted.

Although the development of a single paradigm is our ultimate scientific goal, my reading of our history and immediate future leads me to believe that the devolution to middle-range theory represents an accurate assessment of the present developmental stage of comparative politics: it is our most likely future. I think this forecast holds whether one is using traditional methods of political analysis, behavioral research, or formal modeling approaches. If this prognosis for the future is correct, what does it mean for the field?

In terms of teaching, this perspective suggests that we do not search for a grand theory to orient our students; instead, we describe the history of the field in terms of Kuhnian, Lakatosian, or Mertonian processes of scientific evolution. Since a consensual paradigm of comparative politics does not exist, the major systemic theories can be presented as attempts to develop paradigms as the discipline first developed. In discussing a similar problem in the study of international relations, Hayward Alker and Thomas Biersteker (1984) maintain that introductory courses should be cosmopolitan in their review of these systemic theories (in actual practice, most instructors work within a distinct approach). We still draw our basic orientations and concepts from this theoretical base, and students should realize this (e.g. Almond 1988b). Then, students may be taken island hopping to learn about the significant middle-level theories of the field.

Island hopping may be an effective method of introducing students to the field of comparative politics, but it is less effective as a research

ᒋstrategy. The shift to middle-range research interests develops a large body of knowledge about each island that a scholar must master to achieve standing in the field. Often, this knowledge requires specialized language skills, research expertise, or methodology. Thus, we focus our attention on only one island, or at most a limited number of islands. The positive consequence of this specialization is that it contributes to the rapid expansion of our scientific knowledge—the emphases on middle-range theory has been the corporal sustenance of the field.

∟   At the same time, we realize that middle-level theorizing may narrow our research horizons. It is too easy just to collect facts, without a guiding theoretical (and therefore scientific) interest. It appears to me, for example, that too many studies of public opinion are little more than journalistic accounts of findings, not driven by theoretical interests. Similarly, portions of the political economy field are asking their doctoral students to undertake descriptive case studies of union development or industrial relations that mark a regression in the scope and method of comparative politics. Indeed, at one time or another, all of us probably feel that we are learning more and more about less and less. Excesses of this type fuel the periodic calls for greater attention to theory.

If scholarship continues to follow this middle-range course, this holds certain implications for comparative politics research. I think we have two alternatives before us. One strategy is to focus on incremental growth of each island of theory. The present incentive structure of academia leads us in this direction. Salary and status systems based on numbers of publications and citation counts encourage us to become specialists and individual entrepreneurs. We are very knowledgeable in the political lore of our island and adept in adding incrementally to this knowledge, but limited in the knowledge of other islands. We expand our islands of theory, one small polder at a time.

Γ A second strategy is to consciously build bridges between our islands. This approach would maximize the advantages of our separate areas of specialized knowledge and skills, and minimize the risks of developing too narrow research foci, by attempting to link areas of knowledge together in systematic ways. Given the expansion in our knowledge, however, this bridge building probably lies beyond the abilities of most individuals, and a team approach to research is required. If we are interested in understanding the changing political dynamics of advanced industrial societies, for example, we need to draw upon the expertise of public opinion researchers, social ecologists, economists, historians, policy analysts, and other specialists. Karl Deutsch's study (Deutsch et al. 1971) of the major social science breakthroughs of the twentieth century seems to bear out this point; major advances are more common in institutional settings where resources and a diversity of perspectives intermix. This approach would, in short, harness the strength of the mid-level approach while minimizing its weaknesses through collaborative and interdisciplinary exchange.

The difficulty of this strategy is that it runs counter to the individualist norms of American social science and the institutional trends of the discipline. In an environment in which promotion is based on article productivity and citation counts, individualism is the path to personal security. Even the largest social science research institutes in the United States, such as the Institute for Social Research in Ann Arbor or the National Opinion Research Center in Chicago, are basically individually oriented entrepreneurial organizations.

If we want integrative research that will build bridges between islands, we need different institutional structures in the social sciences. I have consulted with numerous colleagues, and it appears that truly collaborative research settings in the social sciences are quite rare, even if we look to other national experiences. The most notable examples of institutional structures that encourage bridge building may be found in West Germany. The Max Planck institutes, for instance, provide institutional settings for interdisciplinary and team-based research, and in the past decade the Max Planck model has expanded from the natural sciences to include new institutes in the social sciences. Similarly, the integrative and long-term perspective of the Research Center in Berlin led to research activities, such as the Globus project, that simply could not be accomplished in the United States (Bremer et al. 1987). The German Research Foundation also accommodates research proposals for a "special research area," which provides multiyear funding for large, integrative research projects.

Certainly there are potential risks associated with the concentration of research resources; we might turn to the natural sciences or the German experiences for guidance in addressing the potential problems. But taking these risks may be the best method for making fundamental scientific advances.

It is difficult to look into the future, though doing so was the ultimate objective of this essay. Periodic discussions of the vitality or infirmity of the field are probably an inevitable part of the scientific process, as witnessed by the other chapters in this volume. These discussions make us take stock of our progress and think about our future. There is still much more to be done, but I see little cause for pessimism about the status of comparative politics if we continue these introspective discussions. The corporal and spiritual advances of the past generation speak of the basic success and progress of the field, and the future knowledge that is still to be gained.

NOTES

1. S. M. Lipset's documentation of American exceptionalism, for example, directly follows from his broader comparative research orientation (Lipset 1963).

2. See the interesting symposium on growth pattern of the comparative field in *PS* (Summer 1984). Several authors note how the "non-American" content of American political science has ebbed and flowed over the past century (also see Somit and Tanenhaus 1967).

3. These include the Zentralarchiv fuer empirische Sozialforschung in Cologne, the Economic and Social Research Council archive in Essex, the Banque de Données Socio-Politiques in Grenoble, the Steinmetz archive in Amsterdam, the Danish Data Archive in Copenhagen, the Norwegian Data Archive in Bergen, and the BASS in Belgium.

4. The ECPR meetings might provide an even more important forum for research on Western democracies if they were to abandon their quota system, which restricts the number of non-European participants. Nationality quotas are inconsistent with scientific inquiry.

5. Or, as one of the commentators on this chapter recounted, during the early 1960s there was a feeling that the discipline was "waiting for our Newton": the great theorist would synthesize the advances in our scientific knowledge and identify the basic laws of human nature.

6. It should be remembered that the SSRC was a major source of social science research funding at the time, performing the role now occupied by the National Science Foundation. NSF did not become a major source of political science research funding until the mid-1960s.

7. Almond and Coleman (1960); Pye (1963); LaPalombara (1963); Ward and Rustow (1964); Coleman (1965); Pye and Verba (1965); LaPalombara and Weiner (1966); Binder et al. (1971); Tilly (1975).

8. However, Harry Eckstein's attempt (1966) to test his theory of democracy with a critical case study approach may be a significant counterexample.

9. To their credit, this diversity of views is represented in Almond and Verba's (1980) revisitation of the political culture literature.

10. In his earlier work, Inglehart linked the scarcity hypothesis to Abraham Maslow's broader theoretical framework of a hierarchy of human values; the Maslovian framework has become less prominent in Inglehart's more recent writings (e.g. 1990).

11. I would, however, stop well short of Schmitter's (1985, 54ff) claim that neocorporatism has grown into an "associative model of social order," which provides the basic structure of society.

12. The rational choice and social choice approaches would provide other important case studies, as well as resource mobilization theories as applied to political movements.

13. And yet, we carry with us on our journey the concepts and sense of bearing that are drawn from this earlier macrotheorizing. This is one of the sub-

tle lessons in Almond's recent writings (1988a, 1988b) on the intellectual history of political science.

14. Whereas a Marxist approach might once have provided an important framework for the study of Western industrial democracies, it now carries a much more limited scholarly appeal (cf. Alker and Biersteker 1984).

REFERENCES

Aberbach, Joel, Robert Putnam, and Bert Rockman. 1981. *Bureaucrats and Politicians*. Cambridge: Harvard University Press.

Adorno, Theodor, et al. 1950. *The Authoritarian Personality*. New York: Harper.

Alker, Hayward, and Thomas Biersteker. 1984. "The Dialectics of World Order." *International Studies Quarterly* 28:121–42.

Almond, Gabriel. 1954. *The Appeals of Communism*. Princeton: Princeton University Press.

———. 1988a. "Separate Tables: Schools and Sects in Political Science?" *PS* 21: 828–42.

———. 1988b. "Return to the State." *American Political Science Review* 82: 853–74.

Almond, Gabriel, and James Coleman, eds. 1960. *The Politics of Developing Areas*. Princeton: Princeton University Press.

Almond, Gabriel, and Sidney Verba. 1963. *The Civic Culture*. Princeton: Princeton University Press.

Almond, Gabriel, and Sidney Verba, eds. 1980. *The Civic Culture Revisited*. Boston: Little, Brown.

Apter, David. 1965. *The Politics of Modernization*. Chicago: University of Chicago Press.

Arendt, Hannah. 1951. *The Origins of Totalitarianism*. New York: Harcourt & Brace.

Barnes, Samuel. 1977. *Representation in Italy*. Chicago: University of Chicago Press.

Barnes, Samuel, Max Kaase, et al. 1979. *Political Action*. Beverly Hills, Calif.: Sage Publications.

Barry, Brian. 1970. *Sociologists, Economists, and Democracy*. London: Macmillan.

Bell, Daniel. 1973. *The Coming of Post-industrial Society*. New York: Basic Books.

Berger, Suzanne. 1984. "Politics: American and Non-American." *PS* 17: 545–48.

Berger, Suzanne, ed. 1981. *Organizing Interests in Western Europe*. Cambridge: Cambridge University Press.

Binder, Leonard, et al. 1971. *Crises and Sequences in Political Development*. Princeton: Princeton University Press.

Bremer, Stuart, et al. 1987. *The Globus Model*. Boulder: Westview Press.

Buchannan, James, and Gordon Tullock. 1965. *The Calculus of Consent*. Ann Arbor: University of Michigan Press.

Budge, Ian, et al. 1976. *Party Identification and Beyond*. New York: Wiley.

Budge, Ian, David Robertson, and Derek Hearl, eds. 1987. *Ideology, Strategy, and Party Change*. New York: Cambridge University Press.

Buerklin, Wilhelm. 1984. *Gruene Politik. Ideologische Zyklen, Waehler und Parteiensystem*. Opladen: Westdeutscher Verlag.

Campbell, Angus, et al. 1960. *The American Voter*. New York: Wiley.

Cardoso, Fernando, and Enzo Faletto. 1979. *Dependency and Development in Latin America*. Berkeley: University of California Press.

Castles, Frank. 1987. "Neo-corporatism and the 'Happiness' Index, or What the Trade Unions Get for their Cooperation." *European Journal for Political Research* 15:381–93.

Chalmers, Douglas. 1985. "Corporatism and Comparative Politics." In *New Directions in Comparative Politics*, edited by Howard Wiarda. Boulder: Westview Press.

Chilcote, Ronald. 1981. *Theories of Comparative Politics*. Boulder: Westview Press.

Citrin, Jack. 1974. "Comment." *American Political Science Review* 68:973–88.

Coleman, James, ed. 1965. *Education and Political Development*. Princeton: Princeton University Press.

Converse, Phillip, and Roy Pierce. 1986. *Representation in France*. Cambridge: Harvard University Press.

Daalder, Hans, and Ferdinand Mueller-Rommel, eds. 1989. *Cabinet Formations*. London: Sage Publications.

Dahl, Robert, ed. 1966. *Political Oppositions in Western Democracies*. New Haven: Yale University Press.

Dalton, Russell. 1988. *Citizen Politics in Western Democracies*. Chatham, N.J.: Chatham House Publishers.

Dalton, Russell, Scott Flanagan, and Paul Beck, eds. 1984. *Electoral Change in Advanced Industrial Democracies*. Princeton: Princeton University Press.

Dalton, Russell, and Manfred Kuechler, eds. 1990. *Challenging the Political Order*. New York: Oxford University Press; Cambridge: Polity Press.

DeSwaan, Abraham. 1973. *Coalition Theories and Cabinet Formations*. San Francisco: Jossey-Bass.

Deutsch, Karl. 1953. *Nationalism and Social Communication*. New York: MIT Press.

———. 1963. *Nerves of Government*. New York: Free Press.

———. 1966. "The Theoretical Basis of Data Programs." In *Comparing Na-*

tions, edited by Richard Merritt and Stein Rokkan. New Haven: Yale University Press.

Deutsch, Karl, and Lewis Edinger. 1959. *Germany Rejoins the Powers*. Stanford: Stanford University Press.

Deutsch, Karl, John Platt, and Dieter Senghaas. 1971. "Conditions Favoring Major Advances in Social Science." *Science* 171:450–59.

DiPalma, Giuseppe. 1977. *Surviving without Governing*. Berkeley: University of California Press.

Dodd, Larry. 1976. *Coalitions in Parliamentary Government*. Princeton: Princeton University Press.

Downs, Anthony. 1957. *An Economic Theory of Democracy*. New York: Harper & Row.

Easton, David. 1965. *A Systems Analysis of Political Life*. New York: Wiley.

Easton, David, and Jack Dennis. 1969. *Children in the Political System*. New York: McGraw Hill.

Eckstein, Harry. 1960. *Pressure Group Politics: The Case of the British Medical Association*. Stanford: Stanford University Press.

———. 1966. *Division and Cohesion in Democracy*. Princeton: Princeton University Press.

Ehrmann, Henry. 1957. *Organized Business in France*. Princeton: Princeton University Press.

Farah, Barbara. 1980. "Political Representation in West Germany." Ph.D. dissertation, University of Michigan.

Fiorina, Morris. 1981. *Retrospective Voting in American National Elections*. New Haven: Yale University Press.

Flora, Peter, ed. 1986. *Growth to Limits*. 2 vols. Berlin: deGruyter.

Flora, Peter, et al. 1983. *State, Economy and Society in Western Europe, 1918-1975*. Frankfurt: Campus.

Flora, Peter, and Arnold Heidenheimer, eds. 1981. *Development of the Welfare State*. New Brunswick: Transaction Books.

Franklin, Mark, et al. 1991. *Social Structure and Party Choice*. New York: Cambridge University Press.

Frohlich, Norman, and Joe Oppenheimer. 1971. *Political Leadership and Collective Goods*. Princeton: Princeton University Press.

Gourevitch, Peter. 1984. *Unions and the Economic Crisis*. Boston: Allen & Unwin.

———. 1986. *Politics in Hard Times*. Ithaca: Cornell University Press.

Grant, Wyn, ed. 1985. *The Political Economy of Corporatism*. New York: St. Martin's Press.

———. 1987. *Business Interests, Organizational Development and Private Interest Government*. Berlin: deGruyter.

Grew, Raymond, ed. 1978. *Crises of Political Development in Europe and the United States*. Princeton: Princeton University Press.

Harmel, Robert, and Kenneth Janda. 1982. *Parties and Their Environments*. New York: Longman.

Hibbs, Douglas. 1973. *Mass Political Violence*. New York: Wiley.

Hoffmann-Lange, Ursula, et al. 1980. *Konsens und Konflikt zwischen Fuehrungsgruppen in der Bundesrepublik Deutschland*. Frankfurt: Peter Lang.

Holt, Robert, and John Turner, eds. 1970. *The Methodology of Comparative Research*. New York: Free Press.

Huntington, Samuel. 1968. *Political Order in Changing Societies*. New Haven: Yale University Press.

Inglehart, Ronald. 1971. "The Silent Revolution in Europe." *American Political Science Review* 65:991–1017.

———. 1977. *The Silent Revolution*. Princeton: Princeton University Press.

———. 1981. "Postmaterialism in an Environment of Insecurity." *American Political Science Review* 75:880–900.

———. 1984. "Changing Cleavage Alignments in Western Democracies." In *Electoral Change in Advanced Industrial Democracies*, edited by Russell Dalton, Scott Flanagan, and Paul Beck. Princeton: Princeton University Press.

———. 1990. *Culture Shift in Advanced Industrial Society*. Princeton: Princeton University Press.

Jennings, M. Kent, and Jan van Deth, eds. 1989. *Continuities in Political Action*. Berlin: deGruyter.

Katzenstein, Peter. 1984. *Corporatism and Change: Austria, Switzerland, and the Politics of Industry*. Ithaca: Cornell University Press.

———. 1985. *Small States in World Markets: Industrial Policy in Europe*. Ithaca: Cornell University Press.

Klandermans, Bert, ed. 1989. *Organizing for Change: Social Movement Organizations across Cultures*. Greenwich: JAI Press.

LaPalombara, Joseph. 1964. *Interest Groups in Italian Politics*. Princeton: Princeton University Press.

———. 1968. "Macrotheories and Microapplications in Comparative Politics." *Comparative Politics* 1:52–78.

LaPalombara, Joseph, ed. 1963. *Bureaucracy and Political Development*. Princeton: Princeton University Press.

LaPalombara, Joseph, and Myron Weiner, eds. 1966. *Political Parties and Political Development*. Princeton: Princeton University Press.

Lehmbruch, Gerhard, and Philippe Schmitter, eds. 1979. *Patterns of Corporatist Policy Making*. Beverly Hills: Sage Publications.

Lijphart, Arend. 1975. *The Politics of Accommodation: Pluralism and Democracy in the Netherlands*. Berkeley: University of California Press.

———. 1977. *Democracy in Plural Societies*. New Haven: Yale University Press.

Lipset, Seymour Martin. 1959. *Political Man*. New York: Doubleday.

———. 1963. *The First New Nation*. New York: Norton.

Lipset, Seymour Martin, and Earl Raab. 1970. *The Politics of Unreason*. New York: Harper & Row.

Lipset, Seymour Martin, and Stein Rokkan, ed. 1967. *Party Systems and Voter Alignments*. New York: Free Press.

Livingston, Robert, and Uwe Thaysen, eds. 1990. *The Congress and the Bundestag*. Boulder: Westview Press.

Loewenberg, Gerhard, et al. 1985. *Handbook of Legislative Research*. Cambridge: Harvard University Press.

Macridis, Roy. 1968. "Comparative Politics and the Study of Government." *Comparative Politics* 1:79–90.

Markovitz, Andrei. 1984. *Unions and the Economic Crisis*. London: Allen & Unwin.

Mayer, Lawrence. 1989. *Redefining Comparative Politics*. Beverly Hills: Sage Publications.

Merkl, Peter, and Kay Lawson, eds. 1988. *When Parties Fail*. Princeton: Princeton University Press.

Merton, Robert. 1949. *Social Theory and Social Structure*. Glencoe: Free Press.

Milgram, Stanley. 1974. *Obedience to Authority*. New York: Harper & Row.

Miller, Arthur. 1974. "Political Issues and Trust in Government." *American Political Science Review* 68:951–72.

Miller, Warren, and Kent Jennings. 1987. *Party Leadership in Transition*. New York: Russell Sage.

Miller, Warren, and Donald Stokes. 1963. "Constituency Influence in Congress." *American Political Science Review* 57:45–56.

Moe, Terry. 1980. *The Organization of Interests*. Chicago: University of Chicago Press.

Moore, Barrington. 1962. *Social Origins of Dictatorship and Democracy*. Boston: Beacon Press.

Mueller-Rommel, Ferdinand, ed. 1989. *New Politics Parties in Western Europe*. Boulder: Westview Press.

Muller, Edward. 1979. *Aggressive Political Participation*. Princeton: Princeton University Press.

Muller, Edward, and Thomas Jukam. 1977. "On the Meaning of Political Support." *American Political Science Review* 71:1561–95.

Norton, Philip. 1981. *The Commons in Perspective*. New York: Longman.

Offe, Claus. 1984. *Contradictions of the Welfare State*. Cambridge: MIT Press.

Olson, Mancur. 1965. *The Logic of Collective Action*. Cambridge: Harvard University Press.

————. 1982. *The Rise and Decline of Nations*. New Haven: Yale University Press.

Parsons, Talcott, and Edward Shils. 1951. *Toward a General Theory of Action*. New York: Harper & Row.

Pateman, Carole. 1970. *Participation and Democratic Theory*. Cambridge: Cambridge University Press.

Powell, Bingham. 1982. *Contemporary Democracies*. Cambridge: Harvard University Press.

Przeworski, Adam, and Harry Teune. 1970. *Logic of Comparative Social Inquiry*. New York: Wiley.

Putnam, Robert. 1973. *The Beliefs of Politicians*. New Haven: Yale University Press.

Pye, Lucian. 1956. *Guerrilla Communism in Malaya*. Princeton: Princeton University Press.

Pye, Lucian, ed. 1963. *Communications and Political Development*. Princeton: Princeton University Press.

Pye, Lucian, and Sidney Verba, eds. 1965. *Political Culture and Political Development*. Princeton: Princeton University Press.

Riker, William. 1962. *The Theory of Political Coalitions*. New Haven: Yale University Press.

Rochon, Thomas. 1988. "Corporatism and Welfare Retrenchment in Western Europe." Paper presented at the annual meetings of the American Political Science Association.

Rose, Richard, and Derek Urwin. 1970. "Persistence and Change in Western Party Systems since 1945." *Political Studies* 18:287–319.

Rostow, W. W. 1960. *Stages of Economic Growth*. New York: Cambridge University Press.

Schmidt, Manfred. 1979. "Does Corporatism Matter?" In *Patterns of Corporatist Policy Making*, edited by Gerhard Lehmbruch and Philippe Schmitter. Beverly Hills: Sage Publications.

Schmitter, Philippe. 1981. "Interest Intermediation and Regime Governability in Contemporary Western Europe and North America." In *Organizing Interests in Western Europe*, edited by Suzanne Berger. Cambridge: Cambridge University Press.

————. 1982. "Modes of Interest Intermediation and Models of Societal Change in Western Europe." In *Patterns of Corporatist Policy Making*, edited by Gerhard Lehmbruch and Philippe Schmitter. Beverly Hills: Sage Publications.

————. 1985. "Neocorporatism and the State." In *The Political Economy of Corporatism*, edited by Wyn Grant. New York: St. Martin's Press.

Somit, Albert, and Joseph Tanenhaus. 1967. *The Development of Political Science*. Boston: Allyn & Bacon.

Storing, Herbert. 1962. *Essays on the Scientific Study of Politics*. New York: Holt, Rinehart & Winston.

Taageperra, Rein, and Matthew Shugart. 1989. *Seats and Votes*. New Haven: Yale University Press.

Taylor, Charles, and David Jodice. 1983. *World Handbook of Political and Social Indicators*. 3rd ed. New Haven: Yale University Press.

Tilly, Charles, ed. 1975. *The Formation of National States in Western Europe*. Princeton: Princeton University Press.

Verba, Sidney. 1965. "Germany." In *Political Culture and Political Development*, edited by Lucian Pye and Sidney Verba. Princeton: Princeton University Press.

————. 1985. "Comparative Politics." In *New Directions in Comparative Politics*, edited by Howard Wiarda. Boulder: Westview Pres.

Verba, Sidney, et al. 1987. *Elites and the Idea of Inequality*. Cambridge: Harvard University Press.

Ward, Robert, and Dankwart Rustow, eds. 1964. *Political Modernization in Japan and Turkey*. Princeton: Princeton University Press.

Wiarda, Howard, ed. 1985. *New Directions in Comparative Politics*. Boulder: Westview Press.

Wilensky, Harold. 1975. *The Welfare State and Equality*. Berkeley: University of California Press.

2

Paradigms and Sand Castles in Comparative Politics of Developing Areas

Barbara Geddes

[A]s soon as a social phenomenon has been fully explained by a variety of converging approaches and is therefore understood in its majestic inevitability and perhaps even permanence, it vanishes. (Hirschman 1979, 98)

When a phenomenon vanishes, the theories that explained it tend to fall into disrepute. The problem of vanishing phenomena that Hirschman noted is only one of the reasons why theories and paradigms aimed at understanding politics in developing areas tend to rise and fall within short spaces of time, leaving behind little to show that they ever existed. ⚹Other reasons, to be discussed below, include the selective use of available information in building theories, failure to test theories before asserting their validity, and the tendency to focus on trying to explain complex, large-scale outcomes rather than trying to understand the basic processes that underlie such outcomes. In consequence, like an elaborate sand castle, a theory is built with great effort and attention to detail only to be washed away by the tide of the next generation of graduate students, whose research—as it should—batters at the weak points in the structure until eventually the whole thing crumbles and disappears.

A serious question repeatedly confronts those of us who feel a vocation for searching for explanations of politics and development in the

I am very grateful to Barry Ames, Jeff Frieden, Robert Jackman, Michael Lofchie, Dick Sklar, Barbara Stallings, and John Zaller for helpful comments on earlier drafts of this chapter.

Third World: Why have we accumulated so little theoretical—as opposed to factual—knowledge during the last forty years? If we compare our subfield with subfields such as American politics or international relations, the difference in current levels of theoretical coherence and sophistication is striking.

This difference cannot be attributed to any failure of creative theoretical imagination. Rather, it stems from our inability to build on, develop, and extend old theories; we have instead discarded them when anomalies are discovered. This is not to say that we are promiscuous or disloyal to our theories. We cling to our theories with the same fervor and tenacity as do others to theirs. The problem is that our theories disillusion us. Cruel and inconvenient evidence forces us to abandon them. Why does this happen?

⁂ The goal of this chapter is to answer that question. It will begin by sketching the evolution of what I judge to have been the major orienting ideas in comparative politics as applied to developing countries. It will then offer some suggestions about why we feel forced to consign old paradigms to the dustbin of history rather than being able to build on some of their constituent elements even after others have been rejected. And, finally, it will speculate about which current approaches seem to offer the most promise of leading to a more sturdy accumulation of theory in the future.

THE EVOLUTION OF COMPARATIVE POLITICAL ANALYSIS AS APPLIED TO DEVELOPING COUNTRIES

Comparative political analysis of the Third World, with its emphasis on area expertise and its tendency to rely on case studies for data, sometimes gives the impression of being defined in terms of areas of real estate. But, in reality, like other fields, it is defined by a set of central questions, one or more prevailing paradigms (to use the word somewhat loosely) that orient approaches to the central questions, and a research frontier or agenda of issues that at any particular time are considered especially puzzling.

When the Third World first began to receive concentrated attention from political scientists after World War II, the central question for the emerging subfield was: What causes or impedes development? The prevailing paradigm was a loose collection of assumptions, generalizations, and hypotheses referred to, generously, as modernization "theory." I refer to modernization theory as a paradigm because the generalizations, hypotheses, and theories of which it was composed formed a more or less consistent and coherent body.

‰ Modernization theory, as one would expect, reflected the times in which it developed. Some of its central ideas drew on observations of the world at the time, from which observers assumed they could extrapolate into the future, and some drew on academic theories prevailing at the time.

Modernization theorists attributed to some of the empirical relationships they observed the status of lawlike generalizations. One of the most important of these was the correlation between democracy and economic development (Lipset 1959; Jackman 1973). Another was that the diffusion of economic and technological innovations, along with education and the spread of ideas that had originated in Europe, would lead to the rapid transformation of traditional societies and cultures into modern ones (Levy 1966). Expectations about the effects of diffusion were based on historical European experience and the rapidity with which developing societies were embracing certain innovations during the immediate postwar period.

Given the apparent affinity between democracy and economic development in the fifties, theorists viewed modernization as including both a political and an economic dimension, with the political dimension defined as analogous to the economic. That is, analysts expected modern political systems to exhibit characteristics analogous to those associated with modern economic systems: a complex division of labor, occupation by individuals of multiple roles, mobility of resources, including human labor and skills, allocation of resources and goods through an impersonal market rather than by ascription.

A more complex division of labor was expected in the political sphere as well as the economic. That is, political leadership was expected to become more specialized and separate from social, religious, and military leadership. Political roles, like occupational roles, were seen as part-time and changeable, not as lifetime status attributes. Political roles were expected to be allocated by an impersonal procedure analogous to the market: elections. Just as consumers in a modern market economy decide which companies offer the best deal in products, educated modern citizens were expected to participate in elections to decide which candidates would supply the best deal in political goods. This extended analogy provided a theoretical rationale for the belief that democracy was the modern end point of a continuum from traditional to modern political systems just as an industrial economy was the modern end point of the economic continuum. This set of ideas about the centrality of an increasingly complex division of labor and of new ways of organizing it drew basic insights from Durkheim's (1933) analysis of European modernization.

Ideas about the effects of the diffusion of technological innovations, though also based on European experience, drew more heavily from Marx. Observers believed that the diffusion of technology, which could be seen happening rapidly, would quickly lead to economic development, and that cultural and societal modernization would follow automatically as a result of changes in status, expectations, and roles brought about by the resource mobility required by industrialization (W. E. Moore 1963). This emphasis on technological innovation as the deus ex machina that would bring in its wake profound social, political, and cultural changes was consistent with Marx's interpretation of European modernization.

Early modernization theorists, however, gave little attention to the struggle among conflicting interests vested in different stages of development or the possibility that violence might occur in the struggle to overcome interests vested in the traditional order. Their expectations of incremental, peaceful change reflected late nineteenth-century experience in Britain and North America and were consistent with the pluralist image of politics dominant at the time. Their benign view of international economic forces was also consistent with North Atlantic experience and neoclassical economic theory.

Neoclassical economics and pluralism were the two contemporary academic approaches that most influenced modernization theory. The pluralist image of political life contributed to expectations that change would come about incrementally through the interplay of societal interests (cf. Binder 1986). Neoclassical economics supplied theoretical support for a view of the international economy as simply the medium through which resources could flow to their most efficient use and trade, which would enable all parties to capture the gains of specialization based on comparative advantage, could occur.

Challenges to modernization theory arose as a result of anomalies observed by scholars from developing countries and by Northern scholars engaged in research abroad. The "modernization" that modernization theory had sought to explain did not seem to be occurring. Instead of a new crop of prosperous and democratic societies, observers perceived a proliferation of stunted and malformed societal offspring resulting from a careless and exploitative intercourse between advanced and backward nations.

The uneven diffusion of innovations from the advanced to the developing countries had a number of unforeseen consequences. Modern industrial techniques implanted in enclaves by foreign investors failed to spread to the rest of the economy. Agricultural production for the domestic market failed to keep up with industrialization and urbanization, leading to pressure on food prices and an increasing income gap between the rural poor and the rest of society. Industry failed to draw sufficient labor out of the unproductive agricultural sector to improve the distribution of income. Economic growth, though often rapid, failed to generate adequate self-sustained domestic investment, and consequently developing countries remained dependent on foreign sources of capital and technology. Continued dependence on imports led to recurrent and increasingly serious balance-of-payments crises. The spread of medical innovations without compensating increases in agricultural productivity led to fears of deepening poverty as a result of overpopulation. The introduction of Northern political institutions into societies in which traditional modes of personal and political inter-action still prevailed resulted in political systems characterized by nepotism, corruption, and clientelism. In many countries, the line between public and private resources seemed hopelessly blurred. This catalogue of ills could be continued almost indefinitely, but let this list suffice.

Two approaches emerged that were aimed at explaining what was seen as the failure of modernization: dependency theory, and revised versions of modernization theory that stressed the effects of political culture. Revised modernization theory related difficulties encountered during modernization to the persistence of traditional norms and values at variance with the culture traits assumed to be conducive to economic achievement and to honest, efficient government (e.g. Banfield 1958; McClelland 1961). Scholars working within this perspective noted the absence in the developing world of the syndrome of cultural traits—individualism, proceduralism, the work ethic—associated, according to Weber (1958), with the rise of the spirit of capitalism (Lowenthal 1964).

Explanations stressing the effects of political culture typically took the following form. A set of culture traits that had evolved to deal with problems encountered in the traditional society was described. The persistence of these traits, even though the milieu in which they had developed had changed, was then explained by the existence of informal sanctions and rewards that persuaded individuals to continue to behave in culturally approved ways. These sanctions and rewards were not primarily material but were nevertheless compelling. Finally, the consequences of the persistence of traditional behaviors for performance in some modern or modernizing endeavor were described. In other words, these analyses explained the persistence of collectively dysfunctional culture traits in individuals as a consequence of the set of incentives the individuals confront as members of informal, primordial groups.

This approach stressed the utility to individuals, and hence the persistence, of investment in status goods rather than productive endeavors, reluctance to try new agricultural technologies, clientelism, nepotism, and corruption. It offered an explanation based on the clash between personal goals and the goals of organizations intent on fostering development for the frequent mutation and unforeseen consequences of modernization efforts (Riggs 1960, 1964; Price 1975).

Such emphasis on the resistance of society and culture to modernizing change leads, via a route different from that taken by Marx, to a recognition of the role of social revolution in facilitating modernization. Some authors working within the political culture framework saw political violence and revolution as a means of destroying vested interests, both material and ideal, in the traditional order and of changing traditional norms (Jowitt 1971). This extension of modernization theory was thus able to deal with communist as well as capitalist modernization, unlike early modernization theory, which tended to ignore communist countries.

The revised modernization approach, though it challenged the pluralist underpinnings of early modernization theory, did not challenge other basic tenets of the approach. Like earlier versions, it continued to see the international economy as a source of progressive innovations and to focus on explanatory variables located in the domestic society.

Perhaps the most marked revision of modernization theory was the change in the dependent variable it sought to explain. Originally modernization theory had aimed at explaining successful modernization. Revised versions sought to explain failed, distorted, or uneven modernization. The approach offered an explanation for failed or distorted development efforts, but, in the absence of dramatic cultural change, it could not explain development successes.

Dependency theory offered a much more radical challenge to modernization theory. It attributed development problems to the consequences of integration into the international capitalist economy and to exploitation by foreign economic and political interests. Dependency theorists (*dependencistas*) hypothesized two causes of economic difficulties: impersonal economic forces arising from the dependent country's position in the international economy, and the influence of transnational companies and their domestic allies' pursuit of their own interests in opposition to national interests (e.g. Sunkel 1972, 1973; dos Santos 1970; Frank 1967, 1970; Cardoso 1973a; Amin 1964; Barratt-Brown 1963).

The characteristics of a backward country's position in the international economy that *dependencistas* assumed to be detrimental to development included disadvantageous terms of trade for raw materials (e.g. Cardoso and Faletto 1979, 155), excessive vulnerability to changes in international prices because of reliance on a few exports, and reliance on one or a few trading partners and suppliers of aid, investment, and loans.

Dependency theory drew additional arguments from the conflict assumed to exist between the interests of transnational corporations and the developmental needs of host countries. Frequently *dependencistas* pictured transnationals and their host country allies as, in a sense, intervening variables—as the organizations and individual actors through whom international economic forces influenced domestic economic outcomes. This part of the dependency argument attributed slow growth, bottlenecks in the economy, continued dependence, and balance-of-payments crises to the resource drain that resulted from such transnational practices as repatriation of profits, transfer pricing, preference for imported over domestic inputs, and the maintenance of a monopoly on new techniques and the development of innovations (Baran 1957; Evans 1979, 19–38; Leys 1974, 8–18).

Dependency theory relied on the structuralist critique of neoclassical economics for economic theory and interpretations. Central to the structuralist critique is the claim that the distribution of the gains from trade between more and less developed economies disadvantages the less developed (Prebisch 1950; Singer 1950).[1] The fundamental mode of analysis used by *dependencistas* draws on Marx. Dependency theory treats classes as the most salient social actors and class struggle as the means through which political change occurs. Its view of the international economy descends from the writings on imperialism by early neo-Marxists (e.g. Lenin 1968).

Growth rates in developing countries during the past forty years have made it clear that dependence does not prevent growth, contrary to the claims of the earliest dependency theorists (e.g. Frank 1967; Baran 1957). Between 1960 and 1979, the time during which dependency theory was elaborated, disseminated, and became the most influential paradigm in the field of comparative politics, the GNP growth rate in Latin America, whose experience had spawned dependency theory, was 3.3 percent per capita. This compares favorably with an average GNP growth rate in the industrialized countries (excluding Japan) during the same period of 2.9 percent per capita.[2] Moreover, since the rate of population growth in Latin America was two to three times as high as in the industrialized countries, the difference in absolute as opposed to per capita growth rates was even greater.

In other words, the stagnation and slow growth that early dependency theory had sought to explain had certainly vanished from Latin America if it had ever existed. Postindependence growth rates in black Africa came closer to fulfilling the expectations of the dependency/neocolonialist arguments. The average per capita increase in GNP between 1960 and 1979 was only 1.6 percent in black Africa, low by international standards, though higher than that of Southern Asia. Nevertheless, even in Africa, positive growth rates disconfirmed the more extreme stagnationist predictions (cf. Jackman 1982).

Despite respectable growth rates, however, Third World countries continued to experience other very serious economic and political problems, and dependency theorists were understandably reluctant to abandon such an intuitively appealing and deductively compelling set of ideas. Dependency-influenced arguments were extended, modified, and applied to new dependent variables: erratic and crisis-ridden growth, unequal distribution, political instability, authoritarianism, and revolution.

Analysts working in the dependency tradition argued that the "structural" causes of inflation and balance of payments crises inhere in the dependent relationship. Inflation, in the structuralist view, stems largely from two phenomena: reliance on the export of primary products to earn foreign exchange and the existence of a dual economy in the developing country. Reliance on primary product exports carries inflation into the domestic economy and causes balance-of-payments problems, they contend, as a result of deteriorating terms of trade and because primary products are subject to very wide and rapid international price swings.

The defining features of a dual economy include low productivity in a large, traditional agricultural sector and a severely skewed income distribution. The traditional agricultural sector appears to ignore market incentives. In consequence, food production lags behind industrialization, urbanization, and population growth. The increased food imports that then become necessary contribute to the balance-of-payments problem. Profits in the traditional agricultural sector, which should contribute to capital accumulation, remain low and tend not to be invested productively. The skewed distribution of income contributes to the balance-of-payments problem by intensifying the demand for luxury consumption goods, which, even if manufactured inside the country, use imported inputs, imported technology, and imported capital.

Dependencistas link the development of the dual economy to the history of foreign domination of production and trade in dependent countries. They associate the persistence of dualism and the problems it entails, in spite of rapid industrial growth, with the prevalence of transnational corporations in their economies (Sunkel 1973; Cardoso 1973b, 146–48).

Arguments about the effects of the spread of capitalism and colonialism into the Third World also became the backbone of a series of explanations of peasant revolution. Third World revolution moved toward the top of the agenda of the subfield in the late 1960s as a result of an interaction between world events, that is, increasing U.S. involvement in Vietnam, and the development of intellectual tools that seemed to offer some leverage on the problem.

In contrast to modernization theory or classical Marxism, the dependency perspective directed attention to the potentially revolutionary effects of the spread of the market relations and the imposition of colonial systems of property rights and taxation on Third World peoples (Wolf 1969; Scott 1978; Paige 1975). Although arguments differed a good deal with regard to which parts of the peasant population were expected to be most easily moved to revolt and the degree to which economic motivations might be modified by cultural factors, all stressed the importance of changes in material well-being caused by colonial incursions. They argued that the introduction of the international market into subsistence economies led to either a secular decline in peasant welfare or to periodic severe subsistence crises when international commodity prices dropped. This market-induced immiseration was exacerbated by the concentration of landholdings at peasants' expense that accompanied colonial rule in many areas and by the higher levels of effective taxation imposed by colonial rulers as compared to traditional rulers. All the explanations of revolution include factors other than those sketched here, but the idea that peasant desperation induced by incorporation into the international capitalist system makes revolt more likely runs through all of them. These explanations of revolution thus share with the rest of the dependency-influenced tradition the basic assumption that relationships between the more and less developed parts of the world inevitable involve exploitation of the weaker by the stronger.

Dependencistas and others influenced by the dependency perspective also blamed authoritarian interludes on conditions peculiar to dependent countries' interaction with the international capitalist economy. Several arguments were advanced linking authoritarianism to dependency. The best known is the bureaucratic-authoritarian model, which hypothesized that late, dependent industrialization differed from industrialization in the early modernizers in that it entailed two distinct economic-political stages: an easy phase of import substitution based on the production of relatively simple consumption goods during which the amount of capital needed to industrialize would be small; and a "deepening" phase when the demand for simple consumption goods would have been largely supplied and opportunities for further import-substitution industrialization would lie in the production of goods requiring much larger infusions of capital. During the easy phase of import substitution, relatively small capital requirements allow workers to share the benefits of growth and thus permit inclusive political systems in which the working class participates. During this stage, working-class organizations develop and become powerful. As the easy phase is exhausted and capital needs become more urgent, however, the interests of owners and workers diverge. Capitalists then support exclusionary authoritarian regimes that can repress working-class demand-making organizations and suppress wages in order to accumulate capital more rapidly (O'Donnell 1973).

The interest of domestic capitalists in wage reduction coincides with the interest of transnational corporations in a concentrated income distribution, which creates a larger market for the upper income consumer products they produce (Cardoso 1973b). Fear of communism gives the military an interest in repressing working-class political mobilization and encouraging domestic capital accumulation and foreign investment, which they see as necessary to increasing the rate of growth. Growth is doubly desired by the military. On the one hand, it is expected to undercut the appeal of communism to the poor, and, on the other, it is expected to lead to increased geopolitical status and a more secure base of military power (Stepan 1971).

This convergence of interests provides the basis for a coalition of the domestic bourgeoisie, the international bourgeoisie, and the state, dominated by the military and technocrats, which supports the bureaucratic-authoritarian regime and its policies. The bureaucratic-authoritarian argument thus offers an explanation for why several of the more advanced developing countries succumbed to authoritarianism when modernization theory would have predicted that further development would make democracy more likely.

By the early 1980s, both the revised dependency and the bureaucratic-authoritarian approaches had run into a wall of inconvenient facts. For neo-*dependencistas*, the most inconvenient facts came from the Asian newly industrializing countries, which, in spite of being among the most dependent in the world, had experienced about twenty years of rapid, relatively stable growth unmarred by the severe inflationary and balance-of-payments crises that plagued other developing countries, and, what's more, had increased agricultural productivity and maintained relatively equitable income distributions while doing so.

Meanwhile, the bureaucratic-authoritarian model faced an even greater challenge: the disappearance of the phenomenon of bureaucratic authoritarianism. The original bureaucratic-authoritarian regimes were experiencing rapid democratization even though the capital squeeze that had been proposed as the underlying cause of the emergence of bureaucratic authoritarianism had become far worse in the early eighties. And no new conversions to bureaucratic authoritarianism had occurred among the countries that should have been the next to exhaust the easy phase of import substitution.

Since the early eighties, no equally compelling paradigms have arisen to replace those discussed above. Before turning to the various approaches that currently compete for scholarly adherents, let us consider the reasons these appealing theories and paradigms have been discarded in such rapid succession.

CAUSES OF THE DECLINE AND FALL OF THEORIES

The first cause, closely associated with the problem of vanishing phenomena, is the rather remarkable failure of comparativists working on developing areas to make use of readily available information in the formulation of theories. Theories were not data-free, as some critics have charged, but the use of evidence to develop, support, or test theories was selective.

Modernization theorists, for example, exercised considerable selectivity in the choice of European experiences from which to draw. Their image of modernization drew on recent British and North American experience, ignoring earlier civil wars in both countries and the nineteenth-century experience of civil unrest and attempted revolution in several European countries. Moreover, although some recognized that rapid modernization made societies vulnerable to upheaval and revolution, modernization theorists for the most part ignored the nationalist and communist revolutions occurring in developing countries during the postwar era. Analysis of revolution was left for the most part to country specialists working on countries that had experienced revolution. As a result, little in the way of general explanations of revolution relevant to the Third World emerged under the auspices of early modernization theory.

Revisionist modernization theory took into account the strife, unrest, and struggle for power that has accompanied most modernization experiences. In its efforts to explain blocked or distorted transitions, however, it failed to note that several East Asian and Latin American countries were developing quite rapidly and peacefully in spite of the continued prevalence of traditional values and the absence of revolution and Reformation.

Early versions of dependency theory that sought to explain stagnation in developing countries ignored evidence of rapid growth readily available from the World Bank. Later extensions of dependency, including the bureaucratic-authoritarian extension, did recognize that growth was occurring, but, like revisionist modernization theorists, they ignored the evidence from East Asia of growth without the crises and distortions associated with development in Latin America and Africa. They also ignored evidence that the terms of trade for primary products do not inevitably and universally decline over time. And, most seriously, they ignored evidence that common features of import-substitution strategies caused characteristic economic problems, such as recurrent balance-of-payments crises, lagging productivity in the agricultural sector, decreased production for export, an inegalitarian income distribution, and the maintenance of an internationally uncompetitive manufacturing sector. The connection between import-substitution strategies and these unintended consequences was widely perceived among development economists by the late sixties and available to political scientists in readily accessible published sources (Hirschman 1968; Fishlow 1971; Leff 1968, 77–88; Kuczynski 1977). Even so, arguments in the dependency tradition continued to attribute these problems to structural features of the relationship between late-developing countries and the international capitalist economy.

Ideology and aesthetics contributed to this disregard for available information. In Richard Sklar's words, theories are "conceived in ideological sin rather than scientific virtue. They linger for a long time mainly on account of ideological lag."[3] As numerous observers have pointed out, the ideological dispositions of scholars play a role in determining which theories they find inherently plausible and, therefore, which theories they are likely to scrutinize least critically.

Modernization theory had considerable intuitive appeal for many North American social scientists, but it seemed ethnocentric, condescending, and disingenuous to many Third World scholars, who saw it as a rationalization for support of an exploitative international division of labor. Dependency theory and other Marxist-influenced approaches, in contrast, which placed the blame for underdevelopment on the shoulders of exploitative external forces, held much more appeal for many in the Third World. Further, as Robert Tucker (1969) noted, Marx's most powerful image of society, as polarized between the property-owning few and the immiserated masses, has much more resonance for Third World observers who live in societies that approximate this description than for members of advanced industrial societies, who have greater familiarity with more complex class structures.

In short, the intuitive, emotional, and ideological appeals associated with different theories certainly increased their persuasiveness among different groups. When a theory fits with preconceptions and seems highly plausible, scholars feel less motivated to go to what seems like unnecessary trouble to dig up facts to confirm it and, as a result, fail to unearth the facts that would disconfirm it. Ideological predilections have exercised an especially powerful effect on theories in comparative politics because of the absence of subfield norms requiring the rigorous testing of knowledge claims. When there are no well-established norms for selecting the evidence with which to test speculations and when no value attaches to replicating earlier studies, no countervailing force impedes the natural influence of ideology over the choice of which theories to believe.

The aesthetic appeal of compelling deductive theories added further to the tendency to ignore information. A simple, elegant, logically consistent theory muddied by the addition of a lot of sloppy details and exceptions is not a pretty sight. There is some pleasure to be gained from using inconvenient facts to blast a theory into oblivion, but trying to "save" a theory by mucking it up with a bunch of mundane details holds little charm.

As an illustration of the contrast between an elegant, though rather easily disconfirmable, theory and a revision of the theory that is more consistent with facts, though somehow less appealing, compare Guillermo O'Donnell's statement of the bureaucratic-authoritarian model in *Modernization and Bureaucratic-Authoritarianism* (1973) with the revisions to it by Robert Kaufman, David Collier, and Jose Serra in Collier's *The New Authoritarianism in Latin America* (1979). O'Donnell's book is painful to read. The prose is convoluted and turgid. The economic-theory underpinnings of the argument are clearly wrong. And yet, the thing shows so much creativity, its simple logic so delights the mind, that one wants to believe it, to preserve it as an object of beauty. In contrast, the revisions in the Collier volume are clear, well-written, and more consistent with available evidence. But, with the addition of more variables, assorted feedback loops, and the like, they have lost the magic of the original. Consequently, though very well regarded, they did not capture the imagination of the Latin American field the way O'Donnell's original argument did (cf. Binder 1986, 24–26).

In general, I think it safe to say that rewards in the subfield go disproportionately to those who articulate aesthetically and ideologically attractive theories, as compared with those who attempt to test such theories with evidence. In spite of the notions about falsification and hypothesis testing that graduate school attempts to instill into us, most of us respond to these subfield-specific incentives.

To move away from intellectual fads driven by ideological and aesthetic considerations and toward an accumulation of knowledge, we need to begin subjecting our guesses about the way the world works to systematic and repeated empirical tests. I am not suggesting that comparativists can or should become mindless number crunchers. But, whether we use any statistics at all in our research or not, there are some research practices that cannot continue to be standard if we hope to build longer-lived theories. Currently, we gather evidence and use it to make arguments plausible, but we rarely use it to test them. If we want to accumulate knowledge, we cannot continue to avoid even the most rudimentary, nonquantitative tests of basic hypotheses.[4]

An example may make the distinction I am drawing between different uses of evidence more clear. Authors working on stabilization have argued that weak labor movements contribute to the success of structural adjustment policies in developing countries. The argument is plausible and supported by evidence from the countries examined, but it has not been tested. To test it, one would need, first, to define exactly what is meant by a weak labor movement and a successful adjustment. Then one would need to identify the universe of developing countries that face pressure to adjust to the debt. Finally, one would need to array the cases, perhaps in a two by two table with weak/strong labor on one axis and successful/unsuccessful adjustment on the other, to see whether the hypothesized relationship held up. This is the simplest kind of test. A relationship that can be shown between two variables may easily later turn out to be spurious. Nevertheless, even primitive tests such as this would increase the robustness of theories in comparative politics. Most scholars working in the subfield, however, not only fail to carry out tests of this sort but seem not even to realize that they should.

THE CURRENT STATE OF THEORETICAL PLURALISM IN THE SUBFIELD: FROM DATA-FREE THEORY TO THEORY-FREE DATA

In contrast to earlier decades, for the last several years nothing that could loosely be called a paradigm has prevailed or even competed in the subfield of comparative politics of developing areas. Instead, multiple "approaches" compete for adherents. The distinction I am making here between a paradigm and an approach hinges on the role of explanatory hypotheses in each. A paradigm, as I have used it here, is a set of more or less consistent theories and hypotheses that explain various aspects of reality and, taken together, form a coherent worldview. An approach, in contrast, involves, first, a claim that certain factors, for example, states, classes, or political leaders, deserve attention, without articulating specific hypotheses, and, second, the belief that certain research methodologies are the most useful and appropriate means of gaining understanding. I would, for example, call the "new institutionalism" in political science, with its emphasis on the state and other institutions and its advocacy of the comparative historical method, an approach rather than a paradigm.

Such is the pluralism of the subfield at the moment that any two of us might disagree about exactly what the main competing approaches are and how to label them. The following, however, seem to me the most developed.

The New Comparative Historical Sociology, or the New Institutionalism

The new comparative historical sociology differs from the old, most prominently practiced by Barrington Moore (1966) and Reinhard Bendix (1956, 1964, 1978), in its stress on the independent role of states as domestic political actors and in the greater attention it gives to international influences on domestic outcomes (Evans and Stephens 1988). Comparative historical sociology seeks to answer big questions, such as what causes democracy or revolution, by comparing the histories of important cases. Traditional comparative historical sociology looked for relevant causes primarily in the interests of different classes that would lead them to form different kinds of coalitions with other groups and to support one kind of political outcome or another. The new comparative historical sociology has drawn from the strand of the old associated with Moore in its view of the role of classes in history, but it has moved farther from economic determinism. It sees class interests as shaped by culture, social structure, and historical experience as well as economic interests (Evans and Stephens 1988).

The state plays a more explicitly independent role in the new comparative historical sociology than in the old (Skocpol 1973, 1979; Evans, Rueschemeyer, and Skocpol 1985; Evans and Stephens 1988; Ikenberry 1988). Scholars using this approach view the state as a partly autonomous group with an extremely powerful resource base and distinctive interests, shaped in part by international military competition. These distinctive interests and resources give states the reason and the capacity to challenge traditional dominant groups when state elites perceive dominant groups as impeding the achievement of state goals (Skocpol 1979; Trimberger 1977); to form coalitions with particular classes in order to achieve military, geopolitical, or internal security goals (Kurth 1979; Stephens 1987; Stepan 1971); to bargain with and regulate foreign economic actors (Moran 1974; Tugwell 1975; Evans 1979).

The new comparative historical sociology, like the old, relies on path-dependent forms of argument, though it is much more self-conscious about doing so (Krasner 1984; Collier and Collier forthcoming). Path-dependent arguments begin with an initial causal hypothesis, followed by a series of intervening causal hypotheses. At each intervening point, more than one outcome is possible, and whichever outcome occurs limits what may happen in the future.

Because of the multiple contingency points between the initial causal hypothesis and the final outcome, path-dependent arguments tend to be complicated and, in practice though not in principle, inadequately tested empirically. Each link in a path-dependent argument could in principle be tested rigorously by identifying the universe of cases in which a particular hypothesis should hold, randomly choosing a sample from the universe if it is large, and examining the outcomes in those cases to see if they confirm the hypothesis. Reliance on comparative historical case studies as the main form of data, however, precludes this kind of testing procedure. Instead of testing each hypothesis on the universe of cases to which it, though perhaps no other hypothesis in the sequence, should apply, a small number of cases are selected at the beginning and followed in detail. Consequently, all hypotheses are tested on a few, often three, cases—frequently the same cases the author examined in order to develop the hypotheses in the first place. By the end of the analysis, the number of variables almost always exceeds the number of cases. Often, in fact, it seems that at least one new variable has to be introduced to account for each new case. As a result of these methodological shortcomings, much of what claims to be explanation strikes the reader as thick description.

State-Centric Political Economy

What I am calling the state-centric political economy approach shares some features with the new comparative historical sociology. It expects classes and states to be the primary actors of interest, and it gives attention to the role of international economic and geopolitical influences on domestic outcomes. It merits treatment as a separate approach, however, because of some important differences.

In contrast to the sprawling comparative historical sociology, state-centric political economy deals with a narrow range of dependent variables: economic policies and their consequences, most prominently industrialization strategies and stabilization. I have called it state-centric not because most practitioners view the state as the most important independent source of policy, but because state economic policies and their effects are the subject of investigation.

In its treatment of classes, state-centric political economy gives little weight to social structure, ideology, or historical experience on class interests. It generally limits its attention to current economic interests but differs from classical Marxist and dependency approaches in that it gives great weight to the government's role in shaping the interests of private actors. Like the new comparative historical sociology, it treats the state, or government, as an independent actor with distinctive resources, interests, capacities, and economic ideology. Governments interact with private interest groups, sometimes swayed by them, sometimes dominating them, sometimes forming alliances with some against others. Policy outcomes depend on the interplay of these domestic political actors in conjunction with international factors such as global economic crises and aid, advice, and pressure from the United States, the World Bank, and the International Monetary Fund (e.g. Stallings and Kaufman 1989; Kahler 1986; Kaufman 1987; Haggard 1983, 1986).

State-centric political economy approaches "explain" policy outcomes by describing the interplay among these groups and factors. For the most part, explanations are thus highly contingent on specific circumstances, but most analysts would accept the following generalizations about the causes of important policy shifts.

- Challenges arising in the international environment, for example the oil shocks, lead to reassessments of current strategies and searches for improvements.

- State autonomy, meaning that the government has the capacity to ignore the demands of any particular interest group at any particular time and choose its own coalition partners rather than automatically reflecting the interests of dominant groups, grants policymakers the flexibility needed to respond to rapid changes in the economic environment, though it does not guarantee that they will do so.

- Technocratic competence, along with the insulation of technocratic decision-makers from pressures to dissipate state resources in the struggle over political power, contributes to better policy-making and implementation.

- And, most controversially, weakness, repression, or cooptation of labor increases the likelihood that governments will choose and maintain effective policies either to foster growth or to stabilize the economy as the situation may require (Haggard and Kaufman 1989; Haggard, Kim, and Moon 1987; Deyo 1987; but see Geddes 1990).

Analysts have arrived at these generalizations inductively, through examination of Asian, Latin American, and African cases, the preferred methodology. These generalizations are, essentially, verbal assertions of the existence of correlations rather than theories, though implicit theories underlie some of them.

In contrast to the theoretically undeveloped state of explanations of policy choices, the link between policy choices and economic outcomes, which is based on simple, widely accepted elements of neoclassical economic theory, is well understood within the state-centric political economy approach. This literature has introduced the following generalizations drawn from development economics into the mainstream of thought on economic development in political science.

- Equivalued or undervalued exchange rates lead to the increase and diversification of exports and thus overcome the import constraint experienced by many developing countries, reduce pressures on the balance of payments, and reduce vulnerability to international commodity price swings.

- Overvalued exchange rates, along with high across-the-board protection for domestically produced manufactures, result in the creation of an inefficient, internationally uncompetitive manufacturing sector that, because these policies make imported machinery artificially cheap, uses more capital-intensive technology and absorbs less labor than would be efficient given factor endowments. These policies also lead to a shift of investment out of agriculture and into industry, but industry promoted by these means can neither absorb the labor freed from agriculture nor produce exports that could take the place of the agriculture exports which the policies discourage—but which remain crucial to earning foreign exchange.

- Land reform, if accompanied by adequate credit and access to fertilizer, seed, and, where appropriate, machinery, results in a more equal income distribution.

- Development strategies which depend on labor intensive exports lead to higher levels of employment than do import substitution strategies, and therefore put upward pressure on wages even when unions are weak or repressed.

The state-centric political economy approach has made an important contribution to the study of economic development by raising the level of economic sophistication in the subfield. Most scholars working on economic development, whether they favor large-scale or minimal state intervention in the economy, now accept the above, and numerous other, hard facts of economic life.

Contingent Political Decisions

I refer here to explanations that trace the causes of outcomes to the day-to-day decisions of political leaders, party activists, unions, grassroots movements, and other specifically political actors as they respond to their immediate environment. This approach has a long history in journalism and the disciplines of political science and history, but it has recently been explicitly articulated as an alternative to structuralist and economic determinist arguments. To my knowledge, the first explicit defense of the approach, which critics have often dismissed as descriptive and journalistic, appeared in the series edited by Juan Linz and Alfred Stepan, *The Breakdown of Democratic Regimes* (1978).

This series, written in response to the bureaucratic-authoritarian model, contained case studies of the emergence of authoritarian regimes in numerous Latin American and Southern European countries. It showed, first, that the various structural explanations of authoritarianism that had been proposed did not in fact predict outcomes in individual cases, that is, that authoritarianism was not inevitable at certain development stages. Second, it examined in great detail the many contingent and unforeseeable political decisions that had led in the end to military seizures of power. Rather than inherently irreconcilable interests, the series emphasized the role of middle-of-the-road political forces, especially their mistakes, misperceptions, and shortsightedness, in creating unstable and polarized political situations that invited military intervention.

More recently, most studies of redemocratization have taken this approach. Single-country and comparative case studies have continued to make up the bulk of research. Earlier arguments linking regime type to structural features of the internal and international economy have seemed singularly inappropriate for explaining the recent surge in democratization since most of the structural characteristics once believed to have created an affinity for authoritarianism have worsened or remained stable. In consequence, analysts have turned their attention away from structural variables and toward contingent political decisions in the search for explanations. They have produced a large and very interesting descriptive literature (e.g. O'Donnell, Schmitter, and Whitehead 1986; Valenzuela and Valenzuela 1986; Selcher 1986; Peralta-Ramos and Waisman 1987; Stepan 1988, 1989), but compelling theories have yet to emerge.

The New Utilitarianism

This label, coined by Peter Evans and John Stephens (1987), refers to the application of rational choice models to issues salient in developing areas. These arguments, in contrast to comparative historical sociology and state-centric political economy, take the individual as the unit of analysis. They assume that individuals are rational in the sense that, given a set of preferences and a set of alternatives from which to choose, they will choose the alternatives that maximize their chances of achieving their goals. Institutions and other structural features enter rational choice arguments as societal characteristics that influence individual choices. Although the factors that shape preferences are exogenous to the deductive structure of rational choice models (in the sense that the models do not attempt to explain preferences), it is the synthesis of a creative and plausible attribution of preferences to actors with the rational actor assumptions themselves that results in the most compelling instances of this approach.

Rational choice arguments explain the kind of societal outcomes of interest in comparative politics by examining the sometimes nonobvious effects of aggregating individual preferences. The possibility that the aggregation of individually rational behavior can result in socially unfortunate or even collectively irrational behaviors, the best known of which are collective action problems, emerges unambiguously from rational choice models (Schelling 1978; Olson 1965; Hardin 1982; Elster 1979). These arguments thus often lead to quite different expectations about behavior than do arguments that implicitly assume, as many class analytic and interest group arguments do, that group interests will coincide with the interests of members of the group (cf. Bates 1988).

Rational choice arguments differ from contingent political arguments, which also focus on the individual, in that they deal only with systematic patterns of incentives that lead to systematic patterns in outcomes. Contingent political arguments, in contrast, focus on the specific conjunctural circumstances that make particular decisions understandable or "rational" at the time. The strength of such contingent political explanations is that they offer a very complete treatment of events; their weakness is that they do not easily lend themselves to the construction of general theories. Rational choice arguments have the opposite strengths and weaknesses. They invariably omit important details from the analysis, but, by abstracting from the specifics of particular cases, they make theory building possible.

Most compelling rational choice arguments fall into three categories: those that focus on economic incentives to explain economic outcomes; those that focus on the career incentives facing political leaders to explain political outcomes; and those that focus on collective action problems.[5] Individual studies often contain elements of more than one of these categories, but it seems useful to separate them as a way of analyzing different kinds of work.

The first category, the use of economic incentives to explain economic outcomes, simply extends standard economic theory into areas where its implications had not previously been fully appreciated. The literature on rent seeking began this strand of the new utilitarianism. It pointed out that certain government policies created monopoly rents by limiting competition in certain endeavors and that, as a result, "rent seekers" would attempt to buy their way into these protected niches. These attempts would divert resources out of productive investment and result in an inefficient allocation of scarce resources (Buchanan, Tollison, and Tullock 1980). Arguments by Michael Lipton (1977) and Robert Bates (1981) that the fall in African agricultural production can be explained by government policies aimed at keeping the price of food low and at capturing the surplus generated by production for export have been one of the most influential arguments in this category. Recent work by Bates (1989) and Michael Lofchie (1988) has further explored the nuances of African agricultural policy using the same logic and assumptions. Forrest Colburn's (1986) explanation of postrevolutionary agricultural policy in Nicaragua and its effects follows a similar line of argument.

The second strand of rational choice theory, which focuses on the behavior of political leaders whose preferences are structured by the desire to remain in office, involves an extension of ideas developed to explain American Congressional behavior (e.g. Mayhew 1975; Cain, Ferejohn, and Fiorina 1987) into Third World milieus where political institutions are different and far more fluid. Barry Ames (1987) has used presidents' interest in survival in office to explain a host of otherwise unexpected policy decisions in Latin America. The interest of politicians in survival and reelection has also been used to explain the success and failure of different administrative reform strategies (Geddes forthcoming). Africanists have traced the worsening ethnic cleavages in postcolonial nations to strategies pursued by would-be leaders competing for political power (Laitin 1986; Cohen 1974; Bates 1988).

Politicians' interest in survival also explains why in both Africa and

Latin America, policies have been pursued which have impoverished peasant farmers and reduced food production. Politicians have courted the support of urban dwellers, who have more political clout than rural people, by keeping food prices low. These low prices reduce the income of small farmers and decrease their incentives to produce for the market (Bates 1981, 1983; Colburn 1986).

The final, and least explored, strand of the new utilitarianism that deserves comment examines the implications of collective action problems. The idea that individuals will not usually find it rational to expend their resources in order to achieve public goods (i.e. goods that they as members of some target group cannot be excluded from using if the goods become available to the group) explains many outcomes that Marxists, pluralists, and others who expect people to be motivated to political action by their economic interests find surprising. The logic of collective action can, for example, explain why small farmers in Africa, though the majority of the population, fail to make effective demands for agricultural pricing policies that would benefit them (Bates 1988). It can also explain why Latin Americans do not organize to demand administrative reforms that they tell survey researchers they desire (Geddes forthcoming).

The logic of collective action is put to more creative use when it leads to a novel explanation of some event of interest. Samuel Popkin (1979), for example, explains why peasants join communist revolutionary movements by noting, first, the many unsolved collective action problems in traditional peasant villages and then describing the ways in which communist cadres overcome them. In essence, he paints a picture of cadres as political entrepreneurs who exchange help in achieving village-level collective goods for support for the revolutionary struggle, much as legislative political entrepreneurs exchange their votes on environmental issues for their constituents' votes at election time.

The new utilitarianism, like the other perspectives discussed here, is an approach rather than a paradigm. It claims that individuals and the incentives they face should be the focus of attention. Using rational choice models requires the analyst to identify relevant actors, to determine their preferences, and to present a plausible justification for the attribution of preferences. Observers can, of course, make mistakes in their attribution of preferences, but rational choice models do "have the advantage of being naked so that, unlike those of some less explicit theories, [their] limitations are likely to be noticeable" (Schelling 1984). The rational choice approach does not prescribe any particular methodology, but persuasive work combines deductive rational choice arguments with examinations of evidence to see if it conforms to the expectations generated by the model. The main difference between the new utilitarianism and the other approaches discussed here is that, although the former approach is not defined by a set of theories and hypotheses, it consistently produces them. In consequence, the new utilitarianism, unlike the other approaches discussed, has the potential of creating a new paradigm.

THE UNCERTAIN FUTURE OF THE SUBFIELD

The current multiplication of approaches can be traced to two causes: the disconfirmation of many of the central arguments of earlier paradigms and the emergence in the world of urgent questions that so far have not seemed amenable to the kind of simple, elegant theories of which paradigms are constructed. The urgent questions of the middle to late 1980s have to do, first, with democratization and, second, with debt and stabilization.

As numerous developing countries, including most of the bureaucratic-authoritarian cases whose authoritarianism had once been so persuasively explained, have democratized, scholars have sought explanations for the trend. As neither the structural arguments that had figured so large in explanations of authoritarianism nor earlier explanations of democracy (e.g. Moore 1966) seem to offer much help in explaining flipflops between democracy and authoritarianism, scholars have turned to the study of politics for answers. But, since instead of pursuing their comparative advantage and studying the workings of political institutions such as legislatures, parties, elections, and the like, comparative political analysis of developing areas has historically relied on economic, cultural, and social structural variables to explain political outcomes, analysts have found themselves in primitive and uncharted areas when it comes to building theories using political variables to explain political outcomes. The result has been a large descriptive literature on contemporary democratization. Analysts have simply lacked any kind of theoretical foundations about political processes on which to build.

Analyses of stabilization and the debt crisis have been somewhat less atheoretical than treatments of democratization but still have suffered from some of the same rudderless quality. Scholars attempting to explain different countries' response to the debt crisis and pressure for stabilization have gone less far in abandoning variables previously considered important than those studying democratization. Along with contingent political choices, international factors, primarily in the form of pressure from international organizations, and the distribution of domestic economic interests have continued to receive attention (Kaufman 1987; Stallings and Kaufman 1989). Nevertheless, in spite of some efforts at theory building (e.g. Frieden 1989), this literature, like that on democratization, remains largely descriptive and focused on the details of decision-making in different cases. Only if one knows who has power and what they want can one predict outcomes. In short, scholars working on the two topics of highest salience in the developing world today have found the old paradigms wanting but so far have not produced new ones.

The disconfirmation of hypotheses has led to the rejection rather than revision of paradigms because of the broad front along which disconfirmations have occurred. Traditionally, most work in comparative politics of developing areas more or less accepted some prevailing paradigm and reported evidence from particular cases that suggested modifications of elements of the paradigm—though authors sometimes seemed unaware of the implications of their evidence. This process inductively generated pressure for modification of the paradigm along multiple fronts.

A young paradigm is like a river in the spring rushing down out of the mountains over factual obstacles, cutting a new channel through the wilderness. Our ideal of how knowledge should accumulate is that, as factual obstacles build up, the river should be diverted and cut itself a new channel through the mountains. In our subfield, however, an old, much-modified paradigm is like a river that has reached the delta after crossing a broad, flat plain. It begins to dissipate into numerous small channels meandering through the swampy delta until it merges gradually and imperceptibly into the sea of general and commonsensical ideas about the way the world works (cf. Binder 1986, 24).

This, it seems to me, is more than a temporary problem. As knowledge accumulates, it becomes harder and harder to come up with simple theories to explain the kind of large-scale, long-term outcomes on which comparative politics has traditionally focused. Advocates of the new comparative historical sociology accept this inevitability and, in consequence, defend complicated, highly contingent, inelegant, path-dependent explanations as the only kind likely to accurately reflect the causal complexity of the world. In my judgment, this position is tantamount to rejecting "science as a vocation," and I do not think we should settle for such a compromise.

I believe, however, that the inability to accumulate theoretical knowledge will continue to plague us as long as we remain loyal to two time-honored traditions of comparative politics: trying to answer big, ill-defined questions rather than trying to understand the fundamental processes that underlie them; and ignoring the basic principles of research design and hypothesis testing.

We cannot, if we want to accumulate knowledge, continue routinely to select cases on the dependent variable, that is, to select for study cases that have experienced the outcome of interest rather than comparing these cases with cases that have not. No amount of evidence gathered from cases selected on the dependent variable will confirm a hypothesis (cf. Geddes 1990).

Nor can we ever expect to confirm arguments that involve more independent variables than cases. Where these arguments involve a sequence of causes, they need to be broken down into their component parts so that each can be tested on an appropriate universe of cases, rather than attempting to test them all on the same small number of cases, as is done when the comparative case study method is used.

Aside from methodological practices, the tradition that most impedes the development of a body of knowledge in the subfield is, I say with great trepidation, our selection of big, inadequately defined outcomes to explain. Our approach has been like that of a medical researcher who tries to understand the onset of cancer by detailing all the possible symptoms and amassing data on all the dietary, environmental, and hereditary factors that correlate with an increased probability of succumbing to the disease. This strategy results in the accumulation of factual knowledge and results in some inductive generalizations. It does not, however, lead to an understanding of the process through which cancer develops. For that, the researcher must step back from the immediate problem and focus instead on basic mechanisms, for example, on the nature of cells and the principles that regulate cell division. He must focus on the unit within which the process occurs, the cell, rather than on the overall outcome that results, the diseased organism.

In a similar manner, I think we need to seek to understand underlying processes rather than "explaining" large-scale, complex outcomes. And to do so, we need to focus on the fundamental unit of politics, in most cases the individual. This is not to say that the structures and institutions which shape individual behavior are unimportant, but only that we need to look at individual behavior to make sure that institutions and structures really do affect individuals the way we assume they do.

We need to break up the traditional big questions into sets of specific questions that are more theoretically accessible. I am not suggesting a mechanical disaggregation of big questions into smaller ones. Instead, I am advocating a redefinition of the questions of interest in such a way that a focus on individuals and the construction and testing of theories becomes possible. Instead of asking, for example, what causes revolution, we might ask: What causes spontaneous lower-class revolts? What causes peasants to join communist-led revolutionary movements? What causes the leaders of radical movements to choose revolutionary rather than reformist strategies? What causes some members of a dominant elite to desert their erstwhile allies? And so on. These are important questions. They deal with the processes that underlie the final outcome we call revolution.

A focus on understanding these processes leads, in my view, to a more thorough understanding of revolution than does the more usual method of trying to explain revolution or any other big, complex outcome. The usual method is to select some cases that have experienced the outcome and examine their histories and circumstances to see what they have in common. The analyst then hypothesizes that some or all of these common features are the causes of the outcome. This is a methodologically primitive version of the demographic approach to the study of cancer mentioned above. It is a useful exercise in that it will lead to an accumulation of information, but it will not lead to an accumulation of theory.

If one accepts the argument that a focus on process and on the fundamental units of action, in most cases individuals, will increase the likelihood of accumulating a sturdy body of theory, then, of the approaches now competing for adherents, the new utilitarianism is the only one that offers much promise. I would not argue that it is an ideal approach. Rational choice arguments can easily cross the line from simple to simplistic, from creative tautology to mere tautology. Nevertheless, as Churchill said about democracy, though it is a terrible system, it is better than all the others. The new utilitarianism does focus on individual actors. It does lead to a focus on process rather than correlations. And it does regularly yield testable propositions. For these reasons, I think it has the most potential for leading to theoretical development in our field.

NOTES

1. More recent work has called these findings into question. The terms of trade for raw materials vary depending on which time period and which commodities the analyst chooses to examine. The international economy does not invariably disadvantage the producers of primary products (Gonçalves and Barros 1982; Barratt-Brown 1974, 242–48; Haberler 1961, 275–97).

2. These figures were calculated from data available from the World Bank (1981, 134–35).

3. Richard Sklar, personal communication.

4. There are of course some conspicuous exceptions to these strictures, e.g., Jackman 1976, 1978, 1982, and Ames 1987.

5. For an alternative categorization and a more thorough discussion of types of rational choice arguments than is possible here, see Bates 1988.

REFERENCES

Ames, Barry. 1987. *Political Survival: Politicians and Public Policy in Latin America*. Series on Social Choice and Political Economy. Berkeley: University of California Press.

Amin, Samir. 1964 "The Class Struggle in Africa." *Revolution* 1:23–47.

Banfield, Edward. 1958. *The Moral Basis of a Backward Society*. Glencoe, Ill.: Free Press.

Baran, Paul. 1957. *The Political Economy of Growth*. New York: Monthly Review Press.

Barratt-Brown, Michael. 1963. *After Imperialism*. London: Heinemann.

————. 1974. *Economics of Imperialism*. Baltimore: Penguin.

Bates, Robert. 1981. *Markets and States in Tropical Africa: The Political Basis of Agricultural Policies*. Series on Social Choice and Political Economy. Berkeley: University of California Press.

————. 1983. *Essays on the Political Economy of Rural Africa*. Berkeley: University of California Press.

————. 1988. "Macro-Political Economy in the Field of Development." Duke University Program in International Political Economy Working Paper No. 40.

Bates, Robert. 1989. *Beyond the Miracle of the Market: The Political Economy of Agrarian Development in Kenya*. Cambridge: Cambridge University Press.

Bendix, Reinhard. 1956. *Work and Authority in Industry: Ideologies of Management in the Course of Industrialization*. New York: John Wiley.

————. 1964. *Nation-Building and Citizenship: Studies of Our Changing Social Order*. New York: John Wiley.

————. 1978. *Kings or People: Power and the Mandate to Rule*. Berkeley: University of California Press.

Binder, Leonard. 1986. "The Natural History of Development Theory." *Comparative Studies in Society and History* 28:3–33.

Buchanan, James M., Robert D. Tollison, and Gordon Tullock, eds. 1980. *Toward a Theory of the Rent-Seeking Society*. Economics Series No. 4. College Station: Texas A & M University Press.

Cain, Bruce, John Ferejohn, and Morris Fiorina. 1987. *The Personal Vote: Constituency Service and Electoral Independence*. Cambridge: Harvard University Press.

Cardoso, Fernando Henrique. 1973a. "Imperialism and Dependency in Latin America." In *Structures and Dependency*, edited by Frank Bonilla and Robert Girling. Stanford: Institute of Political Studies.

————. 1973b. "Associated Dependent Development: Theoretical and Practical Implications." In *Authoritarian Brazil: Origins, Policies and Future*, edited by Alfred Stepan. New Haven: Yale University Press.

Cardoso, Fernando Henrique, and Enzo Faletto. 1979. *Dependency and Development in Latin America*, translated by Marjory Mattingly Urquidi. Berkeley: University of California Press.

Cohen, Abner. 1974. *Two-Dimensional Man*. Berkeley: University of California Press.

Colburn, Forrest. 1986. *Post-Revolutionary Nicaragua: State, Class, and the Dilemmas of Agrarian Policy*. Series on Social Choice and Political Economy. Berkeley: University of California Press.

Collier, David, ed. 1979. *The New Authoritarianism in Latin America*. Princeton: Princeton University Press.

Collier, Ruth, and David Collier. Forthcoming. *Shaping the Political Arena: Critical Junctures, Trade Unions, and the State in Latin America*. Princeton: Princeton University Press.

DeNardo, James. 1985. *Power in Numbers*. Princeton: Princeton University Press.

Deyo, Frederic. 1987. "Modes of Exclusion in East Asian Development." In his *The Political Economy of the New Asian Industrialism*. Ithaca: Cornell University Press.

dos Santos, Theotônio. 1970. "The Structure of Dependence." *American Economic Review* 60:235–46.

Durkheim, Emile. 1933. *The Division of Labor in Society*. New York: Free Press.

Elster, Jon. 1979. *Ulysses and the Sirens: Studies in Rationality and Irrationality*. Cambridge: Cambridge University Press.

Evans, Peter. 1979. *Dependent Development: The Alliance of Multinational, State, and Local Capital in Brazil*. Princeton: Princeton University Press.

Evans, Peter, Dietrich Rueschemeyer, and Theda Skocpol, eds. 1985. *Bringing the State Back In*. Cambridge: Cambridge University Press.

Evans, Peter, and John D. Stephens. 1987. "Studying Development since the Sixties: The Emergence of a New Comparative Political Economy." Unpublished manuscript.

———. 1988. "Development and the World Economy." In *Handbook of Sociology*, edited by Neil Smelser. Beverly Hills: Sage.

Fishlow, Albert. 1971. "Origins and Consequences of Import Substitution in Brazil." In *International Economics and Development*, edited by Luis DiMarco. New York: Academic Press.

Frank, Andre Gunder. 1967. *Capitalism and Underdevelopment in Latin America: Historical Case Studies of Chile and Brazil*. New York: Monthly Review Press.

———. 1970. "The Development of Underdevelopment." In *Imperialism and Underdevelopment*, edited by Robert I. Rhodes. New York: Monthly Review Press.

Frieden, Jeffry. 1989. "Winners and Losers in the Latin American Debt Crisis: The Political Implications." In *Debt and Democracy in Latin America*, edited by Barbara Stallings and Robert Kaufman. Boulder: Westview.

Geddes, Barbara. 1990. "How the Cases You Choose Affect the Answers You Get: Selection Bias in Comparative Politics." *Political Analysis* 2.

———. Forthcoming. *Politician's Dilemma*. Series on Social Choice and Political Economy. Berkeley: University of California Press.

Gonçalves, Reinaldo, and Amir Coelho Barros. 1982. "Tendências do termos de troca: a tese de Prébisch e a economia brasileira—1850–1979." *Pesquisa e Planejamento Economico* 12:109–31.

Haberler, Gottfried. 1961. "Terms of Trade and Economic Development." In *Economic Development for Latin America,* edited by Howard S. Ellis and Henry C. Wallich. London: Macmillan.

Haggard, Stephan. 1983. "Pathways from the Periphery: The Newly Industrializing Countries in the International System." Ph.D. diss., University of California, Berkeley.

———. 1986. "Newly Industrializing Countries in the International System." *World Politics.* 38:343–70.

Haggard, Stephan, and Robert Kaufman. 1989. "The Politics of Stabilization and Structural Adjustment." In *Debt and Economic Performance: Selected Issues,* edited by Jeffrey Sachs. Chicago: University of Chicago Press.

Haggard, Stephan, Byung-kook Kim, and Chung-in Moon. 1987. "The Transition to Export-Led Growth in Korea, 1954–1966." Paper presented at the Conference on the State and Economic Policy: Republic of Korea, UCLA.

Hardin, Russell. 1982. *Collective Action.* Baltimore: Johns Hopkins University Press.

Hirschman, Albert O. 1968. "The Political Economy of Import-Substituting Industrialization in Latin America." *Quarterly Journal of Economics* 1968: 2–32.

———. 1979. "The Turn to Authoritarianism in Latin America and the Search for Its Economic Determinants." In *The New Authoritarianism in Latin America,* edited by David Collier. Princeton: Princeton University Press.

Ikenberry, G. John. 1988. *Reasons of State: Oil Politics and the Capacities of American Government.* Ithaca: Cornell University Press.

Jackman, Robert W. 1973. "On the Relation of Economic Development to Democratic Performance." *American Journal of Political Science* 17: 611–21.

———. 1976. "Politicians in Uniform: Military Governments and Social Change in the Third World." *American Political Science Review* 70: 1078–97.

———. 1978. "The Predictability of Coups d'etat: A Model with African Data." *American Political Science Review* 72:1262–75.

———. 1982. "Dependence on Foreign Investment and Economic Growth in the Third World." *World Politics* 34:175–96.

Jowitt, Kenneth. 1971. *Revolutionary Breakthroughs and National Development: The Case of Romania, 1944–1965.* Berkeley: University of California Press.

Kahler, Miles, ed. 1986. *The Politics of International Debt.* Ithaca: Cornell University Press.

Kaufman, Robert. 1987. "The Austral and Cruzado Plans in Argentina and Brazil: The Politics of Stabilization in Historical Perspective." Paper presented at the meetings of the American Political Science Association, Chicago, Ill.

Krasner, Stephen. 1984. "Approaches to the State: Alternative Conceptions and Historical Dynamics." *Comparative Politics* 16:223–46.

Kuczynski, Pedro-Pablo. 1977. *Peruvian Democracy under Economic Stress: An Account of the Belaúnde Administration, 1963–1968*. Princeton: Princeton University Press.

Kurth, James. 1979. "Industrial Change and Political Change." In *The New Authoritarianism in Latin America*, edited by David Collier. Princeton: Princeton University Press.

Laitin, David. 1986. *Hegemony and Culture*. Chicago: University of Chicago Press.

Leff, Nathaniel. 1968. *Economic Policy Making and Development in Brazil, 1947–1964*. New York: John Wiley.

Lenin, V. I. 1968. "Imperialism: The Highest Stage of Capitalism." In *Lenin on Politics and Revolution*, edited by James E. O'Connor. New York: Pegasus.

Levy, Marion J. 1966. *Modernization and the Structure of Societies: A Setting for International Affairs*. Princeton: Princeton University Press.

Leys, Colin. 1974. *Underdevelopment in Kenya: The Political Economy of Neo-Colonialism, 1964–1971*. Berkeley: University of California Press.

Linz, Juan, and Alfred Stepan, eds. 1978. *The Breakdown of Democratic Regimes*. 4 vols. Baltimore: Johns Hopkins University Press.

Lipset, Seymour Martin. 1959. "Some Requisites of Democracy." *American Political Science Review* 52:69–105.

Lipton, Michael, 1977. *Why the Poor Stay Poor: A Study of Urban Bias in World Development*. Cambridge: Harvard University Press.

Lofchie, Michael. 1988. *The Policy Factor: Agricultural Performance in Kenya and Tanzania*. Boulder: Lynne Reiner.

Lowenthal, Richard. 1964. "Government in Developing Countries: Its Functions and Its Forms." In *Democracy in a Changing Society* edited by Henry W. Ehrmann. New York: Praeger.

McClelland, David. 1961. *The Achieving Society*. Princeton: Van Nostrand.

Mayhew, David R. 1975. *Congress: The Electoral Connection*. New Haven: Yale University Press.

Moore, Barrington, 1966. *Social Origins of Dictatorship and Democracy: Lord and Peasant in the Making of the Modern World*. Boston: Beacon Press.

Moore, Wilbert E. 1963. "Industrialization and Social Change." In *Industrialization and Society*, edited by Bert F. Hoselitz and Wilbert E. Moore. New York: UNESCO-Mouton.

Moran, Theodore. 1974. *Multinational Corporations and the Politics of Dependency: Copper in Chile*. Princeton: Princeton University Press.

O'Donnell, Guillermo. 1973. *Modernization and Bureaucratic-Authoritarian-*

ism: Studies in South American Politics. Politics of Modernization Series No. 9. Berkeley: Institute of International Studies.

O'Donnell, Guillermo, Philippe Schmitter, and Lawrence Whitehead, eds. *Transitions from Authoritarian Rule*. 4 vols. Baltimore: Johns Hopkins University Press.

Olson, Mancur. 1965. *The Logic of Collective Action: Public Goods and the Theory of Groups*. Cambridge: Harvard University Press.

Paige, Jeffery. 1975. *Agrarian Revolution*. New York: Free Press.

Peralta-Ramos, Mónica, and Carlos Waisman, eds. 1987. *From Military Rule to Liberal Democracy in Argentina*. Boulder: Westview.

Popkin, Samuel. 1979. *The Rational Peasant: The Political Economy of Rural Society in Vietnam*. Berkeley: University of California Press.

Prébisch, Raúl. 1950. *The Economic Development of Latin America and Its Principal Problems*. New York: United Nations.

Price, Robert. 1975. *Society and Bureaucracy in Contemporary Ghana*. Berkeley: University of California Press.

Riggs, Fred. 1960. "Prismatic Society and Financial Administration." *Administrative Science Quarterly* 1:1–46.

———. 1964. *Administration in Developing Countries: The Theory of Prismatic Society*. Boston: Houghton Mifflin.

Schelling, Thomas. 1978. *Micromotives and Macrobehavior*. New York: Norton.

———. 1984. *Choice and Consequence: Perspectives of an Errant Economist*. Cambridge: Harvard University Press.

Scott, James. 1978. *The Moral Economy of the Peasant: Rebellion and Subsistence in Southeast Asia*. New Haven: Yale University Press.

Selcher, Wayne, ed. 1986. *Political Liberalization in Brazil: Dynamics, Dilemmas and Future Prospects*. Boulder: Westview.

Singer, Hans. 1950. "The Distribution of Gains between Investing and Borrowing Countries." *American Economic Review* 40:472–99.

Skocpol, Theda. 1973. "A Critical Review of Barrington Moore's *Social Origins of Dictatorship and Democracy*." *Politics and Society* 4:1–34.

———. 1979. *States and Social Revolutions: A Comparative Analysis of France, Russia and China*. Cambridge: Cambridge University Press.

Stallings, Barbara, and Robert Kaufman, eds. 1989. *Debt and Democracy in Latin America*. Boulder: Westview.

Stepan, Alfred. 1971. *The Military in Politics: Changing Patterns in Brazil*. Princeton: Princeton University Press.

———. 1988. *Rethinking Military Politics: Brazil and the Southern Cone*. Princeton: Princeton University Press.

Stepan, Alfred, ed. 1989. *Democratizing Brazil: Problems of Transition and Consolidation*. New York: Oxford University Press.

Stephens, John. 1987. "The Breakdown of Democracy in Interwar Europe:

A Test of the Moore Thesis." Paper delivered at the meetings of the American Sociological Association, Chicago, Ill.

Sunkel, Osvaldo. 1972. "National Development Policy and External Dependence in Latin America." In *Contemporary Inter-American Relations*, edited by Yale Ferguson. Englewood Cliffs, N.J.: Prentice-Hall.

———. 1973. "Transnational Capitalism and National Disintegration in Latin America." *Social and Economic Studies* 22:132–76.

Trimberger, Ellen Kay. 1977. "State Power and Modes of Production: Implications of the Japanese Transition to Capitalism." *The Insurgent Sociologist* 7: 85–98.

Tucker, Robert. 1969. *The Marxian Revolutionary Idea*. New York: Norton.

Tugwell, Franklin. 1975. *The Politics of Oil in Venezuela*. Stanford: Stanford University Press.

Valenzuela, J. Samuel, and Arturo Valenzuela, eds. 1986. *Military Rule in Chile: Dictatorship and Oppositions*. Baltimore: Johns Hopkins University Press.

Weber, Max. 1958. *The Protestant Ethic and the Spirit of Capitalism*, translated by Talcott Parsons. New York: Scribners.

Wolf, Eric. 1969. *Peasant Wars of the Twentieth Century*. New York: Harper.

World Bank. 1981. *World Development Report, 1981*. New York: Oxford University Press.

3

Where Have We Been and Where Are We Going? Analyzing Post-Socialist Politics in the 1990s

Ellen Comisso

This chapter was written in May 1989. Fortunately, I had the good sense even at that time to realize it was pointless to try to predict what was going to happen next in the socialist states. My reward for resisting the temptation to gaze into a crystal ball (or divine entrails, if the reader prefers) in favor of focusing on questions that would be important regardless of immediate outcomes was that very little of theoretical interest in the essay required revision in July 1990, when the copyedited manuscript arrived on my desk; if anything, the questions posed in the spring of 1989 (from the difference between the breakdowns of military and socialist authoritarianism to the relationship between property forms and political regimes) have simply acquired greater urgency and relevance and proved applicable to a larger number of states than originally intended as a result of the dramatic events of the past year.

Consequently, I decided to leave the review pretty much intact, and merely comment on and update what I had written on the eve of the Great Political Landslide by adding a few footnotes where necessary. The one wholesale change I was tempted to make was one of tense, that is, changing a

I would like to thank Valerie Bunce, Robert Evanson, Joanne Goven, Victor Magagna, Philip Roeder, and William Zimmerman for particularly helpful comments on this manuscript.

discussion of "socialism is" to a discussion of "socialism was." Had this essay been devoted solely to Eastern Europe and the Soviet Union, I would have done so, but given that China—with a population greater than Eastern Europe and the Soviet Union combined—remains firmly in the Leninist camp, where it is at least at this date joined by several other smaller states (Cuba, Vietnam, etc.), even that alteration did not seem entirely appropriate. Nevertheless, readers may wish to make this change mentally for themselves as they go through the review. Otherwise, with the exception of a few paragraphs (see n. 6) and occasional reference to "formerly socialist" states, the chapter remains as it was written in the spring of 1989. That it has stood the test of having the whole world turned upside down while it waited to go to press suggests that the field need not feel as embarrassed at being caught unaware as some have implied.

Hannah Arendt (1958) observed years ago that only "behavior" can be studied scientifically; action cannot. It is hardly surprising, then, that as a discipline political science has long been characterized by a highly ambivalent relation to its primary subject matter, for insofar as politics is a sphere of action *par excellence*, developing a science of it is bound to be an effort somewhat akin to Sisyphus's attempts to roll the rock up the hill in Hades. Thus, almost as soon as we have succeeded in reducing a political phenomenon to a finite set of predictable behavioral patterns, subject to social scientific laws, and specified as an abstract and timeless relationship among variables, our subject matter suddenly appears to revolt, revealing its capacity for creative action by offering us outcomes that only the wide-eyed visionary could have imagined a few years earlier.

The problem created by that irreducible element of contingency inherent in all political action for a discipline that aims at "the accumulation of more or less verifiable propositions about the [political] world" (Riker 1982, 754) may nowadays have become particularly acute for the student of the communist world, but it is by no means unique to it. For example, in reviewing work devoted to the study of the American presidency, a subfield of the discipline far more accessible to analysis than are the inner sanctums of Communist parties, one is struck by the extent to which the entire view of the office and institution changes with each successive occupant of it. And if it is true that "the best single-word description of how scholars evaluate the presidency is confusion" (Nelson 1988), one can hardly berate analysts schooled in the politics of the Brezhnev era for failing to anticipate the emergence of a leadership seriously committed to deep and wide-ranging political and economic reforms in what but a few years earlier was an apparent bastion of socialist conservativism—and this at both elite and popular levels (Barghoorn and Remington 1986; Breslauer 1978; Colton 1984; Connor 1975; Pravda 1982; Shipler 1983; Zaslavsky 1982).

The current politico-economic conjuncture is thus simultaneously the most propitious and the least propitious moment for a reassessment of the comparative communism field, and this chapter will proceed along the following lines. First, I will try to review the main approaches to the study of politics in socialist systems that have evolved over the past seventy years; due to the limits of time, space, and my own knowledge, I will focus primarily on work dealing with the Soviet Union and Eastern Europe, with only occasional reference to the literature on China, Cuba, and less developed socialist states in Africa and Latin America. To narrow an immense field further, I will deal primarily with approaches to the study of domestic politics, giving only the most cursory treatment of the schools of thought that have developed around explaining foreign policy behavior. I make this choice partly because many of the approaches to explaining domestic politics in communist states are in fact also applicable to foreign policy decisions (Evangelista 1989; Hauslohnèr 1981; Roeder 1984), and partly because to the degree foreign policy behavior is determined by factors independent of the domestic situation, it is probably better handled within the framework of the international relations field.[1]

In reviewing the field so defined, I will try to show that although our knowledge and understanding of "actually existing" socialism is far from complete, it is also quite considerable, and that despite a multiplicity of models, characterizations, and labels, there exists a fairly broad consensus as to the essential features of communist systems, the way in which these features vary over time and place, and the causes of the variations. At the same time, I will attempt to assess the utility and relevance of our traditional (and nontraditional) tools of analysis for coming to understand the current situation in socialist states undergoing considerable ferment.

The second part of the chapter will concentrate on the problems and questions that recent moves toward the introduction of market mechanisms and political liberalization pose for the field of "communist politics"—not the least of which is whether or not it will continue to exist should it turn out that the days of the traditionally understood Leninist polity are numbered. Here, I will suggest that whereas the traditional categories of the discipline help us to define the subject matter most in need of research at the present time, the fluidity of the current situation in the socialist world also permits us to ask a series of fundamental questions about the nature and definition of those categories themselves that we have rarely had the opportunity to address in the past. Given this opportunity, I shall argue that the basic task of our field is not so much to concentrate on adapting the methods of political science to predict what socialist societies may be in transition to, as it is to utilize the very basic changes that appear to be taking place in the communist world to illuminate some of the fundamental relationships among political, economic, and social variables that are vital to an understanding of all contemporary states and the emerging international order.

WHAT IS THE FIELD AND
HOW DO WE STUDY IT?

Underlying the evolution of a wide number of models, labels, and characterizations of the "actually existing" socialist state and society is, ironically, a relatively broad consensus as to their essential features, the variations they are capable of, and the causes of those variations. Politically, their hallmark is a single, hegemonic party organized on Leninist lines that faces no electoral constraints, operates according to democratic centralism, and claims an exclusive right to monopolize the means of collective action (Hough 1969; Meyer 1965; Rigby 1976; Schurmann 1968). Construed in principal-agent terms, the party is invariably the principal; the state, the mass organizations, and even the population to varying degrees, its agents (Moe 1984; Shirk 1988).[2]

As is well known, the relationship between the party and the state and the party and the larger society can vary considerably, as can the degree of internal cohesiveness, the social composition of the membership and elite, the level of turnover, and the extent to which the party actually exercises political hegemony in practice. For example, Communist parties that come to power on the heels of an urban revolution tend to look and behave differently from those that come to power by leading a peasant guerrilla movement; whereas the former type of party tends to see itself predominantly (although not exclusively) in class terms, as the vanguard of the proletariat, the latter typically sees its mission much more (although again, far from exclusively) in national terms (Denitch 1976; Johnson 1962; Jowitt 1971; Ulam 1951). Likewise, Communist parties tend to engage in very different activities, have a different social composition, and have a different pattern of elite interaction during so-called "heroic" periods of massive social transformation than they do in periods of more incremental change (Comisso 1986; Hough 1977; Lowenthal 1970).

Finally, despite adherence to a universalistic ideology, Communist parties nevertheless rule specific states, and so their practices cannot help but reflect to a significant degree the national context in which governing takes place. The differences among Communist parties in this respect are most obvious in the sphere of foreign policy, where, say, the factors affecting the international behavior of a major power like the Soviet Union are clearly going to be rather different from those affecting a much smaller state with very different security problems like Vietnam,

Yugoslavia, or Romania. But differences in domestic strategies and organization traceable to the national heterogeneity or homogeneity of the domestic population, its levels of cultural and economic development, and its pre-communist history can be equally marked, as a comparison of the Polish United Workers Party, the Yugoslav League of Communists, and even various republic-level party organizations within the Soviet Union would immediately make evident (Carter 1982; Fischer-Galati 1979; Holmes 1986; Lewis 1989, 1982; Schapiro 1970; Simons and White 1984; White, Gardner, and Schopflin 1982).

The foregoing and other differences notwithstanding, the fact that socialist states are governed by a Leninist party makes socialist authoritarianism (or democracy, as is also claimed) distinctly different from other forms of authoritarian (or democratic) rule. Exactly how different, and different in what specific ways, is a subject of debate to which we shall return after considering the other distinctive feature of the socialist/communist social order, namely, the ownership system.

Here, the economic trademark of the socialist economy is a distinctive set of property rights, whereby the ownership of assets (mobile or immobile) by private individuals is severely restricted and the dominant share of property is owned *de jure* or *de facto* by the state or "society." As such, socialism is first and foremost an ownership system, one that is invariably accompanied by a low degree of differentiation between the state on the one hand and the economy on the other (Bornstein 1974; Comisso and Tyson 1986; Eckstein 1973; Milenkovitch 1971; Neuberger and Duffy 1976). As a result, economic units do not and cannot fully internalize either the costs or the risks of their activities; budget constraints are "soft," such that enterprises are relatively free to compromise on the achievement of economic objectives for the sake of accomplishing the political priorities of their communal owner (Kornai 1981).

If weak differentiation between state/governmental and economic/productive institutions is a defining characteristic of socialism everywhere, there has nevertheless been a fairly wide variation in arrangements prescribing the allocation of resources, the extent of involvement in international trade, investment priorities, growth rates, sectoral proportions and the like. The classic, "Soviet-type" model is typically characterized by centralized, bureaucratic management of the economy with detailed physical planning and supply; a high rate of forced savings; "taut" planning; planning based on priorities, with industry taking priority over agriculture, producer goods over consumer goods, material goods over services; "extensive" development, governed by political preferences for increasing output rather than economically determined comparative advantages; and foreign trade playing largely a "residual" role in the economy (Hewett 1988; Kornai 1959; Nove 1980).

Nevertheless, the specific features of the centrally planned economy (CPE) have varied quite widely over time and place. Planning may be "genetic" or "teleological"; incentives have alternately been "moral" and "material," and the degree of reliance on "volunteers" has changed accordingly (Nove 1982). Enterprise management may have considerably autonomy within plan guidelines or it may be basically subordinated to political/party cadres within the firm; the quality and quantity of management training have also varied a good deal, although the trend has been for management to be drawn from increasingly well-educated groups over time (Baylis 1974; Granick 1975). The degree of tolerance for the remnants of private enterprise in agriculture, retail trade, and even production has also varied widely, as has the relationship between private entrepreneurs and the socialist sector (Aslund 1985; Gabor 1979). Industrial priorities have also changed, as exclusive attention to the growth of heavy industry has been complemented by increased attention to consumer goods production including, of course, agriculture.

Participation in international trade with nonsocialist countries has also varied considerably, ranging from virtually complete insulation (Albania) to a relatively high proportion of national income being realized in international trade (Hungary, Yugoslavia). Needless to add, the willingness to incur external debt to nonsocialist creditors has also varied a great deal, as a comparison of the borrowing practices of Poland and Czechoslovakia in the 1970s makes apparent. So too has the strategy for dealing with debt: if Poland was forced to default, Romania used indebtedness to launch a Draconian austerity campaign.

In some cases, highly centralized management of the economy has given way to more decentralized methods. Here, decentralization as either been geographic (territorial planning, as in China after 1957 or in the Soviet *sovnarkhoz* experiment), bureaucratic (the VVBs in East Germany, *glavki* in the Soviet Union, or WOGs in Poland), or economic (NEM in Hungary) (Eckstein 1977; Perkins 1973; Portes 1968; Woodall 1982). At the extreme, central planning was abandoned altogether in Yugoslavia in the 1960s. Although such a move clearly did not—and, some would argue, could not, given continued "social" ownership and the dominance of the League of Communists—spell the end to a great deal of political intervention in the economy that went well beyond traditional capitalist modes of fiscal and monetary policy and legal regulation, it did apparently have the effect of allowing purely economic goals to play a much more important role in enterprise decisions than had previously been the case (Bajt 1974; Comisso 1979; Estrin 1983; Sirc 1979; Svejnar and Prasnikar 1987; Tyson 1980).

We also have a fairly good, if unsystematic, sense of the consequences of these variations for economic performance (i.e., their effects on the standard of living, price levels, wage levels, income distribution, microeconomic management, innovation and technological diffusion, participation in international trade, etc.) as well (Berliner 1957, 1976; Bornstein 1981; Gomulka 1986; Portes 1976; Pryor 1985a, 1985b). The significance of these variations is a subject of some debate, however, and we shall return to it in the second section of this chapter. Generally, however, they can be thought of as variations in the allocation system, not in the ownership system, which remains communal in one way or another.

The leading role of a Leninist party and the weak differentiation between the state and the economy are, in this author's opinion, the "core" characteristics of the socialist regime, and they (and their variants) are the characteristics from which most other features of these systems can be deduced. The question, however, is whether regimes with these two characteristics are amenable to study drawn from models and frameworks based on systems lacking one or both of the above features.

Historically, the answer to this question has been positive, and the controversies have typically been only about with which systems parallels can be most suitably drawn. Here, even if the debate has been couched in social scientific terms, there has always been an underlying political dimension to it, insofar as utilizing hypotheses about communist systems drawn from, say, Nazi Germany clearly implies a very different evaluation of the systems themselves than does an analysis that seeks to use pluralist theory to illuminate some of the same phenomena (Hough 1972, 1977). Likewise, some of the resistance to accounting for socialist systems as a phenomenon *sui generis* is in part due to the professional interests of those who study it, insofar as excessive emphasis on the unique aspects of such systems could easily confine scholars of the area to an isolated corner of their disciplines (i.e., it would essentially imply that research findings in them could not be generalized in other areas of the discipline).

Thus, the rise and decline of the various models and frameworks that have been used to examine socialist political systems have reflected these conflicting political and disciplinary pressures. Oddly enough, however, the various approaches that have been used tend to complement rather than conflict with each other, largely because a new approach has tended to be coupled with the recognition that a certain subject matter has received insufficient study within the prevailing frameworks. The combined result of amalgamating these approaches is a fairly good and nuanced understanding of how the actually existing socialist systems operate, together with wide disagreement as to the bases on which to evaluate their performance.

Let me now proceed to review the basic approaches to communist politics that have evolved over the years. Critical to the evolution of both the field and the subject matter is the fact that for the first thirty years of its existence, communism was basically a Soviet phenomenon. Consequently, one of the earliest approaches to the field was what might be termed a "national-historical" one, in which the basis for comparison was the prerevolutionary regime. Such an approach was exemplified in the writings of George Kennan, who tended to play down the unique aspects of Bolshevism while stressing the historical continuities the Soviet Union shared with traditional Russian autocracy (Kennan 1961, 1972).

In the foreign policy sphere, such an approach implied that even though the international objectives of socialist states might be stated in terms of a universalistic and revolutionary ideology, they in fact reflected the traditional concern of the particular countries in question and could be countered on those bases. Thus, Soviet hegemony in Eastern Europe was not necessarily part of a desire for world revolution (and thus the initiation of a drive to extend communism to the Atlantic Ocean), but merely the result of historic Russian concerns with securing western borders from the threat of invasion; likewise, in the Sino-Soviet split, ideology was basically a mask for distinct and conflicting national interests. As far as the East European states were concerned, communist leaders could also be expected to pursue traditional national aspirations whenever the opportunity arose: historical ties of pan-Slavism were thus the main explanation for the loyalty of Bulgaria, while long-standing Polish-Russian rivalries would continue to be a source of tension within the Warsaw Pact (Griffiths 1964; Yergin 1977; Ionescu 1965).

Domestically, such an approach was bound to be of more limited utility, but here too, it has had some impact. Alexander Gerschenkron, for example, concluding that "a pattern of economic development which before the First World War seemed to have been relegated to the role of a historical museum piece was reenacted in Soviet Russia," thus observes:

> A resurrected Peter the Great would have . . . quickly recognized the functional resemblance between collectivization and the serfdom of his days, and he would have praised collectivization as the much more efficient and effective system to achieve the same goals—to feed gratis the nonagricultural segments of the economy and at the same time provide a flow of labor for the public works of the government. . . . (1962)

Karl Wittfogel's volume (1957) on the relevance of the "Asiatic mode of production" for our understanding of the contemporary socialist system would appear to be another example of this approach, as do other efforts attempting to explain differences among socialist countries on the basis of differing national traditions (Pipes 1967; Rawin 1970; Brown 1984b; Tucker 1987).

Despite its very valuable insights, the national-historical school of analysis generally fell into disrepute among political scientists by the end of the 1950s, for a number of reasons. First of all, an approach that basically assumed that individual states had certain unique national trajectories was bound to fall into disfavor among social scientists bent on the formulation of generalizable and testable propositions. Thus, even in the foreign policy area, the degree of similarity between Soviet objectives and long-standing Russian security concerns is attributed not so much to national tradition as to the geopolitical position of the state and structural similarities in the international order (Walt 1987; Waltz 1979; Zimmerman 1972).

Second, as socialism extended itself to a larger number of countries at differing levels of development with very different histories and cultures, certain uniformities in their political systems, economies, and societies appeared that clearly could not be explained by national particularities. Even in the foreign policy area, Soviet support for Marxist-Leninist regimes in areas like Cuba and in Africa represented a distinct break with the regional hegemony that had been a primary concern of czarist predecessors.

Equally important, for all their similarities with the *ancien régime*, there were simply too many aspects of the socialist state and society—from the size of the industrial working class and the level of literacy and education of the broad population to the organization of the military and the distribution of income and privileges—that differed from its predecessor to be ignored. Hence, the focus of the field shifted from examining historical continuities to analyzing the ways in which "socialist transformation" implied a break with the past.

Third, although no one could quarrel with the view that a knowledge of the past is necessary for an understanding of the present, neither could anyone argue that a knowledge of the past is necessary and sufficient for an understanding of the present. That is, the fact that certain practices from the past are recreated in the present is itself a phenomenon that must be explained, especially in light of the fact that other practices are abruptly discontinued in the postrevolutionary phase.

Finally, what events, practices, institutions, norms, and the like constitute a national "past" are themselves subject to historical and political interpretation. Ironically, this has led to a resurgence of the national-historical school of thought in an entirely new context: that of the various opposition and reform movements that have sprung up in Eastern Europe and the Soviet Union. Where the early (Western) advocates of this approach stressed the continuity between socialism and the preindustrial order, the newer (native) advocates argue that the establishment of socialism was a distinct break with the past and an (unsuccessful) attempt to eradicate national tradition and society (Michnik 1986; Szelenyi 1988; Gross 1979).

In Eastern Europe, this view has been accompanied by and buttressed with newer histories of the interwar period, portraying it not as simply a period of petty, authoritarian regimes unable to deal with the problems of modernization but also as an episode of emerging social pluralism prematurely ended by World War II and the imposition of an alien regime by an alien force. In such a view, the main impact of communist rule was simply to submerge national consciousness and group identities within an outwardly quiescent society that would rapidly move to articulate them and reclaim its "true" history under the appropriate conditions.

The same type of national-historical understanding appears to have gained in popularity within the Soviet Union as well. Particularly in the case of the non-Russian nationalities—the Baltic states leading the pack for understandable reasons—a vision of autonomous national development as an alternative to Russian-dominated or socialist development frequently appears in nationalist writings, but neither is such a theme absent from Russian discussions. There, however, the subjective and political element present in all choices of which past one wishes to build upon is far more transparent: for some, it is the Russia of the Orthodox Church (Solzhenitsyn); for others, it is the Russia of NEP; for others, it is the Russia of the prerevolutionary liberals or the Social Democrats, for yet others, it is the Russia of Stalin.

As should already be clear, even though the political importance of the new national-historical understanding of the socialist experience is critical to our ability to comprehend the current situation, its heuristic utility is open to some question. On one level, the historical findings this approach has given rise to are extremely rich, and quite correctly call into question many of the stylized accounts of the past. Moreover, the insights of this school of thought do indeed illuminate important limits to the extent of "socialist transformation" and they do offer an explanation as to why nationalism and demands for "citizenship" tend to be coupled in all of the socialist systems today.

On another level, however, to accept that explanation would be to ignore the very active role that the national-historical school of thought itself has played in creating a link between national identity and demands for citizenship. As such, its basic project is not so much the establishment of a new truth as the creation of a new polity, in a context where the power to define the past is a key factor in the ability to control the present. As such, rather than simply accept the historical findings of this current as an "objective" account of the past and present, one must also explain why this mode of thinking has become so popular. That explanation would not see the socialist experience as a "detour" from the national trajectory, but as part and parcel of it, without which the national-historical appeal itself would fall on deaf ears.[3]

The rise, fall, and resurrection of a national-historical approach are analogous to the fate of a second major approach to communist politics that, having been beaten to death over and over again, has also enjoyed a sudden resurgence. As readers have surely guessed, this is none other than the totalitarian school (Friedrich 1954; Friedrich and Brzezinski 1956; Arendt 1951; Wolfe 1961). If the original national-historical school found it fruitful to compare postrevolutionary and prerevolutionary authoritarianism, totalitarian theorists were also comparativists, although the passing of Nazi Germany from the political scene often leads us to forget that they were.

As a theory, totalitarianism's emphasis on the centrality of terror as the basic method of political control caused it to be brought under question after the events beginning in 1956 in the Soviet Union and Eastern Europe. Likewise, its insistence on the rule of a single individual (and not simply a single party, for single-party regimes are found in many states that did not qualify as totalitarian) as an essential characteristic of the communist political system flew in the face of increasing evidence suggesting that decisions were typically accompanied by a good deal of conflict among leaders and bureaucracies. In the Soviet case, neither the relatively "peaceful" replacement of Khrushchev by Brezhnev nor the "stability of cadres" policy followed by the latter conformed to the predictions of the totalitarian school; in Eastern Europe, the relative "demobilization" of society and the waning of "campaign" methods of economic management and social change after the early 1950s also suggested that the applicability of the model was limited (Brown 1974; Cohen 1985; Hough 1972).

In short, once the dust had settled on totalitarianism, the consensus of the field was that while the "leading role" of a Leninist party and the hegemonic role of the state/socially owned sector in the economy may have transformed the nature of politics in socialist states, they had nonetheless not eliminated politics, as the totalitarian model implied. The question that then remained was, of course, to define the nature of that transformation and devise appropriate methods to study it.

Yet just as totalitarianism fell into disfavor among Western social scientists, the term gained new currency among opposition movements, first in Eastern Europe and subsequently in the Soviet Union itself (Michnik 1986; Haraszti 1979; Kolakowski 1971; Rakitsky 1988). In this context, the term acquired the same mythic value in domestic politics that it had attained earlier on the international level at the height of the Cold War: analogous to Sorel's vision of the general strike, it proved to be a potent mobilizer of a mass public. Thus, in one of history's great ironies, it was precisely in the cases where regimes conformed least to the traditional features of the totalitarian model that totalitarianism became the most popular shorthand expression for what needed to be changed. (In Poland, for example, deep divisions virtually paralyzed the party, assertions of its "infallibility" had not been heard for years, there was nowhere near a monopoly of control by the party of the means of communication, it was in large part the absence of central control and direction of the economy that precipitated the economic crisis, and the measures taken after the assassination of Father Popieluszko suggested that even under martial law, police "terror" was hardly a routine event.)

Reconciling a theory of totalitarianism with the existence of a domestic opposition able to apply it required no small sleight of hand. Totalitarianism was consequently redefined from a description of the actual political system to a tendency that Leninist parties aspired to but were necessarily unable to realize in practice. Political life in communist systems could thus be described as how an organization with a totalitarian ideology adapted to a necessarily nontotalitarian situation. As such, it consisted of a series of skirmishes and battles between a party-state seeking to maximize its control over a society bent on expressing its incipient pluralism (Ost 1989).

As a theory, the "new" totalitarianism provides a far more nuanced interpretation of life in socialist systems than did the older version. It can accommodate and explain changes in the pattern of rule, the rise of social movements, the impulse for and frustration of attempts at economic reform, the switch from "moral" to "material" incentives and the consequent emphasis on improving supplies of consumer goods, the party's willingness to tolerate as much diversity as it could co-opt. At the same time, it highlights the ideological barriers to the party's apparent unwillingness to abandon its claim to control state and society even as the reality of that control increasingly declines.

Again, the political importance of the "new" totalitarian school of thought is critical for an understanding of the contemporary political scene in socialist systems, and especially so in Eastern Europe. Yet precisely because the term has become such a catchword of opposition movements wherever they have appeared, it is unclear how great its heuristic value is. Certainly, it gives a neat and consistent account of the current political conjuncture. Yet just as one would hesitate to accept a government's equally neat and consistent account of its actions and those of its opponents, one ought to hesitate to accept uncritically the opposition's account of its own actions and those of the government (even if we are on the opposition's side). In effect, following the opposition in its own terms typically means one will see only what the opposition implicitly is willing to let one see.

Here, one must ask whether or not political life in socialist systems has, in fact, been a series of skirmishes between society on one side and the party-state on the other. Or has it rather been a more complex phenomenon, characterized by cleavages within the party and the state as well? How can it happen that so many members of the party—including quite highly placed officials—come to support the criticisms implied by the totalitarian analysis if the very nature of the organization is to be totalitarian itself? Even more to the point, how can it happen that leaders of a party which "necessarily" tends to total control can themselves take the initiative in calling for pluralization of political processes?

In short, despite the fact that totalitarianism has been redefined from a description of reality into a tendency or an ideal type, the new totalitarianism shares many of the problems that beset the older version: by reifying one "tendency" of Leninism (i.e. its Stalinist variant), it ignores all the other tendencies that are part and parcel of the same intellectual and political heritage. Yet it is precisely all these other tendencies that are now coming to the fore, not despite the Communist party, but because of it. In such a situation, one must ask not simply whether the picture of socialism drawn by the new totalitarian school is accurate, but why it seems to have gained such intellectual prominence recently.

The rise of the "new" totalitarian analysis coincides with the decline of another mode of analysis that had previously enjoyed a good deal of currency in left (if I may use the term in this context) intellectual circles on both banks of the Elbe, namely, Marxist analyses (Djilas 1958; Bahro 1977; Cliff 1970; Konrad and Szelenyi 1979). Like Marxist analyses of capitalist systems, in Marxist understandings of "actually existing" socialism, "class" was a central category. In socialism, however, class lines were drawn not on the basis of property ownership but according to the control of assets. Accordingly, political power was the key to class divisions in socialism, such that the political leadership (also defined as the "bureaucracy") emerged as "ruling class" with a set of interests of its own, distinct from and in contradiction with those of subordinate groups in the society.

Using Marxism to "unmask" Marxism-Leninism was bound to be a popular project: on the right, it allowed hypocrisy to be added to the list of vices of established socialism, whereas on the left, it allowed followers to unburden themselves of justifying the more unpleasant and authoritarian features of "actually existing" socialism without having to abandon Marxism or socialism itself. For the social scientist, the contribution of the "ruling class" paradigms were also nonnegligible, insofar as they drew attention to what appeared to be rather rigid limits to potential economic and political change in socialist states and to rather striking and well-institutionalized political and social inequalities there. And, unlike the totalitarian theorists, ruling-class analyses suggested that authoritarianism did not grow out of a comprehensive ideology, but rather from the power generated by bureaucratic coordination of economic activity, which could be captured by "partial" (i.e. ruling class) interests who then utilized ideology as simply a rationalization for their continued rule.

Nevertheless, ruling-class analyses suffer from several fatal flaws as well (Giddens 1973; Brown 1974; Nove 1975; Staniszkis 1982). For one thing, though such analyses typically posit the political leadership as a class, they either fail to specify a class mission, leaving us in the dark as to what leaders will do, or define a class mission in ways that the actions of the ruling class patently contradict. The first problem is most apparent in Milovan Djilas's analysis, in which directly contradictory policies (collectivization of agriculture or decollectivization of agriculture; centralized economic administration or decentralization of economic processes and use of the market) are held to be equally in the political elite's class interest, thereby making it unclear what the analytic value of calling socialist political elites a "class" is. The second problem plagues "state capitalist" theories, which typically fail to explain why rulers bent on maximizing accumulation or the extraction of surplus routinely select such highly inefficient economic policies.

Furthermore, if socialist political elites are said to constitute a class by virtue of their position in the social structure, it is unclear why political leaders in any country would not also form at least a "potential" class by the same criterion. Certainly, political leaders everywhere try to stay in power and maintain and reinforce the state as they do so; and in performing such activities, leaders act to preserve the state regardless of whether it is pluralist, authoritarian, corporatist, praetorian, or socialist. Thus, whether the appelation "class"—which, at least in its Marxist sense, implies a class mission, interest, and regime-type affinity—can be applied anywhere to describe political elites is questionable.

Finally, although presumably all socialist states have the same class structure and economic system, there are and have nonetheless been important differences in the policies they follow, differences that have a critical impact on the life chances of individuals living in these countries (compare, for example, the structure of opportunities for peasants in Hungary, Romania, and Bulgaria), be they elites or nonelites, and which cannot be explained by a simple dichotomy between rulers and ruled. Here, although class analyses have helped to define and explain revolutionary changes, their analytic power to account for nonrevolutionary changes in individual countries (capitalist or socialist!) is notoriously weak. Yet it is precisely such incremental changes that have the greatest impact in the short term and, one might argue, on long-term evolution of political and social life as well. China in 1989 was a very different place from China of 1969, despite the apparently uninterrupted rule of the same "class." To explain nonrevolutionary change in foreign and domestic policy, some theory of intraclass cleavages and coalitions is required, and here even relatively nuanced "ruling class" theories are normally not very helpful.

In fact, most social scientific analyses of the past two decades or so have indeed focused on explaining precisely such patterns of incremental change in communist systems. Several paradigms emerged, all of which bore an important similarity to Marxist approaches in that they adapted methods of analysis originally articulated in the context of liberal capitalist systems to the study of socialist systems. Here, two basic paradigms seemed to dominate the field: group politics and organizational-bureaucratic politics. Let us examine each in turn.

Theories based on group politics call attention to the cleavages and conflicts within the various political elites of socialist states, suggesting that these conflicts are related in some systematic way to the social differentiation present in the society such elites govern (Skilling 1966; Skilling and Griffiths 1971; Kanet 1978). Until very recently, however, group conflict theories have suffered from a serious lack of empirical support for their key assumption, namely, that social groups in state socialist systems have either the autonomy or the political resources they would require to press their claims on political leaders effectively (Janos 1970).

Certainly, numerous policy measures and reversals in socialist states can be used to show that when individual actions are taken on a broad enough scale, they can influence political choices made by elites: high labor turnover can affect wage regulation, declines in farm output can produce changes in tax and price policy, requests for exit visas may influence emigration and travel policy, consumer rejection of a product can cause its production to be discontinued. Nevertheless, even a large number of individuals using an "exit" option is not equivalent to establishing the common "voice" that is a fundamental requirement for the exercise of genuine political power by groups. For example, political leaders may well respond to high labor turnover or excessive absenteeism with wage increases; yet they can also respond with hiring freezes or increased wage differentiation as well, and have often done so.

Recently, this type of theorizing has been revived in the form of positing an implicit "social compact" between the regime and the population in order to explain the various "welfare state" features common to state socialist systems, and especially their full employment/job security guarantees (Pravda 1981; Hauslohner 1987). Consequently, it is argued, the tendency of economic reform to be accompanied by political changes that would allow more institutionalized forms of consultation between regime and population can be explained by the need to "renegotiate" the social compact: employment guarantees, for example, can be changed or withdrawn only with the consent of the groups affected.

There are both empirical and logical difficulties with the notion that a social compact can be said to exist in state socialism. Empirically, again, there is the problem of exactly who signs such an agreement on behalf of the population, given that the leaders of mass organizations have always been on party *nomenklaturas* and there is a distinct lack of mechanisms by which their membership can hold them to account. Moreover, the only case in which an explicit agreement between a regime and labor force appears to have been concluded—namely, Gierek's agreement to freeze prices in Poland for five years in 1971— suggests that social contracting is an important step in delegitimizing the regime rather than stabilizing it.

In fact, the full employment "guarantees" of socialism appear to be a quite predictable side effect of the "expansion drive" that invariably accompanies the "soft budget" constraints of enterprises in the centrally planned economy rather than an explicit "concession" political leaders make to popular pressures. As such, they are typically accompanied not by increases in workers' bargaining power with either the state or employers—as is the case when full employment is achieved in a capitalist economy—but instead, by increased party intervention into employment practices. Likewise, increased attention to the supply of consumer goods need not be due to fears of delegitimation on the part of political elites; on the contrary, it is the rational counterpart to increased emphasis on material incentives aimed at raising productivity. If there is nothing in the stores to buy with increased earnings, individuals will hardly strive to achieve them.

Logically, the need to posit a social contract is necessitated only if one assumes à la James Madison that leaders will invariably act counter to social interests if they are not accountable to social groups. Yet it is unclear if making such an assumption is justified. "Society"—its development, its needs, its welfare—has always been a key concern of Marxist-Leninist elites; especially once the "heroic" period of social transformation has been completed, there is little need for them to be at war with it.

Nevertheless, this concern for society arises not because society or social groups can push their claims on the political elite or even because the political elite is in constant fear of delegitimation. Rather, the ideology and value system political leaders assume by virtue of entering the elite require society to be the central *object* of decisions at the same time that the same ideology and value system militate against making society the *subject* of decision-making. In short, the fact the "society" is not autonomous does not imply that political leaders do not seek what they judge to be in its best interest; nor does it imply that they do not, in fact, do what is in society's best interest and even what society might very well want them to do. On the contrary, lack of autonomy merely means that society does not have the political mechanisms by which it could make these judgments for itself. Paternalism, not negotiated contracts between equals, is the name of the game.

Nevertheless, if group politics as a theory explaining political outcomes has not made much headway in the past, it has nonetheless been an enormously fruitful framework for research, simply because it pushed scholars to examine aspects of life in socialism that are wider than the top bodies of the party and state and caused them to examine the dynamics of policy decisions that were not examples of "fundamental changes" in the nature of socialism itself. Studies of local government, labor relations, citizen participation, social service delivery, rural change, and the like made tremendous contributions to our understanding of the diversity possible within a polity that remained fundamentally Leninist (Schwartz and Keech 1968; Barry 1964; Mills 1970; Kaplan 1987; Hodnett 1974; Friedgut 1979; Triska 1977; Triska and Gati 1981; Zaslavsky and Brym 1979; Kemeny 1982; Stark 1986; Walder 1987; Zukin 1975; Matthews 1986). If, for the most part, such studies did not show that the conditions underlying a genuine or even limited group pluralism existed, they certainly did show that society was not simply composed of infinitely pliable automatons who simply carried out commands from above in the manner intended and that there was a far greater degree of interaction between political elites and the larger population than could have been anticipated within the older, totalitarianism framework.

Furthermore, the inapplicability of the "group politics" model in the past does not necessarily imply that it is equally irrelevant in the present where, in countries like Hungary, Poland, and the Soviet Union, there has been a meteoric burgeoning of all forms of spontaneous associations, many of which have explicitly political concerns. The problem, however, is that now that we find "real" groups to examine, it turns out that group politics as a theory (Bentley 1908; Truman 1951) tells us dreadfully little about what to say about them—and especially so when the institutional sources of their influence are either unclear or in continual flux. I will return to suggest some questions and approaches to the study of the newly activated social groups that have arisen below.

The second influential paradigm drawn from the Western literature on policy-making was the bureaucratic-organizational model. Here, rather than stress the role of social groups in the decision-making process, the paradigm highlights the role of established organizations as political actors, viewing conflicts among institutional interests for survival and expansion and among organizational elites representing these interests as central factors in policy choices (Hammer 1974; Hough and Fainsod 1979; Rigby 1976; Laky 1979, 1980; Lieberthal and Oksenberg 1988).

The problem with the organizational politics model is clearly not empirical. Bargaining and haggling are endemic to socialist systems; indeed, the lack of an active price mechanism itself means they are the only techniques available for allocating resources at the microeconomic level in a socialist economy. The bureaucratic politics has thus proved to be a powerful tool for unravelling the complexities of "cryptopolitics" in socialist systems, and has led to a wealth of rather sophisticated and illuminating case studies.

The question, however, is whether all politics in socialist states is cryptopolitics or whether there is "real" politics as well. Put in Aristotelian terms, the bureaucratic politics approach offers a great deal of insight into the politics of the household—no small accomplishment in a system that closely resembles One Big Household. Yet there is a real sense in which socialist systems are a polis as well, and to the degree that politics cannot be reduced down to simply a struggle for power but also involves questions of purpose and debates (no matter how esoteric) over the "good life," a bureaucratic politics approach is necessarily limited. It can tell us "who gets what, when, and how," but sheds little light on how the principles determining the allocation of "values" are determined. In effect, it tells us a great deal about the agents, but does so by telling us very little about the principals (Dawisha 1980).

Thus, focusing on the bargaining process alone ignores the fact that the arenas within which bargaining occurs are strictly limited and the issues up for bureaucratic negotiation are tightly restricted.[4] Furthermore, the bargaining partners themselves (e.g. enterprises and ministries) do not determine these limits and restrictions; rather, the political leaders outside them do. If one asks, for example, why the president of the Academy of Sciences in, say, Czechoslovakia lobbies for higher salaries for research workers and improved vacation resorts for them, the bureaucratic politics approach not only has an explanation but can also tell us what strategy he is likely to employ to achieve such goals. But if one asks why the same figure does not lobby for greater intellectual freedom and an end to censorship—clearly an organizational benefit for an academy of sciences—the bureaucratic politics paradigm has no ready answer. Likewise, a bureaucratic politics approach will tell us that the Hungarian steel industry will lobby ferociously to minimize the amount to which investment is cut back in a time of austerity; it will not, however, explain why the industry accepts the need for cutbacks at all, or why it does not seek to cut back employment, wages, or output instead.

Moreover, far from the content of organizational interests being "fixed" once and for all by the "nature" of the organization, organizations have often pursued entirely different goals at different times. For example, trade unions have alternately fought for equalizing wages and for greater differentials, depending on the political priorities of the day. Likewise, individuals within the same organization often differ as to their policy preferences: though the president of the Hungarian National Bank opposed breaking it up into several commercial banks, several of his deputies supported the reform.

Moreover, if organization leaders merely represent organizational interests, it is difficult to understand why the *nomenklatura* exists. However, once we realize that leaders are as likely to play active and creative roles in defining an organization's interests, programs, and missions as they are to be passive transmitters of them, appointments are revealed as a critical mechanism in the ability of higher-level leaders to control the behavior and interests of subordinate units. Thus, there is an important sense in which "where you sit reflects where you stand," rather than the reverse as Graham Allison claimed (1971) in his study of bureaucratic politics in the West.

Finally, it is difficult to explain how "strong" ministries, industries, and mass organizations ever "lose" if policy changes are simply the product of organizational competition. Yet enterprise associations (VVBs) did lose their autonomy in East Germany, the Ministry of Industry was reorganized and cut back in Hungary, and even the Polish United Workers' Party streamlined and reduced its apparatus in Poland in the 1970s.

Analyses of economic reform processes illustrate both the rich insights and the inherent limits to the bureaucratic politics approach in this respect. On the one hand, it leads us to expect a great deal of resistance on the part of ministries and central planning bodies to attempts to introduce market mechanisms to the economy, resistance that appears to have been amply documented in fact. At the same time, if bureaucratic actors are such key political players and stand to lose so much from economic reform, one is at a loss to explain how economic reform gets on the political agenda to start with.

Moreover, it is quite unclear that the problems economic reforms have encountered in the past were due simply to "bureaucratic subversion" in the implementation stage. On the contrary, they appear to be due to inherent contradictions in the reforms themselves. For example, in Hungary, the Ministry of Industry did not invent "supply obligations" in the 1970s all by itself in a grab for power. Rather, it was handed them by a policy-making elite willing to remove constraints from the firms but unwilling to drop them from the economy as whole. Likewise, the Ministry of Finance did not grant tax exemptions nor did the Hungarian Bank grant favorable credit arrangements simply to keep enterprises "dependent"; such measures were typically required by the failure of the reform to create interconnected capital, labor, and product markets, a "policy" failure much more closely related to political compromises than to bureaucratic preferences.

None of the above implies that the study of the behavior of formal, bureaucratic actors in the future is not vital for our understanding of the changes taking place in socialist states. The problem is simply that when the organizational politics model is employed as a paradigm by itself, it inevitably leads to exaggerating bureaucratic constraints to change and underestimating political and economic ones.

A major problem with ruling class, group politics, and bureaucratic politics approaches is that all three rely on theories formulated in the Western context and simply apply them to the socialist systems. As such, the unique characteristics of the key political actor in socialism—namely, the Communist party—are given somewhat short shrift, since such an actor is notably absent from the Western political scene.[5] Two schools of thought, one recent and one more traditional, have tried to surmount this problem, each attempting to formulate a model of politics unique to the socialist systems.

The more recent approach is what might be termed the "civil society versus the state" approach, popular among sociologists and East European opposition movements (Staniszkis 1984; Arato 1981; Havel 1985; Haraszti 1979; Hankiss 1986; Keane 1987, 1988; Judt 1988). The scholarly impulse behind this approach lay in a healthy reaction to what was felt to be too exclusive an emphasis on the "high politics" of the leadership and the established organizations, an emphasis that led observers to ignore or underestimate significant developments and changes in the larger society. In this sense, the approach was the socialist analogue to attempts to "bring the State back" into the study of Western systems. It placed heavy emphasis on the unintended consequences of central decisions, pointing to real limits to the control political leaders were thought to have, and pointed to a great deal of social ferment occurring beneath the surface among a population that appeared apathetic and passive. The growth of the second economy, the rise in nominally apolitical associational activity (from rock groups to environmental discussion clubs), the shop floor activities of workers, the circulation of *samizdat* manuscripts, and changing patterns of social stratification and attitudinal behavior among youth were all topics explored by a view anxious to "bring Society back" into our understanding of contemporary socialist systems.

Politically, the "civil society" approach was the natural complement to the new totalitarianism paradigm. If the political elite's natural tendency was to be "totalitarian," society's natural tendency was to be pluralistic. If the political elite's ideal was the One Big Household of the centrally planned economy, society's counter was to insist on creating a "public space" of political interaction among diverse, "self-organized" groups. It did so by first creating "private spaces" for itself into which the political elite could intervene only at great cost to its own control, the second economy being a case in point. Nevertheless, as society's attempt to create a private sphere in which it governed its own activity increasingly runs up against the regulatory barriers of the established socialist order, private associations become politicized, with the result that a full-fledged "civil society" ultimately emerges which totalitarian elites can no longer suppress.

The "civil society" paradigm is both intellectually and politically powerful, and sheds an enormous amount of light on the factors leading to attempts to reform socialist economies and pluralize political decision-making processes. Moreover, it tells us a tale we love very much to hear: of the triumph of pluralism and democracy over monolithic tyranny, of David over Goliath, of individuals over the State. Alas, precisely because it is such an inspiring account, this cynical observer cannot help but be somewhat skeptical of its claims.

The problem begins with the very definition of "civil society." My own reading of Kant tells me that a civil society is a society governed by laws (Reiss 1970; Rawls 1971). If so, several consequences follow. First of all, insofar as "actually existing" socialism is not and cannot be a society governed by the rule of law (the "leading role" of the party by definition prevents this), the society that emerges from it may become a "civil" society but it cannot be (or even become) one independent of the state that incapsulates it. Hence, the notion that this society can somehow govern itself if the government just leaves it alone appears quite untenable.

Second, insofar as the legal or alegal arrangements that describe the state necessarily condition the social interactions of the individuals within it, it is difficult to understand how "society" 's development and articulation can occur independently of the political and legal structures surrounding it. If Janos planted tomatoes and brought them to the market for sale, he must have had some guarantee that neither his land nor his earnings from the sale would be confiscated—otherwise he might do this once, but not year after year. He must also presumably be able to buy things with the money earned (not to be taken for granted in a shortage economy), and he also must have some expectation that there are consumers willing to pay the price he is asking. If we were to expand this example to include Stanislaw marketing a specially designed computer program to a state enterprise, the need for an explicit regulatory framework is even clearer.

Moreover, let us remember that these activities—at least up to 1989—were going on under state socialism, such that simple legal guarantees were surely insufficient; on the contrary, the real guarantees were political ones, given by whatever party organ was politically responsible for such transactions. As such, we find not a one-sidedly "self-organized" society, but one whose articulations depend very heavily on measures the state and party take (and have taken) for reasons that may or may not be related to social demands. In fact, the "society" that is emerging is very much not a society that "created" itself; nor is it a society very much like the one whose "development" was "interrupted" by socialism in 1917 or 1947. On the contrary, the percentage of blue collar workers, peasants, and intellectuals in the population, the distribution of income, property, and education, the national homogeneity or heterogeneity of the population, and other such features having a major impact on the formation of various groupings today all reflect forty or seventy years of socialism.

Third, Kant's original definition of civil society reminds us sharply that it is not simply a society of voluntary associations. The extraordinary similarities between the Polish experience of 1980–81 and the emergence of bureaucratic-authoritarianism in Latin America in the 1960s suggest equally strongly that the presence of groups making demands on the government (or the party) is not necessarily a prelude to the rule of law and certainly not synonymous with it (Staniszkis 1982; O'Donnell 1979; Huntington 1968). Moreover, the apparently successful transitions of many states in Latin America to competitive political systems in the 1980s suggest that political leadership—on the part of both the outgoing and the incoming regimes—is critical both for the formation of social groups to begin with and for their evolution into responsible political actors (O'Donnell and Schmitter 1986).

With this, we turn to the final school of thought seeking to explain politics under socialism: the political "conflict" school (Roeder 1988). This is a school focusing on patterns of cleavage and conflict within the political leadership itself. As I use the term, it includes a wide range of scholarship, not all of whose practitioners by any means agree with one another (Ploss 1965; Linden 1966; Breslauer 1982; Conquest 1962; Hough and Fainsod 1979; Griffiths 1971; Comisso 1986). The basic assumption of this school is, to quote Carl Linden, that "conflict is a continuous and critical fact of . . . political life" (1966, 12). Whether conflict is simply over power or also over purpose is a subject of some debates, with Kremlinologists tending to stress the former and others stressing the policy implications of competition among the leadership.

Among the latter group, there is normally some attempt to link leaders to constituencies, although in contrast with the bureaucratic politics model, the emphasis is more on leaders mobilizing constituencies than on constituencies choosing among leaders. Social and bureaucratic "interests" thus enter the policy process not because leaders are accountable to them, but because a kind of "virtual" representation takes place. Hence, leaders may be recruited out of bureaucracies (e.g. the KGB), mass organizations (the Komsomol), or territorial organs, but they need not "represent" these interests in the sense of having a mandate from them in broad policy-making party bodies.

The main problem with the political conflict school is precisely the opposite of that of the civil society approach: by focusing overwhelmingly on "high" politics, it tends to obscure what is going on beneath the surface. Yet to the degree political competition has a strong policy parameter, who wins and who loses is going to be affected by the success or lack of success of the measures he or she endorses, even if success itself is defined by the elite making the policy. And here, what the impact of a measure is necessarily requires some attention to its consequences—intended and unintended—on the nonelite population.

Nevertheless, the political conflict approach can be quite illuminating in explaining both the domestic factors that led to political and economic reform in Poland, Hungary, and the Soviet Union and the absence of such factors in Romania, East Germany, and Czechoslovakia. Here, we know that there is nothing like competition for enlarging the size of the market; just as economic competition lowers the cost of commodities, one would expect political competition to reduce the cost of political involvement. And indeed, the secular trend even in oligarchic polities (e.g. the Soviet Union under Brezhnev) was to widen the circle of political consultation, as experts, bureaucracies, territorial officials, and the like were deployed as political resources among rivals.

But what kept the circle relatively narrow was basic agreement among top political elites that the party should resolve conflicts within its own ranks and thereby monopolize the power of the "last say." In Poland, that consensus broke down when the party proved unable to either make decisions or enforce them on its own agents; in Hungary, it broke down as leaders split on the desirability of retaining the party's political monopoly; in the Soviet Union, the circle opened when a leader sought to mobilize popular support as a way of galvanizing the party into his proposed course of action. In East Germany, Czechoslovakia, Romania, and even China, no such split in the established political leadership occurred, and so no one sought to advance his or her position in the party by mobilizing a popular following: the road to acquiring power (and hence accomplishing even democratic and populist purposes) remained that of satisfying the demands of the constituency "above" one in the political hierarchy, and not by creating one below.

Accordingly, the dynamics of the political opening in East Germany, Czechoslovakia, and Bulgaria reveal cases of "external push" rather than "domestic pull."[6] That is, the economic situation in those three countries in 1989 was not nearly so serious as in heavily indebted Poland or Hungary; economic reform was on the agenda only to the degree the Soviet Union had been able to put it there. Nor was the top leadership of the communist parties in those states seriously divided about the undesirabilty of liberalization. Consequently, if a split in the elite was to come, it had to be engineered from outside. It was here that Mikhail Gorbachev and the CPSU provided the spark—whether by supporting (and possibly even encouraging or eliciting) the Hungarian decision to allow East Germans to cross the border into Austria, by (one must assume) denying hard-liners in the GDR access to the kind of force a "Chinese solution" might have required (and when the head of the secret police becomes General Secretary of the East German SED, could the Soviet Union not be involved?), or by reprimanding the Czech party for its intransigence to the point where it permitted the student demonstration that started the opposition ball rolling and, once it was in motion, suddenly publishing Soviet apologies for the 1968 invasion.

Thus, although there is no denying the importance of broad social forces in sweeping away the ancien régime, one must also acknowledge the role forces within the communist parties themselves played in eliciting and channeling those pressures. Bulgaria was perhaps the extreme case in this respect: there, the Communist party literally abandoned its "leading role" before the opposition even requested it to do so.

To the degree political liberalization is a product of splits in the national and/or international ruling elite, the Chinese case becomes particularly interesting. For one thing, it suggests that there is no "automatic" connection between the use of the market and even the institution of private property with political pluralism. Rather, it indicates that as long as elite actors are not internally split over the introduction of structural economic changes, "society" can continue to be excluded from political processes. In effect, then, the link between economic reform and political reform is not that the former somehow "requires" the latter to operate effectively, but rather that disagreements over the pacing, content, and extent of economic reforms can have such extremely divisive effects on Leninist elites that they can give elements in the leadership unusually large incentives to call out mass publics to reinforce their position within the party itself.

The foregoing implies that where "society" 's activation occurred prior to the winter of 1989, it was at least partially politically induced from above. Certainly, it is difficult to understand how *samizdat* in Poland came to be issued by a full-fledged underground printing press (as opposed to hand-reproduced typographical manuscripts) without at least some high-level political support for this type of publication. In Hungary, the fact that Imre Poszgay and not the secret police attended the formative meeting of the Democratic Forum is surely more than coincidental to the public prominence this organization acquired. And in the Soviet Union, when anyone wins by a 90 percent margin in a nominally competitive election, one must ask exactly how serious the competition was before one interprets the result as "society" speaking out all by itself.

This is not to say that the rank-and-file population in places like Poland or Hungary is simply manipulated and that it had nothing to say for itself; merely enumerating all the various campaigns of the past that have swept socialist systems only to fall flat on their face due to societal disinterest indicates quite the contrary. It is, however, to suggest that politics everywhere is more of a "supply-side" phenomenon than we often like to admit. In this regard, one of the main findings of the "regime transition" literature that has arisen around the Asian and Latin American experiences of the 1980s may be quite relevant: it is when the ruling group splits that society enters (O'Donnell and Schmitter 1986). The moral here for the socialist systems appears to be that although political disagreements over the pace and extent of structural economic change can be a major source of elite cleavage—and hence social "opening"—this need not universally be the case.

WHERE DO WE GO FROM HERE?

If the various frameworks and models listed above all have their limits, their collective findings have given us a relatively rich and nuanced knowledge of how the "actually existing" socialist state and society operate and interact with each other, in both ideal-typical and empirically varying forms.[7] Though there are certainly large gaps in our knowledge due to the unavailability of reliable data or to political restrictions on research efforts (be they by foreigners or natives), a fairly complete picture—or perhaps pictures would be the more appropriate term—has emerged, and debates center largely on how to interpret it.

Thus, although the absence of a dominant paradigm has been the source of a great deal of atheoretical, descriptive research, debates that boil down to tussles over definitions, and periodic waves of *samo-kritikas*, as the "field" berates itself for its lack of rigor, it is also responsible for a great deal of flexibility, the growth of a wide variety of research agendas, and attention to a large number of questions, many of which would necessarily be excluded if there were a single Grand Theory of or Approach to State Socialism. Moreover, particularly in light of the difficulties of collecting data in many of the socialist countries, the quality of scholarship is by no means inferior to that in other, more mainstream areas of the discipline; indeed, an analysis of the evolution of such fields as political participation, American government, and international relations would probably even indicate that the degree of "politicization" that has marked the study of communism in American political science is no less and no more than that characterizing other areas of the discipline. As noted at the start of the chapter, there is a real sense in which a "science" of "politics" is a contradiction in terms that even the most careful and astute scholar cannot escape, and so it is hardly surprising that students of communist systems fall victim to it as well.

This much said, there remains much to be done. First of all, even if we are entering a new era, there are some key problems relating to traditional socialism that have generally been ignored or underresearched whose resolution is critical for an understanding of the current situation. In particular, there is the problem of the anomalies.

East Germany is one such case. Here, we are all well aware of the inadequacies of central planning in a modern, sophisticated economy. Why, then, does East Germany seem to prosper under this system?[8] In principle, the drawbacks of central planning should be *most* apparent there (since it is the most developed socialist economy), whereas in practice they seem least apparent. Several suggested explanations have been offered, each of which has its problems and all of which present opportunities for investigation. One suggestion is that the cause is the "special" relationship with West Germany. But insofar as one of the key problems of centrally planned economies has always been characterized as their inability to realize benefits from trade, the ability of East Germany to do so has to be explained. For example, why are East German firms apparently able to satisfy the demands of West German consumers when Polish firms cannot?

Folk wisdom suggests that East Germany does well because "they are Germans." Although we are inclined as social scientists to dismiss such hypotheses, this one suggests a rather fruitful line of inquiry; how do cultural norms get perpetuated when socioeconomic systems change? Here, rather than discuss "Germanness," one could presumably specify a set of behaviors (at work, towards authority, etc.) and investigate the mechanisms that call such behavior forth. Is the difference between, say, the DDR and Poland a different (cultural) understanding and reaction to identical structures and incentives, or are the mechanisms for, say, rewarding high productivity and punishing disobedience themselves different?

Yet a third explanation would suggest that East German performance is only relative, and had central planning never been introduced, East Germany would be far better off than it currently is. Hence, the degree to which the production possibilities frontier has not been attained is as great in East Germany as elsewhere, but the production possibilities frontier itself was much higher to start with. Again, this may be correct, but one longs for some relatively rigorous demonstration of it.

Another anomaly we have little understanding of concerns Yugoslavia. On the one hand, Yugoslavia's dismal economic performance of the last decade or so has been widely interpreted—specially by Yugoslavs nowadays—to signify that the Yugoslav model of labor-managed socialism is itself unworkable. Yet somehow, it has not performed so poorly in Slovenia. Is this due to cultural causes? To initial advantages? To economic policies that have been different from those in other republics? To political causes?

Czechoslovakia is the source of yet a third anomaly. Here, the question is why the socialist state with the strongest democratic tradition was the one with the least political ferment until November 1989? In particular, to the degree political culture has frequently been invoked in explanations of both obedience (the Soviet Union) and resistance (Poland), what does the Czechslovak experience teach us about the relevance (or irrelevance) of this variable?

These are only examples, and surely there are many other anomalies as well. Explaining them would put a great deal of the current ferment in the communist world in perspective, if only by warning us that what "works" and doesn't "work" is far more complex than simple slogans of markets and mixed economies suggest.

Meanwhile, the question that confronts us today is how to come to grips with the situation in communist states that do appear to be undergoing rather substantial changes. In these cases (Poland, Hungary, the Soviet Union, China, Yugoslavia), we confront a situation that simultaneously appears historically unique (to the degree it involves a redefinition of socialism) and all too familial (the erosion of traditional authoritarianism)—and we have no way of knowing which it is.[9]

Put in the terms of this analysis, given the "core" characteristics of socialist states—the leading role of a Leninist party and weak differentiation between state and economy—we simply do not know whether these (one or both) characteristics are merely changing their form, or whether they may be on the verge of disappearing entirely. For a field that has essentially defined its subject matter in terms of these characteristics, this is no small problem. In such a situation, it is hardly surprising—although not very illuminating—that so much debate has centered simply on whether current changes are "fundamental" or "superficial," "permanent" or "reversible," "sufficient" or "not far enough."

Part of the difficulty is that we, for quite understandable reasons, tend to conceptualize political, economic, and social change in terms of mutually exclusive dichotomies: authoritarianism versus democracy, capitalism versus socialism, traditional versus modern, domestic versus international, and so forth. As a result, we can easily exclude by definition the possibility that institutional forms not captured by these dichotomies might emerge (or might not).

Imagine, for example, a Leninist party that retains control of the state and observes democratic centralism but legalizes "factions" within its own ranks. Or imagine a coalition between a Communist party and a grass roots nationalist movement sufficient to give the former a genuine popular base without introducing competitive elections internally or externally. Are these democratic or authoritarian changes? Imagine further an arrangement in which social organizations and institutions (pension funds, universities, research institutes, socialized insurance agencies) rely on endowments composed of shares in socialist firms for a significant portion of their operating revenues. Is this socialism or capitalism? Imagine further a system in which the rate of participation of women in the paid labor force declines at the same time that the percentage of women in top positions increases. Or where access to abortion is more tightly restricted, but contraception is easier to obtain. Is this modern or traditional?

This is not to say that our traditional categories are irrelevant, for they are probably indispensable for our ability to conceptualize the current situation. Yet it is equally critical to remember that the categories are the means, not the end, of understanding, and when events or phenomena don't fit them, it is the category that needs to be subject to question, not the reality. Thus, despite the fact that the biggest question in all of our minds is "Where is all of this going?" this is probably precisely the question we should avoid trying to answer, since we simply lack the means to do so.[10]

Instead, my own sense is that the best strategy to pursue now is one that would recognize the inherent ambiguity of the current conjuncture and seek to exploit it in a genuinely comparative mode. Here, it seems to me, one can begin by using our traditional concepts to define several axes of research; nevertheless, pursuing them successfully may well require redefinition and reconceptualization of our basic concepts themselves.

The first axis of research is the authoritarian/democratic one, that is, an axis focusing on the causes, content, and consequences of changes in the relationship both within and between political elites and the broader population. One potentially fruitful line of approach to such phenomena would be to draw on the recent literature analyzing regime transitions in Latin American and East Asia. The purpose of doing so, it is important to stress, would not necessarily be to find similarities, for it is entirely possible that the "core" characteristics of socialism would make processes of political change under communism very different from those witnessed in other authoritarian regimes. Nevertheless, determining exactly what the differences are can be most precisely discovered by drawing hypotheses from this literature and testing them in the socialist context.

For example, does the fact that the ruling group in socialism is the leadership of a Leninist party rather than a military junta (or a traditional monarch, for that matter) make any difference? Given that Leninist elites are far more directly involved in issues of economic management than are their military counterparts, are they more or less likely to split on economic issues? Are Communist parties more (or less) likely to fall victim to a vertical cleavage between the top and the bottom of the party, or to a horizontal split within the top leadership itself? Or are the factors explaining splits in Leninist elites purely nation (as opposed to regime) specific? Further, given differences between the nature of a political party and a military bureaucracy plus the fact that the former presumably has no barracks to retreat to, is it possible that Leninist elites can lead the transition to a more open and inclusive polity in a way military elites cannot? In effect, both the supply of and demand for political entrepreneurship may be significantly higher in the Leninist system than in the bureaucratic-authoritarian regime; consequently, where the role of the military in a successful transition is to abdicate and leave politics to civilian leaders, the role of the party in a socialist transition may well be creating a broader-based ruling coalition.

On the mass level, if transitions everywhere have been accompanied by a sudden burgeoning of grass roots organizations, is the distribution of political resources among such groups similar in both types of societies? And do similar groups (private entrepreneurs, workers, peasants, etc.) make similar demands across the board? There are a few isolated cases (Poland, South Korea) in which workers and trade unions appear to have been major actors in initiating political reforms, but for the most part they seem to have played a surprisingly secondary role. Why is this the case? Further, if political parties have been the key actors in transitions in authoritarian capitalist regimes, are they equally necessary for opening up the political system to popular pressures in socialist systems?

Another promising line of inquiry would focus on processes of political liberalization within the socialist bloc itself. Here, we have several different configurations: two distinctly different patterns of "top-down" liberalization in the Soviet Union and Yugoslavia (pre-1985); two rather different patterns of "bottom-up" liberalization in Poland and Hungary; and one case in which a rather far-reaching set of economic reforms has been accompanied by minimal changes in elite-mass relationships (China). The consequences of these differences for economic reform, regional economic development, the activation of social groups, the role of the Communist party, labor-management relations, and the like offer a rich field of research.

A second axis of research is the capitalism/socialism dichotomy. Again, this can be analyzed through comparison between socialist systems undergoing "liberalization" and their counterparts among the newly industrialized countries in Latin America, East Asia, and Southern Europe and by comparisons within the socialist economies themselves.

With regard to the first, analysis of the consequences of "deregulation" and "privatization" in socialism and capitalism would appear to be an obvious candidate. What are the consequences of expanding opportunities for private entrepreneurship in a socialist economy and in a regulated capitalist one? Economically, one would expect not only that the distributional consequences of privatization measures would be different, but also that their efficiency effects are different. Likewise, the political consequences of such measures are ambiguous: are the new private entrepreneurs emerging in socialist and formerly socialist economies and the NICs supporters of "neo-liberalism" in politics and economics, or are they the harbingers of a new protectionism? Further, we know that certain "sequences" of liberalization in various sectors of the economy appear to be more successful than others in developing countries; although I am doubtful that the same type of sequencing can be successful in economies lacking the institutions of a market to start with, comparisons along these lines may help to refine our notions of exactly what measures need to be taken to create such institutions in the socialist states. Again, the utility of such comparisons need not be to show similarities; on the contrary, they may indicate the inappropriateness of simply grafting development strategies, ownership arrangements, and economic policies that have worked elsewhere to the socialist economies.

At the same time, the collective experience of the socialist countries that have experimented with economic reforms itself suggests a fairly wide variety of strategies with very different results. Yugoslavia began by introducing labor-managed firms, eliminating central planning of production and supplies, and organizing investment planning on geographical lines; China began its economic reforms in agriculture, a sector in which the presence of numerous buyers and sellers made it relatively easy for markets to operate effectively once property rights were made relatively secure; the Soviet Union's first step appears to have been opening the political arena to create a constituency for reform, whereas Hungary and Poland in the 1980s appear to be concentrating on creating new forms of ownership. A short summary clearly cannot do justice to the range of variations, but it can point to the need for a comparative analysis of the causes and consequences of various reform measures, whether it be by country, by sector, by region, or by social stratum.[11]

Furthermore, the comparative experience of the (present and former) socialist countries can also be mined to shed some light on the barriers to economic reform. While one frequently reads that the main barriers to the creation of effective markets lie in political leaders' (or bureaucracies') unwillingness to give up their control of the economy, the market failures literature suggests that often political leaders intervene in economic processes for quite justifiable reasons. Experience to date suggests that moving from a highly monopolistic centrally planned economy with poorly developed market institutions creates precisely the conditions of market failure. If so, even the most anticommunist political leadership will likely find itself doing exactly what the *ancien régime* did.

A third axis of research is the traditional/modern one. Here, one may explain the impulse to reform partly as a product of the creation of a relatively sophisticated "society" within the shell of a relatively archaic political and economic system (Lewin 1988). At the same time, however, the claims voiced from within some of the nationalist movements in both the Soviet Union and Eastern Europe suggest that more traditional, ascriptive identities are not about to be washed away by the growth of technical (or even legal) rationality. Why has nationalism emerged as such a potent force in "liberalizing" socialist states? In particular, why are groups so prone to form along national lines rather than along dimensions (class, occupation, urban/rural, etc.)? Is it official recognition of national heterogeneity in states like the Soviet Union and Yugoslavia that gives national claims strategic value other claims lack? Is it the fact that individuals depend so heavily on political structures organized on national lines for so many key values (housing, jobs, promotion, etc.) that makes nationalism particularly potent in socialism? Further, nationalism can serve as a convenient label for a wide variety of demands concerning everything from language policy, demographic and family regulation, suffrage arrangements, and economic exchange within and between various national territories. Under what conditions does nationalism assume highly exclusive forms, and when is it harnessed to an inclusive set of demands?

The three axes of research suggested above describe a set of subject matters for research that seem intuitively rather important in the current situation. Proceeding along the lines sketched above will certainly help to clarify what is going on empirically, and may well tell us which independent variables are related to which dependent variables in particular cases, knowledge that will certainly be helpful to have. Nevertheless, it is quite unclear what the broader theoretical significance of such findings will be, and it is here where I would hope that the ferment in the socialist world would allow some insight into issues of more general concern. In this regard, I have no Grand Theory but only Grand Questions on which I hope future research will shed some light.

First of all, even though most students of communist politics tend, with considerable justification, to see the causes of liberalization (political and economic) as being domestic in origin, a glimpse around the world in 1989 suggests that what we seem to be witnessing in the socialist cases is actually a part of a much wider global phenomenon. From the price of bread's being decontrolled in France for the first time since the French Revolution to the selling off of public assets to private owners in areas as unrelated as Great Britain, Turkey, Bangladesh, and Mexico, the popularity of "markets" and "private ownership" has clearly become an international phenomenon. Yet we have very little sense of why markets are suddenly the universal solution (although we can be quite skeptical that they are) when but a few years ago they were widely construed as the universal problem. And surely it is not enough to say that this change has occurred simply because of the efficiency advantages markets have. After all, if efficiency is desirable, so are a whole host of other values, and it is difficult to understand why those values have lost their preeminent position in the public eye.

The importance of the international intellectual hegemony of the competitive market ideal at the current time cannot be underestimated, I think, in the context of the socialist economies. Strong empirical evidence to the effect that economic reform improves the economic performance of socialist economies is extraordinarily weak; even the very good showing put in by Chinese agriculture in the aftermath of reforms in that sector can apparently be attributed as much to three years of good weather and the much-increased availability of fertilizer (thanks to plants constructed under Mao . . .) as to the "responsibility system." And the hard evidence that we do have suggests that there is a very direct link between economic reforms and higher inflation rates and increased income disparities. If this is the case, the conviction of socialist government as to the desirability and necessity of economic reforms is somewhat of a puzzle, as is the virtually unanimous verdict that their problem is simply not having gone "far enough." (After all, isn't it at least possible that they have already gone "too far?" Or that the reform thrust is misplaced, and the solution lies elsewhere?)

Moreover, this is not the first time an international fad seems to have swept the globe. In the 1960s, student movements making remarkably similar demands seized the headlines in the United States, Western Europe, Yugoslavia, Poland, Mexico, and many other countries as well. In the 1970s, the notion of poles of development was fashionable in development strategies all over the world, much as small entrepreneurship seems to be today. What explains these relatively rapid and rather uniform changes in social orientations in areas that have entirely different levels of development, political systems, and socioeconomic structures? Although we have some ideas about the ways in which the international diffusion of ideas occurs, we still understand very little about why what is being diffused changes so rapidly. Unfortunately, the history of ideas does not enjoy a very prominent position in our discipline; perhaps it is time to resurrect it.

Second, one seems to be witnessing (at least in Eastern Europe) the emergence of what, to use Gramsci's terms, can only be described as a new "social-historical bloc" of forces, complete with its own vocabulary ("discourse," if you will), vision of the past, ideology, and general goals: the complementarities illustrated by the "new" national-histori-cal, totalitarian, and civil society approaches described above can be taken as evidence of new intellectual paradigms on the high level and of the new "common sense" on the low level that, according to Gramsci, invariably accompany all such emerging sociohistorical configurations. Indeed, it even comes replete with enough internal political cleavages to be characterized as having a "politics" of its own. Whether and how that "bloc" might become the hegemonic one is a question we cannot answer, but the fact of its existence calls out for some explanation.

Doing so requires rethinking our traditional notions both of how groups form—for here, we have not only a large number of groups, but a large number of groups sharing a similar *weltanschauung*—and of the meaning of political culture. With regard to the former, we have a large number of models and theories explaining interest group interaction and political party competition in Western systems, but a real lack of understanding as to how groups form in the first place, that is, before they are institutionalized organizations.

Here, it seems to me that three lines of approach appear particularly promising. One would involve rethinking the notion of political culture in ways that might accommodate more anthropological and sociological approaches to the phenomenon. Here, insofar as our lack of historical distance from rapidly changing phenomena hinders our ability to make "objective" sense of what appear to be very profound social and cultural changes in values and behavior alike, it becomes increasingly urgent to make some "subjective" sense of them: exactly what do individuals think they are doing when they engage in second economy activities, marches to celebrate resurrected national holidays, celebrations of church masses? A whole host of political symbols has entered (or reentered) the political pantheon: Katyn, Imre Nagy, "civil society," national sovereignty, the Rechtstaat, and so forth. Do these symbols behind which large numbers of people can unite mean the same thing to everyone marching behind them? If not, what do they mean for individual groups and individuals? Such an approach might not only give us some insight into grass roots changes in socialist societies but also allow us to bridge the long-standing gap between subjectivist (attitudes and values) versus objectivist (actions and behaviors) approaches to political culture, by employing the term to describe a continual process of redefining the meaning of symbols in the context of day-to-day political activity.

A second approach is, of course, to employing survey research methods to gauge attitudes and attitudinal changes among large publics. Here, both the Soviet Interview Project (Millar 1987) and survey research conducted within the domestic socialist countries have given us a great deal of insight into generational change and variations among occupational, regional, and other groups as far as their attitudes toward political leaderships, reform programs, economic changes, and the like are concerned. As such, they can offer some clue as to whether and why the established wisdom of socialism seems to be falling on deaf ears whereas the new paradigms seem to "resonate" so well with the larger population (Jowitt 1978).

A third approach to this phenomenon would take off from Mancur Olsen's work (1969) on the logic of collective action, one of the few works that does attempt to confront, in theoretical terms, the problem of how groups get organized in the first place. Unlike the civil society school of thought, Olsen has argued quite persuasively that far from being natural and spontaneous, collective action for political ends is costly and problematic. But if it "pays to let George do it," how then did Solidarity suddenly acquire a mass membership? Are there times in which *not* engaging in collective action is costly? Exactly where do the new political entrepreneurs come from? And who—in quite literal, monetary terms—pays the cost of collective action? Although running an operation large enough to bring thousands of relatively unconnected individuals together in the streets in the Soviet Union or Hungary does not cost as much as winning a senatorial campaign in the United States, it still isn't cheap. Nor does keeping an underground (or aboveground) printing press afloat occur without financial resources. The campaign-financing literature offers a number of intriguing hypotheses about how financial resources are generated and under what conditions they can affect political outcomes; testing some of these hypotheses to analyze the strength of various social movements and their ability to generate and efficiently deploy financial resources (at home and—equally important—from foreign sources) could lead to some highly counterintuitive findings.

A third set of grand questions concerns the relationship between markets, ownership structures, and political systems. Here, we know that private ownership and markets are compatible with a variety of political systems. We also know that all liberal democratic governments are found in economies characterized by private ownership and markets. What we do not know is whether or not there is some "necessary" connection here (as Milton Friedman would claim) or whether that connection is purely the historical product of how Western politico-economic systems have evolved.

Moreover, we have little sense as to whether or not the requirements of democracy themselves can be met by forms of government that are not "liberal-democratic." Here, we know that political systems guaranteeing civil liberties and institutionalizing collective choices through competitive elections are "efficient" solutions to the problem of allowing a mass public to influence government decisions. What we do not know is if they are the only solutions.

Likewise, we know that the institution of private property, whereby private individuals have the right to use, dispose of, and enjoy the income streams from assets the government recognizes their claim to, can be an efficient system of property rights when combined with the competitive markets. Again, the question is whether or not it is the *only* efficient system of property rights or indeed if it would be efficient at all in systems in which the operation of markets has been suspended for years. If not, can one design an "efficient" set of property rights suitable to a socialist economy? And if one can do so, what political conditions would be required for them to be effective?

Here, property rights—whether communal or individual—are first and foremost legal rights; when the rule of law is attenuated by a party playing a leading role, even socialist enterprises lack clear title to the assets they are supposed to control. This suggests that a "rule of law"— whether it be under a single party or a multiparty system—is a requirement for an effective system of public or private property rights to exist. The question then is whether or not one must have democracy as well. Certainly, it is attractive to envision Law as expressing some fundamental social consent, but Western European development suggests that secure legal rights predate universal suffrage by several decades or more. Ironically, if democratization of the political system is a requirement for establishing a rule of law in socialism, it would suggest a rather anomalous pattern of historical evolution.

All of this suggests that there may be an extremely uncomfortable and tenuous relationship between reform of the socialist political system to make it more inclusionary and reform of the economic system to make it more dynamic. One can easily imagine greater democratization rendering impossible the kind of adjustments a major economic reform would necessarily entail, just as one can easily imagine a massive economic restructuring reversing any tendencies toward political opening. Although the communist politics field has done a quite creditable job of coming to grips with the traditional Leninist system, the field—much like its subject matter—is clearly now navigating in distinctly uncharted waters.

NOTES

1. I now regret this decision, insofar as the Great Collapse of East European socialism at the end of 1989 is inexplicable without reference to changes in

Soviet foreign policy priorities. As noted in the text (see pp. 99–100), the role of
the Soviet Union was particularly critical in the collapse of socialist systems in
East Germany and Czechoslovakia (where, to quote a Polish colleague, "once
Gorbachev pulled the plug, all the water just drained out"), as well as in the
changes made in Bulgaria.

On a more general level, my sense is that it was precisely the understandable tendency of the field to concentrate on domestic sources of stability and
change that led many of us (including this author) to underestimate the fragility
of the East European regimes and the degree to which their survival depended
purely on external support.

In this regard, one could actually have seen changes in CPSU attitudes toward "fraternal parties" as early as 1986, when it refused to becomes involved
in conflicts over leadership and program that took place in the Finnish Communist party (as a result, the neo-Stalinist, pro-Soviet wing lost virtually all its clout
in the Finnish party). Nevertheless, given traditional Soviet security concerns
on the European continent, it was unclear that this attitude could be generalized toward ruling communist parties in Warsaw Pact states, and indeed, the
evidence suggests that senior leaders within those parties themselves did not
realize the Brezhnev doctrine was finished until Moscow explicitly informed
them of this. Thus, in Poland, Mieczyslaw Rakowski resigned as prime minister
only after Gorbachev's well-publicized telephone call asking him to do so.

2. In a principal-agent relationship, a principal enters into a contractual
agreement with an agent, expecting that the latter will choose outcomes desired
by the former (e.g., lawyers/clients, doctors/patients, politicians/bureau-
crats). Even if the principal locates a "qualified" agent, the problem does not
stop here, "for there is no guarantee that the agent, once hired, will in fact
choose to pursue the principal's best interests or to do so efficiently. The agent
has his own interests at heart, and is induced to pursue the principal's objectives
only to the extent that the incentive structure imposed in their contract renders
such behavior advantageous. The essence of the principal's problem is [thus] the
design of just such an incentive structure." (Moe 1984, 756.)

Note, then, that seeing the party as principal and the state, the enterprises,
the mass organizations, et cetera as agents by no means implies "automatic"
obedience on the part of the latter. On the contrary, it suggests that control is a
real problem, and will vary depending on how effective the incentive structure
(including monitoring institutions and mechanisms inducing agents to reveal
information) facing agents is.

3. The competitive elections held throughout much of Eastern Europe in
spring 1990 cast a rather interesting light on the insights of the national-historical school. First, consistent with what the thesis of an "interrupted" national
trajectory would predict, the lifting of an externally imposed homogeneity on
the area was accompanied by regional differentiation along lines remarkably
similar to the old, nineteenth-century imperial boundaries: the German Reich
(GDR), the Österreich (Hungary, Czechoslovakia, Poland and northern Yugoslavia), and the Ottoman (southern Yugoslavia, Bulgaria, Romania).

Second, the political spectrum that emerged in the area is—again consistent with the national-historical school—rather different from the political

spectrum we are familiar with in the West. That is, the Western political spectrum typically runs from right to left, and one can conceptualize electoral results as the point at which voters choose to make the efficiency/equality trade-off. In Eastern Europe, by contrast, the political spectrum is structured along *gemeinschaft/geselleschaft* lines and, with the exception of Czechoslovakia, voters typically opted for the parties of national integrity. In such a context, the status of ex-communist parties also differed along the old imperial lines. In the Hapsburg territories, they tended to cast their lots with the westernizers—and did poorly. In the Balkans, however, they posed as parties of *gemeinschaft* and national values and, partly as a result, showed surprising electoral strength.

Finally, it is worth noting that contrary to the predictions of the national-historical school, the parties that emerged victorious in the spring elections were, virtually without exception, parties that did not exist prior to 1945.

4. Politics, on the contrary, "is a process in which the situation is the same as in bargaining—there is intergroup conflict of interest—but the arena of bargaining is *not* taken as fixed by participants." (March and Simon 1958, italics added.)

5. A similar problem characterizes attempts to treat Leninist polities as "state corporatist." Here, however, it appears that the term is somewhat a misnomer for the phenomena usually described. In the Western literature, state corporatism typically refers to the attempts of the government to colonize social groups via the creation or control of monopolistic mass organizations. In the Soviet case, it is usually used to describe the state's relationship with its own agencies (ministries, local governments, etc.) in which case the approach does not differ significantly from that of the bureaucratic politics school (Schmitter 1974; Bunce 1983; Ziegler 1986; Brown 1984).

6. This and the following paragraph were added to the text in July 1990.

7. I still stand by this evaluation in 1990. Certainly, the opening of archives (especially in the Soviet Union) will alter our knowledge of many facts (from Hungary extending sanctuary to individuals wanted as terrorists in the West to new estimates of the deaths associated with Soviet collectivization), but I'm not sure the uncovering of new information is going to alter our understanding of the system very much.

In this regard, there has been an unfortunate tendency to assume that "now that the Soviets are saying it," therefore "it" (usually some highly negative claim) must be true. Unfortunately, *who* says something has nothing to do with whether or not a proposition is empirically valid, particularly in a context in which who is saying what is as politically motivated as it was in the past. Hence, just as no one seriously believed the great accomplishments claimed for the Soviet system in the past, there seems to be little reason to assume a priori that nothing at all was accomplished in the past, regardless of what "the Soviets are saying" about themselves. As noted earlier, the fact that East Europeans and Soviets now routinely refer to state socialism as "totalitarian" tells us a great deal about the contemporary political scene, but it scarcely provides confirmation of the validity of this appellation.

8. Clearly, the next few paragraphs should be read in the past tense! I

realize that it is popular in 1990 to assume that the successful performance of the East German economy up to 1989 was a mirage created by statistical falsification, but it seems to me this is a serious distortion of what was actually the case. That the East German socialist economy collapsed upon amalgamation with the West German capitalist one is *not* evidence of bad performance prior to that amalgamation. On the contrary, it is simply evidence that confirms that economic activities that make sense to conduct under one set of economic arrangements and in one economic environment are no longer advantageous to conduct under a different set of economic arrangements and in a different economic environment. Such an outcome is hardly a surprise, nor is the discovery that East German industry, *designed* not to compete, couldn't compete.

Readers can get a sense of what is involved by imagining that the United States, with its existing industrial structure, natural and factor endowments, population, etc., were suddenly moved to another planet. That many of our most profitable industries and firms would go under in the face of a completely altered external environment they were never before exposed to would by no means imply that those activities were not perfectly rational and efficient when they were conducted within the American economy on planet Earth.

The question raised here that concerns East German economic performance is thus not answered by its (deliberately engineered) inability to compete with the West German economy on an open market. Rather, the question is how, as the most developed socialist economy, it managed to do as well as it did under economic arrangements that are generally though of as antithetical to the creation of a modern economy in any form. That this question is now one of purely historical interest does not make it invalid.

9. That we now obviously know the answer to this question does not invalidate the lines of inquiry raised below.

10. This remains my view in July 1990. The first chapter has been written—and then, only in parts of the (formerly) socialist world—but a good many more remain before "the end of history" is reached.

11. Extrapolating this discussion into the present, it would imply careful comparison of the various strategies for state divestment that have arisen both within Eastern Europe and the Soviet Union and between formerly socialist states and Latin America, Turkey, and Greece.

REFERENCES

Allison, Graham. 1971. *Essence of Decision: Explaining the Cuban Missile Crisis*. Boston: Little, Brown.

Arato, Andrew. 1981. "Civil Society against the State: Poland 1980–81." *Telos* 51:24–47.

Arendt, Hannah. 1951. *The Origins of Totalitarianism*. New York: Harcourt, Brace & World.

———. 1958. *The Human Condition*. Chicago: University of Chicago Press.

Aslund, Anders. 1985. *Private Enterprise in Eastern Europe*. London: Macmillan.

Bahro, Rudolf. 1977. *The Alternative in Eastern Europe*. London: NLB.

Bajt, Alexander. 1974. "Management in Yugoslavia." In *Comparative Economic Systems*, edited by M. Bornstein. 3rd ed. Homewood: Irwin.

Barghoorn, Frederick, and Thomas Remington. 1986. *Politics in the USSR*. 3rd ed. Boston: Little, Brown.

Barry, Donald. 1964. "The Specialist in Soviet Policy-Making: The Adoption of a Law." *Soviet Studies* 16:152–65.

Baylis, Thomas. 1974. *The Technical Intelligentsia and the East German Elite*. Berkeley: University of California Press.

Bentley, Arthur. 1908. *The Process of Government*. Chicago: University of Chicago Press.

Berliner, Joseph. 1957. *Factory and Manager in the USSR*. Cambridge: Harvard University Press.

———. 1976. *The Innovation Decision in Soviet Industry*. Cambridge: MIT Press.

Bornstein, Morris, ed. 1974. *Comparative Economic Systems: Models and Cases*. 3rd ed. Homewood, Ill.: Richard Irwin.

Bornstein, Morris, Zvi Gitelman, and William Zimmerman, eds. 1981. *East-West Relations and the Future of Eastern Europe*. London: Allen & Unwin.

Breslauer, George. 1978. "On the Adaptability of Soviet Welfare-State Authoritarianism." In *Soviet Society and the Communist Party*, edited by Karl Ryavec. Amherst: University of Massachusetts Press.

———. 1982. *Khrushchev and Brezhnev as Leaders: Building Authority in Soviet Politics*. London: Allen & Unwin.

Brown, A. H. 1974. *Soviet Politics and Political Science*. New York: St. Martin's Press.

———. 1984a. "Political Power and the Soviet State: Western and Soviet Approaches." In *The State in Socialist Society*, edited by Neil Harding. Albany: State University of New York Press.

Brown, A. H., ed. 1984b. *Political Culture and Communist Studies*. London: Macmillan.

Bunce, Valerie. 1983. "The Political Economy of the Brezhnev Era: The Rise and Fall of Corporatism." *British Journal of Political Science* 13:129–48.

Carter, April. 1982. *Democratic Reform in Yugoslavia: The Changing Role of the Party*. London: Frances Pinter.

Cliff, Tony. 1970. *Russia: A Marxist Analysis*. 3rd ed. London: International Socialism.

Cohen, Stephen. 1985. *Rethinking the Soviet Experience*. New York: Oxford.

Colton, Timothy. 1984. *The Dilemma of Reform in the Soviet Union*. New York: Council on Foreign Relations.

Comisso, Ellen. 1979. *Workers' Control under Plan and Market*. New Haven: Yale University Press.

————. 1986. "Introduction: State Structures, Political Process, and Collective Choice in CMEA States." *International Organization* 40:195–238.

Comisso, Ellen, and Laura Tyson, eds. 1986. *Power, Purpose and Collective Choice*. Ithaca: Cornell University Press.

Connor, Walter. 1975. "Generations and Politics in the USSR." *Problems of Communism* 24:20–31.

Conquest, Robert. 1982. *Power and Policy in the USSR: The Study of Soviet Dynastics*. London: Macmillan.

Dawisha, Karen. 1980. "The Limits of the Bureaucratic Politics Model: Observations on the Soviet Case." *Studies in Comparative Communism* 13: 300–27.

Denitch, Bogdan. 1976. *The Legimation of a Revolution*. New Haven: Yale University Press.

Djilas, Milovan. 1958. *The New Class*. New York: Praeger.

Eckstein, Alexander. 1977. *China's Economic Revolution*. New York: Cambridge University Press.

Eckstein, Alexander, ed. 1973. *Comparison of Economic Systems*. Berkeley: University of California Press.

Estrin, Saul. 1983. *Self-Management: Economic Theory and Yugoslav Practice*. Cambridge: Cambridge University Press.

Evangelista, Matthew. 1989. "Issue Area and Foreign Policy Revisited." *International Organization* 42:147–73.

Fischer-Galati, Stephen, ed. 1979. *The Communist Parties of Eastern Europe*. New York: Columbia University Press.

Friedgut, Theodore. 1979. *Political Participation in the USSR*. Princeton: Princeton University Press.

Friedrich, Carl, ed. 1954. *Totalitarianism*. Cambridge: Harvard University Press.

Friedrich, Carl, and Zbigniew Brzezinski. 1956. *Totalitarian Dictatorship and Autocracy*. Cambridge: Harvard University Press.

Gabor, Istvan. 1979. "The Second (Secondary) Economy." *Acta Oeconomica* 22:291–311.

Gerschenkron, Alexander. 1962. "Russia: Patterns and Problems of Economic Development, 1861–1958." In *Economic Backwardness in Historical Perspective*, edited by Alexander Gerschenkron. Cambridge: Belknap Press of Harvard University.

Giddens, Anthony. 1973. *The Class Structure of the Advanced Societies*. New York: Harper & Row.

Gomulka, Stanislaw. 1986. *Growth, Innovation and Reform in Eastern Europe*. Madison: University of Wisconsin Press.

Granick, David. 1975. *Enterprise Guidance in Eastern Europe*. Princeton: Princeton University Press.

Griffiths, Franklyn. 1971. "A Tendency Analysis of Soviet Policy-Making." In *Interest Groups in Soviet Politics*, H. Gordon Skilling and Franklyn Griffiths, eds. Princeton: Princeton University Press.

————. 1973. "A Tendency Analysis of Soviet Policy-Making." In *Interest Groups in Soviet Politics*, edited by H. G. Skilling and F. Griffiths. Princeton: Princeton University Press.

Griffiths, William. 1964. *The Sino-Soviet Rift*. Cambridge: MIT Press.

Gross, Jan. 1979. *Polish Society under German Occupation*. Princeton: Princeton University Press.

Hammer, Darrell. 1974. *USSR: The Politics of Oligarchy*. New York: Praeger.

Hankiss, Elemer. 1986. *The "Second Society": Is There a Second Social Paradigm Working in Contemporary Hungary?* Budapest: Institute of Sociology Research Reports.

————. 1989. "Demobilization, Self-Mobilization, and Quasi-Mobilization in Hungary, 1948–1989." *East European Politics and Society* 3:105–52.

Haraszti, Miklos. 1979. *Opposition = 0.1%; extraits du samizdat hongrois*. Paris: Editions du Seuil.

Hauslohner, Peter. 1981. "Prefects as Senators: Soviet Regional Politicians Look to Foreign Policy." *World Politics* 33:197–234.

————. 1987. "Gorbachev's Social Compact." *Soviet Economy* 2:54–79.

Havel, Vaclav. 1985. *The Power of the Powerless*. World Politics. New York: M. E. Sharpe.

Hewett, Edward. 1974. *Foreign Trade Prices in the Council for Mutual Economic Assistance*. Cambridge: Cambridge University Press.

————. 1988. *Reforming the Soviet Economy*. Washington: Brookings Institution.

Hodnett, Grey. 1974. "Technology and Social Change in Soviet Central Asia: The Politics of Cotton Growing." In Henry Morton and Rudolf Tokes, eds. *Soviet Politics and Society in the 1970s*. New York: Free Press, pp. 60–118.

Holmes, Leslie. 1986. *Politics in the Communist World*. Oxford: Clarendon.

Hough, Jerry. 1969. *The Soviet Prefects*. Cambridge: Harvard University Press.

————. 1972. "The Soviet System: Petrification or Pluralism?" *Problems of Communism* 21:23–30.

————. 1977. *The Soviet Union and Social Science Theory*. Cambridge: Harvard University Press.

Hough, Jerry, and Merle Fainsod. 1979. *How the Soviet Union Is Governed*. Cambridge: Harvard University Press.

Huntington, Samuel. 1968. *Political Order in Changing Societies*. New Haven: Yale University Press.

Ionescu, Ghita. 1965. *The Breakup of the Soviet Empire in Eastern Europe*. Baltimore: Penguin.

Janos, Andrew. 1970. "Group Politics in Communist Society: A Second Look at the Pluralist Model." In *Authoritarian Politics in Modern Society: The Dynamics of One-Party Systems*, edited by Samuel Huntington and Clement Moore. New York: Basic Books.

Johnson, Chalmers. 1962. *Peasant Nationalism and Communist Power*. Stanford: Stanford University Press.

Johnson, Chalmers, ed. 1970. *Change in Communist Systems*. Palo Alto: Stanford University Press.

Jowitt, Kenneth. 1971. *Revolutionary Breakthroughs and National Development*. Berkeley: University of California Press.

———. 1978. *The Leninist Response to National Dependency*. Berkeley: Institute of International Studies.

Judt, Tony. 1988. "The Dilemmas of Dissidence: The Politics of Opposition in East-Central Europe." *East European Politics and Societies* 2:185–241.

Kanet, Roger. 1978. "Political Groupings and Their Role in the Process of Change in Eastern Europe." In *Innovation in Communist Societies*, edited by Andrew Gyorgy and James Kuhlmann. Boulder: Westview.

Kaplan, Cynthia. 1987. *The Party and Agricultural Crisis Management in the USSR*. Ithaca: Cornell University Press.

Keane, John. 1987. *The Rediscovery of Civil Society*. London: Verso.

———. 1988. *Civil Society and the State: New European Perspectives*. London: Verso.

Kemeny, Istvan. 1982. "The Unregistered Economy in Hungary." *Soviet Studies* 34:349–66.

Kennan, George. 1961. *Russia and the West under Lenin and Stalin*. Boston: Little, Brown.

———. 1972. *Memoirs*. 2 vols. Boston: Little, Brown.

Kolakowski, Leszek. 1971. "Hope and Hopelessness." *Survey* 17.

Konrad, Gyorgy, and Ivan Szelenyi. 1979. *La marche au pouvoir des intellectuels*. Paris: Editions du Seuil.

Kornai, Janos. 1959. *Overcentralization in Economic Administration*. London: Blackwell.

———. 1981. *The Economics of Shortage*. Amsterdam: North Holland Publishing.

Laky, Terez. 1979. "Enterprises in Bargaining Position." *Acta Oeconomica* 22: 227–46.

———. 1980. "The Hidden Mechanisms of Recentralization in Hungary." *Acta Oeconomica* 24:95–109.

Lewin, Moshe. 1988. *The Gorbachev Phenomenon*. Berkeley: University of California Press.

Lewis, Paul. 1982. "Political Consequences of the Changes in Party-State Structures under Gierek." In *Policy and Politics in Contemporary Poland*, edited by Jean Woodall. London: Pinter.

————. 1989. *Political Authority and Party Secretaries in Poland, 1975–1986*. New York: Cambridge University Press.

Lieberthal, Kenneth, and Michael Oksenberg. 1988. *Policy-Making in China*. Princeton: Princeton University Press.

Linden, Carl. 1966. *Krushchev and the Soviet Leadership, 1957–1964*. Baltimore: Johns Hopkins Press.

Lowenthal, Richard. 1970. "Development v. Utopia in Communist Policy." In *Change in Communist Systems*, edited by Chalmers Johnson. Palo Alto: Stanford University Press.

March, James, and Herbert Simon. 1958. *Organizations*. New York: Wiley & Sons.

Matthews, Mervyn. 1986. *Poverty in the Soviet Union: The Life-Styles of the Underprivileged in Recent Years*. Cambridge: Cambridge University Press.

Meyer, Alfred. 1965. *The Soviet Political System: An Interpretation*. New York: Random House.

Michnik, Adam. 1986. *Letters from Prison and Other Essays*. Berkeley: University of California Press.

Milenkovitch, Deborah. 1971. *Plan and Market in Yugoslav Economic Thought*. New Haven: Yale University Press.

Millar, James, ed. 1987. *Politics, Work and Daily Life in the USSR: A Survey of Former Soviet Citizens*. New York: Cambridge University Press.

Mills, Richard. 1970. "The Formation of the Virgin Lands Policy." *Slavic Review* 29:58–69.

Moe, Terry. 1984. "The New Economics of Organization." *American Journal of Political Science* 28:739–77.

Nelson, Michael. 1988. "Evaluating the Presidency." In *The Presidency and the Political System*, edited by Michael Nelson. 2nd ed. Washington: CQ Press.

Neuberger, Egon, and William Duffy. 1976. *Comparative Economic Systems*. Boston: Allyn & Bacon.

Nove, Alec. 1975. "Is There a Ruling Class in the USSR?" *Soviet Studies* 27: 615–35.

————. 1980. *The Soviet Economic System*. 2nd ed. London: Allen & Unwin.

————. 1982. *An Economic History of the USSR*. Rev. ed. New York: Penguin.

O'Donnell, Guillermo. 1979. *Modernization and Bureaucratic-Authoritarianism*. Berkeley: Institute of International Studies.

O'Donnell, Guillermo, and Phillippe Schmitter. 1986. *Transitions from Authoritarian Rule: Tentative Conclusions about Uncertain Democracies*. Baltimore: Johns Hopkins University Press.

Olsen, Mancur. 1969. *The Logic of Collective Action*. New York: Schocken.

Ost, David. 1989. "Toward a Corporatist Solution in Eastern Europe: The Case of Poland." *East European Politics and Society* 3:152–74.

Perkins, Dwight. 1973. "Plans and Their Implementation in the People's Republic of China." *American Economic Review* 63:224–31.

Pipes, Richard. 1967. "Communism and Russian History." In *Soviet and Chinese Communism: Similarities and Differences*, edited by Donald Treadgold. Seattle: University of Washington Press.

Ploss, Sidney. 1965. *Conflict and Decision-Making in Soviet Russia: A Case Study of Agricultural Policy, 1953–1963*. Princeton: Princeton University Press.

Portes, Richard. 1968. "Hungary: Economic Performance, Policy and Prospects." In *Eastern Europe: Problems and Prospects*, by U.S. Congress, Joint Economic Committee. Washington: U.S. Government Printing Office.

———. 1976. "Inflation under Central Planning." In *The Political Economy of Inflation*, edited by Fred Hirsch and John Goldthorpe. Cambridge: Harvard University Press.

Pravda, Alex. 1981. "East-Western Interdependence and the Social Compact in Eastern Europe." In *East-West Relations and the Future of Eastern Europe*, edited by M. Bornstein, Z. Gitelman and W. Zimmerman. London: Allen & Unwin.

———. 1982. "Is There a Soviet Working Class?" *Problems of Communism* 31: 1–21.

Pryor, Frederick. 1985a. "Growth and Fluctuations of Production in OECD and East European Countries." *World Politics* 37:204–37.

———. 1985b. *A Guidebook to the Comparative Study of Economic Systems*. Englewood Cliffs: Prentice-Hall.

Rakitsky, Boris. 1988. "Market Laws and Specifics in a Distorted Socialist Environment." Paper presented at a conference on Plan and/or Market? December 16–18, Vienna, Austria.

Rawin, S. J. 1970. "Social Values and the Managerial Structure: The Case of Yugoslavia and Poland." *Journal of Comparative Administration* 2:135–49.

Rawls, John. 1971. *A Theory of Justice*. Cambridge: Harvard University Press.

Reiss, Hans, ed. 1970. *Kant's Political Writings*. Cambridge: Cambridge University Press.

Rigby, T. H. 1976. "Politics in the Mono-Organizational Society." In *Authoritarian Politics in Communist Europe*, edited by Andrew Janos. Berkeley: Institute of International Studies.

Riker, William. 1982. "The Two-Party System and Duverger's Law: An Essay on the History of Political Science." *American Political Science Review* 76: 753–67.

Roeder, Philip. 1984. "Soviet Policies and Kremlin Politics." *International Studies Quarterly* 28:171–93.

———. 1988. *Soviet Political Dynamics*. New York: Harper & Row.

Sacks, Steven. 1983. *Self-Management and Efficiency: Large Corporations in Yugoslavia*. London: Allen & Unwin.

Schapiro, Leonard. 1970. *The Communist Party of the Soviet Union*. 2nd ed. London: Blackwell.

Schmitter, Philippe. 1974. "Still the Century of Corporatism?" In *The New*

Corporatism, edited by Frederick Pike and Thomas Stritch. Notre Dame: University of Notre Dame Press.

Schurmann, Franz. 1968. *Ideology and Organization in Communist China*. Berkeley: University of California Press.

Schwartz, Joel, and William Keech. 1968. "Group Influence and the Policy Process in the Soviet Union." *American Political Science Review* 62:840–51.

Shipler, David K. 1983. *Russia: Broken Idols, Solemn Dreams*. New York: NY Times Books.

Shirk, Susan. 1988. "The Chinese Political System and the Political Strategy of Economic Reform." Paper presented at a conference on the Structure of Authority and Bureaucratic Behavior in China, Tucson, Arizona.

Simons, M., and S. White, eds. 1984. *The Party Statutes of the Communist World*. The Hague: Martinus Njihoff.

Sirc, Ljubo. 1979. *The Yugoslav Economy under Self-Management*. London: Macmillan.

Skilling, H. Gordon. 1966. "Interest Groups and Communist Politics." *World Politics* 18:435–61.

Skilling, H. Gordon, and Franklyn Griffiths, eds. 1971. *Interest Groups in Soviet Politics*. Princeton: Princeton University Press.

Staniszkis, Jadwiga. 1982. "Martial Law in Poland." *Telos* 16:85–96.

————. 1984. *Poland's Self-Limiting Revolution*. Princeton: Princeton University Press.

Stark, David. 1986. "Rethinking Internal Labor Markets—New Insights from a Comparative Perspective." *American Sociological Review* 51:492–504.

Svejnar, Jan, and Janez Prasnikar. 1987. "Economic Behavior of Yugoslav Enterprises." *Advances in the Economic Analysis of Participatory and Labor-Managed Firms* 3:3–45.

Szelenyi, Ivan. 1988. *Socialist Entrepreneurs: Embourgeoisement in Rural Hungary*. Madison: University of Wisconsin Press.

Triska, Jan. 1977. "Citizen Participation in Community Decisions in Yugoslavia, Romania, Hungary and Poland." In *Political Development in Eastern Europe*, edited by Jan Triska and Paul Cocks. New York: Praeger.

Triska, Jan, and Charles Gati, eds. 1981. *Blue Collar Workers in Eastern Europe*. London: Allen & Unwin.

Truman, David. 1951. *The Governmental Process: Political Interests and Public Opinion*. New York: Alfred Knopf, Inc.

Tucker, Robert. 1987. *Political Culture and Leadership in Soviet Russia*. New York: Norton.

Tyson, Laura. 1980. *The Yugoslav Economy and Its Performance in the 1970s*. Berkeley: Institute of International Studies.

Ulam, Adam. 1952. *Titoism and the Cominform*. Cambridge: Harvard University Press.

Walder, Andrew. 1987. *Communist Neo-Traditionalism*. Berkeley: University of California Press.

Walt, Stephen. 1987. *The Origins of Alliances*. Ithaca: Cornell University Press.

Waltz, Kenneth. 1979. *Theory of International Politics*. Reading, Mass.: Addison-Wesley.

White, Stephen, John Gardner, and George Schopflin. 1982. *Communist Political Systems*. New York: St. Martin's Press.

Wiles, Peter. 1962. *The Political Economy of Communism*. London: Blackwell.

Wittfogel, Karl. 1957. *Oriental Despotism: A Comparative Study of Total Power*. New York: Vintage.

Wolfe, Bertram. 1961. *Communist Totalitarianism*. Boston: Beacon Press.

Woodall, Jean. 1982. *The Socialist Corporation and Technocratic Power*. Cambridge: Cambridge University Press.

Yergin, Daniel. 1977. *Shattered Peace*. Boston: Houghton Mifflin.

Zaslavsky, Victor. 1982. *The Neo-Stalinist State*. Armonk, N.Y.: M. E. Sharpe.

Zaslavsky, Victor, and Robert Brym. "The Functions of Elections in the USSR." *Soviet Studies* 30:362–71.

Ziegler, Charles. 1986. "Issue Creation and Interest Groups in Soviet Environmental Policy." *Comparative Politics* 21:171–92.

Zimmerman, William. 1972. "Hierarchical Regional Systems and the Politics of System Boundaries." *International Organization* 26:18–36.

Zukin, Sharon. 1975. *Beyond Marx and Tito*. London: Cambridge University Press.

4

Foreign Policy Analysis: Renaissance, Routine, or Rubbish?

Deborah J. Gerner

Imagine a room filled with the individuals from the top twenty North American political science departments who are responsible for graduate and undergraduate education in foreign policy, along with individuals whose self-definition of their research is in the foreign policy field. Now, imagine that the task facing these men and women is to develop a joint statement on what this field of inquiry involves: the central questions, the methodology, the most useful theories. What would be the result? Would there be a consensus?

We can only speculate on whether our group of political scientists would conduct their discussion in a detached and "scholarly" fashion or get into a heated fighting match. But if the range of books and articles published under the rubric of "foreign policy analysis" is any indication, the answer to the second question—is there any consensus?—is a resounding NO: no consensus on the central questions, no consensus on the methodology, no consensus on the most valuable theories. And the problem of finding consensus would only be confounded if members of the foreign policy-making community were included, or if schol-

This chapter has benefited from the insights and advice of Ronald Francisco, Frank Hoole, Valerie Hudson, Bruce Moon, Neil Richardson, Philip Schrodt, and Harvey Starr; as well as from the stimulating discussion that followed its presentation at the Midwest Political Science Association annual meeting in April 1989. Of course, none of the above are responsible for any errors of fact or interpretation that may remain despite their assistance.

123

ars from outside the United States and Canada were also invited to
participate. Thus, it is not surprising that a survey of the foreign policy
literature written some years ago by Bernard C. Cohen and Scott A.
Harris begins: "There is a certain discomfort in writing about foreign
policy, for no two people seem to define it in the same way, disagreements in approach often seem to be deep-seated, and we do not yet
know enough about it to be able to say with confidence whether and
how it may be differentiated from all other areas of public policy"
(1975, 381).

A quick review of recent journals and publishers' catalogues reveals
the range of material being published under the label foreign policy.
Some of the work is descriptive or narrative—current events–style foreign policy analysis of the type found in *Foreign Policy* (published by the
Carnegie Endowment for International Peace) and *Foreign Affairs*
(published by the Council on Foreign Relations)—with few footnotes
or other citations, frequently written by present or former U.S. policymakers. Well represented by books and in the area studies journals, but
relatively uncommon in the mainstream political science journals, are
works about the foreign policy of a single state or small group of states,
either from an idiographic perspective or as a case study in a nomothetic
framework that does not necessarily follow the relatively tight structure
of the quantitative, deductive school (e.g., Beres 1986; Biddle and Stephens 1989; Blachman and Sharpe 1986; Gerner 1990; K. Holsti 1986;
Jentleson 1987; Ng-Quinn 1983; Rubenberg 1986 and 1988; Shinobu
1987; and Spiegel 1987). This type of research is frequently dismissed
by behavioralists as nonrigorous and unscientific, though it is often
thoughtful and carefully documented and is viewed enthusiastically by
area-studies scholars who appreciate the attention to detail, the recognition of multiple sources of foreign policy, and the comprehensiveness.
In addition, there are the statistical studies and modeling exercises of
the comparative foreign policy approach, traditionally represented by
James Rosenau and Charles and Margaret Hermann but also including
a group of younger scholars with various types of training. This work is
scattered throughout the mainstream behavioralist journals (e.g. Hagan
1986; Lamborn 1985; Moon 1985) and an occasional book is published by scholars working in this framework (e.g. Hagan 1990).
Finally, there are issue-specific articles such as a cluster of articles focusing on U.S. foreign policy, human rights, and state terrorism (e.g.
Carleton and Stohl 1987; Cingranelli and Pasquarello 1985; Gerner
1988; McCormick and Mitchell 1988), as well as articles examining a
particular type of potential influence on foreign policy such as the belief
systems of U.S. elites and the public (Ferguson 1986; Holsti and Rosenau 1986a, 1986b; Hurwitz and Peffley 1987; Kegley 1986; Wittkopf
1986).

What accounts for the eclecticism of the field and the lack of consensus? It is always simpler to look back and criticize the unsuccessful paths than to be able to identify those mistakes ahead of time; far easier to identify what has not advanced our understanding of political phenomena than to develop a new approach that will be more successful. In this chapter, I will discuss several factors that may have contributed to the current intellectual dispersion in the foreign policy literature, review some of the significant classical and behavioralist research of the past thirty years to provide anchor points, and suggest several avenues of research that have the potential either to link divergent approaches or to provide insights that may move the field in productive, new directions. But I do this with an awareness that such prescriptions are a bit like being a Monday morning quarterback: it always looks easier from the comfort of an easy chair than it is in practice.

HISTORICAL DEVELOPMENT

Definition of the Field

Although no subfield in political science is completely self-contained, foreign policy analysis is somewhat unusual in that it deals with both the domestic and the international political arenas, jumping from individual to state to systemic levels of analysis, and attempts to integrate all of these aspects into a coherent whole. James N. Rosenau has called foreign policy a "bridging discipline," one with "limitless boundaries" that must somehow deal with "the continuing erosion of the distinction between domestic and foreign issues, between the sociopolitical and economic processes that unfold at home and those that transpire abroad" (1987, 1, 3). The central focus of foreign policy is on the intentions, statements, and actions of an actor—generally a state—that are directed toward the external world and the responses to these intentions, statements, and actions, but unpacking what this focus actually means is a complex task. Foreign policy can be *descriptive*, attempting to establish the actual facts regarding foreign policy decisions made, policies declared publicly by actors, and the relationships among state and non-state international actors. Alternatively, foreign policy *analysis* can attempt to answer the question: Why do states take the actions they do? Such research may focus on the *inputs* that affect the foreign policy process: external, societal, governmental, role and individual factors; or it can examine the *process* by which foreign policy is formulated through theories of decision-making. Finally, foreign policy *evaluation* considers the consequences of foreign policy actions. There is also a wide literature on what might be called "responses to foreign policy"—how people feel about and react to various foreign policy choices. This issue is best left for the general field of public opinion; however, when the issue is phrased in terms of public opinion as a determinant for foreign policy, it comes back under the foreign policy rubric.

The distinction between foreign policy and international relations is not always obvious. For many, there is no clear separation: "Foreign policy is the stuff of international relations," comments one popular textbook (Russett and Starr 1989, 186). Certainly the overlap between the two areas is great. Both are concerned with understanding the actions of nation-states and other players in the international area; both examine issues of conflict and cooperation, military interactions, and economic relations. For purposes of limiting the scope of this chapter, however, boundary lines do need to be drawn. Thus, "international relations" here refers to research that focuses on the total global system as its level of analysis. As J. David Singer explains:

> [This] is the most comprehensive of the levels available, encompassing the totality of interactions which take place within the system and its environment. By focusing on the system, we are enabled to study the patterns of interaction which the system reveals, and to generalize about such phenomena as the creation and dissolution of coalitions, the frequency and duration of specific power configurations, modifications in its stability, its responsiveness to changes in formal political institutions, and the norms and folklore which it manifests as a societal system. (1969b, 22)

"Foreign policy," in contrast, devotes its attention to the nation-state or other international actor as the unit of analysis. There is a greater degree of differentiation among the actors studied than in international relations, and "the entire question of goals, motivations and purposes in national policy" (Singer 1969b, 25) is raised in a way not possible at the systemic level of analysis. Both approaches have the potential to illuminate aspects of the international system: though the systemic-level international relations "produces a more comprehensive and total picture" of the system, foreign policy analysis, with its "atomized and less coherent image produced by the lower level of analysis," is able to provide "richer detail, greater depth, and more intensive portrayal," particularly of the processes that lead to particular decisions being made by international actors (Singer 1969b, 28).

The Pre–World War II Period

The analysis of foreign policy of one sort or another has been occurring since Thucydides set down on paper his monumental history of the Peloponnesian War with its famous debate between the Melians and the *pre World War II Period*

Athenians. As an explicit field of intellectual inquiry, however, its roots are more recent, with the majority of its development coming in the twentieth century (Farr 1988). Prior to this time, neither foreign policy nor international relations constituted a distinct field. Diplomatic history probably came the closest to what we now label as "foreign policy," and much of what we call international relations came under the rubric of international law, institutional analyses, or history.

Within the newly evolving field of political science, the historical-comparative (or historical-legal) method was predominant in the United States, just as it was in Europe. For the study of foreign policy, this essentially meant the study of the international actions of individual state leaders—frequently monarchs—who were believed to have few constraints on their actions other than those imposed by the external situation. Scholars tended not to "look inside" the state—the leaders and the state were for all practical purposes treated as one and the same. Public opinion, interest groups, and domestic economic variables were not considered major factors in the decision calculus of a leader, nor were there large foreign policy bureaucracies to pressure the leader in conflicting directions or to take over significant parts of the foreign policy process. The most significant levels of analysis were the individual and the international system, and the study of foreign policy was in some sense the intersection of these two dimensions: a description of how individuals acted on behalf of states, given the external environment. Realist theory dominated writings of the time, combined with a healthy dose of historical biography of political leaders.

The interwar years were characterized by the increased importance of international relations and foreign policy, which resulted from the desire to understand both the factors that had led to the Great War and the massive changes that were occurring in the 1920s and 1930s in the international environment. Dwight Waldo comments on this period:

> Immediately, the importance of international relations and law was of course underscored. The newly established democratic states provided fresh foreign-comparative materials, however superficial the treatment thereof. The establishment of the League of Nations and its collapse; the creation and endurance of the U.S.S.R.; the rise of Fascism-Nazism; the ominous threats of a new world conflagration—all the important political events flowing from World War I inevitably were reflected in political science to some degree. (1975, 44)

This same impetus to make sense of the world led in the United States to the creation of the journal *Foreign Affairs* by the Council of Foreign Relations in 1922. The Editorial Statement in the first volume of that journal foretold the interdisciplinary direction that the field of foreign policy was to take in the post–World War II era, as well as the continuing tendency of foreign affairs research in the U.S. to focus on current, topical material from a North American perspective:

> We believe there is a place as yet unfilled for a review whose dominant purpose is to promote the discussion of current questions of international interest and to serve as the natural medium for the expression of the best thought, not only of this country, but of Europe when it wishes to address itself on these topics to the American public. . . . The articles in *Foreign Affairs* will deal with questions of international interest today. They will cover a broad range of subjects, not only political but historical and economic. . . . There will be numerous foreign contributors, but the fact that the interest and profit of the American reader are a first consideration will not be forgotten.

What this increased interest reflects is a partial opening up of the discussion regarding alternative foreign policy choices, as well as an expansion of the set of elites who have the ability to affect the final decisions. To be sure, there is not a complete democratization of foreign policy—policy-making is still primarily an activity for a relatively small group of people. But it does signal a recognition that international affairs are no longer strictly the providence of a government's foreign policy elite. This idea, a development of domestic changes within the United States as well as of the increased global role for that country, had the potential to transform the creation of foreign policy. Whether it has actually done so remains a topic of great debate.

Although much of the work done in foreign policy and international relations during the interwar period was, in Waldo's words, "descriptive, hortatory, or legalistic," there was a gradual movement in some quarters toward greater methodological sophistication and a tendency toward being more scientific, setting the stage for the behavioralist-traditionalist battles of the 1950s and 1960s. As the situation on the Continent grew increasingly grim, numerous European scholars migrated to the United States, bringing with them new and often broader perspectives about international relations and foreign policy.

Classical Foreign Policy and Scientific International Relations

The changes in the international system following World War II were mirrored by rapid expansion and change in the fields of foreign policy and international relations.

> [N]ew interests, specializations, and activities emerged [in foreign policy and international relations]; and important interrelations with other disciplines, both in the other social sciences and beyond, were established. Somewhat as public administration had done in the post–World War II period, international relations tended to become a substantial,

varied "world" in itself, with very important relations outside political science and some impulses toward autonomy. (Waldo 1975, 69)

The academic community in the United States was dominant in this process, as it was in the development of the entire field of political science in the postwar period, leading to a "distinctively American stamp [being] placed on the international relations field" (Keohane 1983, 533; see also Hoffman 1977 and Lyons 1982). Thus, to understand the evolution of the field, it is necessary to consider what was occurring in the United States.

To begin with, the global context of international actions had been transformed in the first four decades of the twentieth century. The number of independent actors with which a state's foreign policy had to deal increased massively, as African, Asian, and Middle Eastern countries gained political independence from colonial rule. At the same time, increased international communications and the greater ease of foreign travel brought the world geographically closer together than it had been in the past. The existence of nuclear weapons and the dominant status of the United States during the immediate postwar period were also new. Not only was the United States the major global military power; it was also the preeminent political and economic actor in the capitalist world. In light of these new realities, researchers in the fields of international relations and foreign policy needed to revise a number of assumptions about how the world worked.

The domestic environment of U.S. foreign policy-making was also undergoing alteration. One significant change was the massive expansion of the U.S. foreign policy bureaucracy. James A. Nathan and James K. Oliver (1987, chap. 2) describe the creation in the 1940s and 1950s of a new and powerful foreign policy establishment: there were an expanded Department of State, with the associated Agency for International Development, United States Information Agency, and Arms Control and Disarmament Agency; the International Security Agency and the National Security Agency as part of the newly established Department of Defense; the Central Intelligence Agency; the National Security Council and the position of National Security Advisor. (See also Barnet 1972, especially Part I.) Each of these organizations had an agenda and a mandate that overlapped the responsibilities of other organizations; each saw itself playing an essential role in the formation and implementation of U.S. foreign policy around the world. Bargaining, negotiating, and infighting—both within bureaucratic units and among these agencies and the leaders who spoke on their behalf—became increasingly important factors in understanding the eventual outcome of the foreign policy process. In addition, during these years there was a growth in the number and significance of domestic interest groups, a continuation and logical outgrowth of the process represented by the creation of *Foreign Affairs* nearly three decades earlier. Because of the position the U.S. academic community held in the world, these changes affected the research being conducted outside the United States as well.

In this atmosphere, it is not surprising that a number of scholars began to move away from reliance on the existing grand theories that assumed a unitary state pursuing a clearly specified and agreed-upon national interest, and turned their attention instead to the *process* of foreign policy decision-making. Frameworks were created that specified the factors that could affect this process, efforts were made to clarify the importance of cognition and perception for individual decision-makers, interest group influence was studied, and bureaucracies were examined to better understand how they functioned and the impact their function had on eventual decisions.

At the same time, the behavioralist revolution affecting the whole of political science began to make its mark in international relations and foreign policy. Davis B. Bobrow discusses the creation of this "New IR" and suggests there were "three sets of factors [that] shaped changes in international relations analysis: intellectual objections to what was being done [philosophy of science issues], concern with current international problems [the transformed world discussed above], and opportunities created by new technology [e.g., computers] and research funds" (1972, 6). As a result, the fields of international relations and foreign policy, which had been intertwined, began to pull apart. International relations—or at least a significant subgroup of researchers represented after 1959 by the International Studies Association—became more scientific, with a goal of increasing knowledge through statistical tests and rational and dynamic modeling. Foreign policy theorists, however, were slower to adopt the behavioralist approach, and instead tended to continue in the classical tradition described by Hedley Bull:

> The [classical] approach to theorizing [is one] that derives from philosophy, history, and law, and that is characterized above all by explicit reliance upon the exercise of judgment and by the assumptions that if we confine ourselves to strict standards of verification and proof there is very little of significance that can be said about international relations, that general propositions about this subject must therefore derive from a scientifically imperfect process of perception or intuition, and that these general propositions cannot be accorded anything more than the tentative and inconclusive status appropriate to their doubtful origin. (1966, 361)

There were exceptions, of course, such as the behaviorialist comparative foreign policy group, but in general international relations scholars and foreign policy researchers increasingly found they had little to say to each other.

This separation occurred for a number of reasons. Most fundamentally, early behavioralist studies frequently defined the scientific study of international phenomena in a relatively narrow fashion: the statistical manipulation of quantitative data, often removed from their historical context, to test established theories deductively. This approach was completely at odds with how most scholars interested in foreign policy conducted their research. For example, many of the quantitative data available to researchers in the 1960s (e.g., on internal attributes of nation-states) did not correspond to what were believed to be the most important factors for understanding foreign policy. In particular, the move to quantification and the continuing emphasis on systemic and state-level variables under the assumption of the state as a unitary actor occurred at the same time that there was a growing recognition by many foreign policy scholars that the state was not in fact monolithic and that the decision-making *process* was the key area on which to focus. The behavioralists were testing theoretical propositions that foreign policy analysts thought no longer described contemporary behavior. Furthermore, early statistical techniques had difficulties dealing with the multifaceted explanations that were the basis of detailed, high-quality foreign policy studies. Thus, these explanations could not easily be put to a statistical test, even had the inclination to do so been present. Finally, the deductive method of research demanded by some early behavioralists was counter to the predominantly inductive approach used in much of foreign policy research.

The foreign policy analysts' emphasis on historical factors also put them at odds with some early behavioralists who were attempting to transcend such contextual details in their search for general patterns. Richard Ned Lebow explains the problem he faced in graduate school when he tried to combine interests in political science and history:

> What bothered me the most about the various [behavioralist] models was the assumption that a political system could be analyzed without taking into account the particular historical and cultural experiences which had shaped its society. . . . [On the other hand,] my view of history was different [from members of the history department]. I wanted to study the past to learn about the present, to use history as a laboratory in which to develop and test concepts about political behavior. I was less interested in what was unique about Bismarckian Germany than what it had in common with other societies and states. This was heresy. (1981, ix)

Although Lebow casts his comments in terms of the tension between political science and history, they equally reflect the split between behavioralist international relations and the classical foreign policy approach.

In retrospect, one wonders if this split could have been avoided. Certainly, the restrictive interpretation of "scientific" research was unnecessary, a point made repeatedly by some behavioralists in their dialogue with classically trained and inclined colleagues. (I immediately think of Singer's "The Incompleat Theorist" [1969a], written in response to Bull's 1966 article quoted above.) Empirical research can be either quantitative or qualitative so long as it is explicit and systematic. Certainly there are comparative methodologies appropriate for foreign policy research which do not involve either modeling or the statistical manipulation of numerical data. Furthermore, while scientific research requires logical analysis, there is no intrinsic requirement that this be deductive reasoning. In fact, inductive reasoning based on direct observation or experimentation is an essential step in developing theories which subsequent deductive research tests.

> The most important use of [direct political] observation . . . is *to provide detailed descriptions of a particular social phenomenon* and to use these descriptions to develop theories and formulate hypotheses which can then be tested with other methods. In this sense, direct observation relies primarily upon an inductive strategy of research; that is, one reasons from particular cases (the ones observed) to more general conclusions. (Manheim and Rich 1986, 165)

Thus, it is possible to imagine a scientific-style research orientation that would have been more compatible with the previous practices of foreign policy scholars than the approach actually adopted by the behavioralists.

It would be inaccurate, however, to imply that the only issues separating the classical foreign policy scholars from the behavioralist international relations researchers were those that pertained to interpretations of what it meant to be "scientific." There were other points of divergence as well, less easily attributable to lack of flexibility in epistemology and methodology on the part of the proponents of behavioralism. One such difference was that the early behavioralists placed a heavy emphasis on the acquisition of pure knowledge, uncontaminated by concerns of policy implications, whereas many foreign policy scholars emphasized policy relevance. The postbehavioralist willingness to incorporate policy-relevant issues into the research agenda made this issue less divisive, but by that point the split between the classical foreign policy analysts and the scientific international relations scholars was well established. Despite the findings of J. Martin Rochester and Michael Segalla (1978, 435), who conclude that "contrary to much conventional wisdom, the foreign policy establishment supports a substantial amount of research that is basic . . . , global in scope . . . , international in disciplinary orientation . . . , and temporally open-ended," there was a general belief among foreign policy analysts that studies which were applied, regional, and problem-specific would be of greater value to practitioners. (Whiting 1972 is representative of this perspective; see also Andriole's 1979 response to Rochester and Segalla.)

Complicating the situation is that behavioralist approaches to foreign policy have not caught on with the media and the general public in the way that, for example, studies of electoral behavior have. During the U.S. election season, it is common to see political scientists on television discussing broad topics such as general theories of voting behavior or the role of interest groups. But when a foreign policy analyst is put on television, it is virtually always to discuss a specific political situation in a particular part of the world. What the analyst brings is knowledge of the unique political, economic, historical, and cultural heritage of the country or region of interest. That is her calling card, not the ability to discuss the attributes common to all revolutions or patterns of hostile verbal gestures between two international actors. In this context, it is understandable that foreign policy scholars interested in being policy-relevant resist the idea of generalizable knowledge—it does not appear particularly useful.

Finally, there were—and remain today—many scholars who reject the notion that nomothetic approaches to understanding foreign policy are necessarily superior to, and of greater value than, idiographic approaches. What is wrong, they assert, with attempting to fully understand a particular case for its own sake, because it is of intrinsic interest or because this understanding will result in better policies in the future? Is there not a danger that in the rush to formulate universal laws and test general hypotheses, the unique and distinct will be lost? The tacit assumption underlying this concern

> has been that policies and processes were *sui generis*—that there were no common denominators or classes that could subsume such oranges and apples as the Quai d'Orsay and the British Foreign Office, or United States policy toward Israel and French policy toward Germany [to say nothing of Bolivia's relations with Nigeria or Laos]. (Cohen and Harris 1975, 384)

Not surprisingly, finding the appropriate level at which meaningful comparisons can occur has been one of the major challenges for foreign policy scholars.

Thus, for all these reasons, classical approaches to foreign policy and scientific international relations began to evolve in quite different directions. It is important to keep in mind, however, that the establishment of foreign policy as a separate field was in some senses an incidental outcome of broader epistemological and methodological concerns, rather than of an explicit belief that the intellectual issues addressed by foreign policy analysts were sufficiently different from those examined by international relations scholars to justify an autonomous field. Furthermore, there have always been efforts to bridge the two fields, most notably by those scholars committed to both the substantive issues of foreign policy research and the methodology of scientific international relations.

CLASSICAL AND BEHAVIORAL RESEARCH

Over the past three decades, research in foreign policy and foreign policy decision-making has developed along a series of parallel tracks. These have included variations on rational actor approaches; collective action and bureaucratic analyses; examination of interest groups and public opinion as influences on decision-making; studies of cognition, perception and personality; and decision-making under conditions of crisis. This section will describe examples of each of these approaches.

Frameworks and Classification Schemes

Initial efforts to make foreign policy research more empirical were expressed in the form of typologies and frameworks of foreign policy decision-making: essentially laundry lists of the potentially relevant factors that need to be considered in order to understand the foreign policy process. Underlying such efforts was the growing recognition that the traditional *realpolitik* analysis of foreign policy, with its assumption of a unitary state actor and its focus on national interest, power, and fully rational and efficient decision-making, was inadequate to explain foreign policy decisions. There was also an awareness that if studies of foreign policy were to examine what was occurring within the state structure, they would need to incorporate the insights of the other social sciences—in particular economics, psychology, and sociology.

One of the first attempts to incorporate systematically these ideas is a 1954 monograph by Richard C. Snyder, H. W. Bruck, and Burton Sapin. Drawing on insights from psychology and sociology, Snyder, Bruck, and Sapin propose an action-reaction-interaction approach to foreign policy in which state action is defined as "the action taken by those acting in the name of the state," that is, the decision-makers. This represents a clear departure from the idea of the state as a monolithic actor pursuing its unified "national interests." For Snyder et al. "the key to the explanation of why the state behaves the way it does lies in the way its decision-makers as actors define their situation" (65). That "definition of situation" results from the relationships and interactions of the members of the decision-making unit, existing in a particular international and domestic environment, as well as from each individual's attributes, values, and perceptions. Although decision-maker rationality is not assumed by Snyder, Bruck, and Sapin, there is an *expectation* that their actions are in some sense purposeful. This general framework is applied by Richard C. Snyder and Glenn D. Paige (1958) and by Paige (1968) to the U.S. decision to intervene in Korea. Paige's book includes a meticulous and lengthy chronology similar to that expected in an historical text; his analysis, which is stronger on the sociological variables than on the cognitive and psychological factors, is almost entirely reserved for the end of the volume. At that point, Paige presents a series of propositions and hypothesis and concludes that U.S. policy toward Korea can be understood as either a single, unified decision or a sequence of choices or decisions.

In retrospect, it is easy to criticize the work of Snyder, Bruck, and Sapin for its complexity and its lack of specification as to how the variables are related to one another and are ranked in importance (e.g. Rosenau 1976). At the time, however, the framework was a significant step for behavioralist foreign policy because of its explicit definitions, its indications of underlying assumptions, its effort to untangle the meaning of the actions or decisions of a "state," and its interest in creating a structure within which the foreign policy of any country—not just the United States—can be analyzed.

A second and highly influential attempt to develop a general explanation of foreign policy was James Rosenau's "pre-theory" article, which resulted in the emergence of a distinct, self-conscious group of scholars working under the banner of "comparative foreign policy." In this piece, Rosenau argues that

> foreign policy analysis lacks comprehensive systems of testable generalizations that treat societies as actors subject to stimuli which produce external responses. Stated more succinctly, foreign policy analysis is devoid of general theory. . . . The field has an abundance of frameworks and approaches which cut across societies and conceptualize the ends, means, capabilities, or sources of foreign policy, but no schemes which link up these components of external behavior in causal sequences. No framework has energized inquiry in foreign policy as Rostow's [1960] theory of the stages of economic growth did in the economic development field, as Festinger's [1957] theory of cognitive dissonance did in social psychology, or as Almond's functional model did in comparative politics [Almond and Coleman 1960]. (Rosenau 1966, 32)

Rosenau moves several steps beyond Snyder, Bruck, and Sapin by calling for the generation of testable "if-then" propositions, grouping the multitude of potentially relevant sources of foreign policy decisions into five categories, and proposing ways to rank the importance of these clusters of variables depending on the specific issue and attributes of the state (e.g. size, political accountability, level of development). The five source clusters developed—idiosyncratic (later individual), role, governmental, societal, and systemic variables—serve as the basis for numerous articles, foreign policy textbooks, and collections of readings (e.g. Kegley and Wittkopf 1983) during the decades that followed publication of the original article. Still, Rosenau's "pre-theory" is just that, as Rosenau (1984) is quick to acknowledge: a preliminary approach—a typology—for organizing research on foreign policy, rather than a fully specified model. As such, there is a certain ambiguity in some of the concepts used. For example, the dependent variable—foreign policy behavior—is never clearly specified, and the idiosyncratic category contains a mishmash of variables, some of which pertain to general belief systems, others to the unique attributes of a specific leader.

Another significant effort at developing a framework or organizational structure for understanding foreign policy decision-making is Michael Brecher's case studies of Israel (1972, 1975, 1980). Building on the work of Harold and Margaret Sprout (1956, 1957, 1965), as well as on his own earlier research on political leadership and decision-making in India (1969) and with Blema Steinberg and Janice Stein (1969), Brecher develops an input-process-output model that identifies and classifies the factors that are important in the decision-making process. Of particular interest is the attention given to the relationship between the operational or external environment (military and economic capacity, political structure, interest groups, external factors) and the decision-makers' interpretations or perceptions of that environment. Brecher calls this the psychological environment. Brecher also introduces a descriptive set of policy issue areas (military-security, political-diplomatic, economic-developmental, cultural-status) that he suggests will affect the foreign policy decision. In a positive assessment of Brecher's research, Charles F. Hermann and Gregory Peacock write:

> [Brecher] can be interpreted as asking the question: How do decision makers interpret and integrate the various potential sources of outside influence? The question introduces the assumption that if we can understand those dynamics, decision making can serve as the integrating mechanism for multi-source explanations of foreign policy. . . . [W]e believe this perspective continues to be at the cutting edge of theory-building efforts in the field. (1987, 25)

However, Brecher also stops short of providing specific hypotheses relating the individual variables in the system.

Finally, Cohen and Harris attempt, with some success, to synthesize the major analytical frameworks and approaches that existed as of the mid-1970s in order "to identify the important variables for analysis—to serve as a sort of checklist—and to suggest possible ways in which these variables may be related." Three principal categories of variables are identified and discussed:

1. input variables, consisting of factors present in the political, governmental, or external environments;
2. conversion [or process] variables, which are the means [specific mechanisms] by which policymakers actually choose a course of action when confronted with the various inputs; and
3. output variables, representing the choices made. (1975, 388)

The bulk of their essay focuses on the first of these—the input variables—because that is where the field was devoting the greatest amount of attention in the 1960s and 1970s. But it is clear from the discussion that Cohen and Harris consider the conversion mechanisms—rationality, satisficing, incrementalism, cognitive processes, and bargaining—to be at least as intellectually interesting and important as the input variables, whether as dependent variables or as intervening factors mediating between the independent and the dependent variables.

Curiously, this thoughtful article has received relatively little attention by foreign policy scholars, at least on the international relations side of the fence. One possible explanation can be found in the field specializations of its authors. Cohen writes extensively on foreign policy from the domestic determinants perspective (e.g., *The Press in Foreign Policy* 1963; *The Public's Impact on Foreign Policy* 1973). Neither he nor his coauthor are part of the international relations/foreign policy group. Furthermore, the piece was included in an edited volume on *Policies and Policymaking*, rather than in an international relations book or journal. Lest this alleged parochialism be too quickly dismissed, it is worth recalling that virtually all the foreign policy literature cited by, for example, members of the International Studies Association comes out of the international relations or area studies literatures, rather than from the policy or organizational theory approaches. Though there are exceptions to this tendency—such as the incorporation of insights from David Braybrooke and Charles E. Lindblom (1963) or Herbert Simon (1957, 1985)—the policy literature is generally given less attention by foreign policy scholars than one would expect, given the importance of policy-making in the field of political science as a whole.

Reactions to and Modifications of
the Rational Actor Model

A different approach to the perceived inadequacies of the conventional rational actor model is taken by scholars who modify the parameters of that approach to eliminate or at least reduce its limitations. Among scholars of decision-making, Simon is probably best known for his development of the concepts of bounded rationality and satisficing, which challenge the rational actor framework while working within it. Bounded rationality emphasizes the psychological and intellectual limits of human beings: the normal desire to simplify the world, the tendency to take shortcuts in thinking that violate formal logic, the inability of most people to hold a complex set of variables in their mind simultaneously. Given these human limits, Simon argues, fully rational decision-making is impossible. Instead, people satisfice: they examine sequentially the choices facing them until they come upon one that meets their minimum standards of acceptability, one that will "suffice" and "satisfy."

Simon gives a fresh look at (procedural) bounded rationally—with its basis in cognitive psychology—and also at the global, substantive rationality of economics:

> Using examples drawn from the recent literature of political science, [this article] examines the relative roles played by the rationality principle and by auxiliary assumptions (e.g. assumptions about the content of actors' goals) in explaining human behavior in political contexts, and concludes that the model predictions rest primarily on the auxiliary assumptions rather than from the rationality principle. (1985, 293)

The implication, as Simon points out, is that unless the principle of rationality is "accompanied by extensive empirical research to identify the correct auxiliary assumptions, [it] has little power to make valid predictions about political phenomena" (1985, 293).

Braybrooke and Lindblom also reject the "synoptic conception" of decision-making, which assumes that the values, consequences, and probabilities of all options are known and carefully considered by the decision-maker. Like Simon, they recognize that time and resource constraints may not allow such a comprehensive analysis, even assuming that all the necessary pieces of information can in theory be known. Given this situation, the definition of a problem is crucial in determining the solution chosen; other factors, such as the abilities of the decision-maker and the values held by that person, will also limit the alternatives considered and ultimately chosen. One technique frequently used by policymakers is incremental decision-making, that is, changing only slightly the choices made previously.

Theories on Collective and Bureaucratic Processes

At the same time the comparative foreign policy approach was establishing itself through its classification and theoretical efforts and organizational theorists were refining concepts of rational decision-making, other scholars were pursuing equally significant research on collective and bureaucratic processes, as well as on societal influences on, and individual cognitive and perceptual elements of, foreign policy decision-making. In common with the comparative foreign policy orientation, these theories rejected the realists' assumption of the state as a unitary actor. Beyond that, however, there were clear differences, both between and within each approach.

Among the initial group of bureaucratic policies scholars in the early 1960s were Roger Hilsman (1952, 1959), Richard Neustadt (1960), and Warner Schilling (1962). Robert Art summarizes some of the insights of these researchers:

1. Political power (the ability to get someone to do something he would otherwise not do) is widely dispersed at the national governmental level.

2. Within these institutions, which Schilling termed "quasi-sovereign powers," sit participants in the policy process with differing views on what they would like done on any given issue.

3. Political leadership within or across these institutions is exercised primarily through persuasion, but with persuasion dependent upon the skill with which a figure makes use of the limited power that his position gives him.

4. Foreign policy making is thus a political process of building consensus and support for a policy among those participants who have the power to affect the outcome and who often disagree over what they think the outcome should be.

5. The content of any particular policy reflects as much the necessities of the conditions in which it is forged—what is required to obtain agreement—as it does the substantive merits of that policy. (1973, 468–69)

This set of findings provided essential background for what Art calls the "second wave" of bureaucratic politics scholars; among them Graham T. Allison, Morton H. Halperin, Arnold Kanter, Irving Janis, and Leslie Gelb.

Allison's well-known 1971 volume on the Cuban missile crisis, *Essence of Decision*, proposes three complementary approaches to explain the decision-making process that occurred during the thirteen days in October 1962. The rational, organizational processes, and bureaucratic/governmental politics models are each used to illustrate the insights provided by the varying conceptual lenses. Model 1 (Rational Actor) argues that foreign policy choices are the purposive actions of unified, rational governments, based on plausible calculations of utility and probability, to achieve definable "state goals." Allison does not present the rational actor model as the proverbial straw-person. Despite the previous challenges to this model, its simplicity and parsimony, and the fact that "the information required by the . . . model is likely to be available when the information required by some other conceptual models is not" (Hilsman 1987, 49), continue to make it attractive to many scholars.

Model 2 (Organizational Processes) reflects the theory that foreign policy can best be understood as the choices and outputs of a group of semifeudal, loosely allied organizations within the government that are looking out for their own interests and following standard operating procedures.

> First, the actual occurrences are organizational outputs. . . . Government leaders' decisions can trigger organizational routines. Government leaders can trim the edges of this output and exercise some choice in combining outputs. But the mass of behavior is determined by previously established procedures. Second, existing organizational routines for employing present physical capabilities constitute the effective options open to government leaders confronted with any problem. . . . Third, organizational outputs structure the situation within the narrow constraints of which leaders must contribute their "decision" concerning an issue. Outputs raise the problem, provide the information, and make the initial moves that color the fact of the issue that is turned to the leaders. . . . If one understands the structure of the situation and the fact of the issue—which are determined by the organizational outputs—the formal choice of the leaders is frequently anti-climactic. (Allison 1969, 669)

Model 3 (Bureaucratic/Governmental Politics) suggests that foreign policy is the result of intensive competition among decision-makers and bargaining along regularized channels among players positioned hierarchically within the government bureaucracy, each of whom has his or her own perspective on the issues at hand. It is the "pulling and hauling" of the individual actors that results in the final outcome. In a subsequent article (Allison and Halperin 1972), this conception of Model 3 is further developed by adding the idea that organizations can be included as players in the game of bureaucratic politics and by making a distinction between decision games and action games.

Allison's deductive approach is designed both to test the validity of the three competing theories and to make an important point about the ways theories can influence what evidence is given attention by researchers:

> Thus while at one level three models produce different explanations of the same happening, at a second level the models produce different explanations of quite different occurrences. And indeed, this is my argument. Spectacles magnify one set of factors rather than another and thus not only lead analysts to produce different explanations of

problems that appear, in their summary questions, to be the same, but also influence the character of the analyst's puzzle, the evidence he assumes to be relevant, the concepts he uses in examining the evidence, and what he takes to be an explanation. (1971, 251)

Morton Halperin is one of many scholars who have expanded on and revised the bureaucratic approach; he has combined elements of several models in an effort to find a more comprehensive theory that incorporates the insights of each (e.g. Halperin 1974). In particular, he has tried to classify the participants in the decision-making process, and to examine both the constraints facing actors and the bargaining advantages which they may have available. In an introduction to their book of readings on U.S. foreign policy from a bureaucratic perspective, Halperin and Kanter summarize their conception of this approach:

> The bureaucratic perspective . . . implies (1) that change in the international environment is only one of several stimuli to which participants in the foreign policy process are responding (possibly among the weakest and least important) and (2) that events involving the actions of two or more nations can best be explained and predicted in terms of the actions of two or more *national bureaucracies* whose actions affect the domestic interests and objectives of the other bureaucracies involved. (1973, 3)

One of the best-known efforts to apply bureaucratic decision-making theories to a concrete case is the analysis by Leslie H. Gelb and Richard K. Betts (1979) of the U.S. decision-making processes on Vietnam from World War II until 1968. Gelb and Betts are responding to the common wisdom that says since the U.S. involvement in Vietnam was not "rational," it must have come about through mistakes in the bureaucratic process. Gelb and Betts argue instead that these failures reflect the policy preferences of the various actors influencing the decision-making process:

> The paradox is that the foreign policy failed, but the domestic decision-making system worked. . . . Vietnam was not an aberration of the decision-making system but a logical outcome of the principles that leaders brought with them into it. (2)

> The bureaucratic system did what it was supposed to: select and implement means to a given end. The political system did what a democracy usually does: produce a policy responsive more to the majority and the center than to the minority or the extremes of opinion. And strategic thought, from that of the limited war theorists to the counterinsurgency specialists, did what it was supposed to do: support the general policy of worldwide containment with specific ideas and programs for containment in Vietnam. (354)

In a much shorter piece, Jerel Rosati (1981) applies a modified version of the Allison-Halperin bureaucratic politics model to policymaking behavior regarding SALT I under Johnson and Nixon. He finds that the bureaucratic politics model has explanatory value for the Johnson administration, but for the Nixon administration, which had a chief executive who attempted to control tightly foreign policy from the White House, it is less valuable. Rosati makes an important, if not unique, point that is often lost in discussions of the bureaucratic approach:

> The bureaucratic politics model is dependent upon a simple, two-step, linear relationship between decision structure, decision process, and foreign behavior. In other words, the structure of the decisional unit determines the decision-making process; thereafter, the process determines the decision outcome. However, the existence of a decision-making structure does not solely determine the exact nature of the decision process. . . . (249)

> In sum, to actually determine the nature of the decision-making process, knowledge beyond the decision structure must be considered. The beliefs, personalities, and modes of thinking of the participants will have a direct effect on the decision-making process. In addition, external forces will have an influence on the perceptions of the participants. (251)

The challenge, of course, is to find ways of incorporating all these important factors without becoming overwhelmed with details.

Irving Janis (1982), who develops another effort to understanding the process of collective decision-making, shares Rosati's desire to include individual cognitive factors. As with several scholars previously mentioned, Janis uses a case study approach, based on secondary source materials, as a way of identifying interesting and plausible hypotheses. Janis's interdisciplinary research focuses on seven foreign policy decisions—five fiascos and two successes—and pinpoints elements of the group dynamic process which either interfere with careful decision-making or enhance the decision-making process. Although he gives the greatest attention to the case studies, chapter 10, which presents a summary of the theoretical analysis of groupthink, is arguably the most important. In it, Jaris presents both antecedent conditions of the concurrence-seeking tendency and the observable consequences of this tendency. It is clear from this discussion that even though a researcher using secondary source material will not be able to know everything about the group dynamics of a decision (one of the concerns raised regarding such a methodology), it is possible to accomplish a great deal and gain insights that are at least highly suggestive.

Finally, a number of works explicitly address the interaction of governmental players—the chief executive and his or her staff, the legislative body, the foreign affairs bureaucracy, the Defense Department—and the impact these relationship have on foreign policy. Stephen D. Cohen (1981), Cecil V. Crabb and Kevin Mulcahy (1986), Thomas Cronin (1980), I. M. Destler (1972, 1983), Gelb (1980), and Karl F. Inderfurth and Loch K. Johnson (1988) are representative of this often descriptive and occasionally normative and prescriptive tradition.

The bureaucratic approach to foreign policy analysis has most often been used to describe the decision-making process in the United States; it is more rarely applied to other countries. There are at least two reasons for this. First, bureaucratic analyses require detailed, accurate data about what goes on inside the government: what the standard operating procedures are, how individuals bargain with each other, what agencies have actual (as opposed to official) responsibility for which issues or activities. This information is not easy to obtain even in the relatively open United States. In the case of many countries, it is all but impossible to acquire. Second, bureaucratic factors are most often significant in countries with massive and complex governmental structures. This group is limited at present to a relatively few states.

Societal Sources of Foreign Policy

The decision-making process is affected not only by group dynamics and bureaucratic games, as described above; it also occurs in a particular domestic context. This environment includes not only the values and character of a society but also its physical attributes (size, level of industrialization, and so forth). Among the empirical studies that examine state or national attributes and foreign policy are Maurice East (1978), East and Hermann (1975), David W. Moore (1974), Rudolph J. Rummel (1972), Barbara Salmore and Stephen Salmore (1978), Jonathon Wilkenfeld (1968), and Wilkenfeld et al. (1980). In addition to exploring characteristics of a people or a state, the domestic context must take into account the multiplicity of nongovernmental actors who may attempt to influence the foreign policy choices made by the elites, either through conventional political participation (e.g. voting, responding to public option polls), or through nonconventional means of political expression such as protests, demonstrations, strikes, riots, and coups d'état.

Perhaps because of its initial focus on the unitary, rational actor model, much of the foreign policy literature has ignored domestic factors altogether. When they *are* included, as Cohen and Harris point out, domestic sources are often presented at the grand theory level, or in an effort to make evaluative statements about specific foreign policy decisions:

[S]everal schools of thought, notably those which emphasize national character, historical traditions, or some variant of Marxian analysis, see virtually all of a state's foreign policy as determined by its internal structure and processes. Also, and we think significantly, scholars who are inclined to normative evaluations and interpretations of foreign policy often place great emphasis on the importance of domestic sources (cf. [Ole R.] Holsti, 1974). (1975, 410)

The role of public opinion, particularly in the United States, is discussed briefly here; however, a full consideration of all forms of regular and irregular political participation, as well as other domestic variables, and their impact on foreign policy, goes beyond the scope of this essay.

Gabriel Almond's *The American People and Foreign Policy* (1960) was among the first works to deal systematically and rigorously with the question of the impact of the U.S. public on foreign policy. (See also B. Cohen 1973.) According to Almond, in the post–World War II era the U.S. public is best seen as involving two separate groups: the attentive and non-attentive publics. The latter is by far the larger, consisting of the 70 to 90 percent of the population who "participate in policy making in indirect and primarily passive ways" (Almond 1960, 5). But even the attentive public is relatively constrained in its participation options. Because people feel most secure with opinions grounded in their own experiences, they find it difficult to relate to what is happening halfway around the world (Sanders 1990, chap. 4). Thus, the primary role of the public is not one of active involvement in policy formulation on foreign policy issues. Rather, the public sets "certain policy criteria in the form of widely held values and expectations. It evaluates the results of policies from the point of view of their conformity to these basic values and expectations," and passes judgments on these results at election time (Almond 1960, 5). These judgments, however, are rarely based on a detailed knowledge of foreign realities. Rather, they reflect basic values and expectations that are developed and shaped by events much closer to home.

In many ways, the U.S. public's role has not changed much since Almond first published his seminal work. Its primary function is still to serve as a constraint on policymakers who must take the public's ideas into account when formulating policy. But while the essential role has remained the same, the environment within which this role is played has changed dramatically in several ways. First, the Vietnam War and U.S.-Soviet detente saw a breakdown of foreign policy consensus among U.S. elites (Holsti 1979; Holsti and Rosenau 1979). The post–World War II consensus of internationalism and containment of communism that characterized foreign policy in the United States came under attack from all directions. Whereas previously the public served as a constraint or a check upon a relatively united foreign policy elite that agreed about the general direction of policy, the public now serves as a potential ally in a battle over the direction of policy. Thus, policymakers are more likely to try to drum up support for policies that they want to implement or defeat—for example, the conservative effort to rally public support against the ratification of the Panama Canal treaty in 1978. Today enormous amounts of money and effort may be spent attempting to gain popular support in a policy debate.

In addition, the U.S. public is less likely than it once was to go along automatically with the president in foreign policy matters. Sending troops or other dramatic action usually results in a burst of support for the president—the "rally 'round the flag" phenomenon—but "support for the President in crises . . . can be fickle and depend on the longer-term success of policies or . . . on the absence of long-term negative consequences" (Hughes 1978, 40). If an issue drags on without favorable resolution (for example, the U.S. intervention in Lebanon in the early 1980s), support for presidential initiatives erodes (Mueller 1973, Hughes 1978).

Public interest in foreign policy has been increasing in the United States, particularly in the past ten years: the Chicago Council on Foreign Relations has found steady growth since 1978 in the percentage of people who report they are very interested in news about other countries and in the percentage of people who name a foreign policy problem as one of the biggest problems facing the country today (Rielly 1987, 6). This increased interest in foreign affairs does not, however, mean that Americans are united in their views. To the contrary, mass and attentive public opinion on foreign policy, along with elite opinion, became more divided after Vietnam (Vasquez 1985). As Eugene Wittkopf (1981, 1986, 1987; also Wittkopf and Maggiotto 1983) has shown, a simple internationalism-isolationism dimension no longer captures U.S. attitudes toward the role of the United States in world affairs. Instead, Wittkopf argues, two separate and very different dimensions of internationalism have emerged: militant internationalism and cooperative internationalism. (Similar distinctions are made, using different terms, by Holsti and Rosenau 1984 and by Hughes 1978.) The public disagrees not only about *whether* the United States should get involved outside its borders, but also about *how* it should get involved. Because public opinion is divided and somewhat unpredictable, policymakers have a more difficult time gaining public support.

Finally, and this may be the most important difference between Almond's time and the present, the technology of public opinion measurement has changed. When Almond was writing in the 1950s, public opinion was not measured frequently. Public views on foreign policy issues often went unnoticed—or at least were not systematically monitored—until election time. The feedback that officials got concerning public opinion was sketchy at best, reflected only in the letters they received from highly motivated constituents. Now polls are taken constantly. The public's views on many issues are monitored regularly. When the administration acts, one finds out the next day how the public responds. Because the information is available, policymakers will be judged by how well the public accepts policy decisions: technology has made the impact of the public in developed societies more pressing.

Having said all of this, it must be reiterated that in general the U.S. public does not pay an enormous amount of attention to foreign policy issues, compared with their interest in domestic policy concerns. This is true even when a foreign policy matter is repeatedly presented to the public by the news media. For example, in spite of a very public military presence in the Persian Gulf for over a year, in July of 1988 NBC News reported that a Gallup Poll conducted for the National Geographic Society found that only 25 percent of all Americans could correctly locate the Persian Gulf on a world map (Gerner and Sanders 1988). The percentage of people claiming they are "not sure" about particular policy options in foreign affairs also tends to be much larger than in the area of domestic policy, another reflection of this lack of knowledge.

The increased awareness of and attention to foreign policy, combined with a lack of knowledge of the details of international politics, results in a situation where the public tends to react to foreign policy, just as Almond (1969, 139) wrote thirty years ago, in terms of its "moods, interests and expectations," its opinions heavily shaped by what is currently in the news and by individuals' basic beliefs or general images of foreign relations, structured as these are by early learning experiences. And even though these interests or expectations may be relatively stable, the public's lack of knowledge about details may make attitudes and opinions about particular foreign issues volatile, and give them the appearance of internal inconsistency. The views will tend to reflect a gut reaction based on perceived "American national interest" (that is, the effects on matters close to home) rather than the details of foreign affairs (Clymer 1985; Erikson, Luttbeg, and Tedin 1980; Free and Cantril 1968; Rielly 1983; and Weisberg 1976).

The importance of public opinion as a determinant of foreign policy may well be greater in other countries than it is in the United States. In the latter case, public opinion has become more important as an explanatory factor in recent years only because it is coming from such a small base. Informed discussion of foreign policy requires an esoteric and otherwise useless set of knowledge, and for a powerful state such as the United States, foreign policy issues rarely have an obvious and direct impact on large numbers of people (wars excepted). However, for much of the rest of the world, the connections between foreign and domestic concerns are more obvious and explicit; thus we would expect a higher level of public interest in and awareness of foreign policy issues.

One additional aspect of public opinion and foreign policy should be mentioned. Bruce E. Moon argues that for many Third World states, positive public perceptions of foreign policy become a major source of legitimation for the government, particularly when such legitimacy is difficult to achieve through domestic policies or when the creation of the state was imposed from without.

> Foreign policy enables the state to portray itself as the embodiment of nationalist pride. . . . Legitimating appeals come in a variety of forms, often emphasizing an external enemy against whom the state is seen as a unifying force. . . . Alternative attempts to build state legitimacy through foreign policy consensus involve ideological appeals which gave much of Third World foreign policy its strident rhetorical tone and limited substantive content. . . . This is not to say, of course, that such efforts are either insincere or inappropriate. To the contrary, to command wide support such legitimation appeals must tap and mobilize existing consensus rather than create it artificially. (1989, 14)

Thus, the role of public opinion in defining foreign policy choices needs to be understood in the context of the particular global position of each state and the relationship between the state and the population. In some cases, it sets parameters and constraints; in others it takes on far more significance. The challenge to foreign policy researchers is identifying the circumstances in which public opinion plays a critical role and those in which its impact is more marginal.

Cognitive Processes and Psychological Attributes

Just as it is possible to discuss societal and governmental aspects of foreign policy both in terms of "inputs" (e.g. public opinion) and "processes" (e.g. bureaucratic decision-making), individual-level theories look at the individual actors themselves to understand how their perceptions of the foreign policy situation and their idiosyncratic personal attributes, such as their belief systems, explain eventual foreign policy choices. Initially, research on the cognitive and psychological dimensions of foreign policy decision-making was viewed with some skepticism—it was thought to be outside the realm of political science or a mere residual after systemic, societal, and governmental factors had been taken into account. Thus, there was a tendency for all of the cognitive elements of decision-making to be "black-boxed." Holsti discusses some of the factors that initially limited acceptance of the cognitive processes perspective:

Several theoretical, methodological, and practical problems may have inhibited extensive application of cognitive process perspectives to foreign policy decisionmaking. These include: disillusionment with some previous efforts of related kinds; skepticism about the relevance of psychological theories, insights, and evidence to the analysis of political phenomena; the canon of parsimony; problems of linking beliefs to foreign policy actions; and difficulties of access to data, the laboriousness of coding, and related methodological problems. (1976, 22)

In recent years, however, cognitive processes, beliefs systems, and personality attributes have come to play an increasingly important role in foreign policy research. Often it is difficult to disentangle these different dimensions.

"Belief system" refers to a more or less integrated set of beliefs about man's physical and social environment. In the case of political leaders, beliefs about history and the nature of politics may be especially important. "Cognitive processes" refer to various activities associated with problem solving (broadly conceived) including perception, appraisal, interpretation, search, information processing, strategies for coping with uncertainty, decision rules, verification, and the like. These cognitive activities are assumed to be in an interactive relationship with the individual's belief system, as well as with the environment. (1976, 20)

Alexander George (1975) summarizes eight basic tenets of cognitive psychology that undergird much of the research discussed here. Though lengthy, George's list merits repetition:

1. The mind can be fruitfully viewed as an information-processing system.

2. In order to function, every individual acquires, during the course of his development, a set of beliefs and personal constructs about the physical and social environment (the belief system). These beliefs provide him with a relatively coherent way of organizing and making sense of what would otherwise be a confusing and overwhelming array of signals and clues picked up from the environment by his senses.

3. These beliefs and constructs necessarily simplify and structure the external world.

4. Much of an individual's behavior is shaped by the particular ways in which he perceives, evaluates, and interprets incoming information about events in his environment.

5. Information-processing is selective and subject to bias; the individual's existing beliefs and his "attention-set" at any given time are active agents in determining *what he attends to* and *how he evaluates it.*

6. There is considerable variation among individuals in the richness-complexity as well as the validity of their beliefs and constructs regarding any given portion of the environment.

7. While such beliefs can change, what is noteworthy is that they tend to be relatively stable. They are not easily subject to disconfirmation and to change in response to new information that seems to challenge them.

8. Notwithstanding the preceding tenet, individuals are capable of perceiving the utility of discrepant information and adopting an attitude of openmindedness with regard to new information. (Cited in Starr 1984, 9–10)

One skeptic turned supporter is Richard Snyder, whose work with James Robinson in the 1960s reflects a new interest in the personality attributes of decision-makers such as their "propensity to assume high risks, tolerance of ambiguity and uncertainty, intelligence, creativity, self-esteem, dominance, submissiveness, need for power, need for achievement and need for affiliation" (Robinson and Snyder 1965, 444). In attempting to understand the motivations and attributes of decision-makers, among other ideas, Snyder and Robinson made a distinction between "in order to motives," which are conscious and verbalizable, and "because of motives," which are unconscious or semiconscious.

Margaret Hermann (1983) also considers the personal characteristics of leaders (operational code or view of the world, political style, interest and training in foreign affairs, political socialization, etc.), as well as their constituencies, and the functions they perform in relation to those constituencies. All of these, Hermann argues, need to be examined in order to assess leaders' impact on foreign policy. (An interesting exchange on an earlier version of this research can be found in M. Hermann 1980a; Rasler, Thompson, and Chester 1980; and M. Hermann 1980b.)

Additional research on personality attributes is reported by Graham H. Shepard in a study that replicates Lloyd Etheredge's doctoral research (1978a, 1978b). Shepard (1988, 91) tests two aspects of interpersonal generalization theory "to determine if the personality characteristics of dominance and extroversion-introversion crucially affect the policies advocated by American foreign policy elite" regarding relations with the Soviet Union and the Soviet bloc states between 1969 and 1984. He finds that personality as measured along the extroversion-introversion continuum did not appear to have an impact on the foreign policy decisions he examines. This is counter to Etheredge's conclusion but may be a function of changes over time, since Etheredge's research deals with an earlier period. On the other hand, Shepard identifies support for the hypothesis that the extent of dominance of personality of a member of an elite will affect his or her attitude toward the use of force, confirming Etheredge's original results.

The issue of perception is crucial to any consideration of individual-level sources of foreign policy. Robert Jervis (1968, 1976) is interested in understanding what causes rational decision-making to get sidetracked: how and why does one actor misperceive the actions and intentions of another actor? In "Hypotheses on Misperception," Jervis proposes fourteen hypotheses that, if upheld by empirical evidence, could go a long way toward explaining how conflicts can spiral upward when neither party desires that outcome. Several of these hypotheses address the tendency of decision-makers to recast new information so that it fits into their already established worldview; others deal with the factors that affect perceptions and misperceptions of reality, including the tendency to see other states as more hostile—and their actions more disciplined and coordinated—than is actually the case.

For several years now, Richard Herrmann (1985, 1986) has been investigating systematically the relationship of perceptions and foreign policy choices in the case of the Soviet Union. He uses content analysis to interpret the underlying perceptions and beliefs of Soviet leaders as reflected in their speeches, and also examines Soviet foreign policy actions to see whether there is any connection between the two. Herrmann argues convincingly that although perceptual and motivational variables are not the only factors determining the foreign policy choices of Soviet leaders, they *are* significant and should be given further attention.

Like Jervis, Alexander George (1980) wants to sort out why rational decision-making so often does not occur. He asks the question: How do policymakers deal with the constraints on rational decision-making that they face, particularly when in a crisis situation?

> It is a central thesis . . . that a policymaker often experiences decisional conflicts in attempting to deal with the value complexity and uncertainty imbedded in a problem and that the resulting psychological stress, depending on how the decisionmaker copes with it, can impair adaptive responses to policy issues.
>
> The policymaker can deal with the psychological stress of decision-making in either of two ways: (1) by utilizing *analytical* modes of coping with value-complexity and uncertainty or (2) by resorting to *defensive* modes of coping with the malaise they engender. (491)

George suggests a number of specific methods policymakers use to cope with the uncertainty they face: procrastination, bolstering, satisficing, incrementalism, sequential decision-making, use of historical analogies, consensus politics, and use of ideology. Some, obviously, are more functional than others for making thoughtful foreign policy choices.

Additional insights come from Deborah Welch Larson's (1988) use of social-psychological theories of attitude change to study the origins of the Cold-War belief system of four crucial U.S. leaders. Among Larson's findings are that "Truman did not change his beliefs until after the pressure of events forced him to reorient U.S. foreign policy from cooperation to containment, and that Harriman, Byrnes, and Truman did not have coherent belief systems" (241). This implies that "self-perception theory" (that is, that behavior precedes perception and influences the development of the leader's viewpoint) may be an appropriate psychological explanation, at least in some cases.

Several complementary aspects of individual-level research are woven together in Harvey Starr's study of Henry Kissinger. There is a sensitivity to the governmental and bureaucratic constraints faced by Kissinger and a discussion of how he was able to work around those limitations. Psychohistorical analysis of Kissinger provides the background to the operational-code analysis of Kissinger's belief structure (based on Holsti 1970, *inter alia;* see also George 1969 and Walker 1977), including the way he viewed his opponents. In addition, Starr compares the importance of role factors and idiosyncratic factors in understanding foreign policy, concluding that in the case of Kissinger, "individual or idiosyncratic factors appear to have had much more effect than role did" (1984, 161).

Finally, Rosati's 1987 analysis of the Carter Administration investigates the beliefs of three political leaders (Carter, Brzezinski, and Vance, later replaced by Muskie) in order to determine the extent of consensus or dissensus that existed among them at different points, and to identify the level of stability and change in each individual's attitudes over time. The latter, Rosati argues, is predominantly a function of the individual's personality, external events, and domestic forces. Rosati also examines the relationship between beliefs and behavior over the four years of the Carter Administration. This is important since the belief-behavior linkage is usually assumed rather than systematically tested.

Cognitive research is likely to undergo some changes in the next few years as the effects of the "cognitive revolution" in psychology diffuse into studies of foreign policy. These newer methods emphasize human information processing at a relatively micro level, rather than focusing on more macro concepts such as "personality." Some of these approaches are found in the artificial intelligence literature discussed below, but there are insights about human interpretation and recall of events, attitudes, and assessments of risk (e.g. Kahneman, Slovic, and Tversky 1982) as well as the impact of language, cognitive development, and culture (Sampson 1987) that are relevant to foreign policy analysis even in the absence of computer models of those processes.

Crisis Decision-Making

An explicit emphasis on "crisis" has been important to foreign policy scholars at least since the late 1950s (e.g. Davison 1958; C. Hermann 1969a, 1969b; McClelland 1961, 1962, 1972), in spite of the seemingly endless debate on what defines a crisis and whether "crisis" should be an independent, dependent or intervening variable in the analysis. Of particular interest is Charles McClelland's research in the 1960s, based on an early events data collection. McClelland hypothesized that a crisis can be distinguished from a non-crisis by the amount of entropy in the system: a crisis situation is one that is more uncertain; in other words, one in which there is not a clear patterning of actions.

In order to test this idea, McClelland collected data (initially from the *New York Times* Index, later from the paper itself) on reported events involving two conflict situations: Berlin and the Taiwan Straits. These were grouped into categories of actions and responses, ranging from "yield," "comment," and "consult" on one end of the scale to "expel," "seize," and "force" on the other extreme. (A greatly expanded version of this data set became known as the World Event Interaction Survey or WEIS.) Using H-rel techniques derived from information theory, McClelland established a measure of uncertainty in the system over time, and found that, consistent with his hypotheses, crisis periods could in fact be identified by an increase in the amount of "relative uncertainty" in the system. McCelland's research is an important example of one direction behavioralist foreign policy research has taken: the analysis of events data. The research is also significant because it confirms for many researchers the basic notion that seemingly subjective variables such as crisis can be measured by consistent, objective criteria.

The set of research identified collectively as the Stanford 1914 Crisis Study is one of the earliest efforts to take seriously the goal of an interdisciplinary, scientific approach to foreign policy decision-making. It is also enlightening as its main researchers were originally trained in the classical approach to foreign policy but were working within a scientific method. (Zinnes 1976, chap. 7, contains a nice summary of this research.) The project began in 1958 as an interdisciplinary seminar that included Richard Brody, Philip Buck, Nazli Choucri, Bernard Cohen, Ole Holsti, Robert North, and Dina Zinnes, among others. The goal was to use a single specific crisis—the outbreak of war in 1914—to develop a general model of interstate foreign policy behavior. Initially, the plan was to create a complete minute-by-minute chronology of the period just prior to the beginning of the war. Though this was not completed, the progress that was made allowed researchers to focus on the various perceptions and misperceptions that appeared to trigger further acts.

Holsti, North, and Brody (1968) base their research on this initial research effort. Their approach is to use content analysis within the framework of a stimulus-response model taken from psychology to examine the interaction between decisional units. They begin with the assumption that there was congruence between the stimulus or input and the response or output, but quickly realize that for this to hold true, particularly in a crisis situation, one must incorporate perceptual variables rather than looking only at so-called objective reality. The research finds support for two hypotheses:

> If perceptions of anxiety, fear, threat, or injury [in both verbal communications and actions] are great enough, even the perceptions of one's own inferior capability will fail to deter a nation from going to war.

> In a situation of low involvement, policy response (R) will tend to be at a lower level of violence than the input action (S), whereas in a high involvement situation, the policy response (R) will tend to be at a higher level of violence than the input action (S). (136)

Using this same basic strategy, Holsti, Brody, and North (1964) also examine the Cuban missile crisis. Even though it has been argued that the researchers do not present a true decision-making model because they do not deal with the internal dynamics leading to particular responses, their work does illustrate a keen sensitivity to the psychological issues that underlie contemporary perceptual studies, as well as illuminating how early scientific research looked at crisis.

Two recent works with distinctive methodologies and an explicit focus on decision-making in crisis situations are by Glenn H. Snyder and Paul Diesing (1977), and Richard Ned Lebow (1981). Both books base their analysis on a series of detailed case studies of international crisis situations in the late nineteenth and the twentieth centuries with the goal of building a theory of international crisis behavior. Snyder and Diesing begin with theories and models about aggregate bargaining behaviors, but they also examine "the effects of international system structures and the decision-making activities of the actors on the bargaining process" (xi). Thus, they shift from systemic factors to an examination of perception, group processes, and other individual and domestic level variables. The majority of their investigation deals with sixteen intensive and five less detailed case studies of crises in the period 1898–1970; these were undertaken to provide consistent information on a clear set of common hypotheses and questions.

The most interesting part of the book is the chapter on decision-making, which draws on the research by Jervis (1976) and others. Snyder and Diesing identify fifty cases of strategic decisions that are part of the case studies and use them to test three theories of decision-making:

1. utility maximization (classical rational theory)
2. bounded rationality (from Simon's satisficing model)
3. bureaucratic policies (as defined by Allison and Halperin)

The first two are "problem-solving" theories; the third looks at political processes occurring inside the decision-making unit. Snyder and Diesing argue that utility maximization and bounded rationality may be complementary theories, whereas the bureaucratic politics approach, with its focus on the "internal political imperatives of maintaining and increasing influence and power" (355), should be viewed as supplemental rather than in competition with the other two. Following a suggestion of Robinson and Snyder (1965), Snyder and Diesing also point out that bureaucratic politics, as it is usually discussed, has both rational and nonrational components that are often confused, with the nonrational dimension accounting for attitudes, values, beliefs, and cognitive sensitivities.

After considering the three theories, Snyder and Diesing conclude that although the basic assumptions of utility maximization theory do not hold in crisis situations, "the fit of bounded rationality to crisis bargaining decisions is excellent, especially in the area of strategy revision. . . . [In addition] the bureaucratic theory is in part supplementary to the bounded rationality theory, relating the latter's cybernetic concepts to actual political forces" (1977, 405–07). Bounded rationality and bureaucratic politics theories apply in different circumstances. The former fits best when a limited number of individuals are involved in the decision-making process; as one would expect, the latter is most useful in explaining the coalition-building activities that occur when a large number of actors have input in the decision. Finally, Snyder and Diesing do not find support for the hypothesis—drawn from the Allison-Halperin model of bureaucratic politics—that the attitudes of significant decision-makers are determined to any large extent by the role they play in the bureaucratic structure (408).

Lebow begins his analysis with twenty-six historical crises, dating from the Cuban crisis of 1897–98 to the 1967 Arab-Israeli War. He divides crises into three categories (justification of hostility, spinoff crises, brinksmanship), based on their origins, patterns of development, and probability of resolution. A "justification of hostility" situation is one in which there is a deliberate effort to create a crisis in order to provide the excuse to go to war, whereas "spin-off crises" involve secondary confrontations in which neither party really wants the conflict and will try to resolve the situation in a peaceful fashion if this can be accomplished consistent with protecting the "national interest." Brinkmanship, the most common form of crisis, occurs "when a state knowingly challenges an important commitment of another state in the hope of compelling its adversary to back away from [its] commitment" (Lebow 1981, 57). These three types of crisis are intended to illustrate patterns rather than to predict directly or explain whether a specific crisis will lead to war. Snyder and Diesing come at their material from a bargaining perspective; Lebow, however, is more interested in the political-military environment of the crisis and the thought processes of the decision-makers, in particular cognitive consistency and misperception. He also deals with alternative forms of crisis management.

Artificial Intelligence

In recent years, a number of models of foreign policy have been developed using artificial intelligence (AI) methods; Donald A. Sylvan and Steve Chan (1984), Stephen Cimbala (1987), Valerie Hudson (1991), and Philip A. Schrodt (1991) provide a number of examples. The most common AI technique applied to foreign policy is "rule-based modeling." In the late 1970s, computer scientists discovered that many problems requiring human expertise could be solved by the simple application of a large set of idiosyncratic rules (usually 500 to 5,000 rules). Unlike statistical methods, these "expert systems" also seem to capture some of the characteristics of how humans actually solve problems. Humans are not particularly adept at either statistical reasoning (Kahneman, Slovic, and Tversky 1982) or logical reasoning from first principles; instead, most human problem solving appears to involve the nonstatistical application of idiosyncratic rules.

Rule-based systems are especially attractive when one is modeling the behavior of organizations, since a great deal of organizational behavior is openly and explicitly rule-following. For example, rule-based models appear able to capture many of the standard operating procedures implemented by low-level bureaucrats in the U.S. Departments of State and Defense. These standard operating procedures can be exceedingly complex and idiosyncratic—the response to a kidnapping of a U.S. citizen in Ethiopia, for instance, is very different from the response to a similar kidnapping in Italy—and hence the behavior of the organization is more likely to be captured by a rule-based model than by a more parsimonious and general model. Rule-based models have been less successful, however, in dealing with more complicated problem solving involving crisis situations, or with decisions that involve political controversy or change.

Rule-based models in foreign policy research have generally taken two forms. The most common uses fairly simple versions of the if-then structure of expert systems. Behaviors that have been modeled include Soviet crisis response (Kaw 1989), Chinese foreign policy (Tanaka 1984), Japanese energy security policy (Bobrow, Sylvan, and Ripley

1986), general characteristics of foreign policy behavior (Hudson 1987), and recommendation rules for Vietnam war involvement (Majeski 1987). These systems were coded by the authors' deriving the rules either through interviewing experts or through study, intuition, and experimentation.

Rule-based systems can be extended substantially beyond the if-then rules of expert system, particularly when complicated data structures are introduced that approximate the wealth of information available to a decision-maker. Several AI models have tried to replicate, in part, the actual rules used by multiple actors in an international system thereby attempting to gain process validity as well as outcome validity. Situations that have been modeled using this approach include Saudi Arabian foreign policy (Anderson and Thorson 1982), Japanese energy and foreign policy decision-making (Sylvan, Goel and Chandresekaran 1990), the Cuban Missile Crisis (Thorson and Sylvan 1982), U.S. policy toward Central America (Job, Johnson, and Selbin 1987), U.S. policy toward the Dominican Republic (Job and Johnson 1986), and Middle East international politics (Phillips 1987).

AI modelers are also learning to model the cognitive process itself. The primary approach is the use of analogy or precedent, originally developed in a series of papers by Hayward J. Alker and others (1972, 1976, 1980). Dwain Mefford (1987a, 226) notes that "analogies are recognized as among the most powerful mechanisms devised by the human mind for coping with complex and ambiguous information." Decision-makers seek the "lessons of the past" in dealing with crises, and continually modify those lessons depending on the success or failure of the policy. For example, the CIA overthrow of Mussadegh in Iran in 1953 was used as a precedent for the overthrow of Arbenz in Guatemala in 1954; those successful interventions were then used as the model for the ill-fated Bay of Pigs invasion against Castro in 1961. The failure at the Bay of Pigs was attributed in part to the low level of U.S. military support; this was corrected by the massive use of U.S. troops in invading the Dominican Republic in 1965 and Grenada in 1983. Although the use of historical analogies and metaphors is not without risk, as Taacov Y.I. Vertzberger (1986) points out, humans do so all the time.

The use of historical precedent is probably more prevalent in foreign policy decision-making than in other forms of human information processing because the international system is complex, provides very little feedback, and frequently involves high-risk situations. Decision-makers have little opportunity to experiment actively with different policy options, in contrast to interpersonal or even domestic public policy issues. And because of the risk and complexity of the decisions, hypothetical deductive arguments carry substantially less weight than do actual historical examples. The arguments for precedent are reviewed in John C. Mallery and Roger Hurwitz (1987), Paul A. Anderson (1981), Schrodt (1985), and the various papers employing precedent-based modeling.

A precedent-based computer model involves at least three elements. First, the model must accessibly store information concerning a set of historical precedents. The difficult issue here in knowing what information is held in the computer and how best to set up its data structure. This storage of information is something humans do naturally. Humans acquire precedents through some combination of induction and explicit teaching; part of the socialization in a bureaucracy involves learning which precedents are considered legitimate guides to analyzing situations. It is less straightforward for a computer. A fairly sophisticated design for such a knowledge base using machine-expert collaboration is found in Mefford (1986b); Schrodt (1989) uses a machine learning technique called a Holland classifier to capture a simple form of inductive learning.

Second, there must be an explicit means of comparing a current situation with the information (knowledge) stored in the data base to determine which situation or situations will be employed as the precedent. Mefford (1984, 1987b) has suggested the use of Levenschtein metrics, a technique developed to compare DNA sequences or more complicated techniques (Mefford 1985). This technique has been applied to comparing sequences of international events data in Schrodt (1985, 1991). Finally, the system must have some means of correcting mistaken analogies through feedback and a means of acquiring new information.

In addition to this predominantly precedent-oriented work, many of the rule-based models cited above also use precedent to varying extents. The importance of precedent is almost universally accepted by AI researches in foreign policy, but practical implementations of that principle still appear to be a major challenge. If the technical problems can be overcome, precedent-based AI models may provide a realistic approximation to how decision-makers use history and a systematic means of studying that aspect of the foreign policy process.

MALAISE AND REASSESSMENT: THE SCIENTIFIC COMPARATIVE FOREIGN POLICY

Thus far, the discussion of contrasting and complementary approaches to foreign policy research has deliberately cut across paradigmatic boundaries. For several reasons, this section will explicitly focus attention on "comparative foreign policy" (CFP) approaches. First, over the years a clearly defined group of scholars at various universities have identified with this subfield. Their original intellectual underpinnings are straightforward, driven by the demands and challenges of the behavioral revolution, with its neopositivist orientation and its model of Kuhnian normal science. CFP scholars have an interest in the intersection of domestic and international politics; their goal is the development and empirical verification of comprehensive theories of foreign policy involving multiple sources of explanation that can be applicable to more than one country or actor.

Without minimizing the importance of these basic points of agreement (which would not necessarily be shared by other foreign policy scholars), one must recognize that beyond them there is little sense among CFP researchers of a common theoretical or methodological framework. C. Hermann and Peacock suggest that this lack of a shared understanding of what CFP "means" helps explain the malaise the field has experienced in the 1980s:

> Each of these interpretations of the development of the CFP field is organized around a logic of inquiry (or meta-methodology) that includes not only a particular perspective on scientific activities (rules, prescriptions, etc.), but also a defense of epistemological claims associated with each approach. Thus claims about the growth of knowledge in any scientific endeavor are ineluctably tied to the logic of inquiry adopted. This connection is important for understanding the widespread discontent with CFP research products. (1987, 19)

Nevertheless, with all these caveats, and with the recognition that CFP has evolved over time and is a bit fuzzy at the edges, it is still the case that if one refers to "the CFP group," it is clear who the "core" is and generally what is meant by the term. With the complex intellectual genealogies that exist in all subfields of political science, this is probably the best we can expect in the way of a group identity.

A second reason for looking explicitly at CFP is that its research agenda has been a major motivating factor behind a number of data collection activities, including the creation of events data sets such as Edward Azar's Conflict and Peace Data Bank (COPDAB), the World Event Interaction Survey (WEIS, discussed above), the multi-university Comparative Research on the Events of Nations (CREON), and more recently, Wilkenfeld's International Crisis Behavior Datasets (whose creation is funded by the National Science Foundation through the Data Development in International Relations (DDIR) project. Brody (1975), Robert Burrowes (1975), Charles W. Kegley (1975) and Patrick McGowan (1972) discuss some of the practical and conceptual issues that faced events data collection activities in the 1970s.

What are events data? The classic definition comes from Burgess and Lawton (1972, 6): "Events data is the term that has been coined to refer to words and deed—i.e., verbal and physical actions and reactions—that international actors (such as statesmen, national elites, intergovernmental organizations (IGO's) and nongovernmental international organizations (NGOs)) direct toward their domestic or external environment." These longitudinal collections of daily dyadic international events (CREON is not limited to dyadic interactions), as reported in one or more reliable public sources, indicate type of event, the substance of the event, its intensity, and the extent of cooperation or conflict expressed. A nice discussion of WEIS and COPDAB events data collections can be found in articles written by Llewellyn D. Howell, McClelland, and Jack Vincent, and published as a Symposium in *International Studies Quarterly* (1983).

The original CREON data set is slightly different from other events data collections (see Callahan 1982 and C. Hermann et al. 1973). Unlike WEIS and COPDAB, CREON attempts to develop measures of multiple attributes of foreign policy behavior: the context of the decision, the foreign policy output, and the characteristics of the outcome. In this effort, CREON benefits from the diversity of intellectual training of its main researchers and by the conscious decision to develop multivariate explanations for foreign policy. On the negative side, the non-random sample of states and time periods on which data were collected causes the project to come under some criticism.

Events data research is exciting because it allows scholars to deal in detail with the basic "stuff" of foreign policy in a systematic way. There are problems and limitations with each of these data collections, however. For example, they are expensive and time-consuming to create and maintain. In the current atmosphere of tight funding, there are questions about whether the insights obtained from research using these data justify the investment in time and resources required. The heavy (though not exclusive) focus on nation-states, despite the recognition that non-state actors are often extremely important, causes some to ask whether events data miss crucial events, and raises concerns of unintentional bias of coverage (based in part on the fact that "authoritative data" are scarce outside the Western developed world). There is also a question of defining what "counts" as an event in the first place. How, for example, would one code the Palestinian *intifada*? Finally, there is widespread acknowledgment that this is a methodology ill-suited to a number of crucial foreign policy questions, such as the decision *not* to undertake a particular action. Both non-events and events that cannot be operationalized are left out of these data sets, though they may reflect important facets of a situation. Despite these reservations, events data research continues to hold an important place in CFP; for many, it is one of the identifying trademarks of the CFP approach.

Finally, a third reason for pulling out CFP research for separate attention is that scholars working within this framework have been unusually conscientious—some would say too much so—in assessing the state of the subfield, charting its evolution, measuring its progress against expectations, extolling its virtues, and criticizing its weaknesses. This evaluative aspect has been present from the inception of the subfield: in 1966 Rosenau wrote the "pre-theories" article and a mere two years later came out with his "Fad, Fantasy or Field?" piece to "identify the fad and fantasy dimensions [of CFP] in order to minimize confusion and contradiction as the field evolves" (1968, 68). During the 1970s, Kegley et al. (1975), C. Hermann (1978), and Rosenau (1974, 1975, 1976) engaged in stock-taking activities, and in the past several years East (1987), C. Hermann and Peacock (1987), Gregory A. Raymond (1987), Neil R. Richardson (1987), Rosenau (1984, 1988), Starr (1988), and others have attempted to chart "new directions" for the field. Nor have these evaluative activities been limited to those within the field. Richard Ashley (1976, 1987) has been a critic of CFP for well over a decade, commenting in 1976 that CFP had a "static or degenerating research nucleus" (155); Ib Faurby (1976a, 1976b), Martin Hollis and Steve Smith (1989), Richard Merritt (1987), Donald Munton (1976), and Smith (1987), among others, have also taken CFP seriously enough to criticize. (The article by James A. Caporaso et al. 1987 does not fit neatly into either group; it includes insights from both "insiders" and what might be called "friendly opponents".)

What are the conclusions of these critics? Has CFP accomplished the goals it set for itself? Certainly there have been accomplishments. Caporaso et al. (1987, 35) stress the newness of the field and the progress made during a relatively short period of time: "A field that was once data-poor now has substantial resources in certain areas; vague and imprecise concepts have been replaced by operationalized ones; statistical analyses and their interpretation are far more sophisticated; and there is consensus on why and how hypotheses should be tested." All of this is to the good, but it is primarily foundational. Are there concrete empirical findings that have come out of this research? Regrettably, there have been relatively few empirically based CFP research efforts (at least within the "core"); to a large extent the field is still, after over twenty years, in the process of defining itself. C. Hermann and Peacock (1987, 20) suggest several generalizations identified over the years from the empirical work that *has* been done.

- the importance of a nation's size in differentiating the volume of foreign policy behavior
- the prevalence of 'maintenance' or 'participation' activities in the overall volume of foreign actions of states
- the tendency of decision-making activities to cluster among a small group of top officials in a foreign policy crisis

- the distinction between dyadic behavior and behaviors in which multiple recipients are addressed

- the absence of an unmediated relationship between a country's domestic conflict and international conflict

However, as C. Hermann and Peacock point out, these findings have not been integrated into broader theoretical formations. Thus, there has not been as yet the kind of cumulative growth of knowledge that is considered desirable. Since this is supposed to be CFP's *raison d'être*—the justification for using the CFP approach rather than other methodologies—the lack of cumulative growth of knowledge represents a serious problem. Little wonder that words such as "malaise" (Vasquez 1986, 205) have been used to describe the subfield of foreign policy.

Why has the CFP approach not resulted in the dramatic intellectual breakthroughs originally anticipated? One reason has already been mentioned: a great deal of time and effort has been spent in background activities—creating typologies, operationalizing concepts, and so forth—rather than in actually conducting empirical research. Whether this was necessary or self-indulgent is still unclear, at least to me. But what *is* clear is that frameworks and assessments, although they have an honored and valuable place, do not directly extend knowledge the same way empirical research has the potential to do.

Another issue that constrains comparative foreign policy research is the static conceptualization of many of the frameworks and models developed:

> The macro question "When and why do certain policy activities occur?" leads to an enumeration of potential explanatory sources—the nature of the international system, the immediate policy actions of other actors in the environment, the structure of the actor's society or economy, the nature of the domestic political system, the personal characteristics of leaders. . . . But time, evolutionary processes, system transformations, or primary feedback mechanisms are seldom considered. The impact of foreign policy on the subsequent condition of explanatory variables or the possibility that explanatory variables might respond dynamically to one another is rarely explored. (Caporaso et al. 1987, 37)

The problem with a nondynamic conception of foreign policy is obvious: it is far from reality! Foreign policy is the ultimate interactive activity; there is continuous feedback both within and among international actors. Any approach that is unable to incorporate time and change in foreign policy will have difficulty accurately explaining why foreign policy occurs in the particular ways it does.

Earlier in the essay, I argued that scientific international relations and classical foreign policy have rarely interacted with one another since the behavioral revolution in political science. East points out that this lack of interaction leaves comparative foreign policy researchers in an intellectual limbo:

> [T]he CFP literature by and large has not become part of the main-stream foreign policy literature. It is considered suspect by many of the more "conventional" foreign policy scholars who are skeptical about generalizing across nations or time periods. Area specialists often consider CFP studies lacking in sensitivity to the background and culture of the various countries being studied. And research methodologists and theorists raise questions about the validity of the data, especially events data, and the simplistic ad hoc hypothesizing. (1987, 37)

Munton's (1976) proposed solution is to (re)merge CFP and scientific international relations. To some extent, this has already occurred: in general CFP people talk to international relations scholars more than to classical foreign policy analysts. At the same time, CFP and classical approaches have a great deal to learn from one another and merging CFP and scientific IR makes such cross-fertilization even less likely to occur than it is already. A related critique is raised by Faurby (1967a) and Smith (1987), who object to the way that CFP conceptions of the comparative method and of scientific research on foreign policy have come to be viewed by some as the only appropriate models available. This is surely not the fault of CFP scholars alone; nevertheless, Faurby and Smith make an important point: not only has CFP evolved in a relatively narrow direction methodologically, it has also been unnecessarily restrictive in terms of the substantive issues addressed. In particular, I have in mind the relative lack of "core" CFP research in an international political economy framework; others (e.g. Starr 1988) have also mentioned that CFP has dealt to only a limited extent with the potential importance of issue areas.

FUTURE DIRECTIONS

God has chosen to give the easy problems to the physicists.
—Lave and March (1975, 2)

In his introduction to *New Directions in Comparative Foreign Policy*, Rosenau comments:

> It is perhaps a measure of movement into a new, more mature era of inquiry that philosophical and methodological argumentation is conspicuously absent from these essays. Where earlier works were pervaded with efforts to clarify the epistemological foundations and methodological premises on which the analysis rested, here such mat-

ters are largely taken for granted. Gone are the triumphant paragraphs extolling science, the holier-than-thou espousals of quantification, and the elaborate claims as to the virtues of one method over another. No longer do researchers need to parade their commitment to scientific methods. Now, instead, they just practice them. (1987, 5–6)

The question this raises, however, is whether the lack of epistemological argumentation is good or bad. Obviously, too much introspection is deadly for a field: scholars ought to be doing their research, rather than endlessly debating about it. Kenneth Oye's pithy comment sums it up well: "To avoid studying world politics, study how others study world politics" (1987, 1). At the same time, one of the central challenges facing those who value the scientific study of foreign policy is to figure out why the approach has continually failed to attract the wide participation seen in other subfields of international relations. What is it about foreign policy analysis that makes such a large portion of the academic community apparently resistant to the behavioralist approach? The first part of the chapter suggests some factors leading to the current state of affairs, but it does not fully grapple with whether these factors are immutable or reversible. Thus we cannot duck the epistemological and methodological issues or assume they have been settled. There is a continuing need to go back to those basic debates and ask whether the intellectual assumptions and underpinnings of the scientific study of foreign policy are valid and how behavioral and classical scholars can better make use of each others' skills and insights.

A step in this direction was taken by a number of scholars in the comparative foreign policy tradition, who, with their acceptance of some of the criticisms raised in the 1970s about their approach, have restructured cross-dyadic comparative foreign policy research in some interesting ways. A similar openness and creativity on the part of classical foreign policy scholars would be welcomed. Classical foreign policy analysis is facing a problem. On the one hand, area studies scholars have real and legitimate frustrations with some of the behavioralist theories and empirical tests, wincing at the basic and significant errors made, because of the desire to generalize, when discussing a specific region of the world. The classical, often area studies–trained, scholars have a point when they criticize behavioralists for generalizing at the expense of accuracy. Looking for the big picture may mean dropping out details, but it should not include distorting the landscape beyond recognition. The classical criticism of the behavioralists is not so much that behavioralists are looking at the forest rather than the trees—as the behavioralists often protest—but rather that the behavioralists burn down the forest and then model only the charred stumps that remain. Furthermore, the best classical studies of foreign policy already follow the recommendations being made for improving foreign policy research: they take international political economy variables into account, they are dynamic, with a sense of time and change, they include feedback mechanisms, work at multiple levels, are sensitive to detail and context, and so forth. In short, they are able to address precisely the areas in which the behavioralist research is weak.

At the same time, there *is* a problem with the frequent noncumulativeness of classical foreign policy research, not to mention the lack of common ground with other foreign policy scholars who are not interested in exactly the same region of the world or issue area. Behavioralist research is more easily generalizable, is frequently more precise in its measurement of central concepts, and has been able to uncover bilateral and multilateral relationships that had eluded the classical scholars. It has also challenged some of the conventional wisdom and indicated places where the truisms fail the test of empirical verification, most notably balance of power.

Can the strengths of classical and behavioralist foreign policy analysis be united in some way to enhance both and reduce inadequacies in each? Clearly this is the challenge facing the field of foreign policy in the 1990s. The intellectual problems—and the practical need to better understand the foreign policy process—demand that foreign policy scholars of all varieties be working, if not together, at least on a complementary course. What does this suggest in the way of future directions?

One interesting approach, part of the CREON II project, considers the impact of decision structures on foreign policy (see M. Hermann 1988; C. Hermann 1988; Hagan 1988). Their work attempts to make sense of the diverse theories about who makes foreign policy decisions and what the decision-making process looks like, and suggests that the form of "ultimate decision unit," and the nature of the process within the decision unit, affect both the actual decision and its impact domestically and internationally. Three types of decision units are identified:

- *a predominant leader* ("a single individual has the power to make the choice for the government")
- *a single group* ("all the individuals necessary for allocation decisions participate in the group and the group makes decisions through an interactive process among its members")
- *multiple autonomous actors* ("the decision cannot involve any superior group or individual that can independently resolve differences existing among the groups or that can reverse any decision the groups reach collectively")

An elaborate decision tree is then used to determine the ultimate decision unit in each situation (Hermann, Hermann, and Hagan 1987).

The implication is that different factors will be important for each type of decision unit. When there is a predominant leader, for example, the personality attributes of that individual, his or her sensitivity or insensitivity to the international and domestic environment, and his or her belief systems will be of central importance. Although these factors will also be important for each member of multiple autonomous groups, other factors also enter into the calculus, such as the nature of the relationships among the groups. Research on twenty-five states between 1959 and 1968 suggests that "there are differences in behavior among predominant leaders, single groups, and multiple autonomous actors decision units that can be accentuated depending on whether the particular unit is open (externally influenceable) or closed (self-contained) to forces outside itself in the decision-making process" (Hermann and Hermann 1989, 384). CREON II researchers are now applying this approach to specific countries with a wide variety of attributes.

The CREON II approach is consistent with most of the research on expert systems, virtually all of which operate by asking a small number of general questions first—which narrow down a case to a specific category—and then asking specific questions to figure out the "answer" (to whatever the problem is). So, for example, a medical expert system will ask a few general questions ("Where does it hurt?" "Do you have a fever?") to form a hypothesis about the problem, then narrow down the questions to specifics. In other words, a very different set of questions will be asked if the patient seems to have a cold than if she appears to have appendicitis. This, of course, seems like complete common sense until one realizes that it is *not* the approach used by many of the data analysis projects of the 1960s and 1970s (particularly regression analysis, factor analysis, and other linear models), which used the same data for everything.

Maria Papadakis and Harvey Starr (1987) follow a different angle with their environmental model. After identifying what they see as weaknesses in the CFP literature they set out to remedy these problems through a synthesis of several earlier approaches, including Sprout and Sprout (1957), Singer (1969b), Rosenau (1966), and Starr's (1978; see also Most and Starr 1989) conceptualization of "opportunity" and "willingness."

> The state is an entity in an environment, and the environment may be divided into different levels with different sets of variables characterizing each level. The environment defines the context within which a state may act, but how the state *actually acts* or deals with its environment depends upon a number of factors: the set of opportunities that the characteristics of the sub-environments 'objectively' provide the state, how the state perceives its environment, its willingness to take a particular course of action, and so on. (Papadakis and Starr 1987, 416)

Papadakis and Starr stress that their model, with its focus on foreign policy decision-making within a particular environmental matrix, is more than the traditional set of "significant factors" added up:

> [T]he environment may affect states in different ways, even though they may possess similar environmental factors. . . . constraints implied by one set of factors can be overcome by the opportunities provided by another. . . . This is not to assert that because each nation possesses a different environmental matrix that no theories, generalizations or patterns of foreign policy may be detected. (418–19)

This environmental context approach is used by Papadakis and Starr to explore in a preliminary way whether traditional assumptions about the linkage between size, power, and foreign policy behavior are appropriate for analysis of small states. In modified form, it has also served as the basis for at least one doctoral dissertation: Tarek Chaya's (1989) research on Syrian foreign policy during the regime of Hafez al-Assad.

There are other directions in which the field could move as well. It seems obvious that one very basic step is to include more research that deals with Third World states. At present, the majority of foreign policy research deals with major powers or European states. Even the cross-national aggregate data studies often have an unintentional bias, either due to the unavailability of data for Third World states or because the variables chosen come out of Western conceptions of political processes, structures, and ideologies. The Third World includes countries with cultures, histories, positions in the world economy, and ways of organizing themselves politically that are vastly different from those of advanced industrial societies. These differences must be taken into account as we formulate questions and test hypotheses. It may be premature to expect grand theoretical constructs or even nomothetic intent when it comes to research on foreign policy and the Third World: even idiographic case studies, with no expectation of explicit cumulativeness or intentional comparability, would be a step forward toward a fuller integration of Third World foreign policy goals, decision-making processes, and activities into our knowledge base.

In addition, there is a great need for systematic, empirical foreign policy research that focuses on individual case studies rather than relying solely on large, cross-dyadic correlational studies. This argument is made in different ways by both Rosenau (1987) and Richardson (1987); it is reflective of a more general defense of the value of case studies within a behavioralist tradition (e.g. Verba 1967; Lijphart 1971; Eckstein 1975; George 1979). Rosenau is optimistic about the potential value to come from such research, and believes it could serve as a bridge between the classical area specialists and the behavioralists:

Yet, despite their differences, achieving a theoretical synthesis between the two perspectives is not nearly as difficult as it may seem. All [!!] that is required is a concession on the part of the generalists [behavioralists] that comparing shifts in the key variables that sustain the same system across time is as much a form of scientific inquiry as comparing their operation across different systems, while all the specialists need to concede is that the functioning of any system at any moment in time can derive from generalized dynamics that condition many systems as well as from its unique cultural and historical experiences. . . . Any single-country theory must synthesize idiographic and nomothetic knowledge, that is, the most salient aspects of a country's uniqueness as well as the dynamics it shares with other countries. (1987, 61, 64)

This approach has another advantage: it allows the reintroduction of the interactive dimension of foreign policy behavior called for by Richardson (1987) and others.

Another set of prescriptions has to do with the issues addressed. Although there are no guarantees that any of these areas of research will revolutionize our understanding of foreign policy, their value in related fields suggests further investigation might well be profitable. First, foreign policy research needs to incorporate more of the insights of international political economy. In particular, the implications for foreign policy decision-making of the increased interdependence of national economies need to be more fully developed. This argument has been made persuasively by Caporaso et al. (1987), Moon (1987), Starr (1988) and others, and does not need to be reiterated here.

Greater attention also needs to be given to the role of the state in the development of foreign policy. As Moon points out: "Foreign policy behavior cannot be understood without an appreciation of the goals and priorities, the internal and external constraints, and the perceptions and expectations which guide state action. Thus, any theory of foreign policy behavior must contain within it a theory of the state, however unconscious or incomplete" (1989, 2). Scholars need to formulate more carefully exactly what is meant by the "state" and articulate more clearly the implications of conventional and radical theoretical approaches, a task well begun some years ago by Patrick McGowan and Stephen G. Walker (1981). Does it matter to our conception of the policy process, for example, whether the state is understood as an autonomous entity or as merely an expression of class or other domestic interests? To what extent is the state a reflection of concrete and relatively enduring institutional structures? What is meant by a weak state or a strong state, and what are the implications of these concepts? Does a "state-centered" approach, with its focus on the limits and scope of state action, reveal hitherto unrecognized aspects of foreign policy-making? (For two very different approaches to the importance of the state, see the volumes edited by Ikenberry, Lake, and Mastanduno 1988; and by Evans, Rueschemeyer, and Skocpol 1985.)

Third, research on perception and cognition, including artificial intelligence studies on the process of thinking about foreign policy decisions, is a promising avenue that deserves greater attention, in part because it focuses attention on the notion of *choice* in foreign policy-making. In particular, the AI models employ more case-specific information in their modeling of the foreign policy process than most of the earlier formal models did. They are also capable of modeling complex decision-making processes that involve past actions, bureaucratic bargaining, and information flow, an advance from the simplistic models of maximization by rational unitary actors that characterized many earlier formal models.

The field of foreign policy evaluation introduces another set of issues that have not been fully explored. Though policy evaluation has long been a part of research on domestic public policy (e.g. Cronbach et al. 1980; Haveman and Margolis 1983; Palumbo, Fawcett, and Wright 1981; Nachmias 1980; Weiss 1972), relatively few foreign policy analysts take this approach (e.g. Ashley 1986; Bobrow and Stoker 1981; Hoole 1977; Raymond 1987). There are a number of different types of evaluation research; foreign policy evaluation tends to be closest to summative evaluation, which "focuses on the extent to which policy outcomes contribute to the achievement of goals and objectives" and formative research, which examines "whether and how well a program is implemented" (Palumbo 1988, 127, 131). But specifying "goals" or measuring "success" or "extent of implementation" is not a straightforward task, as evaluation researchers have learned. John A. Vasquez suggests how evaluation research could work in the foreign policy arena:

> At least two standard criteria can be employed in foreign policy evaluation research. The first criterion is that a policy should be based on an understanding of world politics that appears accurate. . . .
>
> A second criterion for evaluation research is that a policy should accomplish what it was intended to do, and that unintended consequences should not outweigh the benefits of the policy. (1986, 5, 9)

Foreign policy evaluation suggests one way in which analysts can bridge the gap between scholar and practitioner. Scholars interested in this approach would be well served, however, by reviewing with care the debates in the public policy literature about the role of evaluation research, controversies regarding its accuracy in measuring the phenomenon it is intended to measure, and concerns about its potential for political manipulation.

Finally, there is a whole set of operationalization and measurement questions that require attention: What is it that we are studying? What counts as evidence? How can the data be improved so we can ask interesting questions rather than being constrained by the variables on which we have information? A key goal must be figuring out ways to deal with foreign policy non-events as well as with events. In addition, with the increase in data available in machine-readable form—for example, the information available from commercial electronic data bases such as NEXUS and large data available on CD-ROM—it may be possible for behavioral studies to incorporate more of the variables that classical theories indicate are important.

Is foreign policy analysis purely rubbish, is it in a rut and engaging in research that is merely routine, or is it experiencing a renaissance? Elements of all three are clearly in evidence at the present time, with the balance tilting in favor of a renaissance. What is exciting is that the potential elements for a reinvigorated field are being put into place: inclusion of Third World states into the analyses; a greater focus on international political economy; more attention to theories of the state; the use of case studies, particularly with sensitivity to theoretical issues; recognition of the importance of individual actors and other decision units; a nudging open of the "black box" through artificial intelligence techniques; a reinterpretation of the decision-making environment.

What many of these factors suggest is that we would be well served by a movement away from grand theory—trying to explain all aspects of foreign policy for all countries at all points in time—in favor of more mid-range theories. This conclusion is not a new one: Benjamin A. Most and Harvey Starr reached a similar judgment several years ago:

> There may well be a variety of social laws, each of which is true, but which should be expected to hold only under certain—perhaps very special—conditions. Although it is possible that universal, always true, laws exist . . . it is difficult to think of very many empirical universals that have been identified even by physical scientists. Thus, it may be useful to recognize that there could very well be laws that are in some sense "good," "domain-specific," or "nice," even though the relationships that they imply are not necessarily empirically general. Rather than assuming that there needs to be a single "always true" law that accounts for a given phenomenon whenever and wherever it has occurred or will occur, it may be more productive to think of several laws, each of which is always true under certain conditions (or within certain domains), but which is only sometimes true empirically because those conditions do not always hold in the empirical world. (1984, 402)

By taking a more modest approach, the field of foreign policy analysis will enhance its prospects of advancing understanding of this large and challenging intellectual problem.

REFERENCES

Alker, Hayward J., and Cheryl Christensen. 1972. "From Causal Modeling to Artificial Intelligence: The Evolving of a UN Peace-Making Simulation." In *Experimentation and Simulation in Political Science*, edited by J. A. LaPonce and P. Smoker. Toronto: University of Toronto Press.

Alker, Hayward J., and W. Greenberg. 1976. "On Simulating Collective Security Regime Alternatives." In *Thought and Action in Foreign Policy*, edited by M. Bonham and M. Shapiro. Basel: Birkhauser Verlag.

Alker, Hayward J., James P. Bennett, and Dwain Mefford. 1980. "Generalized Precedent Logics for Resolving Security Dilemmas." *International Interactions* 7:165–200.

Allison, Graham T. 1969. "Conceptual Models and the Cuban Missile Crisis." *American Political Science Review* 63(3):689–718.

———. 1971. *Essence of Decision: Explaining the Cuban Missile Crisis*. Boston: Little, Brown.

Allison, Graham T., and Morton H. Halperin. 1972. "Bureaucratic Politics: A Paradigm and Some Policy Implications." In *Theory and Policy in International Relations*, edited by Raymond Tanter and Richard H. Ullman. (Published as a Supplement to *World Politics* 24.)

Almond, Gabriel. 1960. *The American People and Foreign Policy*. Rev. ed. New York: Frederick A. Praeger.

Almond, Gabriel, and James S. Coleman, eds. 1960. *The Politics of Developing Areas*. Princeton: Princeton University Press.

Anderson, Paul A. 1981. "Justifications and Precedents as Constraints in Foreign Policy Decision-Making." *American Journal of Political Science* 25(4): 738–61.

Anderson, Paul A., and Stuart Thorson. 1982. "Artificial Intelligence Based Simulations of Foreign Policy Decision-Making." *Behavioral Science* 27: 176–93.

Andriole, Stephen J. 1979. "Another Perspective on Foreign Policy Making and Foreign Policy Research." *International Studies Quarterly* 23(1):155–63.

Art, Robert. 1973. "Bureaucratic Politics and American Foreign Policy: A Critique." *Policy Sciences* 4:467–90. (Reprinted in Robert J. Art and Robert Jervis, eds. *International Politics: Anarchy, Force, Political Economy, and Decision Making*. 2nd ed. Boston: Little, Brown.)

Ashley, Richard K. 1976. "Noticing Pre-Paradigmatic Progress." In *In Search of Global Patterns*, edited by James Rosenau. New York: Free Press.

———. 1986. "At the Impasse: Epistemology and the Scientific Evaluation of Foreign Policy." In *Evaluating U.S. Foreign Policy*, edited by John A. Vasquez. New York: Praeger Publishers.

———. 1987. "Foreign Policy as Political Performance." *International Studies Notes* 13(2):51–54.

Auerbach, Yehudit, and Hemda Ben-Yehuda. 1987. "Attitudes towards an Existence Conflict: Begin and Dayan on the Palestinian Issue." *International Interactions* 13(4):323–51.

Barnet, Richard J. 1972. *Roots of War: The Men and the Institutions behind U.S. Foreign Policy*. New York: Penguin.

Beres, Louis René. 1986. "The End of American Foreign Policy." *Third World Quarterly* 8(4):1253–70.

Biddle, William Jesse, and John D. Stephens. "Dependent Development and Foreign Policy: The Case of Jamaica." *International Studies Quarterly* 33(4):411–34.

Blachman, Morris J., and Kenneth Sharpe. 1986. "De-democratising American Foreign Policy: Dismantling the Post-Vietnam Formula." *Third World Quarterly* 8(4):1271–1308.

Bobrow, Davis B. 1972. *International Relations: New Approaches*. New York: Free Press.

Bobrow, Davis B., Steve Chan, and John A. Kringen. 1979. *Understanding Foreign Policy Decisions: The Chinese Case*. New York: Free Press.

Bobrow, Davis B., and R. Stoker. 1981. "Evaluation of Foreign Policy." In *Cumulation in International Relations Research*. Vol. 18(3), edited by P. T. Hopmann, Dina Zinnes, and J. David Singer. Denver: Monograph Series in World Affairs.

Bobrow, Davis B., Donald A. Sylvan, and Brian Ripley. 1986. "Japanese Supply Security: A Computational Model." Paper presented at the annual meeting of the International Studies Association, Anaheim, Calif.

Braybrooke, David, and Charles E. Lindblom. 1963. *A Strategy of Decision: Policy Evaluation as a Social Process*. New York: Free Press.

Brecher, Michael. 1969. *Political Leadership in India: An Analysis of Elite Attitudes*. New York: Praeger.

———. 1972. *The Foreign Policy System of Israel: Settings, Images, Process*. New Haven: Yale University Press.

———. 1975. *Decisions in Israel's Foreign Policy*. New Haven: Yale University Press.

Brecher, Michael, with Benjamin Geist. 1980. *Decisions in Crisis: Israel, 1967 and 1973*. Berkeley: University of California Press.

Brecher, Michael, Blema Steinberg, and Janice Stein. 1969. "A Framework for Research on Foreign Policy Behavior." *Journal of Conflict Resolution* 13: 75–101.

Brody, Richard A. 1975. "Problems in the Measurement and Analysis of International Events." In *International Events and the Comparative Analysis of Foreign Policy*, edited by Charles W. Kegley Jr., Gregory A. Raymond, Robert Rood, and Richard Skinner. Columbia: University of South Carolina Press.

Bull, Hedley. 1966. "International Theory: The Case for a Classical Approach." *World Politics* 18(3):361–77.

Burgess, P. M., and R. W. Lawton. 1972. *Indicators of International Behavior: An Assessment of Events Data Research.* Beverly Hills: Sage.

Burrowes, Robert. 1975. " 'Mirror, Mirror, on the Wall. . . . ' A Comparison of Events Data Sources." In *Comparing Foreign Policies*, edited by James N. Rosenau. New York: John Wiley & Sons for Sage Publications.

Callahan, Patrick. 1982. "The CREON Project." In *Describing Foreign Policy Behavior*, edited by Patrick Callahan, Linda P. Brady, and Margaret G. Hermann. Beverly Hills: Sage.

Caporaso, James A., Charles F. Hermann, Charles W. Kegley, Jr., James N. Rosenau, and Dina A. Zinnes. 1987. "The Comparative Study of Foreign Policy: Perspectives on the Future." *International Studies Notes* 13(2): 32–46.

Carleton, David, and Michael Stohl. 1987. "The Role of Human Rights in U.S. Foreign Assistance Policy: A Critique and Reappraisal." *American Journal of Political Science* 31(4):1002–18.

Chaya, Tarek. 1989. "An Environmental Approach to the Study of Small States' Foreign Policy: The Case of Syria under the Assad Regime." Ph.D. diss., Northwestern University.

Cimbala, Stephen. 1987. *Artificial Intelligence and National Security.* Lexington: Lexington Books.

Cingranelli, David L., and Thomas E. Pasquarello. 1985. "Human Rights Practices and the Distribution of U.S. Foreign Aid to Latin American Countries." *American Journal of Political Science* 29(3):539–63.

Clymer, Adam. 1985. "Polling Americans." *The New York Times Magazine.* 10 November.

Cohen, Benjamin J. 1985. "International Debt and Linkage Strategies: Some Foreign Policy Implications for the United States." *International Organization* 39(4):699–727.

Cohen, Bernard C. 1963. *The Press and Foreign Policy.* Princeton: Princeton University Press.

———. 1973. *The Public's Impact on Foreign Policy.* Boston: Little, Brown.

Cohen, Bernard C., and Scott A. Harris. 1975. "Foreign Policy." In *Handbook of Political Science.* Vol. 6, *Policies and Policymaking*, edited by Fred I. Greenstein and Nelson Polsby. Reading, Mass.: Addison-Wesley.

Cohen, Stephen D. 1981. *The Making of United States Economic Policy.* 2nd ed. Boulder: Praeger.

Crabb, Cecil V., and Kevin Mulcahy. 1986. *Presidents and Foreign Policy Making.* Baton Rouge: Louisiana State University Press.

Cronbach, Lee J., et al. 1980. *Toward Reform of Program Evaluation: Aims, Methods, and Institutional Arrangements.* San Francisco: Jossey-Bass.

Cronin, Thomas E. 1980. "A Resurgent Congress and the Imperial Presidency." *Political Science Quarterly* 95:209–37.

Davison, W. P. 1958. *The Berlin Blockade*. Princeton: Princeton University Press.

Destler, I. M. 1972. *Presidents, Bureaucrats, and Foreign Policy*. Princeton: Princeton University Press.

————. 1983. "The Rise of the National Security Assistant, 1961–1981." In *Perspectives on American Foreign Policy*, edited by Charles W. Kegley, Jr., and Eugene R. Wittkopf. New York: St. Martin's Press.

Dolan, Michael B., and Brian W. Tomlin. 1984. "Foreign Policy in Asymmetrical Dyads: Theoretical Reformulation and Empirical Analysis, Canada-US Relations, 1963–1972." *International Studies Quarterly* 28(3):349–68.

East, Maurice A. 1978. "National Attributes and Foreign Policy." In *Why Nations Act: Theoretical Perspectives for Comparative Foreign Policy*, edited by Maurice East, Stephen Salmore, and Charles Hermann. Beverly Hills: Sage.

————. 1987. "The Comparative Study of Foreign Policy: We're Not There Yet, But . . . " *International Studies Notes* 13(2):31.

East, Maurice A., and Charles F. Hermann. 1975. "Do Nation Types Account for Foreign Policy Behavior?" In *Comparing Foreign Policies*, edited by James N. Rosenau. New York: John Wiley & Sons for Sage Publications.

Eckstein, Harry. 1975. "Case Study and Theory in Political Science." In *Handbook of Political Science*. Vol. 7, *Strategies of Inquiry*, edited by Fred I. Greenstein and Nelson Polsby. Reading, Mass.: Addison-Wesley.

Erikson, Robert, Norman Luttbeg, and Kent L. Tedin. 1980. *American Public Opinion*. 2nd ed. New York: Wiley.

Etheredge, Lloyd S. 1978a. "Personality Effects on American Foreign Policy, 1898–1968: A Test of Interpersonal Generalization Theory." *American Political Science Review* 72(2):434–51.

————. 1978b. *A World of Men: The Private Sources of American Foreign Policy*. Cambridge: MIT Press.

Evangelista, Matthew. 1989. "Issue-Area and Foreign Policy Revisited." *International Organization* 43(1):147–71.

Evans, Peter, Dietrich Rueschemeyer, and Theda Skocpol, eds. 1985. *Bringing the State Back In*. Cambridge: Cambridge University Press.

Farr, James. 1988. "The History of Political Science." *American Journal of Political Science* 32(4):1175–95.

Faurby, Ib. 1976a. "Premises, Promises, and Problems of Comparative Foreign Policy." *Cooperation and Conflict* 11:139–62.

————. 1976b. "The Lack of Cumulation in Foreign Policy Studies: The Case of Britain and the European Community." *European Journal of Political Research* 4:205–25.

Ferguson, Thomas. 1986. "The Right Consensus? Holsti and Rosenau's New Foreign Policy Belief Surveys." *International Studies Quarterly* 30(4): 411–23.

Festinger, Leon. 1957. *A Theory of Cognitive Dissonance*. Evanston: Row, Peterson.

Free, Lloyd A., and Hedley Cantril. 1968. *The Political Beliefs of Americans*. New York: Simon & Schuster.

Gelb, Leslie H. 1980. "Why Not the State Department?" *The Washington Quarterly*, White Paper, Special Supplement to the Autumn issue.

Gelb, Leslie H., and Richard K. Betts. 1979. *The Irony of Vietnam: The System Worked*. Washington, D.C.: Brookings Institution.

George, Alexander L. 1969. "The 'Operational Code': A Neglected Approach to the Study of Political Leaders and Decision-Making." *International Studies Quarterly* 13(2):190–222.

———. 1975. "The Use of Information." Appendix D. Commission on the Organization of the Government for the Conduct of Foreign Policy. Vol. 2. Washington, D.C.: U.S. Government Printing Office.

———. 1979. "Case Studies and Theory Development: The Method of Structured, Focused Comparison." In *Diplomacy: New Approaches in History, Theory, and Policy*, edited by Paul Gorden Lauren. New York: Free Press.

———. 1980. "Adapting to Constraints on Rational Decisionmaking." In *International Politics: Anarchy, Force, Political Economy, and Decision Making*. 2nd ed. Edited by Robert J. Art and Robert Jervis. Boston: Little, Brown.

Gerner, Deborah J. 1988. "Weapons for Repression? U.S. Arms Transfers and the Third World." In *Terrible beyond Endurance: The Foreign Policy of State Terrorism*, edited by Michael Stohl and George Lopez. Westport, Conn.: Greenwood Press.

———. 1990."Missed Opportunities and Roads Not Taken: The Eisenhower Administration and the Palestinians." *Arab Studies Quarterly* 12(1–2): 67–100.

Gerner, Deborah J., and Arthur Sanders. 1988. "United States Public Opinion towards the Arab States of the Persian Gulf." Paper presented at the annual meeting of the International Studies Association, St. Louis.

Hagan, Joe D. 1986. "Domestic Political Conflict, Issue Areas, and Some Dimensions of Foreign Policy Behavior other than Conflict." *International Interactions* 12(4):291–313.

———. 1988. "The Impact of Multiple Autonomous Actors." Paper presented at the annual meeting of the International Studies Association, St. Louis.

———. 1990. *Political Opposition and Foreign Policy in Comparative Perspective*. Boulder: Lynne Rienner Publishers.

Halperin, Morton H., and Arnold Kanter. 1973. "The Bureaucratic Perspective: A Preliminary Framework." In *Readings in American Foreign Policy*, edited by Halperin and Kanter. Boston: Little, Brown.

Halperin, Morton H., with Priscilla Clapp and Arnold Kanter. 1974. *Bureaucratic Politics and Foreign Policies*. Washington, D.C.: Brookings Institution.

Haveman, Robert H., and Julius Margolis, eds. 1983. *Public Expenditure and Policy Analysis*. 3rd ed. Boston: Houghton Mifflin.

Hermann, Charles F. 1969a. "International Crisis as a Situational Variable." In *International Politics and Foreign Policy*. Rev. ed. Edited by James N. Rosenau. New York: Free Press.

————. 1969b. *Crisis in Foreign Policy*. Indianapolis: Bobbs-Merrill.

————. 1978. "Foreign Policy Behavior: That Which Is to Be Explained." In *Why Nations Act: Theoretical Perspectives for Comparative Foreign Policy*, edited by Maurice East, Stephen Salmore, Charles Hermann. Beverly Hills: Sage.

————. 1988. "The Impact of Single Group Decision Units on Foreign Policy." Paper presented at the annual meeting of the International Studies Association, St. Louis.

Hermann, Charles F., Maurice East, Margaret G. Hermann, Barbara Salmore, and Stephen A. Salmore. 1973. *CREON: A Foreign Events Data Set*. Beverly Hills: Sage.

Hermann, Charles F., Charles W. Kegley, Jr., and James N. Rosenau, eds. 1987. *New Directions in the Study of Foreign Policy*. Boston: Allen & Unwin.

Hermann, Charles F., and Gregory Peacock. 1987. "The Evolution and Future of Theoretical Research in the Comparative Study of Foreign Policy." In *New Directions in the Study of Foreign Policy*, edited by Hermann, Charles W. Kegley, Jr., and James N. Rosenau. Boston: Allen & Unwin.

Hermann, Margaret G. 1980a. "Explaining Foreign Policy Behavior Using the Personal Characteristics of Political Leaders." *International Studies Quarterly* 24(1):7–46.

————. 1980b. "Comments on 'Foreign Policy Makers, Personality Attributes, and Interviews: A Note on Reliability Problems." *International Studies Quarterly* 24(1):67–73.

————. 1983. "Leaders, Leadership, and American Foreign Policy." In *Perspectives on American Foreign Policy*, edited by Charles W. Kegley, Jr., and Eugene R. Wittkopf. New York: St. Martin's Press.

————. 1988. "The Impact of Single Predominant Leaders." Paper presented at the annual meeting of the International Studies Association, St. Louis.

Hermann, Margaret G., and Charles Hermann. 1989. "Who Makes Foreign Policy Decisions and How: An Empirical Inquiry." *International Studies Quarterly* 33(4):361–87.

Hermann, Margaret G., Charles Hermann, and Joe D. Hagan. 1987. "How Decision Units Shape Foreign Policy Behavior." In *New Directions in the Study of Foreign Policy*, edited by Charles Hermann, Charles W. Kegley, Jr., and James N. Rosenau. Boston: Allen & Unwin.

Hermann, Richard K. 1985. *Perceptions and Behavior In Soviet Foreign Policy*. Pittsburgh: University of Pittsburgh Press.

————. 1986. "The Power of Perceptions in Foreign Policy Decision Making:

Do Views of the Soviet Union Determine the Policy Choices of American Leaders?" *American Journal of Political Science* 30(4):841–75.

Hilsman, Roger. 1952. "Intelligence and Policy Making in Foreign Affairs." *World Politics* 5:1–45.

———. 1959. "The Foreign-Policy Consensus: An Interim Report." *Journal of Conflict Resolution* 3:361–82.

———. 1987. *The Politics of Policy Making in Defense and Foreign Affairs: Conceptual Models and Bureaucratic Politics.* Englewood Cliffs, N.J.: Prentice-Hall.

Hoffman, Stanley. 1977. "An American Social Science: International Relations." *Daedalus* (Summer):41–60.

Hollis, Martin, and Steve Smith. 1989. "A Methodological Critique of Comparative Foreign Policy Analysis." Paper presented at the annual meeting of the International Studies Association, London.

Holsti, Kal J. 1986. "Politics in Command: Foreign Trade as National Security Policy." *International Organization* 40(3):643–71.

Holsti, Ole R. 1962. "The Belief System and National Images: A Case Study." *Journal of Conflict Resolution* 6:244–52.

———. 1970. "The 'Operational Code' Approach to the Study of Political Leaders: John Foster Dulles' Philosophical and Instrumental Beliefs." *Canadian Journal of Political Science* 3:123–57.

———. 1974. "The Study of International Politics Makes Strange Bedfellows: Theories of the Radical Right and the Radical Left." *American Political Science Review* 68(1):217–42.

———. 1976. "Foreign Policy Formation Viewed Cognitively." In *Structure of Decision*, edited by Robert Axelrod. Princeton: Princeton University Press.

———. 1979. "The Three Headed Eagle: The United States and System Change." *International Studies Quarterly* 23(3):339–59.

Holsti, Ole R., Richard A. Brody, and Robert C. North. 1964. "Measuring Effect and Action in the International Reaction Models: Empirical Materials from the 1962 Cuban Crisis." *Journal of Peace Research* 1:170–90.

———. 1968. "Perception and Action in the 1914 Crisis." In *Quantitative International Politics*, edited by J. David Singer. New York: Free Press.

Holsti, Ole R., and James N. Rosenau. 1979. "Vietnam, Consensus, and the Belief Systems of American Leaders." *World Politics* 23:1–56.

———. 1984. *American Leadership in World Affairs.* Boston: Allen & Unwin.

———. 1986a. "Consensus Lost. Consensus Regained? Foreign Policy Beliefs of American Leaders, 1976–1980." *International Studies Quarterly* 30(4): 375–409.

———. 1986b. "The Foreign Policy Beliefs of American Leaders: Some Further Thoughts on Theory and Method." *International Studies Quarterly* 30(4): 473–84.

Hoole, Frank W. 1977. "Evaluating the Impact of International Organizations." *International Organization* 31:541–63.

Howell, Llewellyn D. 1983. "A Comparative Study of the WEIS and COPDAB Data Sets." *International Studies Quarterly* 27(2):149–59.

Hudson, Valerie M. 1987. "Using a Rule-Based Production System to Estimate Foreign Policy Behavior." In *Artificial Intelligence and National Security*, edited by Stephen Cimbala. Lexington: Lexington Books.

Hudson, Valerie M., ed. 1991. *Artificial Intelligence and International Politics*. Boulder: Westview Press.

Hughes, Barry. 1978. *The Domestic Context of American Foreign Policy*. San Francisco: W. H. Freeman & Company.

Hurwitz, Jon, and Mark Peffley. 1987. "How Are Foreign Policy Attitudes Structured? A Hierarchical Model." *American Political Science Review* 81(4):1099–1120.

Ikenberry, G. John, David A. Lake, and Michael Mastanduno, eds. 1988. "The State and American Foreign Economic Policy." *International Organization* 41(1). Special Issue.

Inderfurth, Karl F., and Loch K. Johnson, eds. 1988. *Decisions of the Highest Order: Perspectives on the National Security Council*. Pacific Grove: Brooks/Cole.

Janis, Irving. 1982. *Groupthink: Psychological Studies of Policy Decisions and Fiascoes*. Boston: Houghton Mifflin.

Jentleson, Bruce W. 1987. "American Commitments in the Third World: Theory vs. Practice." *International Organization* 41(4):667–704.

Jervis, Robert. 1968. "Hypotheses on Misperception." *World Politics* 20(3): 454–79.

———. 1976. *Perception and Misperception in International Politics*. Princeton: Princeton University Press.

Job, Brian L., and Douglas Johnson. 1986. "A Model of US Foreign Policy Decision Making: The US and the Dominican Republic, 1961–1965." Paper presented at the annual meeting of the International Studies Association, Anaheim.

Job, Brian L., Douglas Johnson, and Eric Selbin. 1987. "A Multi-Agent, Script-Based Model of U.S. Foreign Policy Towards Central America." Paper presented at the annual meeting of the American Political Science Association, Chicago.

Kahneman, Daniel, Paul Slovic, and Amos Tversky. 1982. *Judgement under Uncertainty: Heuristics and Biases*. Cambridge: Cambridge University Press.

Kaw, Marita. 1989. "Predicting Soviet Military Intervention." *Journal of Conflict Resolution* 33(3):402–29.

Kegley, Charles W., Jr. 1975. "Introduction: The Generation and Use of Events Data." In *International Events and the Comparative Analysis of Foreign Pol-*

icy, edited by Kegley, Gregory A. Raymond, Robert M. Rood, and Richard A. Skinner. Columbia: University of South Carolina Press.

———. 1986. "Assumptions and Dilemmas in the Study of Americans' Foreign Policy Beliefs: A Caveat." *International Studies Quarterly* 30(4):447–71.

Kegley, Charles W., Jr., Gregory A. Raymond, Robert M. Rood, and Richard A. Skinner, eds. 1975. *International Events and the Comparative Analysis of Foreign Policy*. Columbia: University of South Carolina Press.

Kegley, Charles W., Jr., and Eugene R. Wittkopf, eds. 1983. *Perspectives on American Foreign Policy*. New York: St. Martin's Press.

Keohane, Robert O. 1983. "Theory of World Politics: Structural Realism and Beyond." In *Political Science: The State of the Discipline*, edited by Ada W. Finifter. Washington, D.C.: American Political Science Association.

Lamborn, Alan C. 1985. "Risk and Foreign Policy Choice." *International Studies Quarterly* 29(4):385–410.

Larson, Deborah Welch. 1988. "Problems of Content Analysis in Foreign Policy Research: Notes from the Study of the Origins of Cold War Belief Systems." *International Studies Quarterly* 32(2):241–55.

Lave, Charles A., and James G. March. 1975. *An Introduction to Models in the Social Science*. New York: Harper & Row.

Lebow, Richard Ned. 1981. *Between Peace and War: The Nature of International Crisis*. Baltimore: Johns Hopkins University Press.

Lijphart, Arend. 1971. "Comparative Politics and the Comparative Method." *American Political Science Review* 65:682–93.

Lyons, Gene M. 1982. "Expanding the Study of International Relations: The French Connection." *World Politics* 35:135–49.

McClelland, Charles. 1961. "The Acute International Crisis." *World Politics* 14(1).

———. 1962. "Decisional Opportunity and Political Controversy: The Quemoy Case." *Journal of Conflict Resolution* 6(3):201–13.

———. 1972. "The Beginning, Curation, and Abatement of International Crises: Comparisons in Two Conflict Arenas." In *International Crises: Insights from Behavioral Research,* edited by Charles F. Hermann. New York: Free Press.

———. 1983. "Let the User Beware." *International Studies Quarterly* 27(2): 169–78.

McClelland, Charles, and Gary D. Hoggard. 1969. "Conflict Patterns in the Interactions Among Nations." In *International Politics and Foreign Policy*. Rev. ed. Edited by James Rosenau. New York: Free Press.

McCormick, James M., and Neil Mitchell. 1988. "Is U.S. Aid Really Linked to Human Rights in Latin America?" *American Journal of Political Science* 32(1):231–39.

McGowan, Patrick. 1972. "A Bayesian Approach to the Problems of Events

Data Validity." In *Comparing Foreign Policies*, edited by James N. Rosenau. New York: John Wiley & Sons for Sage Publications.

McGowan, Patrick, and Stephen G. Walker. 1981. "Radical and Conventional Models of U.S. Foreign Economic Policy Making." *World Politics* 33(3): 347–82.

Majeski, Stephen J. 1987. "A Recommendation Model of War Initiation: The Plausibility and Generalizability of General Cultural Rules." In *Artificial Intelligence and National Security*, edited by Stephen Cimbala. Lexington: Lexington Books.

Mallery, John C., and Roger Hurwitz. 1987. "Analogy and Precedent in Strategic Decision-Making: A Computational Approach." Paper presented at the annual meeting of the American Political Science Association, Chicago.

Manheim, Jarol B., and Richard C. Rich. 1986. *Empirical Political Analysis: Research Methods in Political Science*. New York: Longman.

Mefford, Dwain. 1984. "Formulating Foreign Policy on the Basis of Historical Analogies: An Application of Developments in Artificial Intelligence." Paper presented at the annual meeting of the International Studies Association.

———. 1985. "Inducing Decision Diagrams from Historical Cases: The Implementation of a Scenario-Based Reasoning System." Paper presented at the Merriam Seminar, University of Illinois.

———. 1986a. "What Morton Kaplan Wanted To Do, and Should Have Done: Balance of Power as a Rule-Based System." Paper presented at the annual meeting of the International Studies Association, Anaheim.

———. 1986b. "Using Political Narratives to Structure Decisions and Games: The Design for an Expert System Shell." Paper presented at the annual meeting of the International Studies Association, Anaheim.

———. 1987a. "The Cognitive Elements of a Theory of Foreign Policy: Part I." Paper presented at the annual meeting of the American Political Science Association, Chicago.

———. 1987b. "Analogical Reasoning and the Definition of the Situation: Back to Snyder for Concepts and Forward to Artificial Intelligence for Method." In *New Directions in the Study of Foreign Policy*, edited by Charles F. Hermann, Charles W. Kegley, Jr., and James N. Rosenau. Boston: Allen & Unwin.

Merritt, Richard. 1987. "Levels of Analysis and Data-Based Research." *International Studies Notes* 13(2):49–50.

Moon, Bruce E. 1983. "The Foreign Policy of the Dependent State." *International Studies Quarterly* 27:315–40.

———. 1985. "Consensus or Compliance? Foreign-Policy Change and External Dependence." *International Organization* 39(2):297–329.

———. 1987. "Political Economy Approaches to the Comparative Study of Foreign Policy." In *New Directions in the Study of Foreign Policy*, edited by

Charles F. Hermann, Charles W. Kegley, Jr., and James N. Rosenau. Boston: Allen & Unwin.

———. 1989. "The State in Foreign and Domestic Policy." Lehigh University, unpublished manuscript.

Moon, Bruce E., and William Dixon. 1985. "Politics, the State, and Basic Human Needs: A Cross-National Study." *American Journal of Political Science* 29(4):661–94.

Moore, David W. 1974. "Governmental and Societal Influences on Foreign Policy in Open and Closed Nations." In *Comparing Foreign Policies*, edited by James N. Rosenau. New York: John Wiley & Sons for Sage Publications.

Most, Benjamin A., and Harvey Starr. 1984. "International Relations Theory, Foreign Policy Substitutability, and 'Nice' Laws." *World Politics* 36(3): 383–406.

———. 1989. *Inquiry, Logic and International Politics.* Columbia: University of South Carolina Press.

Mueller, John E. 1973. *War, Presidents and Public Opinion.* New York: John Wiley & Sons.

Munton, Donald. 1976. "Comparative Foreign Policy: Fads, Fantasies, Orthodoxies, Perversities." In *In Search of Global Patterns*, edited by James Rosenau. New York: Free Press.

Nachmias, David, ed. 1980. *The Practice of Policy Evaluation.* New York: St. Martin's Press.

Nathan, James A., and James K. Oliver. 1987. *Foreign Policy Making and the American Political System.* 2nd ed. Boston: Little, Brown.

Neustadt, Richard. 1960. *Presidential Power: The Politics of Leadership.* New York: John Wiley.

Ng-Quinn, Michael. 1983. "The Analytical Study of Chinese Foreign Policy." *International Studies Quarterly* 27(2):203–24.

Oye, Kenneth. 1987. "On Mitigating Deconstructive Destruction." Princeton University, unpublished manuscript.

Paige, Glenn D. 1968. *The Korean Decision, June 24–30, 1950.* New York: Free Press.

Palumbo, Dennis J. 1988. *Public Policy in America: Government in Action.* New York: Harcourt Brace Jovanovich.

Palumbo, Dennis J., Stephen Fawcett, and Paula Wright, eds. 1981. *Evaluating and Optimizing Public Policy.* Lexington: Lexington Books.

Papadakis, Maria, and Harvey Starr. 1987. "Opportunity, Willingness, and Small States: The Relationship Between Environment and Foreign Policy." In *New Directions in the Study of Foreign Policy*, edited by Charles F. Hermann, Charles W. Kegley, Jr., and James N. Rosenau. Boston: Allen & Unwin.

Phillips, Warren R. 1987. "Alternative Futures in the Middle East: The Results from Three Simulations." In *Artificial Intelligence and National Security*, edited by Stephen Cimbala. Lexington: Lexington Books.

Powell, Charles A., Helen E. Purkitt, and James W. Dyson. 1987. "Opening the Black Box: Cognitive Processing and Optimal Choice in Foreign Policy Decision Making." In *New Directions in the Study of Foreign Policy*, edited by Charles F. Hermann, Charles W. Kegley, Jr., and James N. Rosenau. Boston: Allen & Unwin.

Putnam, Robert D. 1988. "Diplomacy and Domestic Politics: The Logic of Two-Level Games." *International Organization* 42(3):427–60.

Rasler, Karen A., William R. Thompson, and Kathleen M. Chester. 1980. "Foreign Policy Makers, Personality Attributes and Interviews: A Note on Reliability Problems." *International Studies Quarterly* 24(1):47–66.

Raymond, Gregory A. 1987. "Evaluation: A Neglected Task for the Comparative Study of Foreign Policy." In *New Directions in the Study of Foreign Policy*, edited by Charles F. Hermann, Charles W. Kegley, Jr., and James N. Rosenau. Boston: Allen & Unwin.

Richardson, Neil R. 1978. *Foreign Policy and Economic Dependence*. Austin: University of Texas Press.

———. 1987. "Dyadic Case Studies in the Comparative Study of Foreign Policy Behavior." In *New Directions in the Study of Foreign Policy*, edited by Charles F. Hermann, Charles W. Kegley, Jr., and James N. Rosenau. Boston: Allen & Unwin.

Richardson, Neil R., and Charles W. Kegley, Jr. 1980. "Trade Dependence and Foreign Policy Compliance: A Longitudinal Analysis." *International Studies Quarterly* 24:191–222.

Rielly, John E. 1983. *American Public Opinion and U.S. Foreign Policy, 1983*. Chicago: Chicago Council on Foreign Relations.

———. 1987. *American Public Opinion and U.S. Foreign Policy, 1987*. Chicago: Chicago Council on Foreign Relations.

Robinson, James A., and Richard S. Snyder. 1965. "Decision-Making in International Politics." In *International Behavior: A Social-Psychological Analysis*, edited by Herbert C. Kelman. New York: Holt, Rinehart & Winston.

Rochester, J. Martin, and Michael Segalla. 1978. "What Foreign Policy Makers Want from Foreign Policy Researchers." *International Studies Quarterly* 22(3):435–61.

Rosati, Jerel A. 1981. "Developing a Systematic Decision-Making Framework: Bureaucratic Politics in Perspective." *World Politics* 33(2):234–52.

———. 1987. *The Carter Administration's Quest for Global Community*. Columbia: University of South Carolina Press.

Rosenau, James N. 1966. "Pre-Theories and Theories of Foreign Policy." In *Approaches to Comparative and International Politics*, edited by R. Barry Farrell. Evanston: Northwestern University Press.

———. 1967. "The Premises and Promises of Decision-Making Analysis." In

Contemporary Political Analysis, edited by James C. Charlesworth. New York: Free Press.

————. 1968. "Comparative Foreign Policy: Fad, Fantasy, or Field?" *International Studies Quarterly* 12:296–329.

————. 1975. "Comparative Foreign Policy: One-Time Fad, Realized Fantasy, and Normal Field." In *International Events and the Comparative Analysis of Foreign Policy*, edited by Charles W. Kegley. Columbia: South Carolina Press.

————. 1984. "A Pre-Theory Revisited: World Politics in an Era of Cascading Interdependence." *International Studies Quarterly* 28(3):245–305.

————. 1987. "Toward Single-Country Theories of Foreign Policy: The Case of the USSR." In *New Directions in the Study of Foreign Policy*, edited by Charles F. Hermann, Charles W. Kegley, Jr., and James N. Rosenau. Boston: Allen & Unwin.

————. 1988. "CFP and IPE: The Anomaly of Mutual Boredom." *International Interactions* 14(1):17–26.

Rosenau, James N., ed. 1974. *Comparing Foreign Policies: Theories, Findings and Methods*. New York: John Wiley & Sons for Sage Publications.

————, ed. 1976. *In Search of Global Patterns*. New York: Free Press.

Rostow, W. W. 1960. *The Stages of Economic Growth*. New York: Cambridge University Press.

Rubenberg, Cheryl A. 1986. "Israeli Foreign Policy in Central America." *Third World Quarterly* 8(3):896–915.

————. 1988. "U.S. Policy toward Nicaragua and Iran and the Iran-Contra Affair: Reflections on the Continuity of American Foreign Policy." *Third World Quarterly* 10(4):1467–1504.

Rummel, Rudolph J. 1972. *The Dimensionality of Nations Project*. Beverly Hills: Sage.

Russett, Bruce, and Harvey Starr. 1989. *World Politics: The Menu for Choice*. 3rd ed. New York: W. H. Freeman & Company.

Salmore, Barbara, and Stephen Salmore. 1978. "Political Regimes and Foreign Policy." In *Why Nations Act: Theoretical Perspectives for Comparative Foreign Policy*, edited by Maurice East, Stephen Salmore, and Charles Hermann. Beverly Hills: Sage.

Sampson, Martin W., III. 1987. "Cultural Influences on Foreign Policy." In *New Directions in the Study of Foreign Policy*, edited by Charles F. Hermann, Charles W. Kegley, Jr., and James N. Rosenau. Boston: Allen & Unwin.

Sanders, Arthur. 1990. *Making Sense of Politics*. Ames: Iowa State University Press.

Schilling, Warner R. 1962. "The Politics of National Defense: Fiscal 1950." In *Strategy, Politics and Defense Budgets*, edited by Warner R. Schilling, Paul T. Hammond, and Glenn H. Snyder. New York: Columbia University Press.

Schrodt, Philip A. 1985. "Precedent-Based Logic and Rational Choice: A Comparison." In *Dynamic Models of International Conflict*, edited by Michael Don Wards and Urs Luterbacher. Boulder: Lynne Rienner Publishers.

———. 1989. "Short Term Prediction of International Events using a Holland Classifier." *Mathematical and Computer Modelling* 12:589–600.

———. 1991. "Pattern Recognition of International Event Sequences: A Machine Learning Approach." In *Artificial Intelligence and International Politics*, edited by Valerie Hudson. Boulder: Westview Press.

———. 1991. *Computational Models of International Politics*. Ann Arbor: University of Michigan Press.

Shepard, Graham H. 1988. "Personality Effects on American Foreign Policy, 1969–84: A Second Test of Interpersonal Generalization Theory." *International Studies Quarterly* 32(1):91–123.

Shinobu, Takashi. 1987. "China's Bilateral Treaties, 1973–82: A Quantitative Study." *International Studies Quarterly* 31(4):439–56.

Simon, Herbert. 1957 (first published in 1955). "A Behavioral Model of Rational Choice." In *Models of Man: Social and Rational*, edited by Herbert Simon. New York: John Wiley & Sons.

———. 1985. "Human Nature in Politics: The Dialogue of Psychology with Political Science." *American Political Science Review* 79(2):293–304.

Singer, J. David. 1969a. "The Incompleat Theorist: Insight without Evidence." In *Contending Approaches to International Politics*, edited by James N. Rosenau and Klauss Knorr. Princeton: Princeton University Press.

———. 1969b. "The Level-of-Analysis Problem in International Relations." In *International Politics and Foreign Policy*. Rev. ed., edited by James N. Rosenau. New York: Free Press.

Smith, Steven. 1981. "Traditionalism, Behavioralism and Change in Foreign Policy Analysis." In *Change and the Study of International Relations: The Evaded Dimension*, edited by Barry Buzan and R. J. Barry Jones. London: Frances Pinter.

———. 1983. "Foreign Policy Analysis: British and American Orientations and Methodologies." *Political Studies* 31:556–65.

———. 1987. "CFP: A Theoretical Critique." *International Studies Notes* 13(2):47–48.

Snyder, Glenn H., and Paul Diesing. 1977. *Conflict among Nations: Bargaining, Decision Making, and System Structure in International Crisis*. Princeton: Princeton University Press.

Snyder, Richard C., H. W. Bruck, and Burton Sapin. 1954. *Decision-Making as an Approach to the Study of International Politics*. Foreign Policy Analysis Series No. 3, Princeton University.

Snyder, Richard C., and Glenn D. Paige. 1958. "The United States Decision to Resist Aggression in Korea: The Application of an Analytical Scheme." *Administrative Science Quarterly* 3:341–78.

Spiegel, Steven L. 1987. "The American Approach to Middle East Conflict Management." *International Interactions* 13(2):145–69.

Sprout, Harold, and Margaret Sprout. 1956. *Man-Milieu Relationship Hypotheses in the Context of International Politics*. Princeton: Princeton University Press.

———. 1957. "Environmental Factors in the Study of International Politics." *Journal of Conflict Resolution* 1:309–28.

———. 1965. *Ecological Perspective on Human Affairs*. Princeton: Princeton University Press.

Starr, Harvey. 1978. " 'Opportunity' and 'Willingness' as Ordering Concepts in the Study of War." *International Interactions* 4:363–87.

———. 1984. *Henry Kissinger: Perceptions of International Politics*. Lexington: University of Kentucky Press.

———. 1988. "Rosenau, Pre-Theories and the Evolution of the Comparative Study of Foreign Policy." *International Interactions* 14(1):3–15.

Steinbruner, John D. 1974. *The Cybernetic Theory of Decision*. Princeton: Princeton University Press.

Sylvan, Donald A., and Steve Chan, eds. 1984. *Foreign Policy Decision Making: Perception, Cognition and Artificial Intelligence*. New York: Praeger.

Sylvan, Donald A., Ashok Goel, and B. Chandresekaran. 1990. "Analyzing Political Decision Making from an Information-Processing Perspective: JESSE." *American Journal of Political Science* 34(1):79–123.

Tanaka, Akihiko. 1984. "China, China Watching and CHINA-WATCHER." In *Foreign Policy Decision Making: Perception, Cognition and Artificial Intelligence*, edited by Donald A. Sylvan and Steve Chan. New York: Praeger.

Thorson, Stuart, and Donald A. Sylvan. 1982. "Counterfactuals and the Cuban Missile Crisis." *International Studies Quarterly* 26:537–71.

Vasquez, John A. 1985. "Domestic Contention on Critical Foreign Policy Issues: The Case of the United States." *International Organization* 39(4): 643–66.

———. 1986. "Explaining and Evaluating Foreign Policy: A New Agenda for Comparative Foreign Policy." In *Evaluating Foreign Policy*, edited by John A. Vasquez. Boulder: Praeger.

Verba, Sidney. 1967. "Some Dilemmas in Comparative Research." *World Politics* 20:111–27.

Vertzberger, Taacov Y. I. 1986. "Foreign Policy Decisionmakers as Practical-Intuitive Historians: Applied History and Its Shortcomings." *International Studies Quarterly* 30(2):223–47.

Vincent, Jack E. 1983. "WIES vs. COPDAB: Correspondence Problems." *International Studies Quarterly* 27(2):160–68.

Waldo, Dwight. 1975. "Political Science: Tradition, Discipline, Profession, Science, Enterprise." In *Handbook of Political Science*. Vol. 1, *Political Science:*

Scope and Theory, edited by Fred I. Greenstein and Nelson W. Polsby. Reading, Mass.: Addison-Wesley.

Walker, Stephen G. 1977. "The Interface between Beliefs and Behavior: Henry Kissinger's Operational Code and the Vietnam War." *Journal of Conflict Resolution* 21(1):129–68.

———. 1987. "Role Theory and the Origins of Foreign Policy." In *New Directions in the Study of Foreign Policy*, edited by Charles F. Hermann, Charles W. Kegley, Jr., and James N. Rosenau. Boston: Allen & Unwin.

Weisberg, Robert. 1976. *Public Opinion and Popular Government*. Englewood Cliffs, N.J.: Prentice-Hall.

Weiss, Carol H. 1972. *Evaluation Research*. Englewood Cliffs, N.J.: Prentice-Hall.

Whiting, A. S. 1972. "The Scholar and the Policy-maker." In *Theory and Policy in International Relations*, edited by Raymond Tanter and Richard H. Ullman. (Published as a Supplement to *World Politics* 24.)

Wilkenfeld, Jonathon. 1968. "Domestic and Foreign Conflict Behavior of Nations." *Journal of Peace Research* 1:56–59.

Wilkenfeld, Jonathon, Gerald W. Hopple, Paul J. Rossa, and Stephen J. Andriole. 1980. *Foreign Policy Behavior: The Interstate Behavior Analysis Model*. Beverly Hills: Sage.

Wittkopf, Eugene. 1981. "The Structure of Foreign Policy Attitudes: An Alternative View." *Social Science Quarterly* 62:108–23.

———. 1986. "On the Foreign Policy Beliefs of the American People: A Critique and Some Evidence." *International Studies Quarterly* 30(4):425–45.

———. 1987. "Elites and Masses: Another Look at Attitudes toward America's World Role." *International Studies Quarterly* 31:131–59.

Wittkopf, Eugene, and James McCormick. 1988. "Was There Ever a Foreign Policy Consensus." Presented at the annual meeting of the American Political Science Association, Washington, D.C., September.

Wittkopf, Eugene, and Michael A. Maggiotto. 1983. "The Two Faces of Internationalism: Public Attitudes toward American Foreign Policy in the 1970s—and Beyond?" *Social Science Quarterly* 64:288–304.

Zinnes, Dina A. 1976. *Contemporary Research in International Relations*. New York: Free Press.

5

The Study of War and Peace: Quo Vadis?

Jacek Kugler

World politics can be divided into two main strands. One strand, broadly defined as the study of war and peace, encompasses the analysis of competition, conflict, and warfare and attempts to account for the waging, prevention, or deterrence of conflict. The second strand deals with all phenomena in international politics other than conflict. This is the broad field of political economy, where topics of interest include political development, integration, trade negotiations, and political demography.

The focus of this chapter is on war and peace because writings in this area have been the prominent concern that defined the field of world politics for many years. Within this field I concentrate on theories that attempt to account for conflict using the state or state leaders as a unit of analysis, partly because much of the literature focuses on these two levels and partly because this work corresponds closely to my research interests.

Let me start this review with important disclaimers. It is impossible in this short space to provide a fair summary of developments in a field as vast as international conflict. But, even if length were not a constraint, any reviewer would distort developments because he is a captive of his own interest and research experience. Like a myopic observer looking at the field through a long time funnel, one is aware of the min-

I wish to thank panel members Bruce Bueno de Mesquita, Brian M. Pollins, and Dina Zinnes for their constructive comments and evaluations of this paper.

utest distinctions among contemporary propositions directly related to one's own research agenda, and one can still see, albeit imprecisely, the contributions of distant predecessors. However, because the funnel is also a blinder, many extensions of work by acknowledged predecessors, which are the contemporary expressions of a common intellectual idea, have evolved in directions so different from those chosen by the reviewer that they no longer attract recognition and are, unfairly, discarded. For these reasons, like most such reviews, this is a personal journey that says more about my own perspective on war and peace than about the development of this branch of world politics. (For recent comprehensive overviews of this field see Midlarsky 1989; Gurr 1980.)

Empirical analysts have also been able to establish consistent relations between conflict and many of its attributes. Evaluations demonstrate consistent patterns of diffusion in international conflicts, show that allies tend to fulfill their commitments, prove that conflicts among allies are less intense than among unattached nations, verify that the consequences of war are intense but temporary and are overcome within two decades, establish that geographic location is not incidental to the frequency of war, or show a direct relationship between the willingness to suffer and the duration of conflict (Most and Starr 1980; Starr and Siverson 1990; Most, Starr, and Siverson 1990; Siverson and King 1980; Bueno de Mesquita 1981, 1983; Organski and Kugler 1980; Kugler and Arbetman 1989; Rosen 1972; Wittman 1979).

THE STATUS OF WAR AND PEACE

The study of war and peace at this early stage of development is chaotic in the sense that it contains a huge, unorganized catalogue of ideas past and present. We are not unlike paleontologists before the advent of bone-dating techniques, who, faced with a bewildering variety of bones of seemingly distinct species, rattled among this enormous legacy until they managed to develop crude but accurate connections and typologies. Analysts of world politics, overburdened by accounts of seemingly distinct and even unique wars and crises past and present, have also managed to classify and order wars, crises, interventions, and conflicts into coherent patterns (Singer and Small 1972; Small and Singer 1982; Levy 1983; George and Smoke 1974; Huth 1988; Taylor and Jodice 1983; Wilkenfeld, Brecker, and Moser 1988; Thompson 1988).[1]

Despite these advances in classification, however, unlike modern paleontologists, who adopted a theory of evolution, analysts of war and peace have not established a coherent paradigm to understand conflict.[2] Recall that once paleontologists acquired the ability to date the age of bones, they were able to determine which species were extinct and which ancestors could be explicitly connected to contemporary expressions within a species. Using this information Darwin (1859) proposed a paradigm of species evaluation which postulates that, despite their size and complexity, members of species and subspecies that disappeared were in one way or another less adapted to survive than exponents of species that live among us. Darwin's macrolevel notions of evolution have received general support from microlevel developments in modern genetics, adding robustness to this theory.[3] In sharp contrast, students of war and peace have not achieved similar closure. Thus, the modern analysis of war has more in common with early paleontology than it has with post-Darwinian developments in that field. In this sense the field of war and peace is a "developing" discipline that lacks some of the key characteristics of a "mature" discipline. Consider some areas that need more agreement before knowledge can advance rapidly.

Analysts of war and peace have not generated a consensus on a common empirical basis for the evaluation of their competing theories.[4] Indeed, theories of war and peace still are judged by the novel insights they suggest, rather than by the conformance of these new insights to empirical evidence that most practitioners will accept. Indeed, because of serious disagreement regarding key variables and the absence of a uniform criteria for falsification, it is difficult to determine whether the propositions advanced today are superior to those advanced by predecessors, and it is hard to decide whether to discard ineffectively specified intellectual strands that retain ardent advocates. Given these limitations, a reviewer of war and peace faces the arduous task of defining anew the criteria he will use to choose viable alternatives from a set of contradictory but internally consistent propositions. Once this choice is made, a reviewer must still face the even more onerous task of justifying the reasons for his or her decisions, which will inevitably be questioned by his cohorts. It is not surprising therefore that in the chaotic field of ideas about war and peace, there is vast disagreement regarding the identity of the intellectual strand that will bear or has borne fruit, and empirical attempts to weed out weaker substrands are mired in controversy.

A major difference between "developing" and "mature" disciplines is that in the latter, evidence can be used to support unpopular positions leading to generate, or to squelch, a controversy. In well-established fields such controversies do not last because replication of established experiments is an agreed-upon means for support or rejection of a new idea.[5] In world politics the evidential approach has not taken hold since experiments can not be carried out and replication is far from easy.

In general, evidence helps in the building of theory when long-held, promising propositions are supported. This has rarely been the case in world politics. Rather, the most important contribution of the empirical literature on war and peace is the falsification of previously widely accepted propositions. Indeed, empirical analysis shows frequently that well-known theoretical constructs are only tenuously consistent or even totally inconsistent with observed reality, while few studies produce strong support for existing structures. (For example, on balance of power and stability see Singer, Bremer, and Stuckey [1972]; Organski and Kugler [1980]; Vasquez [1983]; and Thompson [1988]. On arms races see Zinnes, Gillespie, and Rubinson [1976]; Ostrom [1978]; Kugler, Organski, and Fox [1980]; Ward [1984]; Ostrom and Marra [1986]. On deterrence and stability see Russett [1963]; George and Smoke [1974]; Organski and Kugler [1980]; Kugler [1984]; Huth and Russett [1984, 1988]; Zagare [1986]; Huth [1988].)

It is perhaps because empirical tests do not conform closely with theoretical expectations that so much is still written about the philosophy of scientific research and measurement in world politics. One wonders whether this exercise will ultimately simplify or complicate the enterprise of knowledge creation. However, there is little doubt that the debate regarding a common paradigm and agreed-upon rules of falsification adds complexity to any attempt to define and advance the field.[6] My view is that given the development of the study of war and peace, if vague guidelines for falsification are accepted, knowledge will be clouded in mystery; and, if stringent criteria for rejection are adopted, little worth pursuing will be left upon which to base the study of war and peace. Neither is a palatable choice.

The compromise I favor leans toward ease of rejection by evidence. The study of war and peace is crowded with competing theoretical propositions that account for a limited amount of observed conflict but, in so doing, usually contradict alternative explanations that also seemingly account for the same or largely overlapping portion of this phenomenon. Thus, unless we are willing to agree on criteria for evidential falsification, we are likely to delay the enterprise of knowledge creation. Fundamentally, we need to demand, before new propositions are put forth, that a minimal level of empirical face validity be met and, before complex propositions are advanced, that they provide some improvement over simpler proposals.

These points can be illustrated with axiomatic structures that, despite serious drawbacks, have the unique virtue that their deductions are clear and can be tested empirically when contradictory explanations for the same phenomenon emerge. Several game theoretical representations of the well-known nuclear crisis in Cuba claim to represent consistently the interrelation among decision-makers in that crisis (Snyder and Diesing 1977; Howard 1971; Brams 1985). The real actors during the Cuban crisis had one set of perceived options and this single set was used to resolve that crisis. Therefore, decision-makers could have responded during that crisis using a strategy of short-term gains (Nash solution), a strategy of long-term maximization (nonmyopic), or a forward-looking strategy (sequential), but they could not have applied all three strategies concurrently, particularly since it has been shown that for this crisis the formal results of these three strategies differ fundamentally. Yet, the game theoretical literature on the Cuban crisis provides no explicit guide that demonstrates the superiority of one solution over another; rather, each author shows that the strategy proposed produces plausible results. This lack of cross-study comparisons prevents the creation of cumulative knowledge, since even well-specified formal propositions and well-documented cases do not provide information that can help guide the response of decision-makers in the next intense crisis.

Because of this concern with cumulative, empirically based knowledge I subscribe to the scientific research principles proposed by Lakatos:

> A scientific theory T is falsified if and only if another theory T′ has been proposed with the following characteristics: (1) T′ has excess empirical content over T; that is, it predicts novel facts, that is, facts improbable in the light of, or even forbidden, by T; (2) T′ explains the previous success of T, that is, all the unrefuted content of T is included (within limits of observable error) in the contents of T′, and (3) some of the excess content of T′ is corroborated. (Lakatos 1978, 32)

In Lakatos's view a superior scientific theory is simple and makes definite predictions that can be tested by observation. Clearly, in the absence of a contending theory, systematic, parsimonious statements that seemingly account for a given phenomenon are superior to no statements at all. In world politics, however, where many propositions are advanced to explain the same phenomenon, only agreement on empirical criteria for rejection could permit researchers to choose among the already vast array of competing propositions about conflict. Indeed, like the paleontologists who waited until the discovery of bone-dating techniques to reconstruct connections within species and then used this knowledge to show that Darwin's paradigm of evolution helped to understand the development of species, students of war and peace could use Lakatos's rules of falsification to evaluate alternative explanations and, based on their comprehensiveness, parsimony, and predictive capacity, could choose alternatives that deserve further scrutiny. Analysts of world affairs frequently talk about taking such steps but have, thus far, failed to accept them as a general rule.

I will review the literature on war and peace using the perspective of Lakatos because this simple device allows me to show the progress and potential of the current study of war and peace. Before I do so, however, it seems appropriate to investigate the origins of the main ideas we are developing. Who, in a word, is the common ancestor?

ORIGIN OF PERSPECTIVES
ON WAR AND PEACE

The reason one wishes to identify a common ancestor is simply that it is far easier to summarize a field by tracing from a known origin the most fruitful branches. My reading of the current literature on war and peace suggests it is generally agreed that Thucydides laid out the key elements that still permeate much of the modern work on conflict.[7] Thucydides, an inductive thinker, based his observations regarding the dynamics of interstate relations on an intensive study of competition among Greek states. From these observations he identified the state as the unit of analysis and posited that changes in state power, caused by uneven domestic growth or by the reconstitution of alliances, created conditions for conflict or cooperation. Perhaps most important, Thucydides understood the need to explore the connection between decision-making and state structures. He proposed that leaders and not masses decided the actions of states, that decision patterns were similar whether leaders resided in Athens or Sparta, and that leaders systematically attempted to advance the influence of states they represented but were constrained by the structural resources available to them.[8]

The enduring value of Thucydides' work for current analysts of international politics is, therefore, that his work defined key elements still used in the analysis of war and peace and provided the foundation for the understanding of complex international interactions. The importance of Thucydides' work for the analysis of war and peace is not based on the completeness and accuracy of his insights; rather, his work merits consideration because it provides the initial systematic statement that evolved into the modern study of conflict. Like the insights about our physical environment provided by Aristotle, which were surpassed by Galileo, extended by Newton and in turn by Einstein, and, just as assuredly, will be superseded by an as-yet-unknown physicist who may be already among us, the work of Thucydides has been surpassed without diminishing its impact.[9] In fact, without the foundation laid out long ago by Thucydides one can hardly conceive of the insights on war and peace proposed by Machiavelli, Hobbes, Hume, von Clausewitz, Carr, Von Neumann and Morgenstern, or Morgenthau and their extension or restatement by contemporaries like Organski, Waltz, Allison, Bueno de Mesquita, Keohane, and Gilpin.

The best claim that the work of Thucydides is the common ancestor comes from current writings of many students of war. Hans Morgenthau (1978), for example, in his classic work on realism credits Thucydides with uncovering national self-interest and with connecting such interest to international alignments and stability in world politics. Morgenthau writes that Thucydides discovered that "identity of interests is the surest of bonds whether between states or individuals' " (1978, 10), and he then surmises that these principles were accepted by leaders like George Washington and theorists like Max Weber. A second reason is that statements by Thucydides have inspired numerous writers to propose theories of war and peace that are frequently at odds with each other. Kenneth Waltz (1954), a contemporary advocate of balance of power, gives credit to Thucydides for discovering the foundations of the third image, where many sovereign states, following the dictates of their own ambition, compete and sometimes resort to war. Waltz writes that "Thucydides implies it (the third image) when he wrote that it was 'the growth of the Athenian power, which terrified the Lacedaemonians and forced them into war' " (1954, 159). This argument inspires Waltz to relate balance of power to stability. However, critics of this tradition such as Paul Kennedy (1987, 198), who relates the rise and fall of great powers to war rather than to a balance among powerful nations, also find support in Thucydides' argument that "What made war inevitable was the growth of Athenian power and the fear which this caused in Sparta." Finally, the same passage by the ancient Greek writer inspires Emerson Niou, Peter Ordeshook, and Gregory Rose (1989, chap. 5) to discuss preventive war under balance of power or hegemony. Thus, despite dramatic differences in techniques, underlying assumptions, and notions of the ultimate relations between distribution of power and war or peace, Waltz, Kennedy, and Niou and his colleagues find solace and inspiration in the same passages from their Greek ancestor.

Thucydides' work, like the writings of other influential figures critical to the early development of scientific fields, provides the study of war and peace with a loose framework upon which many builders can construct vastly different structures without contradicting the original writings. The drawback of this long memory is, however, that Thucydides' work receives as much attention today as is given most propositions advanced by contemporaries, yet neither is routinely exposed to Lakatos's criteria to assess constituency in theoretical specification or empirical validity. Unless we alter this approach, the study of war and peace will remain in the stage of paradigm formation rather than refinement because important but vague insights will continue to be called upon to support contradictory positions and many influential but unexplored propositions will remain unchallenged.

In the rest of the chapter I trace the evolution of the paradigm on war and peace that evolved from Thucydides and evaluate divergent strands that have received some empirical scrutiny.

POWER DISTRIBUTION MODELS AS A
PARADIGM TO STUDY WAR AND PEACE

The work of Thucydides fostered a loose paradigm that in its many variants provides a common perspective on war and peace. The element
that unites the many authors who can be drawn under this umbrella is
that power distributions play a central role in the generation of conflict.
Serious dissension emerges on almost all other matters. Power distributions have been connected to conflict by so many complex tracks that it
is impossible to do justice to this vast literature. Nevertheless, power
distribution theories can be simply ordered by observing whether they
stress power interactions among states or power dynamics within states.
(For comprehensive critical overviews see Vasquez 1983; Keohane
1986; Thompson 1988).

Two traditions that have been, perhaps unnecessarily, at odds define
the extremes of interactive power distribution theories. The balance of
power tradition proposes that equality among contending nations is the
necessary condition for peace. On the other hand, preponderance proposes that hegemony or power preponderance rather than equality
ensures peace. Since this divergence is in my view central to recent developments in the war and peace literature, let me succinctly evaluate
the underlying assumptions and show why these differences lead to
competing theoretical expectations about war.

A fundamental assumption of many realist theories is that the international arena, unlike the domestic realm, is an anarchical environment. International outcomes are determined by interaction among
states whose leaders pursue policies guided by national interest unconstrained by formal rules. Thus, such outcomes are ultimately determined by the relative power of competing states. This Hobbesian view
of world politics implies that leaders of preponderant or relatively powerful states can and will initiate conflict in pursuit of their goals when
they anticipate that desired objectives can be attained by war. War is
then, as von Clausewitz contends (1976), the continuation of policy by
other means. Since war is an ever-present possibility, minimizing or pre-
venting conflict is one objective of power distribution theories. Under
anarchy, a prominent conception is that a balance among actors may
inhibit conflict, because, as in a bout between well-matched boxers, the
costs of conflict are high and those of conflict avoidance are low.

An alternative assumption is that the international, like the domestic arena, is a hierarchical environment. In this characterization, governments impose domestic laws or international rules whether individuals
or states agree to them or not. To ensure compliance with the law in
domestic politics, governments monopolize legal coercion and restrict
the use of force to advance private goods. The critical difference be-

tween the domestic and the international environment is that the rule of law is not automatically enforced by international institutions. In the international environment, laws are implicit, and enforcement depends on a power preponderance in the hands of supporters of the status quo. A hegemony of power held by one state or coalition of states that support the status quo minimizes conflict because the cost of challenging the system are very high. In a hierarchical environment, conflict is expected to erupt when dominant states are insufficiently persuasive to create preponderant alliances or insufficiently powerful to prevent confrontations. From this perspective, balance between contenders, like a bout between well-matched boxers, enhances the likelihood of conflict, because when odds are even, despite the high costs of waging war, the rewards from altering the status quo are also very high.

A fundamental implication of viewing the international system as anarchical and the domestic arena as hierarchical is that conflict need not follow similar rules. On the other hand, if the underlying structure of both these systems is hierarchical, conflict should respond to similar incentives. This difference in assumptions and implications can be used to trace the main branches of realist theory.

Most analysts of international politics who assume anarchy argue, like Waltz (1954, 232), that wars occur "because there is nothing to prevent them"[10] and support a balance of power among states. They do not extend this rule to the domestic environment, where preponderance of force ensures that laws are enforced and confrontations are avoided (Thompson 1988, 197–201; Keohane 1986; Grieco 1988). On the other hand, analysts who view the domestic and international environments as hierarchical argue that a preponderance of coercive power leads to stability in both arenas (Organski 1958; Organski and Kugler 1980; Gilpin 1981; Keohane 1984; Kugler and Organski 1989b).

One result of this debate about underlying assumptions is that analysts of international politics who assume hierarchy tend to favor preponderance in order to ensure stability, whereas those who emphasize anarchy tend to stress parity to achieve the same purpose. Grieco (1988), in a recent review of the field, suggests that the new "liberal" realist approach spearheaded by Robert Keohane and Robert Axelrod can be distinguished from the "older" realist tradition led by Kenneth Waltz because the "older" version assumes that competition leads to conflict, dismisses cooperation as unlikely, and proposes that conflict can best be managed by balancing the distributions of power. The new "liberal" realism, on the other hand, assumes that competition leads to cooperation, considers conflict as unlikely, and proposes that institutionalizing preponderance of power leads to stability in the international arena. True to assumptions, then, "liberal" realists propose to replicate the hierarchy of domestic politics in the international arena by strengthening international institutions in the hope that stability can be enhanced. On the other hand, "older" realists oppose attempts to institutionalize hierarchy, arguing that in an anarchical environment such actions will not reduce, but will enhance conflict because state leaders will manipulate institutions to obtain outcomes that maximize national gains, rather than to advance stability per se. The resulting complexity may lead to entanglements and will enhance conflict.

This debate is not new, nor is it restricted to an academic forum. President Woodrow Wilson after World War I was the most influential of many practitioners who effectively argued the advantages of hierarchy over anarchy in world politics. Frustrated with the consequences of anarchical competition among unconstrained states, which in his view led to a devastating war, Wilson proposed that the newly assembled League of Nations ensure stability by creating a legal structure that bound major states to defend international stability against "aggressors." His solution was to institutionalize a collective security alliance whose main objective was to ensure that any "aggressor" defined collectively by the major powers would be punished with overwhelming force. Much like the "liberal" realists of today, who seek to preserve "regimes," Wilson—still incorrectly branded an "idealist"—proposed to institutionalize a power hierarchy in world politics that could force states to alter their behavior and play by new rules.[11]

Given these conflicting expectations, it is not surprising that practitioners who assume anarchy should propose power distributions to ensure stability in world politics very different from those proposed by those who assume hierarchy. What can one say about the empirical fit of these theories? Organski and Kugler (1980), Gilpin (1981), and Keohane (1984) all argue that hegemony leads to stability. The evidence that supports relative stability under hegemony can be challenged in the pre-nuclear era, but in the nuclear post–World War II period evidence supporting this assertion is overwhelming. Indeed, despite disagreements about current rates of decline in the United States, scholars who have attempted this exercise agree that the United States held an overwhelming preponderance in capabilities, alliances, nuclear weapons, and technology after 1945. This hegemony extended into the late 1960s or early 1970s, and the United States remains a preponderant if no longer a hegemonic actor today (Russett 1985; Kennedy 1987; Kugler and Organski 1989b; Huntington 1989). Given this overwhelming evidence, it is puzzling that during the period of hegemony, leading theorists of balance of power were developing notions of balance in bipolar systems to replace the older multipolar conceptions and were not concerned with hegemony. How can we, then, looking at this evidence, have a discussion of the merits of balance of power that does not recognize the fact that a unipolar hegemonic system emerged after 1945?

Why is evidence so far removed from theory that it almost infringes on the ability of scholars to generate new propositions? Why is it that our community is starting to discover its contribution to peace only when hegemony is declining?

TESTING GENERALITY: NUCLEAR DETERRENCE

Lakatos argues that one theory is superior to another when it explains the previous success of that theory and accounts for facts that are improbable or forbidden by the other theory. Social theory is important not only because it conforms to evidence but because it is acted upon. Power distribution theories are pertinent today because they provide the theoretical basis for nuclear deterrence. Deterrence in its most elemental form is "an attempt by party A to prevent party B from undertaking a course of action which A regards as undesirable, by threatening to inflict unacceptable costs upon B in the event the action is taken" (Williams 1975, 67). By itself the absence of nuclear war since the bombing of Hiroshima and Nagasaki provides little evidence for or against nuclear deterrence. The absence of conflict may be due to the addition of nuclear weapons or to the absence of congruence among the many factors that lead to massive confrontations. The jury in this case is still out. However, decision-makers must guide actions by some theory. Nuclear deterrence provides a guide to policy that seems to be derived from consistent and plausible assumptions about the behavior of state actors and has, therefore, been generally embraced. The experience is not new. Ancient navigators feared crossing oceans long after their equipment was adequate for this task because in a flat world their ships would suddenly fall into an immense abyss. Practitioners of nuclear deterrence face a similar dilemma: if they, like the ancient navigators, fear to act, the costs may be immense. On the other hand, if they fear to explore the implications of deterrence in order to assess its congruence with reality, facts not included in the theory may come into play; then, in contrast to Columbus, who discovered the New World because he challenged long-held beliefs, practitioners may endure the very war they wished to avoid because they did not challenge the assumptions of deterrence. These are not pleasant choices, but a comparison of deterrence structures presents a real example of the importance of theory in world politics.

    To start this comparison let me describe how the concept of balance of power, through the efforts of Brodie (1946, 1959), Kaufman (1956), Kissinger (1957) and most recently Intriligator and Brito (1987), evolved into the balance of terror. Balance of power—the dominant realist framework used to understand stability in the international arena—adapts precepts of equilibrium from economists. It argues that balance of power ensures stability, because when opponents or coalitions of opponents are evenly matched, the costs of conflict rise, thus inhibiting conflict. Therefore, since leaders of nuclear nations with assured second strike capabilities anticipate that the net gains from waging war under parity approach zero, the likelihood of conflict should also approach zero. In fact, the policy of mutual deterrence remains at its core the model proposed in a multilateral context by Hume (1742, 1990) and extended by Morgenthau (1948), which was then adapted to a bilateral environment by Waltz (1979) after World War II, and recently formalized using the tools of social choice by Niou, Ordeshook, and Rose (1989).

The basic contention of balance of power is that equality of capabilities reduces the likelihood of war, because informed, well-matched contenders are aware that conflict among them will result in serious damage for both parties while the prospects of victory are minimal. William Riker (1973) provided strong impetus to balance of power notions by deducing that in a multi-actor, interactive environment a minimal winning coalition should form among contending parties because the costs of increasing a coalition beyond the number necessary to win by a small margin are increasingly prohibitive. His results provided a strict justification for the automatic creation of equilibrium among contending alliances in the international arena that did not require purposeful intervention by the actors involved. Following the logic of balance of power, such an equilibrium would ensure stability (for a debate between automatic and purposeful balances see Claude 1962, Morgenthau 1948).

The theoretical beauty of balance of power is its capability to extend and incorporate new demands. Deterrence is the latest in a long series of theoretical perspectives that take cues from balance of power to structure the policies that prevent nuclear war. Mutual Assured Destruction, the policy that we rely on to ensure stability among the superpowers, can be derived almost totally from precepts of balance of power. Intriligator and Brito (1987) provide a clear and graphic outline showing the continuities and the distinctions between a "balance of power" and a "balance of terror" (Figure 5.1).

Intriligator and Brito propose that when a nation anticipates that the costs of war will exceed a threshold above which they are not willing to initiate conflict war is not likely, and when a second threshold is reached above which they no longer are willing to confront an opponent, war is deterred. The possibility of war exists in the gray area where actors cannot fully deter each other. The most stable condition is attained under nuclear parity when both sides choose to yield rather than fight because the costs of war initiation are "unacceptable." The critical

Figure 5.1
The Classic View of Deterrence

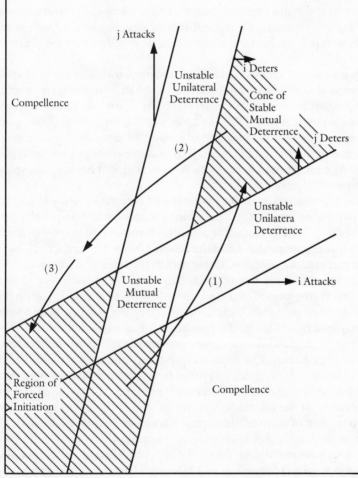

Costs
j can
impose
on i

j Attacks

i Deters

Unstable
Unilateral
Deterrence

Cone of
Stable
Mutual
Deterrence

j Deters

Compellence

(2)

Unstable
Unilatera
Deterrence

(3)

Unstable
Mutual
Deterrence

(1)

i Attacks

Region of
Forced
Initiation

Compellence

Costs i can
impose on j

Source: Intriligator and Brito (1987).

difference between a "balance of power" and a "balance of terror" is that war can be waged under either power parity or preponderance when costs are relatively low, but as war costs increase beyond acceptable thresholds the outcome is compellence under preponderance and mutual deterrence under parity. In fact, once nations reach the cone of stable deterrence, further "overkill" provides a cushion against technological breakthroughs or an uneven deployment of new generations of strategic weapons. Brodie (1946) used precisely such reasoning to reject the long-held dictum of von Clausewitz that war is the continuation of policy by other means; he argued instead that in the nuclear era war must be averted not because it cannot be waged, but because it cannot be won.[12]

An alternative view of deterrence emerges if one assumes that the international system is hierarchically ordered and preponderance or hegemony rather than equality ensures stability. Using the same structures as Intriligator and Brito (1987), Kugler and Zagare (1990) show, using the power transition perspective as a point of departure, that nuclear deterrence has been stable since 1945 because nuclear preponderance was the rule rather than because parity was achieved between these two superpowers (Figure 5.2).

This representation of the evolution of deterrence since 1945 indicates that, in the initial stage, the United States could compel all opponents because it held a massive advantage and the hierarchy in world politics was not disputed. After the Soviet Union, the main challenger, introduced nuclear weapons, stable unilateral deterrence replaced compellence because there was little incentive for the weaker side to challenge the status quo. Since the early 1970s the Soviet Union has achieved rough parity with the United States but has not been able to surpass the latter. This is the condition of mutual deterrence where elites may choose to initiate war or preserve peace. It is not accidental therefore that attempts to limit weapons and diminish tension should occur prior to an overtaking. Fortunately, the post-parity period, in which unstable unilateral deterrence is anticipated, has, thus far, not been reached. If the dissatisfied power overtakes the status quo nation, the probability of war should increase because, despite high costs, the potential for large gains is enormous. Historically, similar conditions were present before World War I, World War II, and the Napoleonic Wars were waged (Houweling and Siccama 1988, Organski and Kugler 1980; for an alternative evaluation see Thompson 1988). In the nuclear period we have not yet undergone a "transition" among the superpowers and, despite the promise of defensive systems, such a transition may be very difficult to achieve.[13]

Practitioners whose argument is based on a balance of power perspective seem to be caught in their actions within the structure of power

Figure 5.2
The Power Transition View of Deterrence

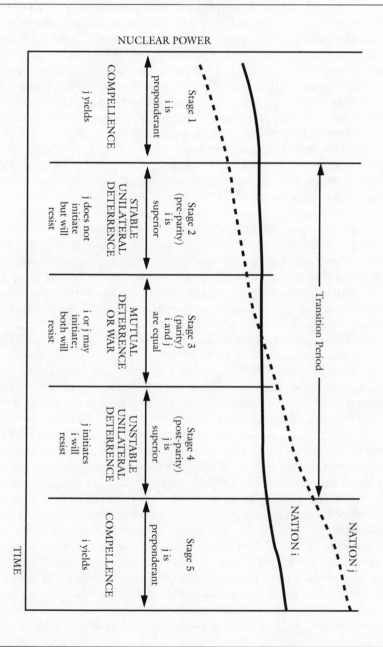

preponderance. Otherwise, why did Secretary of State Dulles threaten but fail to use nuclear weapons to force a withdrawal of Soviet troops from Hungary in 1956? Why did the United States settle for a draw in Korea rather than use nuclear weapons on Chinese troops crossing the Yalu as MacArthur openly argued? Why did the Soviet Union allow the development and deployment of nuclear arsenals by China when the United States did not even recognize that country as a legal entity? And why does Israel, despite its nuclear preponderance, fail to act decisively knowing that in a not too distant future her neighbors will be able to exercise that option on Israel itself? In a word, why do leaders of nations that hold nuclear preponderance maintain peace?

The theoretical rationale that links peace with nuclear preponderance in a nuclear environment was initially suggested by Organski (1958), who posited that preponderance ensures stability because the dominant nation is satisfied with the status quo. In a different context, a very similar argument is made by Keohane (1984) in constructing the notion of hegemonic powers, when he argues that leaders of a regime preserve stability. From a different perspective, Zagare (1986) derives the underlying decision process that ensures stability under preponderance. He shows that a balance of power is sufficient for deterrence if neither party desires a change in the status quo enough to take risks; however, if one side is dissatisfied with the international system, balance provides the conditions under which viable demands can be raised, and the probability of conflict now depends on the risk propensity of the actors involved.

Combining these insights produces a deterrence logic seemingly consistent with empirical record. Figure 5.2 shows that preponderant nuclear nations that support the status quo have no incentive to initiate conflict, and neither does the dissatisfied challenger when the costs of altering the undesirable status quo are prohibitive. This deduction is consistent with the period of Massive Retaliation when the United States could threaten to destroy the Soviet Union with impunity. Only as a challenger starts to deploy nuclear weapons does the stability of Massive Retaliation comes into question. From this perspective it is not unexpected that the series of nuclear crises culminating with the Cuban Crisis coincided with the waning preponderance by the United States. The reason the Soviet Union withdrew missiles under pressure from the United States can presumably be traced directly to the large difference in ultimate costs from a nuclear exchange. Indeed, contrary to the balance perspective, as preponderance disappears, deterrence becomes a tenuous policy.

Hegemony suggests that both war and peace can occur when the costs of conflict are in balance. Peace under these conditions is no longer determined by the size of arsenals but depends directly on the perceptions and actions of leaders in contending states. For example, risk takers may initiate bluffs that can be contested by risk-neutral or risk-acceptant leaders leading to war. In a period of parity, effective negotiations rather than the fear of war prevent conflict (Kugler 1984; Kugler and Zagare 1990; Powell 1989).

The implications for today's world are telling: Mutual Assured Destruction may not be the stable policy balance of power structures imply; rather it may be a tenuous structure that incorporates, concurrently, the conditions for war and peace; the decision to initiate a nuclear war may no longer be determined by the size of arsenals but may depend on the perceptions of national leaders.

EXPLAINING NOVEL IMPLICATIONS: NUCLEAR PROLIFERATION

Lakatos suggests that a theory that in general explains facts not accounted for by a previous theory is a superior theory. Since it is impossible in the absence of a nuclear confrontation to test definitely the validity of either of the above views of deterrence, one may look at secondary implications from each of these competing perspectives. A number of theorists who suggest that mutual deterrence is stable argue— like Waltz (1981), Bueno de Mesquita and Riker (1982), and Intriligator and Brito (1981)—that if one accepts that a balance of nuclear weapons leads to peace among competing superpowers, then peace should also be enhanced by a carefully managed proliferation of such weapons to allies that reduces the risk of accidents. Rosen (1977), perhaps the most explicit and eloquent advocate of the introduction of nuclear weapons, argues that their introduction into the Middle East should have the same salutary effects on the Arab and Israeli contenders that it had on the United States and the Soviet Union at the height of the Cold War. The deduction is clear. If Mutual Assured Destruction is stable, expanding the scope of mutuality should dramatically reduce the likelihood of war whether the contender nations are large or small.

The notion of purposeful proliferation, however, has not gained much practical acceptance. Nuclear nations have restricted access to their technology and have not proliferated nuclear weapons strategically in hopes of enhancing regional stability. Following the dictates of Lakatos, one should question the validity of stable deterrence under parity because the logical implications that flow from this proposition are not implemented. We should, but we do not. Why do we act contrary to theoretical beliefs? Can we do so with impunity?

One explanation for the inconsistency between theory and practice is that leaders of nuclear nations are naive and will follow the more sophisticated strategies proposed by deterrence regarding proliferation only when they are forced to do so. However appealing, this answer fails to meet Lakatos's demand that inferences of a theory should reflect empirical reality, not cause it. A second alternative is to accept inconsistency. This option has been chosen by policy analysts who support the viability of mutual deterrence but reject its logical implication for proliferation. Using Lakatos's criteria, this explanation also fails. Lack of consistency is unacceptable because it allows support for desirable aspects of a theory while rejecting undesirable implications. A third explanation suggests that when behavior does not conform with theory, the theory itself is flawed and should be revised until relevant behavior is accurately assessed. I believe that in order to build theory, only the latter option is viable.

From the perspective of power preponderance, avoiding proliferation of weapons to smaller countries ensures stability. Proliferation would increase the potential for war, since as the number of actors who achieve nuclear parity increase—either in a regional or world context—the probability of nuclear war likewise increases. The proliferation of nuclear weapons, strategic or otherwise, is, as practitioners have long recognized, a very dangerous practice that is unlikely to produce peace. Recall from Figure 5.2 that nuclear deterrence is stable under parity conditions provided that competing actors maximize their long-term stability but leads to war if by accident or design such actors opt for confrontation (see also Zagare 1986 for decision-making arguments). Such deductions suggest that parity may lead to peace or to intense confrontations that terminate only upon the exhaustion of competing parties (e.g. Iran-Iraq) or the unilateral surrender of the defeated side (e.g. Germany and Japan in World War II, Germany in World War I, France in the Napoleonic Wars). Nuclear weapons are, from the hegemonic perspective, as dangerous as their conventional counterparts, and their proliferation enhances the likelihood of nuclear war. Thus far we may not have used nuclear weapons because unilateral destruction is unacceptable. However, if such deductions are accurate, peace under parity will be severely tested in the future.[14]

TESTING THE PRESUMPTIONS OF VALIDITY: ARMS RACES

Lakatos suggests that all theories regardless of intrinsic appeal must conform with empirical necessity. Despite empirical shortcomings, I believe that in this area the discipline is moving vigorously toward a restatement. The case in point is the analysis of arms races. Richardson (1960) proposed prior to World War II in a now-famous monograph that arms races lead to war. He further proposed that when parties reach an equilibrium in arms expenditures they achieve a point tenuously balanced between an arms race that leads to war and disarmament that leads to increased stability. Richardson's empirical work supported his theory, and his studies of the explosive arms race between Germany and the United Kingdom forecasted the initiation of World War II after Richardson suggested that states react to armament buildups by other states, which in turn result in an arms race. Samuel Huntington (1958) added the important consideration that qualitative rather than quantitative races lead to conflict.[15] Much later Paul Smoker (1964) suggested that conflict starts because the weaker nation, unable to compete, is forced to preempt or be left behind.

Since the time of Richardson, numerous evaluations of this very parsimonious and powerful theory have produced an unexpected outcome; domestic factors are generally shown to be powerful determinants of arms buildups, but external factors—which Richardson believed caused arms races—are shown to be far less influential (Ostrom 1978; Kugler, Organski, and Fox 1980; Ward 1984; Ostrom and Marra 1986). What emerges from the empirical literature is that domestic politics fuels arms buildups independent of arms buildups by competitors.

Dina Zinnes, John Gillespie and Michael Rubinson (1976) provide one answer to this dilemma when they explore the implications of domestically driven arms buildups. They formally show that buildups driven by domestic factors are self-regulating and will regress to a common mean after every extensive overexpenditure or underexpenditure. This perspective on arms buildup explains budgetary allocations but, unfortunately provides little assistance in understanding the initiation of conflict.[16] Their prediction seems to have been supported by the empirical literature that associates increases or decreases in arms with the potential for conflict. With the single and well-known exception of Wallace (1979), who found a strong relation between war and arms races, numerous studies that explore the relationship between war and arms races suggest either weak or very confounded results (Smith 1980; Horn 1984; Morrow 1990).

The arms race literature is then an excellent example of the use of empirical investigation of a well-specified theory to reject the original proposition and discover an alternative structure. Of course there is delay in transmitting this information, and not surprisingly this appeal of arms races is still quite strong for practitioners. However, even here many of the implications seem to be dismissed. For example, Gorbachev has initiated many unilateral arms reductions without waiting for a response or obtaining one. Arms negotiators may consider these results in their negotiations to assess whether paired reductions are the most effective way to achieve reductions of tension and ultimately peace.

TESTING CONSISTENCY: FROM
INTERNATIONAL TO DOMESTIC CONFLICT

Lakatos suggests that one theory is superior to another if it can encompass a wider portion of the phenomenon than its alternative. In this respect the propositions emerging from power preponderance have an advantage over balance conceptions because the former assume that conflict in the domestic and international environment responds to similar forces. A.F.K. Organski (1958) was among the first to argue that the pattern of conflict is similar in the domestic and international arenas. Leaders of states, like heads of political groups, are in constant competition over scarce resources and seek to maximize influence using relative differences in power. Cursory evaluations of domestic environments seem to confirm that preponderance ensures stability since successful governments are armed with laws and a monopoly of force to enforce them. In domestic politics, violent political opposition is a viable option only when the government is very weak or when opponents can generate support from other states in order to advance their demands (Kugler 1989). It is not surprising, therefore, that civil war is concentrated in states where governments are weak and opponents are strong. Indeed, the governments of Japan, Germany, the United States, the Soviet Union, and China endure stability because they either persuade populations not to challenge their authority or, if persuasion fails, eradicate rebellion by exercising force concentrated in the hands of the government.[17]

Recent work suggests, however, that it is not necessary to assume preponderance to produce a common model for domestic and international conflict. Bueno de Mesquita (1981) uses expected utility to account for international and domestic instability and demonstrates that the conditions for cooperation and conflict can be derived from a single perspective. Of critical importance to this discussion, Bueno de Mesquita and his colleagues show that the same model that accounts for wars in the international system can account for crisis and revolutions in the domestic environment (Bueno de Mesquita, Newman, and Rabushka 1985; Kugler 1987).[18] Further illuminating the connection between domestic and international conflict are findings from game theory that show, using different assumptions regarding strategies, that players will produce results that are quite different despite consistent assumptions. Frank Zagare (1986), for example, shows that the prisoner's dilemma can be used to represent stable nuclear deterrence if we assume that decision-makers adopt a nonmyopic perspective regarding nuclear conflict suggesting that Mutual Assured Destruction is stable, but tenuously so.[19] Indeed, cooperation under anarchy is not improbable but may be the outcome of more sophisticated calculations of the costs of confrontations (Axelrod 1984; Oye 1986; Niou, Ordeshook, and Rose 1989).

Cooperation in politics may be hard to achieve permanently because political transactions seem to differ fundamentally from the economic transactions that have inspired so many of our current models. Modern economic literature suggests that the market mechanism can achieve effective transactions whether information available to actors is perfect or imperfect and whether governments attempt to adjust outcomes by policy or not. These results reinforce the fundamental theorems of economics that an equilibrium price will provide stable exchange for competing commodities. It is, however, difficult to extend the proposition that an equilibrium among contending political actors will ensure efficient and stable political outcomes, for the reason that economic and political transactions differ fundamentally. Economic transactions are ultimately cooperative, since at the time of a sale, both the buyer and seller must agree on the price and, at least during the instant of transaction, must be fully satisfied and cooperate in its execution. Bueno de Mesquita and his colleagues (1985) persuasively argue that political transactions—both domestic and international—differ fundamentally from economic ones because political transactions are intrinsically coercive. At the point of a political transaction there is no cooperation between the parties; rather, demands are imposed by one state on another or by the government on individuals when a disagreement occurs. Unlike economic transactions, in political transactions the weak party cannot walk out of the store, but must accept the offer or resist the demand or law violation and pay the consequences of dissent. Just as a murderer cannot escape sentence for his transgression because he refuses to cooperate, nation-states cannot avoid the repercussion of challenges when opponents choose not to cooperate and must opt for conflict or appeasement. Thus, since political transactions can be completed without cooperation, a balance among competing parties does not necessarily lead to cooperative solutions similar to those encountered in economic markets.

Returning to the earlier evaluations of power distribution, "liberals" may have correctly suggested that in political transactions preponderance is required to avert conflict because compliance under equilibrium can be successfully resisted. It is not essential to assume, as "older" realists do, that equilibrium leads to cooperation or preponderance leads to conflict. Indeed a general theory of conflict may emerge in a not-too-distant future, if war and peace at the international level follow rules that are no different from insurgency and revolution at the domestic level. (For work in this area see Wilkenfeld, Bracher, and Moser 1988; Bueno de Mesquita et al. 1985; Kugler 1989).

ALTERNATIVE SPECIFICATIONS:
NEW HORIZONS WITHIN THE STATE

I hope to have persuaded the reader that current theories of conflict are still tenuous and imprecise. The best proposals suggest necessary but not sufficient conditions, and a search for "sufficiency" is afoot in different directions. Under such conditions Lakatos suggests that alternative specifications that alter the presumed relation among variables can sometimes produce key insights. Indeed, the revolution caused by Copernicus was not based on new variables but on a rearrangement of relations between the earth and the sun.

In power distribution, one promising area reconsiders the interactive aspect of power and concentrates on domestic interactions. Modelsky (1987), Thompson (1988), and Doran (1990) suggest that internal dynamics are responsible for conflict in the international arena. Nations, particularly large nations, undergo a cycle of relative growth in relation to competitors, followed by a leveling-off period and ending in decline as others catch up. This well-documented phenomenon is found in the history of ancient empires; in more recent times it is documented in the cases of Portugal, the Netherlands, Spain, France, and the United Kingdom (Targepara 1986; Kennedy 1987; Thompson 1988). The fundamental assumption of internal distribution theories is that an association exists between stages in this internal cycle and the decisions of leaders to initiate war. There is still serious debate about what point on this cycle is related to war, with some suggesting before and others suggesting after the apex has been reached. Yet, cycle theory departs fundamentally from other power distribution models because it proposes that the interaction between states is not related to conflict: rather, internal dynamics generates stable and unstable behavior by nations within the international systems. Empirical evidence thus far is mixed. In their early work Doran and Parsons (1980) suggested a strong relation of cycles to war, but more recent reviews tend to discount or diffuse this finding (Thompson 1988).

Another approach associates conflict with the rise and decline of economic fortunes in the overall international system. This proposition, advanced prominently by Kondratieff and promulgated by Modelsky (1987), proposes that an international economic cycle accounts for conflict. This theory does not relate war to domestic performance; rather, nations are mere pawns of the systemic changes in fortunes that are the real underlying reason for conflict. The empirical jury on these propositions is still out (Goldstein 1985; Thompson 1988).

Note that as in the case of power preponderance and balance of power, internal power distribution theories completely recast the relation of power to conflict in ways not congruent with or anticipated by either of these interactive theories. Such recastings may yet produce fruitful results, but it is too early to pass judgment.

THE THEORY OF WAR AND PEACE: QUO VADIS?

Can we say that there is progress in the study of war and peace? The answer is a tentative yes. As part of this exercise, I read random articles on international conflict, starting with the end of World War II in the *American Political Science Review, World Politics, Foreign Affairs*, and more recently in the *Journal of Conflict Resolution*. In those written in the 1940s and 1950s and even in the late 1960s, I found few attempts to conceptualize theories of conflict or to go beyond simple case studies. Not surprisingly, few current writers refer to this almost purely descriptive work. However, a distinct change occurred after empirical results emerged in the *Journal of Conflict Resolution*. Although empirical work is seldom accepted when propositions are rejected, the results are used to temper theory formation, to support theories radically different from the accepted norm, and to provide some clarity to the field.

Empirical analysts have shown diffusion of international conflicts, rejected a direct link between domestic and international conflict, demonstrated that allies tend to fulfill their commitments, established that conflict among allies is less intense than among unattached nations, shown that the consequences of war are intense but can be overcome within two decades, established that geographic location is not incidental to the frequency of war, and challenged the validity of links between arms races and war. This body of work has been less successful in demonstrating the validity of competing theories. However, the development of power distribution theories is encouraging because numerous refinements and restatements of this concept of powers have led to substantial agreement regarding its measurement and empirical reviews of power distribution alternatives have narrowed the debate (Stoll and Ward 1989). It is encouraging that empirical tests, though still inadequate, are helping to resolve scientific disputes in our field.

The discipline is also beginning to develop more encompassing theories of war and peace. It is possible that conflict starts because individuals manipulate the environment—as decision-making models generally suggest (Allison 1969; Bueno de Mesquita et al. 1985; Zagare 1986)—or because of systemic changes that cannot be easily deflected by human effort—as structural theories usually imply (Thompson 1988; Doran and Parsons 1980; Organski and Kugler 1980; Waltz 1979). Yet we will gain little understanding of war unless we gain a similar and explicit understanding of the systematic and individual reasons for war. Moreo-

ver, theory still frequently concentrates on either war or peace. Muller
(1988) writes a gripping book on deterrence that poses the puzzling
question: Why did peace break out and no one notice? Achen and
Snidel (1989) challenge deterrence theory to account for the resolution
of the crisis that should have emerged and did not. Axelrod (1984) and
Keohane (1984) make important contributions to the study of war because they concentrate on cooperation. Thus far, however, studies of
conflict have concentrated on specifying the necessary conditions for
war and escalation of conflict, with promising results (Bueno de Mesquita and Lalman 1986; Houweling and Siccama 1988; Organski and
Kugler 1980). However, to gain a fuller understanding of war and
peace, we need to pay much more attention to the conditions under
which cooperation and peace break out.

Have we departed far from Thucydides? The answer is both yes and
no. The paradigm in use is still directly related to the structure outlined
by this classic writer, but increasingly theory is moving farther and farther away from his generalizations. Empirical work has helped to accept
some notions and to reject most others. It is my belief that the next
generation of scholars will be far more dependent on their own cohorts
than on their ancestors. The reason is that improved specification and
empirical developments now permit the rejection of most propositions
and the preservation of plausible ones. As we move into the future, and
as larger well-documented data sets become available to students of politics, it seems only logical that current work will be dramatically revised
and superseded. Improvements in data banks, formal structures that
have only started in the last decade, will undoubtedly expand and allow
us to integrate larger sections of the field. Nevertheless, our generation
can take credit for being the first to face the scientific challenge and explore—admittedly very incompletely—the propositions generated by
generations of students of war and peace.

NOTES

1. Recently many of these data collections have been extended under the
auspices of the Merriam Laboratory for Analytical Political Research as part of
the Data Development for International Relations project headed by Dina
Zinnes and Richard Merritt. Important extensions include Ted Robert Gurr,
National Capabilities; Jack Levy, Great Power Wars; Manus Midlarsky, Major–Minor Powers Wars; John Wilkenfeld, International Crisis Behavior; and
Frederic Parson, Interventions. These data sets should become available to the
community through the ICPSR at the University of Michigan in 1990.

2. Thomas Kuhn (1962) proposed the notion of a paradigm but con-
ceded that it has been used in various ways. In later work he argues that a paradigm "stands for the entire constellation of beliefs, values, techniques, shared

by the members of a given community. On the other hand, it denotes one sort of element in that constellation, the concrete puzzle-solutions which, employed as models or examples, can replace explicit rules as a basis for the solution of the remaining puzzles of normal science" (Kuhn 1962, 175). Here I employ paradigm in the first sense defined by Kuhn. For an effective and enlightening discussion with world politics applications, see Vasquez (1983, 1–12).

3. In no area is the difficulty of establishing a paradigm more apparent than in the study of human evolution. Darwin's notions were in sharp contrast to the prevailing theory of human creation held by the Western church, and the debate on the evidence is still being fought to this day. For example, "scientific" creationists challenge bone-dating techniques in an attempt to show that all species were concurrently created. However, the modern study of genetics has independently confirmed the validity of bone-dating techniques, lending further credence to Darwin's main insight about the mechanics of evolution without necessarily supporting each detail of his original proposal.

4. For a particularly heated discussion of data and paradigm in the context of deterrence see Richard Ned Lebow and Janice Gross Stein (1989) and Achen and Snidel (1989).

5. Yet that this arrangement is far from perfect is well exemplified in the current controversy over the creation of energy from fusion by chemical means. The ability to create low temperature fusion seems to have been rejected a mere six months after it was presented. *New York Times*, July 13, 1989, 1.

6. I note in passing that the more advanced the field the stronger is the consensus on rules of falsification. Note that Stephen Hawking, despite the enormous complexity of his ideas on time and space, accepts with little discussion Lakatos's criteria and through their application is able to reject complex alternatives (Hawking 1988, 9–13 and 47–49).

7. Perhaps Kautilya, who wrote his classic *Arthasastra* sometime between 321 and 296 B.C., deserves equal credit. This work antecedes, and parallels in many respects, the critical elements of Thucydides' postulates on conflict. However, I know of no evidence that Thucydides was aware of Kautilya's work, or that Western thinkers like Machiavelli, Hobbes, or Morgenthau, who laid the foundations of contemporary conflict theory and were familiar with the work of Thucydides, discovered the writings of Kautilya. (See Kautilya 1967.)

8. In a recent article on Thucydides and neorealism, Daniel Garst (1989) argues that the credit given to that writer by neorealists is misplaced and results from a misreading of that author's intent and content. In the conclusion of his extensive review Garst writes: "In writing *The Peloponnesian War*, Thucydides hoped to create a work for all times. This article has argued that Thucydides' enduring insights on international relations were primarily political rather than scientific. Thucydides' history does not point to general laws explaining international conflict, nor did its author intend it to do so. What *The Peloponnesian War* does provide are timeless insights into the basis of political power and hegemony." It is difficult to reconcile Garst's claim that Thucydides "does not point to general laws" since one definition of a law is a relation that applies to all times. Moreover, it is difficult to understand why enduring insights about

politics are not scientific. I believe that here terminology and content are confounded. Moreover, regardless of the validity of Garst's claim, it is important to note that neorealists and many realists before them who influenced the current generation of international relations specialists—i.e. Waltz, Gilpin, Keohane, Bueno de Mesquita, Kissinger—read Thucydides' work in the same way and gave him credit for identifying the elements critical to their analysis.

9. The development of physics is outlined in a clear and brilliant manner by Hawking (1988), who may well be the contemporary Galileo.

10. Aron (1966, 6) likewise concludes that international relations "present one original feature which distinguishes them from all other social relations: they take place within the shadow of war."

11. Woodrow Wilson should be labeled a "realist" rather than an "idealist," in my view, because he was as aware of the use of power as any of his predecessors. The accusation of "idealism" was motivated by his rejection of balance of power as a source of stability in an anarchical world and his attempt to create a hierarchy to ensure peace. Wilson was quite aware of power distributions and hoped to create a binding alliance among the major powers to ensure stability of all borders, including those of the major powers. His solution—once national self-determination was used to establish the legitimate distribution of territories in contested areas—was to use preponderant force against any violator of existing arrangements. Indeed, like the nation-state, Wilson wanted to allocate to the League of Nations the exclusive right to determine the rules and back up such rules with overwhelming power to help implement them. Thus, while the collective security would not amount to monopoly of legal coercion in the international arena, as is the case in the domestic environment, it would amount to a preponderance of coercive capabilities imposed by the combination of major powers. (For alternative views see Claude 1962; Carr 1940).

12. Deterrence is generally consistent with balance of power. An exception—not justified under an assumption of anarchy—is that a preponderant nuclear nation should wait to retaliate against attack rather than initiate an attack when it has a temporary preponderance (Brodie 1946). This inconsistency makes it difficult to operationalize unilateral and mutual deterrence in similar terms with consistent assumptions about the antagonists (Kugler 1984; Mayer 1988).

13. John Muller (1988) brings vividly to our attention an oversight present in most deterrence theories: the conditions for peace are effectively and fully elaborated, but those for war are simply noted without evaluation. This tendency is present in the treatment of nuclear deterrence by Intriligator and Brito (1987), who elaborate extensively the conditions for peace but fail to label the logical conditions their model suggests will lead to conflict. Indeed, their model suggests that since 1945 during transitions from the cone of war to compellence or from compellence to mutual deterrence a nuclear war should have been waged. The lack of nuclear conflict under such conditions is—after the fact—dismissed or attributed to luck. This emphasis on the partial outcome one wishes to explore is reversed by Organski and Kugler (1980), who define conditions for instability under parity and transition but fail to elaborate with equal precision the reasons for stability under preponderance.

14. For an alternative view of deterrence not based on balance of terror, see Muller (1988).

15. Michael McGinnis (1989) provides a complete evaluation of the growing literature on Richardson's arms race models.

16. Note that the predictions of Zinnes and Gillespie are consistent with models of bureaucratic politics proposed and extensively tested by Crecine, Kanter, and Wildawski.

17. Since this paper was written, events in China have confirmed that preponderant power can be used to enforce the wishes of a government.

18. Somewhat paradoxically E. H. Carr (1940, 109), a devoted realist, assumed anarchy in international politics and presumably hierarchy in domestic politics but nevertheless suggested that war "lurks in the background of international politics just as revolution lurks in the background of domestic politics."

19. Similar results are obtained when the prisoner's dilemma is played over a number of iterations (Rappaport and Chammah 1965) or when one adopts a strategy of tit-for-tat in repeated games (Axelrod 1984). However, unlike Zagere's results, Rappaport and Axelrod suggest that several failures occur before the cooperation quadrant is chosen. In the nuclear world such a learning curve would empirically require that a number of nuclear wars be waged before stability is fully understood.

REFERENCES

Achen, Christopher, and Duncan Snidel. 1989. "Rational Deterrence Theory and Comparative Case Studies." *World Politics* 41(2):19.

Allison, Graham T. 1969. "Conceptual Models and the Cuban Missile Crisis." *American Political Science Review* 63(3):689–718.

Aron, Raymond. 1966. *Peace and War: A Theory of International Relations*. Garden City, N.J.: Doubleday.

Axelrod, Robert. 1984. *The Evolution of Cooperation*. New York: Basic Books.

Brams, Steven. 1985. *Superpower Games: Applying Game Theory to Superpower Conflict*. New Haven: Yale University Press.

Brodie, Bernard. 1946. *The Absolute Weapon: Atomic Power and World Order*. New York: Harcourt, Brace & Company.

———. 1959. *Strategy in the Missile Age*. Princeton: Princeton University Press.

Bueno de Mesquita, Bruce. 1981. *The War Trap*. New Haven: Yale University Press.

———. 1983. "The Costs of War: A Rational Expectations Approach." *American Political Science Review* 77(2):347–56.

Bueno de Mesquita, Bruce, David Newman, and Alvin Rabushka. 1985. *Forecasting Political Events*. New Haven: Yale University Press.

Bueno de Mesquita, Bruce, and Riker, William. 1982. "An Assessment of the Merits of Nuclear Proliferation." *Journal of Conflict Resolution*.

Bueno de Mesquita, Bruce, and David Lalman. 1986. "Reason and War." *American Political Science Review* 80(4):1113–50.

Carr, Edward. 1940. *The Twenty Years' Crisis, 1919–1939: An Introduction to the Study of International Relations*. London: Macmillan.

Claude, Inis. 1962. *Power and International Relations*. New York: Random House.

Clausewitz, Carl von. 1976. *On War*. Princeton: Princeton University Press.

Darwin, Charles. 1859. *On the Origin of the Species by Means of Natural Selection*. London: S. Murray.

Doran, Charles. 1990. *Systems in Crisis: New Imperatives of High Politics at Century's End*. Forthcoming.

Doran, Charles, and Parsons, W. 1980. "War and the Cycle of Relative Power." *American Political Science Review* 14:947–65.

Garst, Daniel. 1989. "Thucydides and Neorealism." *International Studies Quarterly* 33(1):3–27.

George, Alexander, and Richard Smoke. 1974. *Deterrence in American Foreign Policy Theory and Practice*. New York: Columbia University Press.

Gilpen, Robert. 1981. *War and Change in World Politics*. Cambridge: Cambridge University Press.

Goldstein, Joshua. 1985. "War and the Kondratieff Upswing." *International Studies Quarterly* 29:411–41.

Grieco, Joseph. 1988. "Anarchy and the Limits of Cooperation." *International Organizations* 42(3):485–507.

Gurr, Ted R., ed. 1980. *Handbook of Political Conflict: Theory and Research*. New York: Free Press.

Hawking, Stephen W. 1988. *A Brief History of Time*. New York: Bantam.

Horn, Michael. 1984. "Arms Races and the Likelihood of War." Mimeo.

Houweling, H., and Siccama, J. G. 1988. "Power Transition as Cause of War." *Journal of Conflict Resolution* 32:87–102.

Howard, Nigel. 1971. *Paradoxes of Rationality: Theory of Metagames and Political Behavior*. Cambridge, Mass.: MIT Press.

Hume, David. 1742. "Of the Balance of Power." In *Classics of International Relations*, edited by John Vasquez. Englewood Cliffs, N.J: Prentice Hall, 1990.

Huntington, Samuel. 1958. "Arms Races: Prerequisites and Results." *Public Policy* 8:41–86.

———. 1989. "The U.S.—Decline or Renewal?" *World Politics* 67(2):76–96.

Huth, Paul. 1988. *Extended Deterrence and the Prevention of War*. New Haven: Yale University Press.

Huth, Paul, and Bruce Russett. 1984. "What Makes Deterrence Work? Cases from 1900 to 1980." *World Politics* 36:496–526.

———. 1988. "Deterrence Failure and Crisis Escalation." *International Studies Quarterly.*

Intriligator, Michael, and D. Brito. 1981. "Nuclear Proliferation and the Probability of War." *Public Choice* 37:247–60.

———. 1987. "The Stability of Mutual Deterrence." In *Exploring the Stability of Deterrence*, edited by Jacek Kugler and Frank Zagare. Boulder: Lynne Rienner.

Kaufman, William. 1956. *Military Policy and National Security.* Princeton: Princeton University Press.

Kautilya. 1967. *Arthasastra.* Mysore, India: Mysore Printing.

Kennedy, Paul. 1987. *The Rise and Fall of Great Powers.* New York: Random House.

Keohane, Robert. 1984. *After Hegemony: Cooperation and Discord in the World Political Order.* Princeton: Princeton University Press.

———. 1986. *Neorealism and Its Critics.* New York: Columbia University Press.

Kissinger, Henry. 1957. *Nuclear Weapons and Foreign Policy.* New York: Harper.

Kugler, Jacek. 1984. "Terror without Deterrence? Reassessing the Role of Nuclear Weapons." *Journal of Conflict Resolution* 28(3).

———. 1987. "The Politics of Foreign Debt in Latin America." *International Interactions* 13(2).

———. 1989. "Anticipating Domestic Violence with Measures of Political Capacity." Mimeo.

Kugler, Jacek, and Marina Arbetman. 1989. "Exploring the 'Phoenix Factor' with the Collective Goods Perspective." *Journal of Conflict Resolution* 33(1):84–122.

Kugler, Jacek, and A. F. K. Organski. 1989. "The End of Hegemony?" *International Interactions* 15(2):113–28.

———. 1989b. "The Power Transition: A Retrospective and Prospective Evaluation." In *Handbook of War Studies*, edited by Manus Midlarsky. Boston: Unwin Hyman.

Kugler, Jacek, A. F. K. Organski, and Daniel Fox. 1980. "Deterrence and the Arms Race: The Impotence of Power." *International Security* 11(2).

Kugler, Jacek, and Frank Zagare. 1990. "The Long Term Stability of Deterrence." *International Interactions* 15(3/4):255–78.

Kuhn, Thomas. 1962. *The Structure of Scientific Revolution.* Chicago: University of Chicago Press.

Lakatos, Imre. 1978. *The Methodology of Scientific Research Programmes.* Cambridge: Cambridge University Press.

Lebow, Richard Ned, and Janice Gross Stein. 1989. "When Does Deterrence Succeed and How Do We Know?" Mimeo.

Levy, Jack. 1983. *War in the Great Power System: 1495–1975*. Lexington: University Press of Kentucky.

McGinnis, Michael. 1989. "Richardson and the Political Concept of Arms Race Models: From Simplicity to Diversity." Presented at the American Political Science Association meetings, Atlanta.

Mayer, Thomas. 1988. "Arms Races and War Initiation: Some Alternatives to the Intriligator-Brito Model." *Journal of Conflict Resolution* 30(1):3–28.

Midlarsky, Manus, ed. 1989. *Handbook of War Studies*. Boston: Unwin Hyman.

Modelski, George. 1987. *Long Cycles in World Politics*. Seattle: University of Washington Press.

Morgenthau, Hans. 1948, 1978. *Politics Among Nations: The Struggle for Power and Peace*. New York: Knopf.

Morrow, James. 1990. "A Twist of Truth: A Re-examination of the Effects of Arms Races on the Occurrence of War." *Journal of Conflict Resolution*.

Most, Benjamin, and Harvey Starr. 1980. "Diffusion, Reinforcement, Geopolitics and the Spread of War." *American Political Science Review* 74:932–46.

Most, Benjamin, Harvey Starr, and Randolph Siverson. 1990. "The Logic and Study of the Diffusion of International Conflict." In *Handbook of War Studies*, edited by Manus Midlarsky. Boston: Unwin Hyman.

Muller, John. 1988. *Retreat from Doomsday*. New York: Basic Books.

Niou, Emerson, Peter Ordeshook, and Gregory Rose. 1989. *The Balance of Power: Stability and Instability in International Systems*. New York: Cambridge University Press.

Organski, A. F. K. 1958. *World Politics*. New York: Knopf.

Organski, A. F. K., and Jacek Kugler. 1980. *The War Ledger*. Chicago: University of Chicago Press.

Ostrom, Charles. 1978. "A Reactive Link Model of the U.S. Defense Expenditure Policy-Making Process." *American Political Science Review* 72:941–57.

Ostrom, Charles, and Robin Marra. 1986. "U.S. Defense Spending and the Soviet Estimate." *American Political Science Review* 80(3):821–41.

Oye, Kenneth. 1986. *Cooperation under Anarchy*. Princeton: Princeton University Press.

Powell, Robert. 1989. "Crisis Stability in the Nuclear Age." *American Political Science Review* 83(1):61–76.

Rappaport, Anatol, and H. Chammah. 1965. *Prisoner's Dilemma: A Study of Conflict and Cooperation*. Ann Arbor: University of Michigan Press.

Richardson, Lewis. 1960. *Arms and Insecurity: A Mathematical Study of the Causes and Origins of War*. Pittsburgh: Boxwood Press.

Riker, William. 1973. *An Introduction to Positive Political Theory*. Englewood Cliffs, N.J.: Prentice-Hall.

Rosen, Steven. 1972. "War Power and the Willingness to Suffer." In *Peace, War and Numbers*, edited by Bruce Russett. Beverly Hills: Sage.

————. 1977. "A Stable System of Mutual Nuclear Deterrence in the Arab-Israeli Conflict." *American Political Science Review* 71:1367–83.

Russett, Bruce. 1963. "The Calculus of Deterrence." *Journal of Conflict Resolution* 7:97–109.

————. 1985. "America's Continuing Strengths." *International Organization* 39(2) (Spring).

Singer, David, Stuart Bremer, and John Stuckey. 1972. "Capability Distribution, Uncertainty, and Major Power War, 1980–1965." In *Peace, War and Numbers*, edited by Bruce Russett. Beverly Hills: Sage.

Singer, David, and Melvin Small. 1972. *The Wages of War*. New York: John Wiley.

Siverson, Randolph, and Joel King. 1980. "Alliances and the Expansion of War." In *To Augur Well: Early Warning Indicators in World Politics*, edited by J.D. Singer and M.D. Wallace. Beverly Hills: Sage.

Small, Melvin, and David Singer. 1982. *Resort to Arms*. Beverly Hills: Sage.

Smith, T. 1980. "Arms Race Instability and War." *Journal of Conflict Resolution* 24:253–84.

Smoker, Paul. 1964. "Fear in the Arms Race." *Journal of Peace Research* 1: 55–63.

Snyder, Glenn. 1977. *Conflict Among Nations: Bargaining and Decision Making in International Crises*. Princeton: Princeton University Press.

Snyder, G.H., and P. Diesing. 1977. *Conflict Among Nations: Bargaining, Decisionmaking System Structure in International Crisis*. Princeton, N.J.: Princeton University Press.

Starr, Harvey, and Randolph Siverson. 1990. "Opportunity, Willingness and the Diffusion of War, 1816–1965." *American Political Science Review* 84.

Stoll, Richard, and Michael Ward, eds. 1989. *Power in World Politics*. Boulder: Lynne Rienner Publishers.

Targepara, Rein. 1986. "Growth and Decline of Empires since 600 A.D." Presented at the International Studies Association meeting, Anaheim.

Taylor, Charles, and David Jodice. 1983. *World Handbook of Political and Social Indicators*. 3rd ed., 2 vols. New Haven: Yale University Press.

Thompson, William. 1988. *On Global War: Historical-Structural Approaches to World Politics*. Columbia: University of South Carolina Press.

Thucydides. 1985. *The Pelopennesian War*, translated by R. Crawley. New York: Modern Library College Editions.

Vasquez, John. 1983. *The Power of Power Politics*. New Brunswick, N.J.: Rutgers University Press.

Wallace, M. D. 1979. "Arms Races and Escalation: Some New Evidence." *Journal of Conflict Resolution* 23:3–16.

Waltz, Kenneth. 1954. *Man, the State and War*. New York: Columbia University Press.

————. 1979. *A Theory of International Politics*. Reading, Mass.: Addison-Wesley.

————. 1981. "The Spread of Nuclear Weapons: More May Be Better." Adelphi paper no. 171. London: The International Institute for Strategic Studies.

Ward, Michael Don. 1984. "Differential Paths to Parity: A Study of the Contemporary Arms Race." *American Political Science Review* 78:297–317.

Wilkenfeld, Jonathon, Michael Brecher, and Sheila Moser. 1988. *Crises in the Twentieth Century*. Vol. 2. New York: Pergamon Press.

Williams, P. 1975. "Deterrence." In *Contemporary Strategies*, edited by John Bayle et al. New York: Holms & Meir.

Wittman, D. 1979. "How a War Ends: A Rational Model Approach." *Journal of Conflict Resolution* 23:743–63.

Zagare, Frank. 1986. *The Dynamics of Deterrence*. Chicago: University of Chicago Press.

Zinnes, Dina, John Gillespie, and Michael Rubinson. 1976. "A Reinterpretation of the Richardson Arms Race Model." In *Mathematical Models in International Politics*, edited by Dina Zinnes and John Gillespie. New York: Praeger.

6

Political Economy
within Nations

William R. Keech, Robert H. Bates,
and Peter Lange

As the nineteenth-century name for what is now known as economics, political economy once suggested the possibility of a single discipline that integrated political and economic phenomena. Instead, two disciplines, economics and political science, have developed quite separately. These disciplines have had rather little in common intellectually, in spite of substantial common ground in their subject matter. More recently, however, economists have paid increasing attention to political phenomena, and political scientists have done the same to economic phenomena. Although some of this work continues on quite separate tracks, members of the two disciplines are sharing ideas to an unprecedented degree.

We find this sharing constructive, and we wish to use this essay to illustrate some of its benefits for political science. These benefits are twofold. The scope of our discipline is expanded when we recognize the ways that politics affects economic phenomena, and vice versa. Also, economic concepts and choice-theoretic reasoning can contribute to deeper explanation and better understanding. Accordingly, there are two themes to our chapter. One is the utility of a kind of reasoning that is shared by most economists and many political scientists. We call this choice-theoretic reasoning. The second is the substantive relationship

We would like to acknowledge the advice of Douglas Nelson, John Conybeare, Ronald Herring, and the Comparative Politics Group at the University of North Carolina.

between political and economic phenomena, and between government and markets.

The two themes can easily go together, but they do not necessarily do so. Many studies of the relationship between politics and economics do not involve choice-theoretic reasoning. This chapter will emphasize those that do. Such studies serve as a promising basis for a more comprehensive social science by uniting market and nonmarket phenomena in a common framework (Denzau et al. 1985, 1117). With some leavening from psychology and elsewhere, we hope to show that there is more to this than intellectual imperialism from economics. Each discipline can be enhanced by the insights of the other. By identifying common ground and by merging diverse disciplinary solutions to similar problems, we broaden our perspectives and enhance the power of our knowledge.

The term political economy means many things to many people in our discipline, ranging from Marxist analysis to neoclassical microeconomic studies of politics. We do not presume that our analysis will satisfy all practitioners or identifiers, nor do we claim that our description is authoritative, let alone inclusive.

Our chapter is about the application of choice-theoretic reasoning to three areas of political science. As such we are discussing the utility of an epistemological and methodological approach. Since this approach is used in both economics and political science, one might describe our enterprise as political economy on this ground. In each section we discuss to at least some degree the substantive relationship between politics and states, on the one hand, and economics and markets on the other. Here is a second ground on which the subject of our chapter might be called political economy. Even though the approach and the substance both provide grounds for inclusion in a chapter on political economy, these grounds are conceptually independent and separable. We have chosen to emphasize the relation of the one to the other.

In the first section we identify three fundamental characteristics of choice-theoretic reasoning and their applicability to politics. Three substantive sections follow, written respectively by specialists in American, European, and Third World politics, and reflecting the literature in those areas.

Just as we hope this chapter will undermine the intellectual boundaries between political science and economics, we also mean to undermine the intellectual boundaries between the studies of American, European, and Third World politics. We do so by using a common intellectual approach, and by suggesting that some research that grows out of one geographic area is applicable in another. The second section of the chapter, which reflects the literature in American politics, deals with the democratic political process in a setting in which the analytical distinction between government and markets is often considered a viable one. Much of the work reported there on voting and on legislative behavior is applicable in Europe.

The third section, which reflects the literature on Western European politics, deals with issues of the meaning of democracy in a setting in which the analytical distinction between markets and government is often considered less viable. Here we emphasize the interpenetration of institutions, government, and markets, and stress the contributions that choice-theoretic reasoning has made to the understanding of these phenomena. Since sections 2 and 3 each deal with democratic systems, much of the discussion of section 3 applies to both the United States and other advanced industrial democracies. Accordingly, we have for the most part eschewed geographic references in these sections.

Section 4 reflects the literature on political development and the Third World. Here we return to a more clearcut distinction between states and markets in a setting in which such a distinction is controversial. Although we do not have a section on international relations, political economy is thriving in that setting in both senses of approach and substance.[1]

1. CHOICE-THEORETIC REASONING ABOUT POLITICS

Three themes characterize choice-theoretic reasoning. One is an emphasis on individuals and their choices. The second is a concern with the aggregation of individual preferences by way of markets, elections, and collective action, and with the relative desirability of various patterns of aggregation. The third is a concern with costs and with constraints on possible outcomes.

Individuals and Choices

Individuals are the basic unit of analysis in choice-theoretic reasoning, and individual choices are a central variable. This feature is both realistic and constructive. We believe that individual choices are a truly fundamental unit of analysis of social and political phenomena, and that explanations of such phenomena that are rooted in the analysis of individual choice and behavior are likely to be deeper than those that are not.

As Elster (1985, 5–8) explains, such "methodological individualism" does not presuppose selfishness or even rationality, and it can even be used as a basis for Marxist theory (see Elster 1985; Roemer 1982). Elster defends it as a form of reductionism that is designed to reduce the time span between cause and effect and thus to avoid spurious explanation.

Much of choice-theoretic reasoning does in fact go beyond individualism in the broad sense just expressed to the assumptions of selfishness and rationality. A traditional view is that economic phenomena can be explained in terms of rational, utility-maximizing behavior, where utility is grounded in individual tastes. Such tastes are often considered to be exogenous to all economic arguments. They are typically taken to be subject to explanation only by other disciplines, such as psychology, but to be fixed, or stable, as well as exogenous to economic explanations.

In the broader and more eclectic view that we present here, these presumptions are not necessary. In our view, individual preferences are fluid, capable of redefinition, subject to influence, and often subject to serious internal conflict and inconsistency (see March 1978; Elster 1979, 1983; Schelling 1984; and Rhoads 1985).[2] In short, although it is perfectly reasonable to consider preferences as exogenous and fixed for purposes of a particular analysis, a broader view will acknowledge that preferences are endogenous. This perspective allows political economists to take advantage of and contribute to the considerable body of research in political science on the sources of preferences.

Narrow presumptions of rationality are also not necessary to our view. Simon (1976) distinguishes between what he calls substantive and procedural rationality. The former is behavior that is "appropriate to the achievement of given goals within the limits imposed by given conditions and constraints," and the latter is "the outcome of appropriate deliberation."

A prominent version of the former is "subjective expected utility maximization," which probably characterizes the professional worldview of most economists. Most holders of this view would argue that, even though people may make mistakes, they do not make systematic and repeated mistakes, and that they do not behave inconsistently. This view is challenged by Kahneman, Tversky, and their colleagues, who do find systematic biases in human decision-making.[3] Quattrone and Tversky (1988) have identified several that are especially relevant to politics. We accept such findings, and do not believe that they threaten the utility of choice-theoretic reasoning in political economy.

What is more important and constructive is the view that individuals are intelligent beings who make choices. Their cognitive capacities may be limited, and their goals may be neither clear nor fixed. Still, their behavior can be better understood with the assumption that they have some goals and that they are making choices among available alternatives. We will show below how this presumption leads to increased understanding in several settings.

The Problems of Aggregation and Optimization

Political economy offers three models for understanding how individual preferences may be aggregated and for analyzing how the outcomes of such aggregation might be evaluated from a social point of view. They are markets, elections, and voluntary collective action.

Markets One of the central problems of economics is how individual preferences are aggregated in markets to determine prices and quantities of goods and services. Microeconomics is the theory of such aggregation, and microeconomic theory identifies conditions under which markets maximize social welfare. That is, microeconomic theory is a theory not only of distribution but of optimal distribution, emphasizing efficiency criteria. It offers not only a theory of market success but also a theory of market failure and thereby an implicit theory of government. Originally, this was a theory of benevolent government's applying the wisdom of economics to rectify market failure. Increasingly, a theory of government is developing in both disciplines that recognizes that public officials may not always reliably correct market failures in the way economists would recommend. (See Rhoads 1985, chap. 5.)

Elections One of the central problems of politics is the aggregation of individual political preferences outside of markets. Voting and elections in democracies have long been a central topic in political science. But political science has not had a theory of the optimal aggregation of preferences, which might *define* the public interest. Nor has our discipline had a widely accepted theory of the public interest independent of the aggregation of preferences. Major advances on both counts have come from economics, where optimizing is a much more central theme.

Kenneth Arrow (1951, 1963) identified a fundamental limitation on the possibility of using electoral procedures to aggregate preferences into an authoritative definition of general welfare or the public interest. He showed that when there are more than two alternatives, any voting method or decision rule must fail simultaneously to fulfill a few basic and seemingly innocuous criteria. The implication is that even if all votes are taken as legitimate expressions of individual preference, all election methods are at best somewhat arbitrary.

An interdisciplinary theory of social choice developed in the wake of Arrow's research, but it operated for a long time on the fringes of both political science and economics.[4] More recently, William Riker (1982) has provided "a confrontation between the theory of democracy and the theory of social choice." His book provides a survey of social choice theory in the context of traditional concerns of democratic theory, such as participation, liberty, and equality. Riker argues that modern social choice theory is in fact quite compatible with a liberal or Madisonian version of democratic theory, such as that found in *The Federalist Papers*, and that it undermines other, more populist theories of democracy. As such, this brand of political economy can contribute to normative political theory.

Voluntary action Just as Arrow gave political scientists fundamental insights about elections, another economist, Mancur Olson (1965, 1971), gave us fundamental insights about the possibilities of achieving political goals through voluntary action. Olson applied the economic theory of collective goods to issues of groups and organizations. He argued that under common circumstances, "rational, self-interested individuals will not act to achieve their common or group interests" (1971, 2).

While Olson's theory has not been the last word on interest groups (see for example Moe 1980; Walker 1983), the application of this point has had enormous impact on many areas of political science. It seriously undermined pluralist theory, which was once the discipline's dominant view of American politics, and all contemporary studies of group politics must address his insight.

Olson was identifying the generic collective action problem in the context of interest groups. This problem is commonly known as a prisoner's dilemma type of situation, and its applications range from the interaction of pairs of individuals to the provision of national-level public goods such as defense, and to the interactions among nations.

The prisoner's dilemma, or collective action problem, is an abstraction of situations in which individually "rational" behavior leads to collective outcomes that are undesirable for the individuals involved. This model is useful both as an explanation of behavior and for the identification of the nature of social problems to be overcome. The collective action problem is not the unique property of political economy, but it is so generally important as to be a common theme in psychology and sociology as well as in political science and economics.

The possibility that coercion might solve such collective action problems is an insight at least as old as Thomas Hobbes, and there is renewed awareness that the collective action problem can be a rationale for government itself. But of course coercion has its own problems, and a major theme of current research is the identification of conditions under which desirable cooperation can emerge without coercion (see Axelrod 1984). The contrast between theory of markets and theory of collective action makes it apparent that selfish individual behavior may sometimes maximize welfare and at other times lead to suboptimal results.[5] And social choice theory makes it clear that elections cannot be assumed to assure the maximization of social welfare.

Costs and Constraints

A third fundamental feature of choice-theoretic thinking is attention to costs and constraints. The economist views individuals as making choices among alternative commodities with different prices or costs and a budget or resource constraint. Choice-theoretic reasoning about politics also considers the costs of alternative choices, whether in terms of their prices or their consequences. The absence of a price system in the political world makes such issues less quantifiable, but this fact does not lessen the importance of the issue. Choices are made and consequences are experienced under real world constraints on what is possible. Whether or not these constraints are clearly perceived or well understood by political actors is an open question, but they are of interest to the analyst in either case.

Costs and constraints are especially prominent in policy analysis, in the form of benefit-cost analysis, an effort to apply "objective" economic reasoning to policy choice.[6] As its proponents recognize, objective measurement of costs and benefits is not always possible, and, as Ferejohn (1974) shows, benefit-cost analysis can readily become just another politically manipulated element of a much less objective political interaction.

Another area of political economy in which models of constraints on possible outcomes are especially relevant is in the politics of macroeconomic policy. Macroeconomic theory identifies limits on possible macroeconomic outcomes, though explicit attention is given to this problem in only a few articles.[7]

2. APPLICATIONS IN DOMESTIC POLITICAL PROCESSES

Although the subfield of American politics is in some respects an "area study," it is probably the part of political science in which democratic political behavior, institutions, processes, and outcomes have been studied in greatest depth.

The Demand for Public Policy: Examples from the Study of Voting

Choice-theoretic reasoning has contributed importantly to the study of voting, which is perhaps the quintessential democratic act. Anthony Downs's *An Economic Theory of Democracy* (1957) introduced the idea that parties compete with each other by taking positions relative to voters in issue space. This was a political application of the economic idea that firms may compete by choosing optimal locations relative to customers in geographical space. The construct of the median voter has been used to explain the incentives of each of two parties to move toward the center in order to win when elections are contested in a one-dimensional issue space.

Donald Stokes (1963) pointed out that elections are much more complicated than that. For one thing, more than one issue dimension may be involved. For another, electoral competition often hinges on "valence" issues, such as prosperity or corruption, about which there is not disagreement regarding what is desirable. The question is which party is associated with a condition that is agreed to be desirable or undesirable.

Political economy has responded to each of these challenges, with a theory of voting in multidimensional issue space, and with a theory of retrospective voting, respectively. The spatial theory of voting provides the basis for understanding the behavior of both candidates and voters in n-dimensional issue spaces (Enelow and Hinich 1984). This theory presumes that all voters' preferences can be understood as being arrayed in such a mathematical space, and that the voters choose among candidates by picking the one that is closest to them. Candidates are typically presumed to choose positions in the space so as to maximize their prospects of winning votes, but spatial theory also lends itself to the study of the consequences of other candidate motivations, such as policy goals.[8]

Empirical spatial models have been used to map the preferences of voters (Poole and Rosenthal 1984), to study the process of electoral change (Rabinowitz et al. 1984), and to study the competition over issues in particular elections (Page and Brody 1972). Abstract spatial models have been used to show how electoral outcomes in multidimensional issue spaces can be manipulated by those who control the agenda (McKelvey 1976; Riker 1982). Recently, Rabinowitz and Macdonald (1989) have shown that the predictive ability of the basic spatial model may be enhanced by linking it with some psychological premises about the direction of preferences as well as distance.

Theory about retrospective voting has addressed Stokes's other major challenge to Downs's theory. The idea that voters respond to their evaluation of incumbent government performance had been the basis for Key's (1966) challenge to then-dominant social-psychological models of voting. Kramer (1971) presented a more self-consciously choice-theoretic elaboration of retrospective performance evaluation as a basis for voting. In fact, Kramer's model built on Downs's own idea that a reasonable expectation of the future performance of incumbents could be projected from their past performance, and could be compared to a less informed guess about the future performance of an alternative party. Fiorina (1981) has developed these ideas and tested them empirically in an in-depth study of contemporary American voting behavior.

The Supply of Public Policy:
Examples from the Study of Legislatures

The methods of political economy have contributed to the study of legislative behavior, principally by introducing the method of assuming a goal orientation and inferring from it hypotheses about behavior. Richard Fenno and David Mayhew pioneered this approach. Mayhew (1974) posited a goal of reelection and showed how the institutions of Congress might be better understood if scholars asked how they were designed to help fulfill that goal for its members.

Richard Fenno (1973) observed that congressmen are motivated by a desire for influence in the legislature and for good public policy, as well as by the desire for reelection. The mix of these and other goals will vary among legislators. Fenno argued that different committees help congressmen fulfill different goals, and that members seek membership on committees that will help them fulfill their own goals. He showed that these premises helped to understand the decision-making behavior and the policy outcomes of different committees. Richard Hall (1987) extended this logic to the individual level. He found that congressmen's goals could be measured, and that they vary across members and legislative options within a given committee. This variation can be used to explain variation in participation in committee decision-making.

Legislative behavior and institutions can also be understood in the context of spatial models such as those mentioned above for the study of voting. Different issue preferences can be modeled as positions in an n-dimensional issue space. Shepsle and Weingast (1987) show how spatial models can be used to illustrate the nature of committee power in two ways. Committees can influence the outcome of floor votes by their strategic choice of what bills to report, and they can do so by their influence over the decisions of conference committees.

Congressional roll call voting has been modeled in diverse choice-theoretic terms. Kingdon's cognitive processing model (1981) is probably the leading theory of legislative voting in political science, but economists have recently entered this area of study with utility-maximizing models of economic self-interest. For example, Peltzman (1985) interprets historical changes in roll call voting in terms of changes in the economic interests of the districts.

Markets and Governments:
Rationales for Change at the Margin

Political economy provides intellectual tools for evaluating the policies voters might want or legislatures might consider. For example, how much should society depend on markets and how much on governments in making collective decisions and in allocating resources? Modern neoclassical microeconomic theory establishes convincingly that under the highly restrictive (and rare) conditions of perfect competition, market systems are efficient and welfare-maximizing. Advocates of markets are influenced by an understanding of how markets work under favorable conditions.

In fact, economic theories of market *failure* provide some of the most compelling rationales for government. Conditions of perfect markets are often not met. First, collective goods, such as national defense, are not always adequately provided by markets, because of the free rider problem. Government can address this problem by coercing citizens to pay for such collective goods through taxation.

Second, some markets involve increasing returns to scale. Concentration of production in a few large firms may allow more efficient production than is possible in many smaller firms. Under such conditions, firms may produce less or charge more than they could if they lacked the market power that comes from concentration. Government can address this problem by producing the goods itself, by regulation of the industry, or by antitrust policy.

Third, when the quality of products cannot be readily evaluated by the consumer, as in the case of food and drugs, government can protect the consumer by inspection or licensing. Or when incentives to create new products may be undermined by possibilities of imitation, government can protect those incentives by issuing patents.

Fourth, markets do not assure fairness. Even the most efficient markets may create great inequities in the distribution of income or wealth. Government may seek to redress some of these inequities through progressive income taxation or transfer payments.[9]

Finally, the macroeconomy does not always perform satisfactorily. Government stabilization policy is seen as a possible solution to problems of inflation and of unemployment.

In the form of the above points, the analysis of markets in economics has provided some of the most compelling rationales for government activity. Such theory deserves a prominent place in political science. There is no irony in the fact that economics has been the main source of theory about the desirable qualities of markets, and thus about the rationales for using markets as a method of allocating resources. It is, however, perhaps ironic that economic theory of market failure is such an important source of theoretical rationales for government.

Many economists have assumed that the government that steps in to resolve market failure is itself benevolent and knows how to maximize welfare, usually using the concepts of economics. But political science has not had a theory of *government failure* to identify the comparable liabilities of government when it is not at its best. Political economy is responding to this gap. For example, Charles Wolf details the conditions of the demand and of the supply of government activity, and puts them together in a theory of the sources of "non-market failure" (1988, chaps. 3–4).

Work in public choice has long emphasized that government may not be a reliable solution to market failure, because governments are operated by humans who are interested in maximizing their own utility, as well as the general welfare. That is, public choice took the premise of selfish, utility-maximizing behavior that characterizes economic models and applied it to models of government behavior. The resulting models show how public officials who maximize their own utility may make policy that is not in the public interest.

A leading early example was Niskanen (1971), who showed that bureaucrats seeking to maximize their budgets could cause government to become larger than is optimal. Nordhaus (1975) showed how vote-maximizing public officials might create a politically induced business cycle and suboptimal economic outcomes. Shepsle and Weingast (1981) showed how geographic representation and the economics of public projects could lead to provision of inefficient projects whose benefits are less than their costs.[10]

Each of these studies identified a process by which market failure might *not* be resolved by government intervention. Furthermore, they suggested that democratic government might actually make things worse. In general, they provided a scholarly basis for skepticism about government as a solution to market failure, but they did not directly address the question of whether the government failure was worse than no government intervention. Surely not all government interventions are still worse than all market failures.

Shepsle and Weingast (1984) address this question in the context of their above-noted model of distributive politics and geographic representation. They identify circumstances in which democratically produced public policies improve on market failures and others in which the politically determined results are even worse than the original market failure. Applying this question to other areas of market failure will be an important topic for political economy to pursue.

Political Economy and the Study of Institutions

Shepsle (1979) showed that institutional procedures might induce predictable equilibria in the outcome of voting situations that might otherwise be unpredictable because of the problems identified by Arrow (1963). The studies by Shepsle and Weingast noted above are studies that consciously model institutions, such as geographically based representation and a legislative committee system.

Charles Stewart (1988) has shown how one important result about institutions may be specific to a particular setting. Shepsle and Weingast (1981, 1984) have developed a theme in which preferences for high government spending flourish in an environment where decision-making is fragmented, as in the committee system of the U.S. Congress. The implicit alternative is lower spending and more centralized decision-making. Stewart points out that there are several other possibilities imaginable in abstract, and observable in American history. For example, he shows that expansionary impulses have been achieved by centralization and retrenching policy goals have been achieved by decentralization. The effect of institutions may be contingent on other features of the environment.

Modern choice-theoretic analyses of the design and selection of institutions go back at least to Buchanan and Tullock's abstract study of the choice of constitutional rules (1962) and Vincent Ostrom's analytical study of *The Federalist Papers* (1971, 1987). The current flourishing of studies includes very abstract game-theoretic studies of the choice of institutions (Tsebelis 1989), evaluations of alternative decision rules (Merrill 1988), and empirical studies of actual constitutional choice (McGuire and Ohsfeldt 1989).

Combining Models of Supply, Demand and Institutions: The Politics of Macroeconomic Policy

Macroeconomic indicators have been perhaps the most commonly used standards for the evaluation of government performance, and a rich literature has grown up detailing the topic. The scholarly recognition that elections may hinge on economic performance led to another advance. Studies began to investigate the interaction between electoral incentives and economic policy-making. The hypothesis of the political business cycle expressed the idea that public officials might manipulate economic policy to win elections. This idea was elaborated in a tightly reasoned theoretical model (Nordhaus 1975) and in a more empirical application (Tufte 1978).

Nordhaus, an economist, presented a major challenge to political scientists, arguing that democratic policy-making might be systematically suboptimal: "democratic systems will choose a policy . . . that has lower unemployment and higher inflation than is optimal" (1975, 178). The question of optimizing definable and measurable goals is characteristic of economic thinking, but still rather rare in political science, which has not responded much to Nordhaus's challenge about the characteristics of democratic policy choice.[11] The main response to his article has been in a spate of empirical studies of political business cycles that have for the most part generated negative results (see Alt and Chrystal 1983 and Hibbs 1987 for reviews).

The dominant theme of this literature has shifted from political business cycles to differences between political parties (Hibbs 1987). Numerous studies have found systematic differences between parties in unemployment rates. They have led political scientists to be much more conscious of the differences between choices on policy instruments, such as those of monetary and fiscal policy, and policy outcomes, such as unemployment and inflation. For the most part, systematic party differences in instruments have been less than the differences in outcomes attributed to parties, leading Woolley (1988) to identify a "macropolitics paradox." Several studies have inferred party differences in output or unemployment from party differences in choices of monetary policy instruments as simulated through models of the economy as a constraint on possible outcomes.[12] The studies that have explicitly taken into account the way that the structure of the economy limits possible outcomes have found party differences to be small.

The study of the politics of macroeconomic policy has increased awareness of the role that alternative institutions play in structuring the incentives and behavior of political actors. Relevant institutions include the length of electoral terms, the separation of powers in the legislative process for fiscal policy, the independence of the Federal Reserve, and the possibility of rules such as balanced budget amendments and line item vetoes.

3. APPLICATIONS IN ADVANCED INDUSTRIAL DEMOCRACIES

Macro and Micro Levels of Political Economy

Political economy, and especially questions of the linkages between mass democracy, capitalism, and state institutions, have assumed prominence in the study of the advanced industrial democracies in the last two decades.[13] This research has predominantly been concerned with *macro* political economic issues: the role of politics and political and market institutions in the determination of economic processes and outcomes, and the role of market forces in political institutions and processes in economies dominated by private control over the means of production. In contrast to most of the macro political economic literature on the United States, two features of this work stand out. First, it has given prominence to economic class, class divisions, organizations built on class lines, and the potential for conflict that these imply under capitalism. The focus has been on how the politics of class intersects with the politics of democracy to affect class relations, democratic processes and outcomes, and the nature and performance of capitalism.[14] Second, analysis has focused on the institutional, rather than individual, level.

The application of choice-theoretic analysis and the search for individual-level "microfoundations" of macro outcomes have often played little or no role in these studies. More recently, however, methodological individualism, individual choices under constraints, and the collective action problem, and their implications for understanding the relationship between politics and markets, have received greater attention.[15] The attempts to establish microfoundations for a number of the most important macro outcomes demonstrate the potential, and the difficulties and challenges, of attempting to link these two levels and forms of analysis in the comparative study of political economic choices and outcomes in the institutional contexts of the advanced capitalist democracies.[16]

In the pages that follow, we will discuss some themes of macro political economy and the ways in which choice-theoretic analysis has recently been brought into play. We begin with a discussion of the particular challenge that the character of European societies poses for those interested in establishing rational microfoundations for macro political economic outcomes.

The Challenge of Historical Institutionalist Analysis

Historical institutions and collective actors in the European political economies have seemed all-pervasive and highly resilient to the effects of economic, social, and political change.[17] Whether conceived of narrowly—as particular political parties or interest group structures, for instance—or more broadly—as configurations of state institutions, social classes, and cleavage structures, or even as national patterns of policy-making and class compromise—institutions have played a central role in analyses of the European political economies.

Thus they have profoundly affected how macro political economic outcomes and their causes have been studied. At the macro level, the inescapable interpenetration of political and social institutions with the market has been highlighted. From Polanyi's *The Great Transformation* (1944, 1957) to Shonfield's *Modern Capitalism* (1965) and Gerschenkron's *Economic Backwardness in Historical Perspective* (1966) to more contemporary studies, the inseparability of state structures, social institutions and the market, and political and economic processes has been emphasized.[18] The central research tasks have been the description, explanation, and delineation of the consequences of cross-national differences in these interpenetrated institutions and processes, and of the changes over time in the "boundaries of the political" (Maier 1987).

The notion of "free" markets separate from political processes—common in much of the American literature—has been foreign to most of this work on Europe. Much of it has, instead, stressed the *positive* contribution to distribution, welfare, and even aggregate economic performance and efficiency made by *some forms* of national political economic institutional arrangements and state interventions.

The pervasiveness of institutions has also had a profound impact on the use of choice-theoretic approaches to the political economies of the advanced industrial democracies. There has been a widespread belief among those studying the macro political economy that the undeniable role of institutions has made application of choice-theoretic analysis and the search for microfoundations of little use at best and fundamentally misguided at worst. Similarly, in contrast to the assumption of the centrality of individuals, rationality, and choice, the emphasis has been on collective actors, including the state, on the historical and institutional conditioning of actors' beliefs, norms, and (resultant) preferences and behavior and thus on the highly constrained nature of the "choices" that actors make. The "value added" of adopting a choice-theoretic rather than a causal (or functional) perspective has seemed small and the loss in richness of understanding potentially large. (For an excellent discussion see March and Olsen 1984.)

A similar implicit, and sometimes explicit, critique has been made of the application of Olson's (1971) treatment of the collective action problem to groups and social movements. Again, the assumption has been that historically and institutionally grounded norms and ties of solidarity make the assumption of narrowly self-interested individuals and of free riding fundamentally misplaced. A much more historical and sociological perspective on the individual has been offered in counterpoint. The challenge these critiques represent for the role of choice-theoretic reasoning in political economy is clear (March and Olsen 1984).

What is less evident but also true, however, is that this challenge also represents a major opportunity. Notions of the rational pursuit of interests, strategy, and intended and unintended consequences appear often in these historical-institutionalist studies. Governments, bureaucrats, interest groups and their leaders, political parties and politicians, and even social classes and economic sectors are often implicitly (and sometimes explicitly) interpreted as behaving in boundedly rational ways in pursuit of their own and/or some collective interest. National institutional arrangements and specific policies are frequently explained in terms of how they serve the interests of actors as well as how they constrain their behavior. In fact, the view that institutions chosen instrumentally (although not always with the intended consequence) at one point act as constraints on subsequent choices is a central tenet of this literature (Krasner 1984).

These are conceptualizations that invite the application of the tools of choice-theoretic analysis, albeit in ways that are sensitive to the endogeneity of preferences, to hysteresis and the power of institutional constraints on action, and to the appropriateness (and efficiency) of treating collectivities as "actors" despite the violation of methodological individualism and ignoring of aggregation problems that may be entailed in doing so. It is, thus, in working out what we think are potentially powerful intersections and overlaps of the two approaches in the context of the advanced industrial democracies that significant gains are to be made. Some contemporary examples drawn from work on the relationship between capitalism, collective actors, and democracy can illustrate this potential.

Class Compromise

Certainly one of the classic themes of both nineteenth- and twentieth-century political economy has been the relationship between the class division of capitalism and democratic politics. From the expectation that industrial capitalism would produce a working-class revolution, and overthrow both capitalism and "bourgeois democracy," to the belief that, when combined with mass democracy, it would lead to the evolutionary socialization of the economy, the central question gradually became why, despite these expectations, did democratic capitalism endure and even win the apparent consent of the working class.

There is, of course, a vast literature on the topic. Much of it has concentrated on the ways in which forms of capitalist hegemony (Gramsci 1971) or capitalist state action (O'Connor 1973), or democratic legitimacy and state action, or affluence or values other than class loyalty and consciousness (Lipset 1960) have dulled or diverted the class conflict rooted in the structure of modern capitalism. To a large extent, such work has not directly examined the long-standing assumption that the rational pursuit of class interest by the working class under capitalism would promote class conflict, were it not for the effects of other factors.[19]

Drawing on rational choice assumptions and formal and game theoretic analyses, however, Przeworski and Wallerstein (1982; Przeworski 1985; see also Schott 1984a and Lancaster 1973) have shown that class compromise under democratic capitalism can be beneficial for both workers and capitalists. Recognizing the basic economic logic of capitalism that links current investment by capitalists to future growth of the economic product from which both wages and further funds for investment may be drawn, they have shown the conditions under which it may be rational for workers to restrain their current wage militancy, to accept limitations on their share of the product, to allow capitalists discretion over profits, to support state policies which promote investment in exchange for the right to organize, and to use democratic processes to enhance their security and well-being over time within the structural confines of capitalism.

This work challenges the assumed economic irrationality of class compromise under capitalism. The challenge is both to the left and the right, for it questions both whether class confrontation is always in the interests of workers and whether its absence is necessarily attributable to socialization and values, rather than to the strategic pursuit of economic self-interest.

Like all formal models, that of Przeworski and Wallerstein makes assumptions that enhance its theoretical power but represent substantial simplifications of empirical reality. One of the most important of these is that the social classes whose behavior the model purports to portray are monopolistically represented by class organizations—"bilateral monopoly." This assumption is both empirically and theoretically hazardous, for it accords neither with the experiences of unions and business associations in the advanced capitalist democracies nor with the implications of the collective action problem or other theories of intraclass differentiation of interests.

To the extent that our interest is in explaining cross-national differences in forms of democratic class compromise and their consequences, it is at this point that there are important intersections with the historical-institutionalist perspective. The explanation of differences in the outcomes of the class compromise "game" specified by Przeworski and Wallerstein is, as they clearly recognize, that it is played by actors whose internal characteristics and preferences are historically and institutionally produced. The payoffs for class cooperation or conflict are also significantly determined by structural features of the historically given national (and international) contexts in which the game is played as well as by the particular economic and political conjunctures in which the class organizations confront one another (Lange 1984b; Masters and Robertson 1988).[20]

The rational choice, game-theoretic approach provides us with the fundamental insight that democratic class compromise can be economically rational for workers as a class, thereby altering the premises with which much of the earlier analyses have operated. It also underlines that cooperation is the result of strategic interaction and thereby points to the contingent character of outcomes that from the historical or functional standpoint seem inevitable. And it provides a framework for the systematic analysis and explanation of such outcomes that, while focusing on the rational choices of actors, recognizes the critical role of context defined historically—through institutions and preferences—but also conjuncturally—by contingent economic and political conditions.

The work of Przeworski and Wallerstein, therefore, provides us with tools for the systematic, comparative analysis of class relations under democracy. At the same time, however, it raises issues that test our ability to find syntheses between the historical-institutionalist and choice-theoretic approaches to these issues. For those committed to the potential of the application of the latter, it directs our attention back onto the institutions themselves and to the explanation of their origins and the exploration of how they constrain contemporary choices and outcomes. For those committed to more historical analysis, it lays down the challenge to avoid the facile invocation of "history" to explain contemporary outcomes, to explore the mechanisms that translate past events into contemporary outcomes, and to recognize the contingency of those outcomes when they are seen as products of sequential strategic interactions.

Corporatism

The theory of class compromise addresses the relationship between democracy and social classes at the most abstract—and reified—level. The work on corporatism looks more concretely at the role of interest organizations representing components of social classes (and other interests) in mediating the relationship between citizens and the contemporary democratic state.

The corporatism "growth industry" (Panitch 1981) emerged from a discontent with the application of pluralist theory to the relationship between interest groups and the democratic state in Western Europe (Schmitter 1974; Berger 1981; Almond 1983).[21] Taking off from Schmitter's seminal article (1974), a vast number of studies have sought to understand how interests are organized and articulated with the institutions of the state in different countries, why these patterns exist, and what their consequences are for political and economic performance and democratic values. Although the original corporatism studies (collected in Schmitter and Lehmbruch 1979) made claims to describe whole national systems of interest intermediation,[22] the focus soon became primarily the organizations of labor and business and how they interacted with the state in a bi- or tri-partite pattern of economic policy-making (Lehmbruch and Schmitter 1982). Empirical work became concentrated on unions and on incomes policies, the latter viewed as the quintessential corporatist policy outcomes (Goldthorpe 1984; Flanagan, Soskice, and Ulman 1983; Golden 1988; Swenson 1989; Lange, Ross, and Vannicelli 1982; Gourevitch, Martin, and Ross et al. 1984).

From the outset, two types of corporatism—state and societal—were distinguished (Schmitter 1974). For the former, the authoritarian state was identified as prime mover in the establishment and control of functionally organized interest associations—as under fascism and in several Latin American cases. In societal corporatism, superficially similar patterns of interest organization were analyzed as the product of long sequences of societal development in response to domestic and international threats and opportunities (Cameron 1978; Katzenstein 1984, 1985). They were, where they existed, path-dependent outcomes, and because of their societal roots, generally compatible with a balance between society and state appropriate to democracy.

This work was largely in tune with the traditional historical-institutionalist themes and approaches of European political economy. More recently, however, some of the questions raised in the corporatism literature have been treated with choice-theoretic formulations. Two innovations on the first generation of corporatism studies have stimulated this recent work.

First, much of the early work assumed that though corporatist forms of interest intermediation were functional to capitalism, especially when labor was organizationally and politically strong, they operated at the expense of the interests of workers (Panitch 1979, 1980, 1981).[23] In this case, the ability of workers to advance their interest under corporatist democracy was impugned. The second generation of studies, however, shifted the focus to the corporatist actors, and their interests and strategies under democratic conditions. They sought to identify costs and benefits of corporatist participation and to explain why the interest organizations, rationally pursuing their interests, chose to participate in corporatist networks. (See a number of essays in Goldthorpe 1984.)

Second, and relatedly, the new work separated the issue of how interests were organized (corporatism) from the question of how and why they cooperated in the formulation and implementation of policy (Schmitter 1982). This latter work on "concertation" had close ties to the broader work on class compromise as well as with long-standing efforts in comparative politics to explain cross-national differences in elite cooperation (as we see in a number of essays in Goldthorpe 1984).

These developments have underlined the contingency of concerted outcomes and raised questions about when cooperation occurs that can be substantially informed by choice-theoretic reasoning. It has led to analyses of the processes and networks of institutions through which the *horizontal* relationships between the peak organizations of labor and capital are articulated in the process of national—and, more recently, subnational and even firm-level—economic policy-making and the role that the structure and policy of the democratic state can play in facilitating or impeding concerted outcomes (Streeck and Schmitter 1985; Cawson 1985; Grant 1986; Schmitter 1986; Esping-Andersen 1985). The processes are particularly susceptible to analysis using game theory and institutional theories borrowed from economics (Williamson 1985).

It has also directed attention to the problems concertation raises for the aggregation of interests *vertically*, within the organizations, and thus for the ability of the organizations—especially unions—to gain the cooperation of those for whom they supposedly speak (Offe and Wiesenthal 1980; Lange 1984a, 1984b). Here the collective action problem, Arrow's paradox, and rational choice approaches to organization theory are highly germane. And, finally, it has implied that these two levels and forms of cooperation may be substantially related to one another, thus raising issues that can be substantially informed by the work on nested games (Tsebelis 1989; Golden 1988).

Interestingly, however, exploration of these issues with such tools has shown levels and forms of cooperation that are not easily understood in a unalloyedly rationalist framework (Elster 1989), and has highlighted the fragile and problematic nature of equilibria predicted by models drawing on such a framework. The role of institutions and norms in explaining forms of both horizontal and vertical cooperation has, not surprisingly, come to the fore. At the same time, this work on the microfoundations of corporatism and concertation has established the conditions under which such forms of interest intermediation and economic policy-making might be compatible with democratic norms of representation and citizen consent and identified the features of the democratic process likely to foster or impede corporatist concertation. Thus, the cross-fertilization and potential for mutual enrichment between the historical institutionalist and choice-theoretic approaches have been considerable and offer promise of more in the future.

Economic Performance

A third central issue in the research on the political economy of the advanced industrial democracies has been the potential tension between democratic rights and effective national economic performance arising out of the ability of citizens to vote and organize and thereby to use interest group, party, and electoral politics to alter the distributional outcomes that would be produced by the efficient operation of markets.[24] Does this tension imply that democratic societies are doomed to economic inefficiency? Are there forms of societal and political organization in democracies that are more consistent with better economic performance than others? Furthermore, how do different democratic institutional configurations influence the distribution of economic goods across social groups?[25]

It is impossible here to deal with all the findings in this rich, complex, and sometimes contradictory research. We want, instead, to highlight work on two issues of great importance to democratic theory—the relationship of the number and structure of organized interests, and of "who governs," to economic performance—to which choice-theoretic reasoning has been fruitfully applied or in which the possibilities for doing so seem particularly promising.

(1) Since the widespread labor militancy and more general social mobilization of the late 1960s, scholars have been concerned with the impact of distributional struggle among ever more widely and better organized economic interests on the ability of democratic government to manage the economy and to make the strategic choices in economic policy requiring the sacrifice of current consumption for future growth (Crozier, Huntington, and Watanuki 1975; Rose and Peters 1978; Offe 1981; O'Connor 1973; Hirsch and Goldthorpe 1978; Lindberg and Maier 1985; Skidelsky 1979). The implication has been that "too much democracy" or at least too much pluralism was incompatible with effective economic management and performance in the advanced industrial democracies.[26]

A great deal of empirical work has explored the impact of how interests—especially trade unions—are organized for different performance outcomes. This research has generally been either historical-institutionalist or econometric in character, but it has more recently become linked to efforts to develop microfoundations for the relationships discovered.

Both the historical-institutionalist and the statistical research has raised significant doubts about any general argument that the mobilized organization of interests necessarily has deleterious consequences for economic performance. On the one hand, the former has shown that cross-national differences in the structure of interest organizations and state institutions have significant effects on how interest organizations pressure governments, the specific policies they pursue, the access they gain to the policy formulating and implementing processes, and the ways democratically elected and appointed officials are likely to respond (Katzenstein 1978, 1984, 1985; Hall 1986; Steinmo 1986; Berger 1981; Esping-Andersen 1985). These studies underline the importance of the structure of interest organizations and of the institutional context in which they pursue their activity. The small number of cases examined, however, limits the generalizations about policy impacts that can be drawn.

On the other hand, statistical associations have been found that also support the linkage between differences in the character of interest organization and policy outputs and outcomes. Such studies have primarily focused on trade unions. They reveal strong correlations between very high levels of union density and centralization and low levels of strikes, low unemployment, and high state expenditures on social policies that reduce the risks faced by workers from market fluctuations. Societies with such configurations of labor organizations also do not appear to have unusually high rates of inflation and appear to have performed relatively well, by international standards, during the stagflationary period following the oil crisis of 1974 (Cameron 1984; Schmidt 1982, 1983; Korpi and Shalev 1979; Bruno and Sachs 1985; Lange and Garrett 1985, 1987; Garrett and Lange 1986; Alvarez, Garrett, and Lange 1991).

These studies offer an important corrective to facile generalizations about the relationship between pluralism, mobilized interests, and economic performance in democratic systems. They do not, however, fully explain the relationships found, for they fail to provide the mechanisms linking interest organization, institutional context, and interest organization behavior. Providing such microfoundations has made progress, but substantial work remains.

The most thorough attempt to build a choice-theoretic understanding of the relationship between groups and policy under democracy is that of Mancur Olson (1982; see also Mueller 1983). Extending his theory of collective action in groups to the societal level, Olson argued that the greater the extent of interest organization in the society, the more likely economic growth would suffer.[27] Each individual interest group would have an incentive to press the state for protective policies, but the accumulated effect of such policies would be to impede the efficient allocation of resources in the economy. Such an argument was wholly consistent with the most pessimistic views of the impact of pluralist democracy.

Olson did, however, make an exception for "encompassing" organizations, that is, ones so large that the net effect of their pressure for protective policies would be to damage the interests of their own members. Where interests are encompassing, public interest–regarding policy pressures might be anticipated and economic performance might be less damaged by organizational action.[28] This argument is consistent with the empirical findings regarding dense and centralized trade unions (see above and Jankowski 1988) and weakens the negative conclusions about the relationship between democratic pluralism and performance.

Olson's theory offers a starting point for the development of microfoundations for the explanation of the effects of group action on aggregate economic performance. He says nothing, however, about the role of political parties and state institutions in his theory, nor does he discuss the contribution of international political economic variables to different levels of performance (Cameron 1988). Yet, these factors emerge as quite important in the historical-institutionalist studies already cited, and they need to be incorporated into a choice-theoretic explanation if the actual influence of the distributional policies of interest groups on growth is to be understood (Cameron 1988; Lange and Garrett 1985; Garrett and Lange 1989; Scharpf 1988). Further integration of the institutionalist and choice-theoretic arguments and findings is necessary if we are to develop a thorough understanding of the role of interest groups in explaining economic performance.

(2) A second major issue addressed in the literature on the relationship between democratic politics and economic performance has been equally central to democratic theory: does who governs make a difference? A great deal of sophisticated cross-national statistical research in recent years has explored whether which party controls government influences numerous features of economic performance.

This work was to a substantial extent kindled by Hibbs's (1977) seminal studies exploring the relationship between control of government by political parties of the left and right and the (assumed) Phillips curve tradeoff between unemployment and inflation. A very large number of subsequent sophisticated time series studies have examined the relationship of political control to the outcomes Hibbs examined and numerous others. It has, in general, discovered small but significant partisan effects. Furthermore, to the extent that effects of partisanship have been discovered, they have tended to be concentrated in the immediate postelection period, fading as the government's term extends toward the next election (Alt 1985; Alesina 1989). Nonetheless, the weight of evidence is that the partisanship of government does make some difference, especially in combination with other factors including the organization of interest groups and the structure of state institutions.

A somewhat parallel set of studies has focused on similar issues but used aggregate, cross-sectional analyses or more detailed, comparative case study analyses. This work has tended to find more distinct partisan effects for similar performance outcomes, as well as for a range of specific policies. In particular, distinct associations have been found between sustained government by the left and low rates of unemployment, higher levels of state expenditures and transfers (Cameron 1984, 1982; Schmidt 1982, 1983; Schott 1984b). Weak or nonexistent associations appear with regard to the relationship between government partisanship and inflation. There has also been substantial controversy about the relationship between government partisanship and economic growth (Whitely 1983; Lange and Garrett 1985, 1987; Garrett and Lange 1986, 1989; Hicks and Patterson 1989; Hicks 1988; Jackman 1986, 1987, 1989; Alvarez, Garrett, and Lange 1991). It is noteworthy that the systems that appear to do best in cross-national studies of performance are those that have the combination of corporatist institutional arrangements, left governments, concerted forms of economic policy-making, and highly developed and institutionalized forms of class compromise.

For the most part, these studies have treated such outcomes as the effects of rational, reelection-oriented behavior on the part of governments under conditions of democratic electoral competition. Some have also stressed the role of constraints on policy effectiveness deriving from the structure of government institutions and of interest groups (Masters and Robertson 1986; Garrett and Lange 1989). The choice-theoretic analysis has promoted systematic evaluation of the conditions under which parties might be expected to differ in their policy choices, given their desire to win elections and thereby once again introduced contingency into the explanation of outcomes. Interestingly, however, the role of domestic institutional factors—including the structure of government institutions, of the party system, and of the type of government—as well as conditions in the international economy emerge as significant constraints on parties' pursuit of their preferred policies (Alt 1985). In addition, attention has necessarily been focused on the organizational and ideological factors that influence the parties' policy preferences and their relationship to the historically given institutional context. Thus, this work has once again intersected the historical-institutionalist work on European political parties and party and interest group systems, on the one hand, and the more abstract application of choice-theoretic reasoning to party competition and interest group behavior, on the other.

To conclude this discussion, let us return to the question of the relationship between democratic rights and economic performance. It is clear that there is no empirical or theoretical foundation for the view that the organized mobilization of social interests, especially of the working class and the pursuit of those interests through market action and through partisan politics, necessarily leads to highly inefficient economic outcomes, even when it affects distributional outcomes. Rather, a great deal depends on how those interests are organized, both economically and politically, and on the institutional context within which they operate. Each of these clusters of variables affects the way the organizations perceive their interests and the contexts within which they develop and pursue strategies to further those interests.

The distinctive contribution of the application of choice-theoretic analysis to these issues is both to explain why the actors act as they do— underexploiting their market and political power, for instance—and to indicate the contingency of those cooperative outcomes and the factors that may contribute to their breakdown. By highlighting the ways in which institutions and policies affect the strategic calculi of the actors and their interactions, such reasoning allows us to analyze national policy and performance configurations in ways that both combine a sensitivity to national histories and institutions with analytical tools that are broadly comparative and allow us to discover the "mechanisms" linking context to behavior and, eventually, back to contingent outcomes and subsequent context. Thus, they once again direct our attention to the interpenetrations between institutions, states, and markets that are an inescapable part of the political economy of the advanced industrial democracies.

4. APPLICATIONS IN POLITICAL DEVELOPMENT AND THE THIRD WORLD
Political Development and Rural Radicalism

Political development emerged as a recognized subfield in the 1950s. Increasingly, it too has adapted choice-theoretic foundations. A major reason has been the field's inability to cope with the growth of rural radicalism in the developing areas.

According to the theories employed in the development field, rural dwellers should have fulfilled the role of subjects (Almond and Verba 1963) rather than participants in politics (Lerner 1958; Deutsch 1961; Rogers 1962). According to the modernization paradigm, rural dwellers were uneducated and illiterate and lacked exposure to the mass media; they therefore lacked political opinions and a sense of political efficacy and were unwilling or unable to participate in politics. Largely as a result of successful rural rebellions in Vietnam, those working in the development field learned that such claims were wrong. As Mao Tse-tung and Ché Guevara (Miller and Aya 1971) had long contended, rather than being politically passive, rural dwellers could seize the political initiative; they could, as Barrington Moore had claimed, provide the revolutionary class of our time (Moore 1966).

For many, the insurgencies of the 1970s precipitated a move to radical political economy. Returning to Lenin, Hobson, and their latterday interpreters (Lenin 1984; Hobson 1982; Baran 1957), radical political economists reconceptualized the growth of capitalism within the framework of the theory of imperialism. They thereby sought to explain why political revolutions took place in the relatively rural Third World rather than in the advanced industrial nations of the First World, and why they were opposed by the armies of major industrial powers (Palma 1978).

Radical political economy contained a variety of schools that differed greatly in content (Palma 1978). Some theorists (Bodenheimer 1970; Frank 1969) saw in the prosperity of the First World the causes for the poverty in the Third and explored mechanisms for the forceful expropriation and redistribution of resources. Others (Prebisch 1950; Emmanuel 1972) focused on the characteristics of trade relations between North and South, arguing that shifts in relative prices between primary and manufactured goods and differences in the relative magnitude of embodied labor power help to account for differences in the real value of incomes. Still others, such as Gereffi (1978), Hymer (1979), and Evans (1979), focus on factors that shape the relative rates of technical change and productivity growth in the developing and developed nations.

These and other works contend that conditions in the developing world are decisively shaped by their relations with the developed. As argued perhaps most vigorously by Wallerstein (1974), underdevelopment is structurally determined: where a society is located in the global division of labor largely determines the life chances of those within it.

The great strength of the *dependencia* approach was that it helped to account for the rise of revolutionary violence in poor, agrarian countries. In addition to taking place within nations, capitalist accumulation also took place on the global level, it argued. Protests against the extraction of surplus could therefore take the form of struggles between as well as within nations. The class struggle could take international form. It could assume the form of anti-imperialist revolutions.

A second major form of radical political economy sought to account for agrarian violence. It focused on the internal rather than external setting of Third World nations and in particular upon the structural transformations characteristic of economic growth. In the tradition of classical economics, this tradition stressed the tensions between town and country in the process of development (for a review, see Bates 1987). In Marxian form, this literature focused on the struggle between the rising commercial and industrial classes centered in the towns and the agrarian elite and peasantry dwelling in the rural areas (Brenner 1976; Moore 1966; Skocpol 1979). In the course of development, political and economic struggles among these interests focused on the terms of trade between town and country; tariffs and trade regimes; and contests over the structure of markets for labor, land, and capital. Rural violence, this literature held, represented an outgrowth of the internal class struggle. It was a by-product of the process of primitive accumulation, wherein resources were extracted from the agrarian sector and vested in the industrial.

For many scholars, radical political economy did not prove satisfying, for it ignored one of the basic problems that bedeviled modernization theory: the lack of appropriate microfoundations. A major lesson of the power of rural violence was, after all, that the model of individual behavior characteristic of modernization theory was wrong; peasants possessed preferences and could chose in accord with them. The dependency school in particular failed to build upon this lesson; it simply had very little to say about human behavior at the microlevel. In addition, it offered little latitude for choice. Rather, outcomes were to a great degree structurally determined.

For the dependency school, where a society was located in the global division of labor largely determined the life chances of those within it. The weakness in this position became apparent in the 1970s. Clearly, societies that were similarly situated *did* possess a range of discretion and choice concerning how they inserted themselves into the world economy. Some, such as those in Africa and Latin America, sought to shelter themselves from world markets; but others, such as those in Asia, aggressively positioned themselves to take advantage of market forces (Balassa 1982, 1981). Domestic political forces within Third World nations played a significant role in explaining these differences (Alavi 1972; Trimberger 1972; Warren 1973; Bates 1981). Clearly, the field needed models that admitted the significance of, and the power of, choice. And though these studies admitted a role for classes or sectors in accounting for variations in policy regimes, they failed to disaggregate their explanations to the individual level. Elsewhere in radical political economy, this step was being taken (Elster 1985; Przeworski 1985; Roemer 1982). But it was not taken by theorists working in the radical tradition in the developing areas.

The literature that located the sources of Third World violence internal to the developing world possessed more explicit microfoundations. It did not require that rural dwellers respond to some disembodied world capitalist system; rather, in these works, they possessed clear class enemies and well defined arenas for political combat. Nonetheless, further steps in the argument were clearly needed to account for how individual preferences could generate collective outcomes. As argued by Elster (1985), Przeworski (1985), and others (Olson 1965), social theorists must supply the intermediate steps that link individual wants to the creation and behavior of collective aggregates. As we shall see, one of the strengths of the development literature is that it has recognized the need for such links and has attempted to provide them. We shall also see that in key branches of the field such links are missing, thus frustrating the development of fully satisfying theories of the political economy of development.

Microfoundations for the Development Field

Two kinds of theories sought to provide choice-theoretic foundations for the development field. One was based upon decision theory; the other upon market economics. Despite fundamental disagreement on ethical issues—in particular on the desirability of markets—they shared a common weakness, and this proved to be their undoing. Both lacked an adequate theory of preference aggregation.

Decision-theoretic approaches Illustrative of the decision-theoretic approach is the work of James Scott (1976). In his *The Moral Economy of the Peasant*, Scott established the micro-foundations for a theory of peasant revolution. Stressing that peasants are risk averse, Scott employed this insight to account for a broad range of peasant behaviors, above all, their propensity to rebel. Under imperialism, he argued, the market and the state violated the peasant's assurance of subsistence; in the market, those who lacked wealth could starve, and the state's need for taxes proved unforgiving, sometimes driving people below the subsistence margin. Peasant rebellion represented an attempt to reinstate a moral community, where social institutions would protect people against the risk of death resulting from the lack of material possessions.

Part of the power of Scott's work was that it provided the microfoundations to link the structural fact of imperialism to the political fact of peasant violence. Much of the power of Scott's leading critic, Samuel Popkin, was that he demonstrated that additional steps were necessary. A revolution, Popkin argued (1979), is a public good; following the revolution, all will be free of oppressive taxes, for example, whether or not they sacrificed for the insurrection. As a consequence, there are incentives to let others sacrifice and then to consume the benefits for free. Revolutions must therefore be organized; for if all seek a free ride, the revolution must fail. Organization requires the application of selective incentives that make it in the private interests of individuals to make choices that are consistent with the collective good. Based on the analysis of public goods, Popkin thus criticized Scott for his lack of an adequate theory of aggregation.

Neoclassical political economy Neoclassical political economy (Colander 1984; Srinivasan 1985; Lal 1984; Krueger 1974) also assumes that individuals are rational choice makers. The question it then confronts is: why, then, do the poor countries remain poor? The neoclassicists assume that if left to their own devices, individuals would interact in such a way that their private decisions would generate socially desirable outcomes and the resultant allocation of resources would be efficient. Many of the problems of the developing world, the neoclassicists argue, are a consequence of the reluctance of governments to let market prices shape individual decisions (Lal 1983; Little 1982). Inefficient use of scarce resources, distorted patterns of development, and slow growth—all are held to result from inappropriate forms of government intervention.

As a reader of *The Moral Economy of the Peasant* will note, Scott advances a passionate condemnation of the market; by contrast, neoclassical political economy represents an enthusiastic celebration of market forces. It is ironic that neoclassical political economy shares the weakness of Scott's argument: the lack of an adequate theory of aggregation.

Scott's theory foundered because revolutions represent public goods. Public goods constitute but one of several circumstances in which rational choices by individuals will fail to aggregate into socially desirable outcomes. Broadly speaking, such failures of aggregation will occur whenever individual actions are interdependent, that is, whenever the value of the outcome of an individual decision depends not only on the choice made by that individual but also upon choices made by others. In such circumstances, rational individuals will possess an incentive to behave *strategically*. The way in which they will make choices will depend not only on what they prefer but also upon their anticipation of the action of others. As a consequence, the analyst cannot infer social outcomes from individual preferences. Popkin exposed the dangers of doing so in the case of Scott. The dangers are equally great in the case of the neoclassicists.

The neo-classicists stress the desirability of markets. But markets in the Third World, just as in the First, will fail to aggregate individual preferences into welfare-maximizing outcomes when individual decisions are interdependent, whether through utility functions, as in the case of public goods; through production functions, as in the case of externalities; or because of the number and size of actors, as in the case of imperfect competition. The reasons for the failure of individual decisions to aggregate into socially desirable outcomes are deeply understood; the study of market failures constitutes one of the most productive branches of contemporary economics (Starrett 1988).

Neoclassicists stress the role of markets on the one hand; on the other, they stress the role of the state. The state, they contend, seeks to maximize revenues, subject to some constraint; alternatively, it seeks to maximize the value of the rents that accrue to selected influentials. In either case, the state employs policy instruments to fulfill its objectives in a way that distorts market prices, leading to welfare losses and undermining economic growth.

The neoclassical political economists, we have argued, fail to develop an adequate theory of markets because they do not pay sufficient attention to problems of market failure. By positing a major role for "the state," they also exhibit a lack of a theory of politics. Beginning with the assumption of rational individuals, they fail to examine how these preferences aggregate into public policy; rather, they invoke a unitary political actor, labeled "the state," thereby shortcutting political analysis.

This analytic sleight of hand not only represents a failure of omission; it also represents a failure of commission. One of the most significant theoretical contributions to neoclassical thought is Arrow's impossibility theorem (Arrow 1951), which shows that no coherent rendering of the social interest can be built up from individual preferences in ways that systematically satisfy easily defensible technical and ethical requirements. His theorem, of course, applies not only to social welfare functions but also to the "ill-fare" functions attributed to governments by the neo-classical development economists.

The lesson is clear: like their welfare-oriented predecessors whom the neoclassical development economists criticize, the neoclassicists fail to provide a theory that explains how individual preferences aggregate into public policies. Alternatively, their analysis applies only to pure dictatorships. And the Arrovian criterion for a dictatorship—that the dictator be able to impose his will even though he is opposed by everyone else in society—is so demanding as to leave their theory applicable almost nowhere.

Analytically—although, of course, not normatively—neoclassical development economists are simply old-fashioned welfare economists in disguise. Traditional welfare economists thought markets to be imperfect and governments benevolent. The neoclassicists regard markets as benevolent and governments as pernicious. The basic problem of aggregation that crippled the evolution of welfare economics remains: the problem of accounting for—and justifying—market outcomes (given market imperfections) and political outcomes (given Arrow's impossibility theorem). Beginning with the assumption of individually rational behavior, neither the market nor the state can behave in the way that the neoclassicists contend.

5. CONCLUSION

This chapter has emphasized the relationship between two separable and independent themes of political economy: choice-theoretic reasoning and the relationship between government and markets. We have tried to show that political science can learn from economics and vice versa, and that there is a substantial area of common interest between the two disciplines. We have shown that choice-theoretic reasoning can help us understand politics as well as economics. We have shown that it can help us understand how democracy works and why, and that it can also help us understand political behavior and outcomes in nondemocratic systems. Its place in political science seems secure.

NOTES

1. For evidence, see Keohane (1984b), Gilpin (1987), and McKeown (1986).

2. Clever economists, such as Stigler and Becker (1977), are capable of arguing that even the most apparently fluid preferences are actually based in stable tastes, but we do not take this view. See Stigler (1988) for a useful collec-

tion of essays in this tradition. In our view, the utility of these essays is not contingent on the reality of narrow assumptions about tastes and preferences.

3. See Kahneman et al. (1982). See also Hogarth and Reder (1987), and Elster (1986). See Simon (1985) for a discussion of substantive and procedural rationality in the context of political science.

4. This field is perhaps best identified by the journal *Public Choice*, whose masthead says that the field "deals with the intersection of economics and political science. It started when economists and political scientists became interested in the application of essentially economic methods to problems normally dealt with by political scientists. It has retained strong traces of economic methodology, but new and fruitful techniques have been developed which are not recognizable by economists." See Mueller (1989) for a survey.

5. Game theory is a growing field that abstracts the essentials of such alternative situations and studies the consequences of alternative courses of action. See Friedman (1986), Ordeshook (1986), and Tsebelis (1989) for general treatments.

6. See Stokey and Zeckhauser (1978, chap. 9); MacRae and Wilde (1979); and Gramlich (1981).

7. See, for example, Alesina and Sachs (1988) and Chappell and Keech (1985, 1988).

8. See Wittman (1983) and Chappell and Keech (1986) for examples.

9. This discussion draws on Wolf (1988), who draws on Bator (1958).

10. Miller and Moe (1983) and Berry and Lowery (1987) have responded to Niskanen's challenge with theoretical refinements and empirical tests, which weaken the original claim. We deal briefly with literature responding to the identification of the other two pathologies below.

11. However, see Keech and Simon (1985) for an argument that Nordhaus's observations about democracy are not generic, even in terms of his own model of political and economic behavior.

12. See Alesina and Sachs (1988) and Chappell and Keech (1988).

13. In this section we will refer almost exclusively to research on the advanced industrial capitalist democracies of Western Europe.

14. It should be underlined that this agenda in no way implies acceptance of the predominant role of class in explaining actual outcomes but only its potential role and/or an effort to demonstrate what role class does or does not play and why.

15. Choice-theoretic reasoning has also been assuming a larger role in studies devoted to political processes outside the political economy but at the heart of democratic theory (Tsebelis 1989; Laver and Schofield 1989; Przeworski and Sprague 1986). The economic rationality of voting behavior, extending studies done on the United States, has also begun to be extensively explored in a wide variety of European settings (Eulau and Lewis-Beck 1985). For reasons of space and their overlap with other chapters in this volume, we do not discuss these here.

16. Though there is much to be said for most different systems designs, at the present state of our theoretical and empirical knowledge, comparative analysis within the partially similar settings of the advanced industrial democracies of Western Europe has much to recommend it.

17. There are significant similarities between what we here refer to as historical-institutionalist analysis and what some scholars refer to as the "new institutionalism" (March and Olsen 1984). The problem with the latter term is that it has been appropriated both by some of those who use the type of analysis we discuss in this section and by some who apply to politics the type of institutional analysis in economics most often associated with the work of Oliver Williamson (1985) and/or who explore the role of institutions in explaining stable equilibria in situations in which the "pure" play of individualistic rational choice would produce "chaos," and the production of public goods when the rational choices of individuals would be expected to lead to substantial shortfalls in their production.

18. Some of the most germane of these include Berger (1981), Katzenstein (1978, 1984, 1985), P. Hall (1986), Esping-Andersen (1985), Gourevitch (1986), Zysman (1983), Skocpol et al. (1985), Maier (1987), and Lange and Regini (1989). There has also been some concern, largely at the theoretical level, with the ways capitalism constrains or conditions the potential outcomes of the democratic process (Lindblom 1977; Elkin 1985).

19. Inherent in this view is also the idea that democratic institutions and policies will reflect the need for the capitalist state to contain such conflict within boundaries consistent with capitalist accumulation. The possibility that class relations under capitalism can be a positive-sum rather than a zero-sum game does not mean that class relations are not reflected in state institutions and policies. Rather, this possibility changes the range of these which are possible and likely, given different configurations of class relationships and/or political institutions.

20. The relevant political context includes factors such as the character of the democratic state and its policies, the nature of the party system, and who is governing. It is important to note that, for Przeworski and Wallerstein, the class compromise game is not iterated but is repeatedly played anew, each time in a possibly new conjuncture that can affect its outcome.

21. The concept of corporatism has been prefaced with several modifiers, including liberal and neo-, to distinguish it from the corporatist doctrine and forms of interest organization found under fascism. In the current text, we will simply use the word corporatism to apply to the phenomenon in the advanced industrial democracies and attach qualifiers when referring to other systems.

22. Recently, Streeck and Schmitter have reproposed a general framework in which societal regulation by "association" is compared to social orders based on regulation by community, market, and state (1985).

23. This argument was sometimes posed in terms of functionalist Marxism and sometimes in terms of the advantages that accrued to union elites in corporatist arrangements. For a critique, see Schmitter (1982) and Lange (1984b).

24. This is a tension that caused concern among liberals as early as the mid-

nineteenth century. For a discussion, see Hirsch (1976). Much of the contemporary research has focused on variables that have also figured prominently in the work on class compromise and corporatism. Whereas in that work these were treated as outcomes to be explained, here, however, they become causes whose effects on unemployment, inflation, economic growth, economic policies, and other features of economic performance are being examined.

Many have also argued that the electoral process itself is a likely source of incentives for politicians to seek to influence economic outcomes for political purposes in ways detrimental to good economic performance. The electoral business cycle literature discussed above is the most prominent form of this argument. The support for such a cycle in the European context is extremely weak. In this connection, see Paldam (1978), Alt and Chrystal (1983), Alesina (1989), and Barry (1985). For reasons of space, we do not discuss it here.

25. These questions were inherent in some of the seminal studies on modern capitalism cited at the outset of this section. They have become of more pressing concern over the last twenty years with the end of the "golden age" of postwar democratic capitalism and the subsequent pressures for economic adjustment under conditions of reduced rates of economic growth and the increasing pace of integration and reorganization of the world economy (Keohane 1984a; Piore and Sabel 1984; Bruno and Sachs 1985).

26. Interestingly, this view was found quite often in studies by scholars on both the political right and left, although obviously with differing perspectives on the conclusions to be drawn and remedies to be adopted.

27. Olson linked this argument to a historical one about the relationship between major political and social upheavals and the density of organizations and "distributional coalitions" in the society. One need not, however, accept this historical argument to acknowledge possible merits of the argument regarding the relationship between the organizational density and economic growth.

28. Olson argues that the size and resultant slowness to respond to changes in market incentives would nonetheless make encompassing organizations less conducive to economic growth than systems with relatively lower levels of group organization.

REFERENCES

Alavi, H. 1972. "The State in Post Colonial Societies." *New Left Review* 74: 59–81.

Alchian, A., and H. Demsetz. 1972. "Production, Information Costs, and Economic Organization." *American Economic Review* 2:777–95.

Alesina, Alberto. 1989. "Politics and Business Cycles in Industrial Democracies." *Economic Policy* 8:55–98.

Alesina, Alberto, and Jeffrey Sachs. 1988. "Political Parties and the Business Cycle in the United States, 1948–1984." *Journal of Money, Credit and Banking* 20:63–82.

Almond, G. A. 1983. "Corporatism, Pluralism, and Professional Memory." *World Politics* 35:245–260.

Almond, G. A., and S. Verba. 1963. *The Civic Culture*. Princeton: Princeton University Press.

Alt, James. 1985. "Political Parties, World Demand, and Unemployment." *American Political Science Review* 79:1016–40.

———. 1987. "Crude Politics: Oil and the Political Economy of Unemployment in Britain and Norway, 1970–1985." *British Journal of Political Science* 17:149–99.

Alt, James, and Alec Chrystal. 1983. *Political Economics*. Berkeley: University of California Press.

Alvarez, R. Michael, Geoffrey Garrett, and Peter Lange. 1991. "Government Partnership, Labor Organization and Macroeconomic Performance, 1967–1984." *American Political Science Review* 85.

Arrow, Kenneth. 1951, 1963. *Social Choice and Individual Values*. New York: John Wiley.

Austen-Smith, David, and Jeffrey Banks. 1988. "Elections, Coalitions and Legislative Outcomes." *American Political Science Review* 82:405–22.

Axelrod, Robert M. 1984. *The Evolution of Cooperation*. New York: Basic Books.

Balassa, B. 1981. "Trade in Manufactured Goods: Patterns of Change" *World Development* 9:263–75.

———. 1982. "The Newly-Industrializing Developing Countries after the Oil Crisis." *Weltwirtschaftiches Archiv* 10 (1982):1027–38.

Baran, P. A. 1957. *The Political Economy of Growth*. New York: Monthly Review Press.

Barry, Brian. 1985. "Does Democracy Cause Inflation? Political Ideas of Some Economists." In *The Politics of Inflation and Economic Stagnation*, edited by L. Lindberg and C. Maier. Washington, D.C.: Brookings.

Bates, R. H. 1981. *Markets and States in Tropical Africa*. Berkeley and Los Angeles: University of California Press.

———. 1986. *Essays on the Political Economy of Rural Africa*. Berkeley and Los Angeles: University of California Press.

———. 1987. "Agrarian Politics." In *Understanding Political Development*, edited by Myron Weiner and Samuel P. Huntington. Boston: Little, Brown.

———. 1988. *Toward a Political Economy of Development*. Berkeley and Los Angeles: University of California Press.

———. 1989. *Beyond the Miracle of the Market: The Institutional Foundations of Agrarian Development in Kenya*. Cambridge: Cambridge University Press.

Bator, Francis M. 1958. "The Anatomy of Market Failure." *Quarterly Journal of Economics* 72:351.

Benjamin, Roger, and Stephen Elkin. 1985. *The Democratic State*. Lawrence: University Press of Kansas.

Berger, Suzanne, ed. 1981. *Organizing Interests in Western Europe*. New York: Cambridge University Press.

Berry, William D., and David Lowery. 1987. *Understanding United States Government Growth*. New York: Praeger.

Bodenheimer, Suzanne. 1970. " The Ideology of Developmentalism." *Berkeley Journal of Sociology* 95–137.

Boltho, Andrea. 1982. *The European Economy: Growth and Crisis*. Oxford: Oxford University Press.

Brenner, Robert. 1976. "Agrarian Class Structure and Economic Development in Pre-Industrial Europe." *Past and Present* 30–75.

Bruno, Michael, and Jeffery Sachs. 1985. *Economics of Worldwide Stagflation*. Cambridge: Harvard University Press.

Buchanan, James M., and Gordon Tullock. 1962. *The Calculus of Consent*. Ann Arbor: University of Michigan Press.

Cameron, David. 1978. "The Expansion of the Political Economy." *American Political Science Review* 72:1242–61.

———. 1982. "On the Limits of the Public Economy." *The Annals of the American Academy of Political and Social Science* 459:46–62.

———. 1984. "Social Democracy, Corporatism, Labour Quiescence, and the Representation of Economic Interest in Advanced Capitalist Society." In *Order and Conflict in Contemporary Capitalism*, edited by J. Goldthorpe. New York: Oxford University Press.

———. 1988. "Distributional Coalitions and Other Sources of Economic Stagnation: On Olson's *Rise and Decline of Nations*." *International Organization* 42:561–603.

Cardoso, Fernando H., and Enzo Falletto. 1979. *Dependency and Development*. Berkeley and Los Angeles: University of California Press.

Castles, Francis. 1978. *The Social Democratic Image of Society*. London: Routledge & Kegan Paul.

———. 1982. *The Impact of Parties*. Beverly Hills: Sage.

Cawson, Alan, ed. 1985. *Organized Interests and the State*. Beverly Hills: Sage.

Chappell, Henry W., Jr., and William R. Keech. 1985. "A New View of Political Accountability for Economic Performance." *American Political Science Review* 79:10–27.

———. 1986. "Policy Motivation and Party Differences in a Dynamic Spatial Model of Party Competition." *American Political Science Review* 80:881–99.

———. 1988. "The Unemployment Rate Consequences of Partisan Monetary Policies." *Southern Economic Journal* 55:107–22.

Cohen, G. A. 1978. *Karl Marx's Theory of History: A Defense*. Princeton: Princeton University Press.

Colander, D. C. 1984. *Neoclassical Political Economy*. Cambridge, Mass.: Ballinger Publishers.

Collier, D. 1979. *The New Authoritarianism in Latin America*. Princeton: Princeton University Press.

Crozier, Michel, Samuel P. Huntington, and Joji Watanuki. 1975. *The Crisis of Democracy*. New York: New York University Press.

Denzau, Arthur, William Riker, and Kenneth Shepsle. 1985. "Farquharson and Fenno: Sophisticated Voting and Home Style." *American Political Science Review* 79:1117–34.

Deutsch, Karl 1961. "Social Mobilization and Political Development." *American Political Science Review* 55(3):493–514.

Downs, Anthony. 1957. *An Economic Theory of Democracy*. New York: Harper.

Elkin, Steven. 1985. "Pluralism in Its Place." In *The Democratic State*, edited by R. Benjamin and S. Elkin. Lawrence: University Press of Kansas.

Elster, John. 1979. *Ulysses and the Sirens*. Cambridge: Cambridge University Press.

———. 1983a. *Sour Grapes*. Cambridge: Cambridge University Press.

———. 1983b. *Explaining Technical Change*. Cambridge: Cambridge University Press.

———. 1985. *Making Sense of Marx*. Cambridge: Cambridge University Press.

———. 1989. *The Cement of Society*. New York: Cambridge University Press.

Elster, John, ed. 1986. *Rational Choice*. New York: New York University Press.

Emmanuel, Arghiri. 1972. *Unequal Exchange: A Study of the Imperialism of Trade*. New York: Monthly Review Press.

Enelow, James M., and Melvin J. Hinich. 1984. *The Spatial Theory of Voting*. Cambridge: Cambridge University Press.

Esping-Andersen, Gosta. 1985. *Politics against Markets*. Princeton: Princeton University Press.

Eulau, Heinz, and Michael S. Lewis-Beck, eds. 1985. *Economic Conditions and Electoral Outcomes: The United States and Western Europe*. New York: Agathon Press.

Evans, Peter. 1979. *Dependent Development*. Princeton: Princeton University Press.

Fenno, Richard F. 1973. *Congressmen in Committees*. Boston: Little, Brown.

Ferejohn, John. 1974. *Pork Barrel Politics*. Stanford: Stanford University Press.

Fiorina, Morris P. 1981. *Retrospective Voting in American National Elections*. New Haven: Yale University Press.

Flanagan, Robert, David Soskice, and Lloyd Ulman, eds. 1983. *Unionism, Economic Stabilization, and Income Policies: European Experience*. Washington D.C.: Brookings.

Frank, Andre Gunder. 1969. *Capitalism and Underdevelopment*. New York: Monthly Review Press.

Friedland, Roger, and Jimy Sanders. 1985. "The Public Economy and Economic Growth in Western Market Economies." *American Sociological Review* 50:421–37.

Friedman, James W. 1986. *Game Theory with Applications to Economics*. New York: Oxford University Press.

Garrett, Geoffrey, and Peter Lange. 1986. "Performance in a Hostile World: Domestic and International Determinants of Economic Growth in the Advanced Capitalist Democracies, 1974–1982." *World Politics* 38:517–45.

———. 1989. "Government Partisanship and Economic Performance: When and How 'Who Governs?' Matter." *Journal of Politics* 51:676–93.

Geertz, C. 1983. *Local Knowledge*. New York: Basic Books.

Gereffi, Gary. 1978. "Drug Firms and Dependency in Mexico." *International Organization* 237–86.

Gerschenkron, Alexander. 1966. *Economic Backwardness in Historical Perspective*. Cambridge, Mass.: Harvard University Press.

Gilpin, Robert. 1987. *The Political Economy of International Relations*. Princeton: Princeton University Press.

Goffman, I. 1959. *The Presentation of the Self in Everyday Life*. New York: Doubleday Anchor.

Golden, Miriam. 1988. *Labor Divided: Austerity and Working-Class Politics in Contemporary Italy*. Ithaca: Cornell University Press.

Goldthorpe, John, ed. *1984. Order and Conflict in Contemporary Capitalism*. New York: Oxford University Press.

Gourevitch, Peter. 1986. *Politics in Hard Times*. Ithaca: Cornell University Press.

Gourevitch, Peter, Andrew Martin, George Ross, et al. 1984. *Unions and Economic Crisis: Britain, West Germany, and Sweden*. London: Allen & Unwin.

Gramlich, Edward M. 1981. *Benefit-Cost Analysis of Government Programs*. Englewood Cliffs, N.J.: Prentice-Hall.

Gramsci, Antonio. 1971. *Selections from the Prison Notebooks*. New York: International Publishers.

Grant, Wyn. 1986. *The Political Economy of Corporatism*. New York: St. Martin's Press.

Greenberg, Joseph, and Kenneth Shepsle. 1987. "The Effects of Electoral Rewards in Multiparty Competition with Entry." *American Political Science Review* 81:525–39.

Hall, Peter. 1986. *Governing the Economy: The Politics of State Intervention in Britain and France*. Cambridge: Polity Press.

Hall, Richard L. 1987. "Participation and Purpose in Committee Decision-Making." *American Political Science Review* 81:105–28.

Hibbs, Douglas. 1977. "Political Parties and Macroeconomic Policies." *American Political Science Review* 71:1467–87.

————. 1978. "On the Political Economy of Long-Run Trends in Strike Activity." *British Journal of Political Science* 8:153–75.

————. 1987. *The American Political Economy*. Cambridge: Harvard University Press.

Hicks, Alexander. 1988. "Social Democratic Corporatism and Economic Growth." *Journal of Politics* 50:677–704.

Hicks, Alexander, and William Patterson. 1989. "On the Robustness of the Left Corporatist Model of Economic Growth." *Journal of Politics*. 51: 662–675.

Hicks, Alexander, and Duane Swank. 1984. "On the Political Economy of Welfare Expansion." *Comparative Political Studies* 17:81–118.

Hirsch, Fred. 1976. *Social Limits of Growth*. Cambridge: Harvard University Press.

Hirsch, Fred, and John Goldthorpe, eds. 1978. *The Political Economy of Inflation*. London: Martin Robertson.

Hobson, J. A. 1982. *Imperialism*. Ann Arbor: University of Michigan Press.

Hogarth, Robin M., and Melvin W. Reder. 1987. *Rational Choice: The Contrast between Economics and Psychology*. Chicago: University of Chicago Press.

Hymer, Stephen. 1979. *The Multinational Corporation: A Radical Approach*. Cambridge: Cambridge University Press.

Jackman, Robert. 1986. "Elections and the Democratic Class Struggle." *World Politics* 39:123–46.

————. 1987. "The Politics of Economic Growth in the Industrial Democracies, 1974–1980." *Journal of Politics* 49:242–56.

————. 1989. "The Politics of Growth, Once Again." *Journal of Politics* 51: 646–61.

Jankowski, Richard. 1988. "Preference Aggregation in Political Parties and Interest Groups: A Synthesis of Corporatist and Encompassing Organization Theory." *American Journal of Political Science* 32:105–25.

Kahneman, Daniel, Paul Slovic, and Amos Tversky. 1982. *Judgment under Uncertainty: Heuristics and Biases*. Cambridge: Cambridge University Press.

Katzenstein, Peter. 1978. *Between Power and Plenty*. Madison: University of Wisconsin Press.

————. 1984. *Corporatism and Change*. Ithaca: Cornell University Press.

————. 1985. *Small States in World Markets*. Ithaca: Cornell University Press.

Keech, William R., and Carl P. Simon. 1985. "Electoral and Welfare Consequences of Political Manipulation of the Economy." *Journal of Economic Behavior and Organization* 6:177–202.

Keohane, Robert. 1984a. "The World Political Economy and the Crisis of Embedded Liberalism." In *Order and Conflict in Contemporary Capitalism*, edited by J. Goldthorpe. New York: Oxford University Press.

———. 1984b. *After Hegemony: Cooperation and Discord in World Political Economy*. Boston: Little, Brown.

Key, V. O., Jr. 1966. *The Responsible Electorate*. Cambridge, Mass.: Harvard University Press.

Kingdon, John W. 1981. *Congressmen's Voting Decisions*. 2nd ed. New York: Harper & Row.

Korpi, Walter, and Michael Shalev. 1979. "Strikes, Industrial Relations and Class Conflict in Capitalist Societies." *British Journal of Sociology* 30.

Kramer, Gerald H. 1971. "Short-Term Fluctuations in U.S. Voting Behavior, 1896–1964." *American Political Science Review* 71:131–43.

Krasner, Stephen D. 1984. "Approaches to the State: Alternative Conceptions and Historical Dynamics." *Comparative Politics* 16:223–46.

Krueger, A. O. 1974. "The Political Economy of the Rent Seeking Society." *American Economic Review* 64:291–303.

Lal, D. 1983. *The Poverty of 'Development Economics'*. Hobart Paperback 16. London: The Institute of Economic Affairs.

———. 1984. "The Political Economy of the Predatory State." Discussion Paper, Development Research Department, World Bank.

Lancaster, Kelvin. 1973. "The Dynamic Inefficiency of Capitalism." *Journal of Political Economy* 81.

Lange, Peter 1984a. *Union Democracy and Liberal Corporatism: Exit, Voice and Wage Regulation in Postwar Europe*. Ithaca: Cornell Studies in International Affairs, Western Societies Papers.

Lange, Peter. 1984b. "Unions, Workers and Wage Regulation: The Rational Bases of Consent." In *Order and Conflict in Contemporary Capitalism*, edited by J. Goldthorpe. New York: Oxford University Press.

Lange, Peter, and Geoffrey Garrett. 1985. "The Politics of Growth: Strategic Interaction and Economic Performance in the Advanced Industrial Democracies, 1974–1980." *Journal of Politics* 47:792–827.

———. 1987. "The Politics of Growth Reconsidered." *Journal of Politics* 49: 257–74.

Lange, Peter, and Marino Regini, eds. 1989. *State, Market and Social Regulation: New Perspectives on Italy*. New York: Cambridge University Press.

Lange, Peter, George Ross, and Maurizio Vannicelli. 1982. *Unions, Change and Crisis: French and Italian Union Strategy and the Political Economy, 1945–1980*. Boston: George Allen & Unwin.

Laver, Michael, and Norman Schofield. 1989. *Multiparty Government: The Politics of Coalition in Europe*. New York: Oxford.

Lehmbruch, Gerhard. 1979. "Liberal Corporatism and Party Government." In *Trends toward Corporatist Intermediation*, edited by P. Schmitter and G. Lehmbruch. London: Sage.

———. 1982. "Introduction: Neo-Corporatism in Comparative Perspective."

In *Patterns of Corporatist Policy-Making*, edited by G. Lehmbruch and P. Schmitter. London: Sage.

Lehmbruch, Gerhard, and Philippe Schmitter, eds. 1982. *Patterns of Corporatist Policy-Making*. London: Sage.

Lenin, V. I. 1984. *Imperialism: The Highest Stage of Capitalism*. New York: International Publishers.

Lerner, D. 1958. *The Passing of Traditional Society*. New York: Free Press.

Lindberg, Leon, and Charles Maier, eds. 1985. *The Politics of Inflation and Economic Stagnation*. Washington D.C.: Brookings.

Lijphart, Arend. 1984. *Democracies*. New Haven: Yale University Press.

Lindblom, Charles. 1977. *Politics and Markets*. New York: Basic Books.

Lipset, Seymour. 1963. *Political Man*. New York: Anchor Books.

Little, I. M. D. 1982. *Economic Development: Theory, Practice, and International Relations*. New York: Basic Books.

McGuire, Robert A., and Robert L. Ohsfeldt. 1989. "Self-Interest, Agency Theory, and Political Voting Behavior: The Ratification of the United States Constitution." *American Economic Review* 79:219–34.

McKelvey, Richard. 1976. "Intransitivities in Multidimensional Voting Models and Some Implications for Agenda Control." *Journal of Economic Theory* 12:472–82.

McKeown, Timothy J. 1986. "The Limitations of 'Structural' Theories of Commercial Policy." *International Organization* 40:43–64.

MacRae, Duncan, Jr., and James A. Wilde. 1979. *Policy Analysis or Public Decisions*. Belmont, Calif.: Wadsworth.

Maier, Charles, ed. 1987. *Changing Boundaries of the Political*. Cambridge: Cambridge University Press.

March, James G. 1978. "Bounded Rationality, Ambiguity and the Engineering of Choice." *Bell Journal of Economics* 9:587–608.

March, James G., and Johan P. Olsen. 1984. "The New Institutionalism: Organizational Factors in Political Life." *American Political Science Review* 78: 734–49.

Marx, K., and F. Engels. 1979. *Pre-Capitalist Socio-economic Formations: A Collection*. London: Lawrence & Wishart.

Masters, Marick F., and John Robertson. 1988. "Class Compromise in Industrial Democracies." *American Political Science Review* 82:1183–1202.

Mayhew, David R. 1974. *Congress: The Electoral Connection*. New Haven: Yale University Press.

Meillassoux, C. 1972. "From Production to Reproduction: A Marxist Approach to Economic Anthropology." *Economy and Society* 1:93–105.

Merrill, Samuel, III. 1988. *Making Multicandidate Elections More Democratic*. Princeton: Princeton University Press.

Miller, Gary, and Terry Moe. 1983. "Bureaucrats, Legislators and the Size of Government." *American Political Science Review* 77:297–322.

Miller, N., and R. Aya. 1971. *National Liberation: Revolution in the Third World*. New York: Free Press.

Moe, Terry. 1980. *The Organization of Interests*. Chicago: University of Chicago Press.

Moore, Barrington. 1966. *The Social Origins of Dictatorship and Democracy*. Boston: Beacon Press.

Mueller, Dennis C. 1989. *Public Choice*. Vol. 2. Cambridge: Cambridge University Press.

————. 1983. *The Political Economy of Growth*. New Haven: Yale University Press.

Niskanen, William. 1971. *Bureaucracy and Representative Government*. Chicago: Aldine.

Nordhaus, William D. 1975. "The Political Business Cycle." *Review of Economic Studies* 42:169–90.

O'Connor, James. 1973. *The Fiscal Crisis of State*. New York: St. Martin's Press.

O'Donnell, G. 1973. *Modernization and Bureaucratic Authoritarianism: Studies in South American Politics*. Berkeley: Institute of International Studies.

Offe, Claus. 1981. "The Attribution of Public Status to Interest Groups: Observations on the West German Case." In *Organizing Interests in Western Europe*, edited by Suzanne Berger. Cambridge: Cambridge University Press.

Offe, Claus, and Helmut Wiesenthal. 1980. "Two Logics of Collective Action." In *Political Power and Social Theory*, edited by M. Zeitlin. Greenwich, Conn.: JAI Press.

Olson, Mancur, Jr. 1965, 1971. *The Logic of Collective Action*. Cambridge: Harvard University Press.

————. 1982. *The Rise and Decline of Nations*. New Haven: Yale University Press.

Ordeshook, Peter. 1986. *Game Theory and Political Theory*. Cambridge: Cambridge University Press.

Ostrom, Vincent. 1971, 1987. *The Political Theory of a Compound Republic*. 2nd ed. Lincoln: University of Nebraska Press.

Page, Benjamin I., and Richard A. Brody. 1972. "Policy Voting and the Electoral Process: The Vietnam War Issue." *American Political Science Review* 66:979–95.

Paldam, Martin. 1978. "Is There an Electoral Cycle? A Comparative Study of National Accounts." *Scandinavian Journal Of Economics* 81.

Palfrey, Thomas. 1984. "Spatial Equilibrium with Entry." *Review of Economic Studies* 51:139–56.

Palma, G. 1978. "Dependency: A Formal Theory of Underdevelopment or a

Methodology for the Analysis of Concrete Situations of Underdevelopment." *World Development* 6:881–924.

Panitch, Leo. 1979. "The Development of Corporatism in Liberal Democracies." In *Trends toward Corporatist Intermediation*, edited by P. Schmitter and G. Lehmbruch. London: Sage.

———. 1980. "Recent Theorizations of Corporatism: Reflections on a Growth Industry." *British Journal of Sociology* 31.

———. 1981. "Trade Unions in the Capitalist State." *New Left Review* 125.

Peltzman, Sam. 1985. "An Economic Interpretation of the History of Congressional Voting in the Twentieth Century." *American Economic Review* 75: 656–75.

Piore, Michael, and Charles Sabel. 1984. *The Second Industrial Divide*. New York: Basic Books.

Polanyi, Karl. 1944, 1957. *The Great Transformation*. Boston: Beacon Press.

Poole, Keith, and Howard Rosenthal. 1984. "U.S. Presidential Elections 1968–1980: A Spatial Analysis." *American Journal of Political Science* 28: 282–312.

Popkin, S. L. 1979. *The Rational Peasant*. Berkeley and Los Angeles: University of California Press.

Posner, R. 1980. "A Theory of Primitive Society, with Special Relevance to Law." *The Journal of Law and Economics* 23:1–53.

Prebisch, Raul. 1950. *The Economic Development of Latin America and its Principal Problems*. New York: United Nations.

Przeworski, Adam. 1985. *Capitalism and Social Democracy*. Cambridge: Cambridge University Press.

Przeworski, Adam, and Michael Wallerstein. 1982. "The Structure of Class Conflict in Democratic Capitalist Societies." *American Political Science Review* 76.

Przeworski, Adam, and John Sprague. 1986. *Paper Stones: A History of Electoral Socialism*. Chicago: University of Chicago Press.

Putterman, L. 1987. *The Nature of the Firm*. Cambridge: Cambridge University Press.

Quattrone, George A., and Amos Tversky. 1988. "Contrasting Rational and Psychological Analyses of Political Choice." *American Political Science Review* 82:719–36.

Rabinowitz, George, Paul-Henri Gurian, and Stuart Elaine Macdonald. 1984. "The Structure of Presidential Elections and the Process of Realignment." *American Journal of Political Science* 28:611–35.

Rabinowitz, George, and Stuart Macdonald. 1989. "A Directional Theory of Issue Voting." *American Political Science Review* 83:93–121.

Rhoads, Steven E. 1985. *The Economist's View of the World: Government, Markets and Public Policy*. Cambridge: Cambridge University Press.

Riker, William H. 1982. *Liberalism against Populism*. San Francisco: W. H. Freeman.

Robertson, David. 1976. *A Theory of Party Competition*. New York: Wiley & Sons.

Roemer, J. E. 1982. *A General Theory of Class and Exploitation*. Cambridge: Harvard University Press.

Rogers, E. 1962. *Diffusion of Innovations*. New York: Free Press.

Rose, Richard. 1984. *Do Parties Make a Difference?* 2nd ed. London: Chatham House.

Rose, Richard, and Guy Peters. 1978. *Can Government Go Bankrupt?* New York: Basic Books.

Scharpf, Fritz. 1984. "Economic and Institutional Constraints on Full Employment Strategies: Sweden, Austria, and West Germany, 1973–1982." In *Order and Conflict in Contemporary Capitalism*, edited by J. Goldthorpe. New York: Oxford University Press.

———. 1988. "A Game-Theoretical Interpretation of Inflation and Unemployment in Western Europe." *Journal of Public Policy* 7:227–57.

Schelling, Thomas C. 1984. *Choice and Consequence*. Cambridge: Harvard University Press.

Schmidt, Manfred. 1982. "The Role of Parties in Shaping Macroeconomic Policy." In *The Impact of Parties*, edited by F. Castles. Beverly Hills: Sage.

———. 1983. "The Welfare State and the Economy in Periods of Economic Crisis." *European Journal of Political Research* 11:1–26.

Schmitter, Philippe. 1974. "Still the Century of Corporatism?" *Review of Politics* 36.

———. 1981. "Interest Intermediation and Regime Governability in Contemporary Western Europe and North America." In *Organizing Interests in Western Europe*, edited by S. Berger. New York: Cambridge University Press.

———. 1982. "Reflections on Where the Theory of Neo-corporatism Has Gone and Where the Praxis of Neo-corporatism May Be Going." *Patterns of Corporatist Policy-Making*, edited by G. Lehmbruch and P. Schmitter. London: Sage.

———. 1986. "Neo-corporatism and the State." In *The Political Economy of Corporatism*, edited by Wyn Grant. New York: St. Martin's Press.

Schmitter, Philippe, and Gerhard Lehmbruch, eds. 1979. *Trends toward Corporatist Intermediation*. London: Sage.

Schott, Kerry. 1984a. "Investment, Order, and Conflict in a Simple Dynamic Model of Capitalism." In *Order and Conflict in Contemporary Capitalism*, edited by J. Goldthorpe. New York: Oxford University Press.

———. 1984b. *Policy, Power and Order: The Persistence of Economic Problems in Capitalist States*. New Haven: Yale University Press.

Scott, J. C. 1976. *The Moral Economy of the Peasant*. New Haven and London: Yale University Press.

Shepsle, Kenneth. 1979. "Institutional Arrangements and Equilibrium in Multidimensional Voting Models." *American Journal of Political Science* 23: 27–59.

Shepsle, Kenneth, and Barry Weingast. 1981. "Political Preferences for the Pork Barrel: A Generalization." *American Journal of Political Science* 25:96–112.

———. 1984. "Political Solutions to Market Problems." *American Political Science Review* 78:417–34.

———. 1987. "The Institutional Foundations of Committee Power." *American Political Science Review* 81:85–104.

Shonfield, Andrew. 1965. *Modern Capitalism*. New York: Oxford University Press.

Simon, Herbert A. 1976. "From Substantive to Procedural Rationality." In *Method and Appraisal in Economics* edited by S. J. Latsis. Cambridge: Cambridge University Press.

———. 1981. *The Sciences of the Artificial*. Cambridge: MIT Press.

———. 1985. "Human Nature in Politics: The Dialogue of Psychology with Political Science." *American Political Science Review* 79:293–304.

Skidelsky, Robert. 1979. "The Decline of Keynesian Politics." In *State and Economy in Contemporary Capitalism*, edited by Colin Crouch. New York: St. Martin's Press.

Skocpol, Theda. 1979. *States and Social Revolutions: A Comparative Analysis of France, Russia and China*. Cambridge: Cambridge University Press.

Skocpol, Theda, et al., eds. 1985. *Bringing the State Back In*. Cambridge: Cambridge University Press.

Srinivasan, T. N. 1985. "Neoclassical Political Economy, the State, and Economic Development." *Asian Development Review* 3:35–58.

Starrett, D. A. 1988. *Foundations of Public Economics*. Cambridge: Cambridge University Press.

Steinmo, Sven Holger. 1986. *Taxes, Institutions and the Mobilization of Bias: The Political Economy of Taxation in Britain, Sweden, and the United States*. Ph.D. diss. Department of Political Science, University of California, Berkeley.

Stewart, Charles, III. 1988. "Budget Reform as Strategic Legislative Action." *Journal of Politics* 50:292–321.

Stigler, George J. ed. 1988. *Chicago Studies in Political Economy*. Chicago: University of Chicago Press.

Stigler, George J., and Gary S. Becker. 1977. "De Gustibus Non Est Disputandum." *American Economic Review* 67:76–90.

Stokes, Donald E. 1963. "Spatial Models of Party Competition." *American Political Science Review* 57:368–77.

Stokey, Edith, and Richard Zeckhauser. 1978. *A Primer for Policy Analysis*. New York: Norton.

Streeck, Wolfgang, and Philippe Schmitter, eds. 1985. *Private Interest Government*. London: Sage.

Swenson, Peter. 1989. *Fair Shares: Unions, Pay, and Politics in Sweden and West Germany*. Ithaca: Cornell University Press.

Trimberger, E. K. 1972. "A Theory of Elite Revolutions." *Studies in International Comparative Development* 7:191–207.

Tsebelis, George. 1989. *Nested Games*. Berkeley: University of California Press.

Tufte, Edward R. 1978. *Political Control of the Economy*. Princeton: Princeton University Press.

Walker, Jack L. 1983. "The Origin and Maintenance of Interest Groups in America." *American Political Science Review* 77:390–406.

Wallerstein, Immanuel. 1974. *The Modern World System*. New York: Academic Press.

Warren, B. 1973. "Imperialism and Capitalist Industrialization." *New Left Review* 81:3–44.

Whiteley, Paul. 1983. "The Political Economy of Economic Growth." *European Journal of Political Research* 11:197–213.

Wilks, I. 1975. *Asante in the Nineteenth Century: The Structure and Evolution of a Political Order*. Cambridge: Cambridge University Press.

Williamson, Oliver. 1985. *The Economic Institutions of Capitalism*. New York: Free Press.

Wittman, Donald. 1983. "Candidate Motivation: A Synthesis of Alternative Theories." *American Political Science Review* 77:142–58.

Wolf, Charles, Jr. 1988. *Markets or Governments: Choosing between Imperfect Alternatives*. Cambridge: MIT Press.

Woolley, John. 1984. *Monetary Politics*. Cambridge: Cambridge University Press.

———. 1988. "Partisan Manipulation of the Economy: Another Look at Monetary Policy with Moving Regression." *Journal of Politics* 50:335–60.

Zysman, John. 1983. *Governments, Markets and Growth: Financial Systems and the Politics of Industrial Change*. Ithaca: Cornell University Press.

7

Public Policy: Toward Better Theories of the Policy Process

Paul A. Sabatier

Although political scientists who are policy scholars often trace their lineage back to the pioneering work of Lerner and Lasswell (1951), public policy did not emerge as a significant subfield within the discipline of political science until the late 1960s or early 1970s. There were at least three important stimuli: (1) social and political pressures to apply the discipline's accumulated knowledge to the amelioration of pressing social problems such as racial discrimination, poverty, the arms race, and environmental pollution; (2) the challenge posed by the Dawson and Robinson article (1963) indicating that governmental policy decisions were less the result of traditional disciplinary concerns such as public opinion and party composition than of socioeconomic factors such as income, education, and unemployment levels; and (3) the efforts of David Easton, whose *Systems Analysis of Political Life* (1965; also Easton 1953) provided an intellectual framework focusing the various concerns of the discipline on their contributions to policy outputs and impacts, and whose 1968 APSA presidential address (Easton 1969) encouraged the discipline to apply its knowledge to policy problems.

Over the past twenty years, policy research by political scientists can be divided into four types, depending upon the principal focus:

1. *Substantive area research.* Here the focus is on understanding the politics of a specific policy area, such as health, education, transpor-

The author would like to thank Hank Jenkins-Smith, Joseph Stewart, Jr., Theodore Lowi, Aaron Wildavsky, Virginia Gray, John Kingdon, and Michael Rich for their constructive criticisms of previous drafts of this chapter.

tation, natural resources, or foreign policy. Most of the work in this tradition has consisted of detailed, largely atheoretical, case studies. Examples would include the work of Derthick (1979) on social security, Moynihan (1970) on anti-poverty programs, and Bailey and Mosher (1968) on federal aid to education. Such studies are very useful to practitioners and policy activists in these areas, as well as providing potentially useful information for inductive theory building. In terms of the profession as a whole, however, they are probably less useful than theoretical case studies—such as Pressman and Wildavsky (1973) on implementation or Nelson (1986) on agenda-setting—which use a specific case to illustrate or test theories of important aspects of the policy process.

2. *Evaluation and impact studies*. Most evaluation research is based on contributions from other disciplines. The basic features of quasi-experimental research designs were established by Campbell and Stanley (1963); the statistical techniques for modeling the effects of policy interventions in time-series analysis were developed by Box and Jenkins (1970); and the normative assumptions and analytical frameworks for policy evaluations rely heavily upon welfare economics (Stokey and Zeckhauser 1978; Jenkins-Smith 1990).

   Policy scholars trained as political scientists have, however, broadened the criteria of evaluation from traditional social welfare functions to include process criteria, such as opportunities for effective citizen participation (Rosenbaum 1976; Pierce and Doerksen 1976). They have focused attention on the distribution of impacts among various constituencies (MacRae 1989). They have criticized traditional techniques of benefit-cost analysis on many grounds (Meier 1984; MacRae and Whittington 1988). Most important, under the leadership of Aaron Wildavsky, they have sought to integrate evaluation studies into research on the policy process by examining the use and non-use of policy analysis in the real world (Wildavsky 1966; Dunn 1980) and by analyzing the bureaucratic and other political factors affecting policy impacts (Pressman and Wildavsky 1973).

3. *Policy process*. Two decades ago, both Ranney (1968) and Sharkansky (1970) urged political scientists interested in public policy to focus on the policy process, i.e. the factors affecting policy formulation and implementation, as well as the subsequent political effects of policy impacts. In their view, focusing on substantive policy areas risked falling into the relatively fruitless realm of atheoretical case studies, and evaluation research offered little promise for a discipline without clear normative standards of what constitutes good policy. On the other hand, a focus on the policy process would provide many opportunities for applying and integrating the disci-

pline's accumulated knowledge concerning political behavior in various institutional settings. That advice was remarkably prescient, and the bulk of this chapter will seek to summarize what has been learned.

4. *Policy design*. The most recent of the four research foci, it has tended to deal with such topics as the efficacy of different types of policy instruments (Salamon 1989; Linder and Peters 1989). Some scholars within this orientation propose a quite radical departure from the behavioral traditions of the discipline (Bobrow and Dryzek 1987); others seek to build upon and extend work by policy-oriented political scientists over the past twenty years (Schneider and Ingram 1990). The latter strikes us as a far more sensible strategy. Thus policy design will be discussed in the concluding section, when we address the prospects for using our accumulated knowledge to develop a *prospective* policy science.

Though all have made some contributions, the third has been the most fruitful.

Before turning to a review of work on the policy process, I should make some mention of tensions that have emerged between traditional political scientists and the subfield of policy scholars (see Sabatier 1991 for a more extended discussion). Several are essentially normative, arising from policy scholars' tendency to be political activists and to view government in instrumental terms (Hofferbert 1986). The most serious strain arises, however, from the perception of many political scientists that policy scholars have made only very modest contributions to the development of reasonably clear, generalizable, and empirically verified theories of the policy process (Eulau 1977; Landau 1977). In some respects, this indictment strikes me as quite valid. Much of what passes as policy research—particularly by substantive area specialists—consists of essentially descriptive analyses of specific institutions or decisions relying upon subjective methods of data acquisition and analysis, with minimal attention to the theoretical assumptions underlying the research and little concern for the potential generalizability of the findings.

In addition, the dominant paradigm of the policy process—the stages heuristic of Jones (1970), Anderson (1975), and Peters (1986)—is not really a *causal* theory. Instead, it divides the policy process into several stages—agenda setting, formulation and adoption, implementation, and evaluation—and discusses some of the things going on in each stage, but contains no coherent assumptions about what forces are driving the process from stage to stage and very few falsifiable hypotheses.[1] The stages heuristic has been helpful in dividing the incredibly complex policy process into more manageable units of analysis, but researchers have tended to focus on one of the stages with little recognition of work in other stages. The result is little theoretical coherence across stages. Even within stages (such as implementation) where there has been a great deal of empirical research, disagreement exists as to how much has actually been learned over the past twenty years (see Sabatier 1986 and O'Toole 1986 for contrasting reviews). Finally, Nakamura (1987) and others have noted that the real world process often does not fit the sequence of stages envisaged.

On the other hand, a great deal of policy research—particularly within the policy process tradition—has been methodologically sophisticated and guided by explicit theory. Examples would include Kingdon (1984) and Nelson (1986) on agenda-setting; Pressman and Wildavsky (1973), Rodgers and Bullock (1976), Mazmanian and Sabatier (1981, 1989), and Goggin (1987) on implementation; Browning et al. (1984) on long-term policy change; and Ostrom (1990) on institutional arrangements for managing common property resources. More important, as I hope to show in the next section, in several areas policy scholars have made major contributions to our knowledge of the policy process, while also questioning some of the basic assumptions of many political scientists. In short, though the criticisms of Eulau and Landau were largely justified a decade ago, they are less valid today.

INNOVATIONS BY POLICY SCHOLARS IN UNDERSTANDING THE POLICY PROCESS

At least since World War II, most political scientists at any given point in their careers have tended to focus either on a specific type of institution (legislatures, the presidency, courts, interest groups, administrative agencies, local governments, political parties) or on specific types of political behavior outside those institutions (public opinion, voting, political socialization). These have become the standard subfields within the discipline.

In contrast, scholars interested in public policy have not been able to stay within these subfields because the policy process usually involves nearly all of the above. In the course of their empirical work, policy scholars have highlighted a number of phenomena that political scientists without a policy focus have often neglected. These include:

1. The importance of policy communities/networks/subsystems involving actors from numerous public and private institutions and from multiple levels of government;

2. The importance of substantive policy information;

3. The critical role of policy elites vis-à-vis the general public;

4. The desirability of longitudinal studies of a decade or more;

5. Differences in political behavior across policy types.

Each will be discussed in turn in this section. The next section will then explore a number of recent efforts to combine these and other factors into theories of the policy process.

The Importance of Intergovernmental Policy Communities/Subsystems

Traditionally, political scientists have been preoccupied with either a single type of institution or with "iron triangles" at a single level of government. The separate, and neglected, field of intergovernmental relations has focused on legal relationships and political culture (Elazar 1984).

Numerous strands of policy research have clearly demonstrated the inadequacy of this focus on single, or very small groups of, institutions. Virtually all implementation research, from the early studies of Murphy (1973), Pressman and Wildavsky (1973), and Van Horn (1979) to more recent work by Hjern and Porter (1981), Mazmanian and Sabatier (1981, 1989), Scholz and Wei (1986), and Goggin (1987) has clearly demonstrated that the development and execution of virtually all domestic policy in the United States and Western Europe involve numerous agencies and interest groups at all levels of government. This has been confirmed by studies of fiscal federalism (Reagan 1972; Nathan and Adams 1977; ACIR 1984); by research on the relationship between federal and state laws within a specific policy area (Gray 1973; Rose 1973; Kemp 1978; Lester and Bowman 1989); and by the growing literature on intergovernmental relations in Western Europe (Hanf and Scharpf 1978; Rhodes and Wright 1987; Page and Goldsmith 1987).

In addition, studies of agenda setting (Kingdon 1984; Cook and Skogan 1989), implementation (Sharpe 1985; Mazmanian and Sabatier 1989, chap. 6), deregulation (Derthick and Quirk 1985), and the entire literature on the use of policy analysis (Weiss 1977a; Nelkin 1979; Mazur 1981) have demonstrated that researchers, specialist reporters, and professional associations need to be added to the list of active participants within policy communities. There is also considerable evidence that policy specialists in the chief executive's office (e.g., the Office of Management and Budget at the federal level) need to be added to the list of actors within policy communities (White 1981; Vig and Kraft 1984).

Thus one of the clearest conclusions to emerge from the policy literature is that understanding the policy process requires looking at an intergovernmental policy community or subsystem—composed of bureaucrats, legislative personnel, interest group leaders, researchers, and specialist reporters within a substantive policy area—as the basic unit of study. Political scientists' traditional focus on single institutions, or even single levels of government, will help in understanding the effects of institutional rules on behavior and, at times, in understanding specific decisions. But it is usually inadequate for understanding the policy process over any length of time (Jones 1975; Heclo 1978; Kingdon 1984; Sabatier 1988).

The Importance of Substantive Policy Information

Political scientists have traditionally sought explanations of behavior in the preferences, interests, and resources of the actors involved, in institutional rules, and in background socioeconomic conditions. The topic of the amount and quality of information used in choice situations has been neglected—except in voting studies, where the public clearly are cognitive misers (Lau and Sears 1986).

In contrast, numerous strands of public policy research have demonstrated the importance of substantive policy information. Virtually all studies of specific policy areas have shown that most participants spend a great deal of time discussing relatively technical topics such as the magnitude of the problems involved, the relative importance of various factors affecting the problem(s), the impacts of past policies, and the probable future consequences of policy alternatives (Heclo 1974; Derthick 1979; Nelson 1986; Greenberger et al. 1983). This is precisely why subsystems are critical. One must specialize in a particular policy area in order to understand the substantive debates; actors outside the subsystem tend to take cues from those within (Matthews and Stimson 1975; Kingdon 1981).

The influence of such information on policy decisions has been the subject of extensive research. Several conclusions have tentatively emerged. First, substantive policy information is typically used in an advocacy fashion, that is, to buttress one's position or to attack an opponent's (Wildavsky and Tenenbaum 1981; Mazur 1981; Jenkins-Smith 1990; Heintz 1988). Second, only rarely does a specific piece of research strongly influence a major policy decision. When that happens, it is usually because a source respected by all participants has done an excellent job (Whiteman 1985; Songer 1988; Cook and Skogan 1989). Instead, the more normal pattern is for a process of "enlightenment" whereby the accumulation of findings over time gradually alters decision-makers' perceptions of the seriousness of the problems, the importance of various causal factors, and the impacts of major policy programs (Caplan et al. 1975; Weiss 1977a, 1977b; Derthick and Quirk 1985).

Finally, the importance of substantive policy information suggests that our conception of the content of elite belief systems needs to be broadened beyond the traditional focus on normative and ideological beliefs (Putnam 1976) to include perceptions of problem severity and causal relationships in the policy areas in which elites are specialists (Greenberger et al. 1983; Sabatier and Hunter 1989).

The Critical Role of Policy Elites vis-à-vis the Public

Over the past thirty years, political scientists have spent an enormous amount of time and resources seeking to understand public opinion and voting behavior. Both Walker (1972) and Palumbo (1989) found this was either the first or second most frequent category of articles in the major disciplinary journals (theory being the other). There has also been a great deal of attention to the congruence between constituent preferences and legislative floor voting.

Several decades of policy research suggest, however, that the general public plays a more modest role in the formulation and implementation of governmental policy than in the discipline's research priorities. On the one hand, there is a fairly strong correlation between important shifts in public opinion and changes in the *general direction* of governmental policy (Page and Shapiro 1983). Popular influence is further enhanced if one includes citizen complaints to agency and legislative officials (Verba and Nie 1972; Johannes 1984) and grass roots response to interest group lobbying campaigns (Loomis 1983). But affecting the general direction of policy and the disposition of a small percentage of specific cases still leaves some enormous voids. In air pollution policy, for example, the major issues over the past decade have included such topics as the effects of command-and-control strategies versus economic incentives; the question of whether to set the national air quality standard for ozone at .10 ppm or .08 ppm; the consequences of using tall stacks and scrubbers as control techniques for utilities; the sources and consequences of acid rain; and the importance of inspection and maintenance programs for controlling automotive emissions (White 1981; Liroff 1986). All of these topics require much greater substantive information than the general public (or more legislators) have at their disposal, a knowledge of precisely when and where to intervene, and the ability and willingness to sustain that intervention over many years. It is the members of the air pollution policy community who have that knowledge and commitment and, thus, the ability to actually shape policy over an extended period of time.

The Desirability of Longitudinal Studies
of a Decade or More

In this instance, political scientists and policy scholars have pursued similar paths. During the 1960s and early 1970s, most research in both areas involved either cross-sectional designs or short-term case studies of specific decisions or institutions. Recently, both groups of scholars have given much greater attention to longitudinal designs involving a decade or more.

From a policy perspective, the desirability of a longer time perspective has arisen for several reasons. First, many of the early implementation studies using time frames of three to four years resulted in premature assessments of program performance; much fairer evaluations came after a decade or so (Kirst and Jung 1983; Sabatier 1986). Second, if the dominant use of substantive policy information is via the "enlightenment function," that obviously requires a time frame of a decade or more—one of the best examples being the gradual accumulation of economic critiques of the inefficiencies of airline regulation by the Civil Aeronautics Board (Derthick and Quirk 1985). Third, there is a recognition that understanding the significance of particular policy innovations, as well as the relative importance of factors such as changing socioeconomic conditions and policy-oriented learning, requires time spans of several decades (Heclo 1974; Derthick 1979; Nelson 1986; Burstein 1985).

Of course, the optimal strategy is to use pooled cross-sectional, longitudinal designs (Goggin 1986). In policy research, doing so is complicated by difficulties in obtaining good data across numerous governmental units over a decade or more on anything besides legislative roll calls and government expenditures. But recently scholars have become more adept at obtaining data on, for instance, enforcement actions, from government agencies. When linked to changes in socioeconomic and political conditions, statutes, and policy impacts/outcomes, these offer the prospect of more sophisticated analyses (Scholz and Wei 1986; Lester and Bowman 1989; Wood 1990).

Differences in Political Behavior across Policy Types

Of all the work in public policy over the past two decades, Lowi's (1964, 1972) argument that political behavior varies across policy types—distributive, redistributive, regulatory—has probably had the greatest effect on the discipline of political science.[2] For example, it forms a major organizing principle in several texts on both congressional and bureaucratic behavior (Ripley and Franklin 1980, 1982; Meier 1987).

The basic argument has been subjected to considerable criticism, including ambiguities in the precise causal process by which behavioral differences are associated with policy types and difficulties in applying the typology to particular policy decisions (Heclo 1972; Greenberg et al. 1977; May 1986). These problems can probably be remedied, however, by focusing on the distribution of costs and benefits across policy categories (Wilson 1973, chap. 16; Ingram 1978) and by acknowledging that a law can contain quite different policy types. Lowi would simply predict quite different forms of political behavior regarding different parts of many statutes, which is precisely what Mann (1975) found in examining the passage of the 1972 Federal Water Pollution Control Act.

SYNTHESIZING THEORIES OF THE POLICY PROCESS

The fundamental arguments of this chapter are, first, that political scientists and policy scholars share a common interest in developing better theories of the policy process than the stages heuristic and, second, that such theories should seek to integrate many of the contributions by policy scholars discussed in the previous section with political scientists' traditional focus on the preferences, interests, and resources of various actors, institutional rules, and background socioeconomic conditions.

This section briefly analyzes four such efforts. They cover the range of approaches that address most of those topics, which apply to significant portions of the policy process, and have proven useful in a variety of empirical settings:

1. The open-systems framework of Richard Hofferbert;
2. An approach involving rational actors within institutions developed by Elinor Ostrom and her colleagues;
3. John Kingdon's "policy streams" framework;
4. The "advocacy coalition" framework recently developed by Sabatier.

All but the first were developed during the 1980s, suggesting that alternatives to the stages heuristic are finally emerging. Though these strike us as the most promising approaches, others have also proven useful. They include Ripley's (1985) synthesis of the stages heuristic with a modified version of Lowi's arenas of power and Wildavsky's "cultural" explanations of policy change (Wildavsky 1982, 1987; Coyle and Wildavsky 1987).

An Open Systems (Funnel of Causality) Approach

Fifteen years ago, Hofferbert (1974) developed a conceptual framework of the policy process with policy outputs (governmental decisions) as the dependent variable. As indicated in Figure 7.1, these were seen as a direct and indirect function of historical-geographic conditions, socioeconomic conditions, mass political behavior, governmental institutions, and—most directly—elite behavior.

Figure 7.1
Hofferbert's model for comparative study of policy formation*

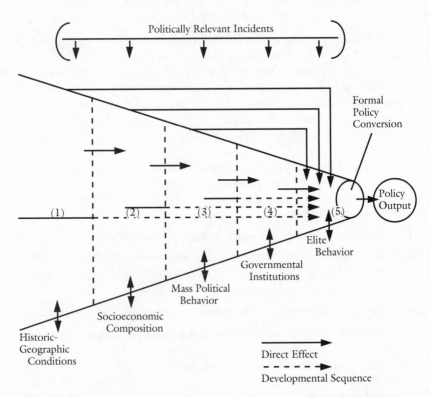

*This is a slightly truncated reproduction of the model. The numerous direct and indirect paths between sectors 2–5 have been deleted (Hofferbert 1974, figure VII-1).

Source: Mazmanian and Sabatier (1980, 441).

This is a slightly truncated reproduction of the model. The numerous direct and indirect paths between sectors 2–5 have been deleted (Hofferbert 1974, figure VII–1).

Source: Mazmanian and Sabatier (1980, 441).

This approach has proven useful in guiding research involving cross-sectional comparisons of policy outputs across states and localities. On the other hand, it has been criticized for its "black box" approach to governmental institutions and elite behavior, and for its neglect of an intergovernmental dimension (Rose 1973; Eyestone 1977). Although subsequent research has partially resolved these problems (Mazmanian and Sabatier 1980; Hofferbert and Urice 1985), the highly aggregated nature of the variables—and the consequent neglect of individual-level processes—means that the Hofferbert approach has inherent limitations when dealing with such topics as the role of substantive information and interactions within intergovernmental policy communities. In addition, the framework would have to add policy impacts and feedback loops to be useful in longitudinal studies. Finally, Hofferbert assumed that socioeconomic conditions and mass political behavior—as mediated by governmental institutions and elite behavior—drove policy outputs, a view that runs counter to a fair amount of research concerning the ability of governmental elites to manipulate popular opinion (Dye and Zeigler 1975; Cobb et al. 1976).

Despite these limitations, the Hofferbert approach constitutes a parsimonious view of the policy process with clear (if perhaps not always valid) driving forces. It continues to be a useful starting point for cross-sectional comparisons and may still be the dominant paradigm in comparative policy research (Leichter 1979; Lundqvist 1980).

Rational Actors within Institutions

In direct contrast to the systems approach of Hofferbert, a large group of "rational choice" scholars over the past twenty years have started with individual actors—their preferences, interests, and resources—as the basic unit of analysis and then have examined how institutional rules can affect behavior (March and Olsen 1984; for a review, see the chapter by Keech et al. in this volume.) From a policy perspective, the most useful body of work within this tradition has been that of Elinor Ostrom and her colleagues, because it combines an actor-based perspective with attention to institutional rules, intergovernmental relations, and policy outputs.

The basic approach is found in Kiser and Ostrom (1982). As can be seen in Part A of Figure 7.2, it views individual actions as a function of both the attributes (values and resources) of the individual and the attributes of his or her decision situation. The latter is, in turn, a product of institutional rules, the nature of the relevant good, and the attributes of the community (which would include Hofferbert's socioeconomic conditions and community opinion). The principal insight of this approach is that the same individual will behave differently in different

Figure 7.2
Ostrom's framework for institutional analysis

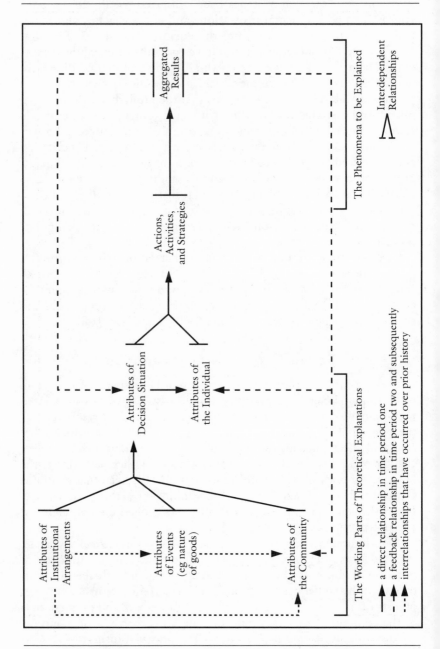

Part A: The working parts of institutional analysis

Figure 7.2 cont.

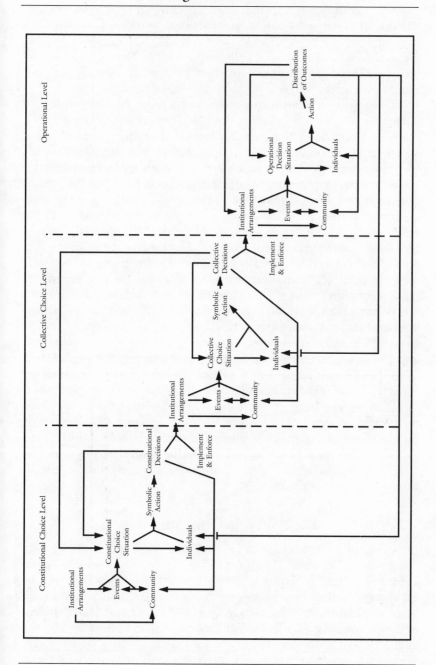

Part B: Three levels of institutional analysis

decision situations. The focus has been, first, on developing a classification of institutional rules that delineate entry and exit to various positions, the scope of authority for each position, permissible communication among actors in various roles, and means for aggregating individual actions into a collective decision. Next, empirical and theoretical work has demonstrated how changes in a specific rule can significantly affect behavior (Ostrom 1986a, 1986b).

This approach to institutional analysis is given a policy perspective in Part B of Figure 7.2. It defines three levels of institutional analysis—the operational level (e.g., agency permit decisions), the collective choice (e.g., the statute governing the agency), and the constitutional (the constitution governing the legislature). There are two fundamental insights: First, that the outputs of a given level basically set the institutional rules of the next lower level. Thus a constitution sets the basic institutional rules for a legislature, while a legislative statute sets the basic rules governing agency permit decisions. Second, it is primarily the outputs of the operational level that directly affect citizens; the outputs of higher levels are basically instructions to lower levels. This statement is perfectly consistent with the findings from a decade of implementation research: what happens in Washington or Sacramento is little more than words on paper until it affects the behavior of "street-level bureaucrats" and, ultimately, target groups.

This is a superb framework for thinking about the effects of individuals and institutions on governmental policy outputs/decisions. It has, of course, some limitations. The role of substantive policy information is neglected, as is the range of factors intervening between policy outputs and societal impacts. Although "community characteristics" are mentioned as one of the three sets of factors affecting a decision situation, they have largely been neglected in the work to date. Finally, the focus on individual behavior within specific institutions renders this framework a little unwieldy for dealing with the multitude of institutions in a policy community.

The Policy Streams Approach

Drawing upon the "garbage can model" of organizational choice (Cohen et al. 1972), John Kingdon (1984) has developed an interesting approach to agenda setting and policy formulation that may well be expandable to the entire policy process. In his view, policy-making can be conceptualized as three largely unrelated "streams": (1) a problem stream, consisting of information about real world problems and the effects of past governmental interventions; (2) a policy stream/community composed of researchers, advocates, and other specialists who analyze problems and formulate possible alternatives; and (3) a political stream, consisting of elections, legislative leadership contests, and so on. According to Kingdon, major policy reforms result when "a window of opportunity" joins the three streams: in response to a recognized problem, the policy community develops a proposal that is financially and technically feasible, and politicians find it advantageous to approve it.

The Kingdon approach has many praiseworthy features. It incorporates an enlarged view of policy communities. It gives a prominent role to substantive policy information about real world problems and the impacts of previous governmental interventions. It gets beyond the rather rigid institutionalism in which many political scientists confine themselves. And it acknowledges the role of serendipity in the policy process.

On the other hand, several aspects need further development. The conditions under which windows of opportunity arise merit further analysis, and Jones (1987) has recently made some suggestions in this regard. As will become apparent shortly, Sabatier would contend that Kingdon views policy analysts and researchers as being too neutral, thus neglecting the role of advocacy analysis and putting too much distance between the "policy" and the "political" streams. Finally, if the framework is to be expanded to include the entire policy process, more attention needs to be given to bureaucracies and courts in implementing those reforms, and more recognition needs to be accorded the intergovernmental dimension in both formulation and implementation.

The Advocacy Coalition Approach

Recently Sabatier (1988) has developed a conceptual framework of the policy process that synthesizes many of the features discussed in this chapter. It views policy change over time as a function of three sets of factors:

1. *The interaction of competing advocacy coalitions within a policy subsystem/community.* An advocacy coalition consists of actors from a variety of public and private organizations at all levels of government who share a set of basic beliefs (policy goals plus causal and other perceptions) and who seek to manipulate the rules of various governmental institutions in order to achieve those goals over time. Conflict among coalitions is mediated by "policy brokers," i.e. actors more concerned with system stability than with achieving policy goals.

2. *Changes external to the subsystem* in socioeconomic conditions, system-wide governing coalitions, and outputs from other policy subsystems. Since 1970, for example, U.S. air pollution policy has been

affected by changes in petroleum prices, by Republican electoral victories in 1980, and by outputs from the tax and energy subsystems.

3. *The effects of stable system parameters*—such as basic social structure and constitutional rules—on the constraints and resources of various actors. The strategies available to advocacy coalitions in air pollution policy, for example, are obviously constrained by federalism.

With respect to both belief systems and public policies, the framework distinguishes "core" from "secondary" elements. Coalitions are assumed to organize around common beliefs in core elements, such as the proper scope of governmental versus market activity and the proper distribution of authority among various levels of government. Since these core beliefs are hypothesized to be relatively stable over periods of a decade or more, so too is coalition composition. Coalitions seek to learn about how the world operates and the effects of various governmental interventions in order to realize their goals over time. Because of resistance to changing core beliefs, such policy-oriented learning is usually confined to the secondary aspects of belief systems.[3] Changes in the core elements of public policies require the replacement of a dominant coalition by another, which is hypothesized to result primarily from changes external to the subsystem (i.e., from the second set of factors).

The advocacy coalition framework has been applied to a number of policy areas, primarily dealing with energy and environmental policy (McLaughlin and Sabatier 1987; Jenkins-Smith 1988; Heintz 1988; Weyent 1988; Jenkins-Smith and Sabatier 1990). Thus far, the arguments concerning coalition stability and the prevalence of advocacy analysis have generally been confirmed; however, doubts have been raised about the hierarchical structure of belief systems and the framework's neglect of actor interests (as opposed to beliefs). Although further testing will almost certainly suggest additional modifications and elaborations, the advocacy coalition framework's ability to integrate the concerns of policy scholars with much of the political science literature makes it a promising new approach to the policy process. It shares several similarities with Wildavsky's (1982, 1987) "cultural" explanations, but gives more attention to the nature of belief systems and the respective roles of policy learning and exogenous factors in policy change.

FUTURE DIRECTIONS

Public policy shares a characteristic of many subfields within political science: the absence of a commonly accepted, clearly articulated, and empirically verified body of theory. This can partially be attributed to the complexity of the policy process and the recent emergence of the

Figure 7.3
General model of policy change focusing on competing advocacy coalitions within policy subsystems

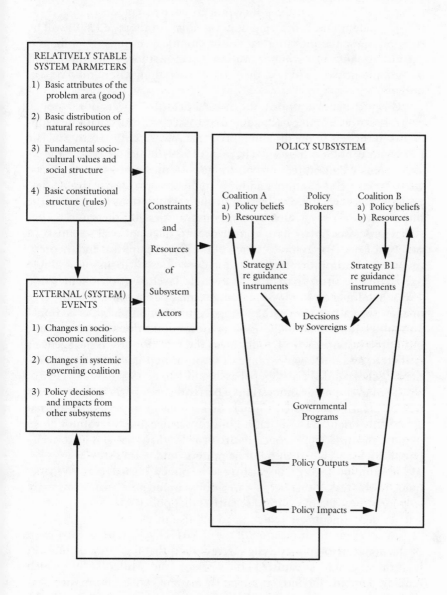

Source: Sabatier (1988, 132).

subfield. The 1970s and early 1980s were dominated by largely atheoretical work in substantive policy areas and by research in specific policy stages, particularly formulation and implementation. In the last five to ten years, however, a number of causal theories (or metatheories) of substantial portions of the policy process have emerged.

The paramount task facing policy scholars during the 1990s will be to apply these theories in a variety of empirical settings, refining and expanding those that seem promising, rejecting those that do not, and developing new ones to take their place. Everything else should be secondary.

Given the contributions of other subfields to aspects of the policy process, however, policy scholars need to keep in touch with developments in the rest of the discipline. For example, recent work by Sinclair (1989) and by Smith and Maltzman (1989) indicates that congressional policy committees are no longer as autonomous as they once were. If this trend continues and if it applies to other legislative bodies, policy scholars will need to reexamine their assumptions concerning the importance of policy subsystems/communities. By the same token, policy process scholars have a great deal to offer political scientists in other subfields. For example, much of the recent empirical and theoretical work in administrative behavior continues to focus on a single agency or on "iron triangles" at a single level of government (Moe 1985; Bendor and Moe 1985). Doing so may be appropriate in the case of a few federal agencies with monopoly jurisdiction (e.g., the National Labor Relations Board, the Federal Communications Commission), but in the vast majority of policy areas the behavior of specific agencies is affected by a much wider range of actors at multiple levels of government (Scholz and Wei 1986; Sabatier and Pelkey 1987; Wood 1990).

The development and testing of better theories of the policy process will be greatly accelerated if interested scholars can develop a journal specifically oriented to this task. Political science journals cannot do so because the discipline's concerns are broader than that and historically have been preoccupied with public opinion and voting studies (Walker 1972; Palumbo 1989). The existing set of policy journals are also inadequate to this task, either because of a different focus or because most are so poorly regarded by political scientists that policy scholars in political science departments are reluctant to publish in them.[4]

Another important feature of the 1990s is likely to be an expansion of the literature on policy design. At present, that literature includes at least three separate streams: (1) the work of Trudi Miller (1989), which seeks to combine modern empirical theory and explicit normative concerns in order to fundamentally redesign social institutions; (2) the work of Dryzek (1989; Bobrow and Dryzek 1987), which is highly critical of behavioral social science and instead seeks to develop very situation-specific, adaptive approaches to policy design; and (3) the work of scholars like Salamon (1989), Schneider and Ingram (1988, 1990), and Linder and Peters (1989), which tends to focus on the efficacy of different policy instruments.

In our view, the fruitfulness of various approaches to policy design will depend heavily upon their ability to incorporate existing (and future) research on the policy process. Design involves the self-conscious attempt to alter governmental policies in order to achieve one or more objectives. It makes all sorts of causal assumptions that pushing specific "levers" will have certain effects; such assumptions are, in turn, based on theories of how bureaucracies, courts, legislators, interest groups, and so forth will react.

Policy design scholars thus need to involve themselves in the fundamental task of testing and refining various theories of the policy process. The design approach is probably most compatible with the institutional rational choice perspective of Ostrom. Her categorization of "institutional rules" and Schneider and Ingram's (1990) categorization of "policy instruments" show some similarities, but they could also benefit from some self-conscious integration. Other theories would caution against placing too much faith in the efficacy of altering specific instruments. Hofferbert, for example, would predict that the effects would vary greatly across communities with different socioeconomic conditions and, hence, political support for the perceived implications of instrument choice. The advocacy coalition framework views instrument choice as an aspect of the policy core, and thus would anticipate great resistance to changing from, for example, command-and-control to economic incentives as the dominant policy instrument. It would also suggest, however, that the overall minority coalition might be in control of some governmental units, and thus be able to experiment with new instruments; even though favorable results would be contested by members of the majority coalition, a learning process would take place under certain conditions. The experience with the use of economic incentives in air pollution control would seem to support many of these reservations (Liroff 1986), but additional work certainly needs to be done.

In conclusion, the policy process is complicated. Unless we are willing to make explicit our assumptions about how it works and to subject those assumptions to empirical testing, we are unlikely to learn very much. As Pogo might say, "Better to be clear and risk being wrong than be mushy and think you're always right."

NOTES

1. This criticism is less valid for Anderson (1975). His first two chapters discuss a variety of socioeconomic conditions and types of actors that affect the policy process, and he briefly reviews several approaches. But nowhere does he

elaborate one or more frameworks and then seek to apply them throughout the book. Ripley (1985) proposes a somewhat similar framework, although his arguments derive primarily from Lowi's arenas of power.

On the other hand, the stages heuristic—which distinguishes a major policy decision, such as a statute, from what emerges in the implementation and reformulation stages—is one means of dealing with several of the problems mentioned by Greenberg et al. (1977).

2. The only other candidates would be the policy output studies (Dawson and Robinson 1963; Sharkansky 1970; Hofferbert 1974) and the work of Wildavsky (1974) on budgeting.

3. Sabatier (1988, 149–57) hypothesizes that policy-oriented learning is more likely to occur *between* coalitions when the issues are technically tractable, when they deal with important secondary aspects of belief systems, and when coalitions are forced to confront each other in relatively professionalized fora. See Jenkins-Smith (1988) for very similar arguments developed independently.

4. This argument is developed more fully in Sabatier (1990). None of the existing public policy journals have developed a focus on the policy process. Some have been preoccupied with techniques of policy evaluation (*Journal of Policy Analysis and Management*); many deal with specific policy areas; the rest have attempted to deal with the broad range of policy scholars' interests, with much of the work consisting of techniques useful to practitioners or of atheoretical studies of a particular policy area (*Policy Sciences, Journal of Public Policy, Policy Studies Journal*, and *Policy Studies Review*).

REFERENCES

Advisory Commission on Intergovernmental Relations (ACIR). 1984. *Significant Features of Fiscal Federalism, 1982–83 Edition*. Washington, D.C.: ACIR.

Anderson, James. 1975. *Public Policy-Making*. New York: Praeger.

Bailey, Stephen, and Edith Mosher. 1968. *ESEA: The Office of Education Administers a Law*. Syracuse: Syracuse University Press.

Bardach, Eugene. 1974. *The Implementation Game*. Cambridge: MIT Press.

Bendor, Jonathan, and Terry Moe. 1985. "An Adaptive Model of Bureaucratic Politics." *American Political Science Review* 79 (Sept.):755–74.

Bobrow, Davis, and John Dryzek. 1987. *Policy Analysis by Design*. Pittsburgh: University of Pittsburgh Press.

Box, G. E. P., and Gwilyn Jenkins. 1970. *Time Series Analysis*. San Francisco: Holden-Day.

Browning, Rufus, Dale Rogers Marshall, and David Tabb. 1984. *Protest Is Not Enough: The Struggle of Blacks and Hispanics for Equality in Urban Politics*. Berkeley: University of California Press.

Burstein, Paul. 1985. *Discrimination, Jobs, and Politics*. Chicago: University of Chicago Press.

Campbell, Donald, and Julian Stanley. 1963. *Experimental and Quasi-Experimental Designs for Research*. Boston: Houghton-Mifflin Co.

Caplan, Nathan, et al. 1975. *The Use of Social Science Knowledge in Policy Decisions at the National Level*. Ann Arbor: Institute of Social Research.

Cobb, Roger, et al. 1976. "Agenda Building as a Comparative Process." *American Political Science Review* 70 (Mar.):126–38.

Cohen, Michael, James March, and Johen Olsen. 1972. "A Garbage Can Model of Organizational Choice." *Administrative Science Quarterly* 17 (Mar.): 1–25.

Cook, Fay Lomax, and Wesley Skogan. 1989. "Agenda Setting: Contingent and Divergent Voice Models of the Rise and Fall of Policy Issues." Unpublished paper, Northwestern University.

Coyle, Dennis, and Aaron Wildavsky. 1987. "Requisites of Radical Reform: Income Maintenance Versus Tax Preferences." *Journal of Policy Analysis and Management* 7 (Fall):1–16.

Culhane, Paul. 1981. *Public Lands Politics*. Baltimore: Johns Hopkins University Press.

Dawson, Richard, and James Robinson. 1963. "Interparty Competition, Economic Variables, and Welfare Policies in the American States." *Journal of Politics* 25 (May):265–89.

deLeon, Peter. 1988. *Advice and Consent: The Development of the Policy Sciences*. New York: Russell Sage Foundation.

Derthick, Martha, 1979. *Policymaking for Social Security*. Washington, D.C.: Brookings.

Derthick, Martha, and Paul Quirk. 1985. *The Politics of Deregulation*. Washington, D.C.: Brookings.

Dryzek, John. 1989. "Don't Toss Coins in Garbage Cans: A Prologue to Policy Design." *Journal of Public Policy* 3 (Oct.):345–68.

Dunn, William. 1980. "The Two-Communities Metaphor and Models of Knowledge Use." *Knowledge* 1 (June):515–36.

Dye, Thomas. 1972. *Understanding Public Policy*. Englewood Cliffs, N.J.: Prentice-Hall.

Dye, Thomas, and L. Harmon Zeigler. 1975. *The Irony of Democracy*. 3rd ed. North Scitate, Mass.: Duxbury Press.

Easton, David. 1953. *The Political System*. New York: Alfred Knopf.

———. 1965. *A Systems Analysis of Political Life*. New York: John Wiley & Sons.

———. 1969. "The New Revolution in Political Science." *American Political Science Review* 63 (Dec.):1051–61.

Elazar, Daniel. 1984. *American Federalism: A View from the States*. 3rd ed. New York: Harper & Row.

Eulau, Heinz. 1977. "The Interventionist Synthesis." *American Journal of Political Science* 21 (May):419–23.

Eyestone, Robert. 1977. "Confusion, Diffusion, and Innovation." *American Political Science Review* 71 (June):441–47.

Giles, Michael, Franzie Mizell, and David Patterson. 1989. "Political Scientists' Journal Evaluations Revisited." *PS* 22 (Sept.):613–17.

Goggin, Malcolm. 1986. "The 'Too Few Cases/Too Many Variables' Problem in Implementation Research." *Western Political Quarterly* 38 (June): 328–47.

———. 1987. *Policy Design and the Politics of Implementation.* Knoxville: University of Tennessee Press.

Gormley, William. 1987. "Institutional Policy Analysis." *Journal of Policy Analysis and Management* 6 (Winter):153–69.

Gray, Virginia. 1973. "Innovation in the States: A Diffusion Study." *American Political Science Review* 67 (Dec.):1174–85.

Greenberg, George, Jeffrey Miller, Lawrence Mohr, and Bruce Vladeck. 1977. "Developing Public Policy Theory Perspectives from Empirical Research." *American Political Science Review* 71 (Dec.):1532–43.

Greenberger, Martin, Garry Brewer, William Hogan, and Milton Russell. 1983. *Caught Unawares: The Energy Decade in Retrospect.* Cambridge, Mass.: Ballinger.

Hanf, Kenneth, and Fritz Scharpf, eds. 1978. *Interorganizational Policy Making.* London: Sage.

Heclo, Hugh. 1972. "Review Article: Policy Analysis." *British Journal of Political Science* 2 (Jan.):83–108.

———. 1974. *Social Policy in Britain and Sweden.* New Haven: Yale University Press.

———. 1978. "Issue Networks and the Executive Establishment." In *The New American Political System*, edited by A. King. Washington, D.C.: American Enterprise Institute.

Heintz, H. Theodore. 1988. "Advocacy Coalitions and the OCS Leasing Debate." *Policy Sciences* 21 (Fall):213–38.

Hjern, Benny, and David Porter. 1981. "Implementation Structures: A New Unit of Administrative Analysis." *Organization Studies* 2:211–27.

Hofferbert, Richard. 1974. *The Study of Public Policy.* Indianapolis: Bobbs-Merrill.

———. 1986. "Policy Evaluation, Democratic Theory, and the Division of Scholarly Labor." *Policy Studies Review* 5 (Feb.):511–19.

Hofferbert, Richard, and John Urice. 1985. "Small Scale Policy: The Federal Stimulus versus Competing Explanations for State Funding of the Arts." *American Journal of Political Science* 29 (May):308–29.

Huntington, Samuel. 1988. "One Soul at a Time: Political Science and Political Reform." *American Political Science Review* 82 (Mar.):3–10.

Ingram, Helen. 1978. "The Political Rationality of Innovation." In *Approaches to Controlling Air Pollution,* edited by Ann Friedlaender. Cambridge: MIT Press.

Ingram, Helen, Nancy Laney, and John McCain. 1980. *A Policy Approach to Political Representation: Lessons from the Four Corners States.* Baltimore: Johns Hopkins University Press.

Jenkins-Smith, Hank. 1988. "Analytical Debates and Policy Learning." *Policy Sciences* 21 (Fall):169–212.

――. 1990. *Democratic Politics and Policy Analysis.* Monterey, Calif.: Brooks/ Cole.

Jenkins-Smith, Hank, and Paul Sabatier, eds. 1990. *An Advocacy Coalition Model of Policy Change and Learning.* Manuscript submitted for publication.

Johannes, John. 1984. "Congress, the Bureaucracy, and Casework." *Administration and Society* 16 (May):41–69.

Jones, Charles. 1970. *An Introduction to the Study of Public Policy.* Belmont, Calif.: Wadsworth.

――. 1975. *Clean Air.* Pittsburgh: University of Pittsburgh Press.

――. 1987. "Presidents and Agendas: Who Defines What for Whom?" Unpublished paper, University of Virginia.

Kemp, Kathleen. 1978. "Nationalization of the American States: A Test of the Thesis." *American Politics Quarterly* 6 (Apr.):237–47.

Kingdon, John. 1981. *Congressmen's Voting Decisions,* 2nd ed. New York: Harper & Row.

――. 1984. *Agendas, Alternatives, and Public Policies.* Boston: Little, Brown.

Kirst, Michael, and Richard Jung. 1983. "The Utility of a Longitudinal Approach in Assessing Implementation: A Thirteen-Year View of Title I, ESEA." In *Studying Implementation,* edited by Walter Williams. Chatham, N.J.: Chatham House.

Kiser, Larry, and Elinor Ostrom. 1982. "The Three Worlds of Action." In *Strategies of Political Inquiry,* edited by E. Ostrom. Beverly Hills: Sage.

Landau, Martin. 1977. "The Proper Domain of Policy Analysis." *American Journal of Political Science* 21 (May):423–27.

Lau, Richard, and David Sears, eds. 1986. *Political Cognition.* Hillsdale, N.J.: Lawrence Erlbaum Assoc.

Leichter, Howard. 1979. *A Comparative Approach to Policy Analysis.* Cambridge: Cambridge University Press.

Lerner, Daniel, and Harold Lasswell, eds. 1951. *The Policy Sciences.* Stanford: Stanford University Press.

Lester, James, and Ann Bowman. 1989. "Implementing Intergovernmental Policy." *Polity* 21 (Summer):731–53.

Lindblom, Charles. 1964. *The Intelligence of Democracy.* New York: Macmillan.

Linder, Stephen, and B. Guy Peters. 1989. "Instruments of Government: Perceptions and Contexts." *Journal of Public Policy* 9 (1):35–58.

Liroff, Richard. 1986. *Reforming Air Pollution Regulation*. Washington, D.C.: Conservation Foundation.

Loomis, Burdett. 1983. "A New Era: Groups and the Grass Roots." In *Interest Group Politics*, edited by A. J. Cigler and B. A. Loomis. Washington, D.C.: Congressional Quarterly Press.

Lowi, Theodore. 1964. "American Business, Public Policy, Case Studies, and Political Theory." *World Politics* 16 (June):677–715.

———. 1972. "Four Systems of Policy, Politics, and Choice." *Public Administration Review* 32 (July/Aug.):298–310.

Lundqvist, Lennart. 1980. *The Hare and the Tortoise: Clean Air Policies in the U.S. and Sweden*. Ann Arbor: University of Michigan Press.

Luttbeg, Norman, ed. 1968. *Public Opinion and Public Policy: Models of Political Linkages*. Homewood, Ill.: Dorsey.

McLaughlin, Susan, and Paul Sabatier. 1987. "Elite Beliefs and Policy Change: Environmental Politics at Lake Tahoe, 1970–84." Paper presented at the Meetings of the American Political Science Association, Chicago.

MacRae, Duncan. 1989. "Social Science and Policy Advice." Paper presented at the PSO/APSA Conference on Advances in Public Policy Studies, Atlanta.

MacRae, Duncan, and Dale Whittington. 1988. "Assessing Preferences in Cost-Benefit Analysis." *Journal of Policy Analysis and Management* 7 (Winter): 246–63.

Mann, Dean. 1975. "Political Incentives in U.S. Water Policy: Relationships between Distributive and Regulatory Politics." In *What Government Does*, edited by Matthew Holden and Dennis Dresang. Beverly Hills: Sage.

March, James, and Johan Olsen. 1984. "The New Institutionalism: Organizational Factors in Political Life." *American Political Science Review* 78 (Sept.):734–49.

Matthews, Donald, and James Stimson. 1975. *Yeas and Nays*. New York: Wiley.

May, Peter. 1986. "Politics and Policy Analysis." *Political Science Quarterly* 101 (1):109–25.

Mazmanian, Daniel, and Paul Sabatier. 1980. "A Multivariate Model of Public Policy-Making." *American Journal of Political Science* 24 (Aug.):439–68.

———, eds. 1989. *Implementation and Public Policy*. Rev. ed. Lanham, Md.: University Press of America.

———. 1981. *Effective Policy Implementation*. Lexington, Mass.: D. C. Heath.

Mazur, Allan. 1981. *The Dynamics of Technical Controversy*. Washington, D.C.: Communications Press.

Meier, Kenneth. 1975. "Representative Bureaucracy: An Empirical Analysis." *American Political Science Review* 69 (June):526–42.

———. 1984. "The Limits of Cost-Benefit Analysis." In *Decision-Making in the Public Sector*, edited by Lloyn Nigro. New York: Marcel Dekker.

————. 1987. *Politics and the Bureaucracy*. 2nd ed. Monterey, Calif.: Brooks/ Cole.

Miller, Trudi. 1989. "Design Science as a Unifying Paradigm." Paper presented at the PSO/APSA Conference on Advances in Policy Studies, Atlanta.

Miller, Warren, and Donald Stokes. "Constituency Influence on Congress." *American Political Science Review* 57 (Mar.):45–56.

Moe, Terry. 1985. "Control and Feedback in Economic Regulation: The Case of the NLRB." *American Political Science Review* 79 (Dec.):1094–1116.

Moynihan, Daniel. 1970. *Maximum Feasible Misunderstanding*. New York: Free Press.

Murphy, Jerome. 1973. "The Education Bureaucracies Implement Novel Policy: The Politics of Title I of ESEA." In *Policy and Politics in America*, edited by Allan Sindler. Boston: Little, Brown.

Nakamura, Robert. 1987. "The Textbook Policy Process and Implementation Research." *Policy Studies Review* 7 (1):142–54.

Nathan, Richard, and Charles Adams. 1977. *Revenue Sharing: The Second Round*. Washington, D.C.: Brookings.

Nelkin, Dorothy. 1979. *Controversy: Politics of Technical Decisions*. Beverly Hills: Sage.

Nelson, Barbara J. 1986. *Making an Issue of Child Abuse*. Chicago: University of Chicago Press.

Ostrom, Elinor. 1986a. "An Agenda for the Study of Institution." *Public Choice* 48:3–25.

————. 1986b. "A Method of Institutional Analysis." In *Guidance, Control, and Evaluation in the Public Sector,* edited by F. X. Kaufman, G. Majone, and V. Ostrom. Berlin: de Gruyter.

————. 1990. *Governing the Commons*. Cambridge: Cambridge University Press.

O'Toole, Laurence. 1986. "Policy Recommendations for Multi-Actor Implementation: An Assessment of the Field." *Journal of Public Policy* 6 (Apr.): 181–210.

Page, Benjamin, and Robert Shapiro. 1983. "Effects of Public Opinion on Policy." *American Political Science Review* 77 (Mar.):175–90.

Page, Edward, and Michael Goldsmith, eds. 1987. *Central and Local Government Relations: A Comparative Analysis of West European Unitary States*. London: Sage.

Palumbo, Dennis. 1989. "Bucking the Tide: Policy Studies in Political Science, 1978–88." Paper presented at the PSO Conference on Advances in Policy Studies, Atlanta.

Peters, B. Guy. 1986. *American Public Policy: Promise and Performance*. 2nd ed. Chatham, N.J.: Chatham House.

Pierce, John, and Harvey Doerksen, eds. 1976. *Water Politics and Public Involvement*. Ann Arbor: Ann Arbor Science.

Pressman, Jeffrey, and Aaron Wildavsky. 1973. *Implementation*. Berkeley: University of California Press.

Putnam, Robert. 1976. *The Comparative Study of Political Elites*. Englewood Cliffs, N.J.: Prentice-Hall.

Ranney, Austin, ed. 1968. *Political Science and Public Policy*. Chicago: Markham.

Reagan, Michael. 1972. *The New Federalism*. New York: Oxford University Press.

Rhodes, R. A. W., and Vincent Wright, eds. 1987. *Tensions in the Territorial Politics of Western Europe*. London: Frank Cass & Co.

Ripley, Randall. 1985. *Policy Analysis in Political Science*. Chicago: Nelson-Hall.

Ripley, Randall, and Grace Franklin. 1980. *Congress, the Bureaucracy, and Public Policy*. Homewood, Ill.: Dorsey.

———. 1982. *Bureaucracy and Policy Implementation*. Homewood, Ill.: Dorsey.

Rodgers, Harrell, and Charles Bullock. 1976. *Coercion to Compliance*. Lexington, Mass.: D. C. Heath.

Rose, Douglas. 1973. "National and Local Forces in State Politics: The Implications of Multi-Level Analysis." *American Political Science Review* 67 (Dec.): 1162–73.

Rosenbaum, Walter. 1976. "The Paradoxes of Public Participation." *Administration and Society* 8 (Nov.):355–83.

Sabatier, Paul. 1986. "Top-Down and Bottom-Up Models of Policy Implementation: A Critical Analysis and Suggested Synthesis." *Journal of Public Policy* 6 (Jan.):21–48.

———. 1988. "An Advocacy Coalition Framework of Policy Change and the Role of Policy-Oriented Learning Therein." *Policy Sciences* 21 (Fall): 129–68.

———. 1991. "Political Science and Public Policy: Despite Strains, Mutual Contributions to Understanding the Policy Process." *PS* forthcoming.

Sabatier, Paul, and Daniel Mazmanian. 1983. *Can Regulation Work? The Implementation of the 1972 California Coastal Initiative*. New York: Plenum.

Sabatier, Paul, and Susan Hunter. 1989. "The Incorporation of Causal Perceptions into Models of Elite Belief Systems." *Western Political Quarterly* 42 (Sept.):229–61.

Sabatier, Paul, and Neil Pelkey. 1987. "Incorporating Multiple Actors and Guidance Instruments into Models of Regulatory Policymaking." *Administration and Society* 19 (Sept.):236–63.

Salamon, Lester, ed. 1989. *Beyond Privatization: The Tools of Government*. Washington, D.C.: The Urban Institute.

Salisbury, Robert. 1968. "The Analysis of Public Policy." In *Political Science and Public Policy*, edited by A. Ranney. Chicago: Markham.

Schneider, Anne, and Helen Ingram. 1988. "Systematically Pinching Ideas: A

Comparative Approach to Policy Design." *Journal of Public Policy* 8 (1): 61–80.

———. 1990. "Behavioral Assumptions of Policy Tools." *Journal of Politics* 52 (May):510–29.

Scholz, John, and Feng Hieng Wei. 1986. "Regulatory Enforcement in a Federalist System." *American Political Science Review* 80 (Dec.):1249–70.

Sharkansky, Ira, ed. 1970. *Policy Analysis in Political Science*. Chicago: Markham.

Sharpe, L. J. 1985. "Central Coordination and the Policy Network." *Political Studies* 33 (Sept.):361–81.

Sinclair, Barbara. 1989. *The Transformation of the U.S. Senate*. Baltimore: Johns Hopkins University Press.

Smith, Steven, and Forrest Maltzman. 1989. "Declining Committee Power in the House of Representatives." Paper presented at the APSA Annual Meeting, Atlanta, September.

Songer, David. 1988. "The Influence of Empirical Research: Committee vs. Floor Decision Making." *Legislative Studies Quarterly* 13 (Aug.):375–92.

Stokey, Edith, and Richard Zeckhauser. 1978. *A Primer for Policy Analysis*. New York: W. W. Norton.

Van Horn, Carl. 1979. *Policy Implementation in the Federal System*. Lexington, Mass.: D. C. Heath.

Verba, Sidney, and Norman Nie. 1972. *Participation in America*. New York: Harper & Row.

Vig, Norman, and Michael Kraft, eds. 1984. *Environmental Policy in the 1980s*. Washington, D.C.: Congressional Quarterly Press.

Walker, Jack. 1972. "Brother, Can You Paradigm?" *Political Science and Politics* 3 (Fall):419–22.

Weiss, Carol. 1977a. *Using Social Research in Public Policy Making*. Lexington, Mass.: D. C. Heath.

———. 1977b. "Research for Policy's Sake: The Enlightenment Function of Social Research." *Policy Analysis* 3 (Fall):531–45.

Weyent, John. 1988. "Is There Policy-Oriented Learning in the Analysis of Natural Gas Policy Issues?" *Policy Sciences* 21 (Fall):239–62.

White, Lawrence J. 1981. *Reforming Regulation*. Englewood Cliffs, N.J.: Prentice-Hall.

Whiteman, David. 1985. "The Fate of Policy Analysis in Congressional Decision Making." *Western Political Quarterly* 38 (June): 294–311.

Wildavsky, Aaron. 1966. "The Political Economy of Efficiency: Cost-Benefit Analysis, Systems Analysis, and Program Budgeting." *Public Administration Review* 26 (Dec.):292–310.

———. 1974. *The Politics of the Budgetary Process*. 2nd ed. Boston: Little, Brown.

————. 1982. "The Three Cultures: Explaining Anomalies in the American Welfare State." *The Public Interest* 69 (Fall):45–58.

————. 1987. "Choosing Preferences by Constructing Institutions: A Cultural Theory of Preference Formation." *American Political Science Review* 81 (Mar.):3–22.

Wildavsky, Aaron, and Ellen Tenenbaum. 1981. *The Politics of Mistrust*. Beverly Hills: Sage.

Wilson, James Q. 1973. *Political Organizations*. New York: Basic Books.

Wood, B. Dan. 1990. "Modeling Federal Policy Structures with Dynamic Structural Equations." Paper delivered at the 1989 Meetings of the Midwest Political Science Association, Chicago.

Notes on Contributors

Robert H. Bates is Henry R. Luce Professor in the Department of Political Science and director of the Center in Political Economy at Duke University. He received his Ph.D. from the Massachusetts Institute of Technology in 1969 and then taught at the California Institute of Technology until 1985. He is author of several books, including *Beyond the Miracle of the Market* (1989) and *Essays on the Political Economy of Rural Africa* (1986). His edited books include *Toward a Political Economy of Development* (1988). From 1989 to 1990, he served as Vice President of the American Political Science Association.

Ellen Comisso is professor of political science at the University of California, San Diego. She received her Ph.D. from Yale University in 1977. She is the author of *Workers' Control Under Plan and Market* (1979) and has edited *Power, Purpose and Collective Choice* (1986). She has also published articles in *International Organization, World Politics,* and other scholarly journals and edited volumes.

William Crotty is professor of political science at Northwestern University. He received his Ph.D. from the University of North Carolina at Chapel Hill in 1964. His areas of interest include political parties and election processes, policy-making, and American and comparative governing institutions. He has served as president of the Political Organizations and Parties Section of the American Political Science Organization, the Midwest Political Science Association, and the Policy Studies Organization. He is the author of a number of articles and books, including *Decision for the Democrats* (1978), *Party Reform* (1983), *The Party Game* (1985), *American Parties in Decline* (co-author, 1980, 1984), *Presidential Primaries and Nominations* (co-author, 1985), and *Political Parties in Local Areas* (co-author, 1987). Professor Crotty has been the recipient of an American Political Science Association Fellowship to study the national political parties and he has served as a member of a number of commissions invited to observe elections and democratic processes in Latin America.

Russell J. Dalton teaches in the Department of Politics and Society at the University of California at Irvine. He received his Ph.D. from the University of Michigan in 1978. He has been a Fulbright Professor at the University of Mannheim and worked at the Zentralarchiv fuer empirische Sozialforschung at the University of Cologne. Among his authored and edited books are *Germany Transformed* (1981), *Electoral Change in Advanced Industrial Democracies* (1984), *Citizen Politics in Western Democracies* (1988), *Politics in West Germany* (1989), and *Challenging the Political Order* (1990).

Barbara Geddes teaches Latin American politics and comparative politics at the University of California, Los Angeles. She received her Ph.D. from the University of California, Berkeley, in 1986. She has published articles on economic development and administrative reform in Latin America, on popular attitudes toward authoritarian regimes, and on methodology in the study of comparative politics. Her book, *Politician's Dilemma*, will soon be available from University of California Press.

Deborah J. Gerner received her B.A. from Earlham College and her M.A. and Ph.D. from Northwestern University; she now teaches at the University of Kansas. Her areas of interest include U.S. and comparative foreign policy, Middle East politics, and international political economy. She is the author of *One Land, Two Peoples: The Conflict over Palestine* (1991) and a wide variety of articles dealing with foreign policy broadly defined; she is currently analyzing consistency and change in U.S. foreign policy relations with the Arab world using a combination of statistical methods and archival research. Gerner was chair of the foreign policy analysis section of the International Studies Association in 1991.

William R. Keech has been teaching political science at the University of North Carolina at Chapel Hill for twenty-five years, since he received his Ph.D. from the University of Wisconsin. His publications include *The Impact of Negro Voting: The Role of the Vote in the Quest for Equality* (1968), *The Party's Choice* (1976), and numerous articles on the politics of macroeconomic policy in political science and economics journals. Recently he served as president of the Southern Political Science Association. His presidential address was entitled "Politics, Economics, and Politics Again."

Jacek Kugler teaches political science at Vanderbilt University. He received his Ph.D. from the University of Michigan in 1973. He is the co-author of *The War Ledger* (1980) *Births, Deaths and Taxes* (1984), co-editor of *Exploring the Stability of Deterrence* (1987), and has published numerous scholarly articles in the *American Political Science Review, Journal of Conflict Resolution, International Interactions*, and *Comparative Political Studies*, among others.

Peter Lange teaches political science at Duke University. He received his Ph.D. from the Massachusetts Institute of Technology in 1975. He has published *Unions, Change and Crisis: French and Italian Union Strategy and the Political Economy, 1945–1980* (1982) (with George Ross and Maurizio Vannicelli), *Union Democracy and Liberal Corporatism: Exit, Voice and Wage Regulation in Postwar Europe* (1984) and *State, Market and Social Regulation: New Perspectives on Italy* (1989) (with Marino Regini) as well as numerous scholarly articles published in major disciplinary journals. He is President of the Conference Group on Italian Politics and Society and Chair of the Organized Section in Comparative Politics of the American Political Science Association and Editor of the Cambridge Studies in Comparative Politics of Cambridge University Press.

Paul A. Sabatier teaches environmental policy at the University of California, Davis. He received his Ph.D. in political science from the University of Chicago in 1974. He is the co-author of several books on policy implementation, and has published articles on policy change, administrative policy-making, elite belief systems, and interest group dynamics in journals such as *Policy Sciences*, the *American Journal of Political Science*, the *Journal of Politics*, and the *Western Political Quarterly*.